BUILDING NATIONS FROM DIVERSITY

McGILL-QUEEN'S STUDIES IN ETHNIC HISTORY
SERIES ONE   DONALD HARMAN AKENSON, EDITOR

McGILL-QUEEN'S STUDIES IN ETHNIC HISTORY
SERIES TWO   JOHN ZUCCHI, EDITOR

Building Nations from Diversity

Canadian and American Experience Compared

GARTH STEVENSON

McGill-Queen's University Press
Montreal & Kingston · London · Ithaca

© McGill-Queen's University Press 2014

ISBN 978-0-7735-4385-0 (cloth)
ISBN 978-0-7735-4386-7 (paper)
ISBN 978-0-7735-8320-7 (ePDF)
ISBN 978-0-7735-8321-4 (ePUB)

Legal deposit fourth quarter 2014
Bibliothèque nationale du Québec

Printed in Canada on acid-free paper that is 100% ancient forest free
(100% post-consumer recycled), processed chlorine free

McGill-Queen's University Press acknowledges the support of the Canada
Council for the Arts for our publishing program. We also acknowledge the
financial support of the Government of Canada through the Canada Book
Fund for our publishing activities.

Library and Archives Canada Cataloguing in Publication

Stevenson, Garth, 1943–, author
    Building nations from diversity: Canadian and American
experience compared / Garth Stevenson.

(McGill-Queen's studies in ethnic history. Series two; 35)
Includes bibliographical references and index.
Issued in print and electronic formats.
ISBN 978-0-7735-4385-0 (bound). – ISBN 978-0-7735-4386-7 (pbk.). –
ISBN 978-0-7735-8320-7 (ePDF). – ISBN 978-0-7735-8321-4 (ePUB)

    1. Multiculturalism – Canada – History. 2. Cultural pluralism –
United States – History. 3. Immigrants – Government policy – Canada –
History. 4. Immigrants – Government policy – United States – History.
5. Canada – Emigration and immigration – History. 6. United States –
Emigration and immigration – History. 7. Canada – Ethnic relations –
History. 8. United States – Ethnic relations – History. I. Title. II. Series:
McGill-Queen's studies in ethnic history. Series two; 35

FC105.M8S74 2014   305.800971   C2013-908677-3
                                          C2013-908678-1

This book was typeset by Interscript in 10.5 / 13 Sabon.

Contents

Acknowledgments

The research for this project could not have been conducted without the assistance of the Social Sciences and Humanities Research Council of Canada, which supported it with research grant #410–2007–0379. Its completion was accelerated by the fact that Brock University freed me from scheduled teaching responsibilities during the last semester before my retirement on 30 June 2012. Two research assistants, Mai Nguyen and Melanie Bishop, assisted in the collection of data. Both began as MA students in political science at Brock. Mai continued as my research assistant after entering the PhD program at York University. The tedious task of preparing the index was effectively performed by Meagan Collins, also a student in Brock's MA program in political science. The project also benefitted from the assistance of staff at the following archives: Library and Archives Canada in Ottawa, the Diefenbaker Canada Centre in Saskatoon, the Franklin D. Roosevelt Presidential Library in Hyde Park, the Harry S. Truman Presidential Library in Independence, the John F. Kennedy Presidential Library in Boston, the Lyndon B. Johnson Presidential Library in Austin, the Richard M. Nixon Presidential Library in Yorba Linda, the Gerald R. Ford Presidential Library in Ann Arbor, and the Immigration History Research Center at the University of Minnesota in Minneapolis. Philip Cercone of McGill-Queen's University Press, with whom I have now worked on six books, was, as always, a helpful and supportive editor.

Some material that found its way into the book was presented at the annual meetings of the Canadian Political Science Association at the University of British Columbia (2008) and at Concordia University (2010) and at the triennial conference of the Association for Canadian Studies in the United States at San Diego in 2009. The paper presented at U B C in 2008 was co-authored with Mai Nguyen, my research assistant at the time.

This book is dedicated to my dear wife, Aillen Santos Stevenson, a new addition to the Canadian mosaic, who provided much encouragement and inspiration during the writing of the manuscript. Although I met her after I began the collection of data for the book, she has contributed much more to it than she realizes.

Garth Stevenson
Grimsby, Ontario
10 June 2013

BUILDING NATIONS FROM DIVERSITY

1

Introduction

Canada and the United States are often said to have more in common with one another than any two countries in the modern world. Whether or not this is true, comparisons between the two countries are a staple commodity of everyday conversation, media discourse, political rhetoric, and scholarly analysis, at least in Canada. (The fact that Americans are less preoccupied with Canada than Canadians are with the United States seems to offend some Canadians, while others take delight in ridiculing American ignorance about Canada, but the disproportion in size and influence between the two countries makes it inevitable.) There is, however, at least one way in which the two neighbours are alleged by many Canadians to be different, so much so in fact that the alleged contrast has become a cliché. This alleged contrast is perceived in the response of the two countries to ethnic diversity, particularly the diversity that results from immigration. Canadian "multiculturalism" or, as it was known before 1971, the "Canadian mosaic" is frequently contrasted with the American "melting pot."

Neither of these metaphors is of recent origin. The "melting pot," both the phrase and the concept, apparently first surfaced in a play of the same name by Israel Zangwill, a Jewish immigrant from the United Kingdom, which was first performed in Washington, DC, in 1908.[1] The play's rather improbable plot concerns a romance between a Jew and a Christian who agree to transcend their religious and cultural differences through a common devotion to the American way of life.

The reference to Canada, and particularly western Canada, as a "mosaic" is almost as old. It apparently made its first appearance in a travel book by Victoria Hayward published in 1922. It subsequently appeared in the titles of two other books about Canada, by Kate Foster and John Murray Gibbon, which were published, respectively, in 1926 and 1938.[2] (Gibbon, the director of public relations for Canadian Pacific, was responsible for two of our national myths, since his earlier book, *Steel of Empire*, may have been the first to celebrate the transcontinental railway as a symbol of national achievement.)

According to these familiar stereotypes, which early in the present millennium were even incorporated in a beer commercial, immigrants in Canada are encouraged to retain their distinct characteristics and identities more or less indefinitely while immigrants in the United States face pressure to conform to American cultural patterns and to lose their distinct characteristics as rapidly as possible. (The fact that the beer in question, Molson's Canadian, is indistinguishable from American mass-market lager was an irony that apparently escaped most of the audience.)

Particularly in urban Ontario and among persons born since "multiculturalism" was proclaimed as an official doctrine of the Canadian state in 1971, these contrasting stereotypes have become so firmly established as articles of belief that anyone who questions them is viewed with suspicion. Like the once-accepted belief among Japanese people that they were descended from the sun goddess, the belief that Canadians invented a uniquely successful, civilized, and un-American approach to the management of diversity appears to provide a warm glow of satisfaction to the people concerned, however slight its empirical foundation. Canadians frequently cite the alleged contrast between "mosaic" and "melting pot" as evidence of Canada's moral superiority over its nearest neighbour. In fact, the celebration of "multiculturalism" has become a virtual cottage industry among English-speaking Canadian journalists and academics, particularly political philosophers, and has spawned an extensive literature.[3]

For those Canadians who worry about their collective identity vis-à-vis the neighbouring country whose culture, entertainment, and way of life they largely share, Prime Minister Pierre Trudeau's endorsement of "multiculturalism" in 1971 and the incorporation of "multicultural heritage" in the Constitution a decade later were very conveniently timed. In fact, it has been argued that the primary purpose of the multiculturalism myth was to differentiate Canada from the United States.[4] Others argue that its primary purpose was to combat Quebec nationalism.[5] Whichever explanation, if either, is correct, the proposition that Canada's "identity" consists in having no identity greater than the sum of its parts is rather problematical for Canadian nationalists, as a few have pointed out.[6]

Although many Canadians, especially politicians, intellectuals, and spokespersons for various ethnic lobbies, still cherish the "mosaic" or "multiculturalism" as a badge of national identity, the American "melting pot" no longer enjoys the popularity and respectability of its early years. It is hard to imagine an American president endorsing the expression today, as Theodore Roosevelt did after attending the first performance of Zangwill's play. In fact, John F. Kennedy, while he resembled the first President Roosevelt in many ways, set the new trend by writing a short book that conveyed a very different message.[7] The African-American civil rights movement of the 1960s, the counter-movement of European-American "ethnics" in the 1970s, the major reform of immigration policy for which Kennedy was largely responsible, and the rapid increase in the number of educated and articulate Americans with non-European roots have combined to make it increasingly problematical.

Identity politics and the cultivation and celebration of ethnicity are at least as widespread and conspicuous in the present-day United States as in Canada, contrary to what most Canadians believe. Even the word "multiculturalism" has entered the American discourse.[8] The Reverend Jesse Jackson was one of the first prominent politicians to use it with approval. Admittedly, it is not universally accepted as a part of the American creed, but it is not universally accepted in Canada either. Indeed, some polling data suggest that Canadians are more likely, not less likely, than Americans to agree with the proposition that immigrants should adapt to the cultural norms of their adopted country.[9] Americans nowadays are far more likely to use the term "melting pot" in an ironic or derogatory sense, or as a label for something that no longer exists, than to celebrate it as their ancestors did a century ago. It is also interesting that Americans are far less likely to list their ethnicity as "American" in the census than Canadians are to list their ethnicity as "Canadian."

Pope Leo XIII observed in one of his encyclicals that every error contains a grain of truth, and the alleged contrast between Canadian mosaic and American melting pot is no exception, as will be shown in the pages that follow. Initially, there really were some differences between Canadian and American attitudes and policies regarding ethnicity, even if they have tended to fade away over time. But there were important similarities as well. The United States, like Canada, was until very recent times a "vertical mosaic," to use John Porter's expression, in which Protestants of British ancestry enjoyed pride of place.[10] There was also never a time in which the ethnic and cultural diversity of the American people was in any way invisible. In fact, in the first half of the twentieth century such diversity was actually more visible in the United States than in Canada. Mackenzie King commented after a ride on the New York subway in 1943 that the people he saw were "mostly all of foreign descent, many Jews."[11]

Differences of this kind at any point in time are heavily influenced by the foreign-born and non-British percentages of the population in the two countries. For many years, the United States was a far more attractive magnet for immigrants of all kinds than Canada, as well as being somewhat more welcoming toward European immigrants of non-British ancestry. On the other hand, as will be explained elsewhere in this book, the United States instituted a very restrictive immigration policy toward people from outside the Western Hemisphere after World War I, which significantly reduced the foreign-born percentage of its population over the next several decades. When the policy was abandoned in 1965, the United States quickly began to catch up with Canada in the foreign-born percentage of its population and in the cultural diversity of its major cities. Conversely, Canada, which had difficulty attracting immigrants for much of its history, attracted a great many after World War II when Canada was much easier to enter as a landed immigrant than the United States. In recent years, the rate at which immigrants are assimilated in the two countries seems, for better or for worse, to be much the same.

As noted above, both Canada and the United States were dominated for most of their history by Protestants of British ancestry, and some would say that this is still the case. This hegemony by the dominant ethnocultural group certainly lasted after the group in question ceased to be a majority of the population, which happened in the United States by about 1890 and in Canada about half a century later. In Canada, British Protestant economic, social, and political dominance actually began *before* the British became a majority of the population, which they did about the middle of the nineteenth century, almost a century after Canada was transferred from the French to the British Empire. In both countries, contrary to the Canadian official myth, Anglo-conformity was considered essential until very recently, even by such progressive persons as J.S. Woodsworth, the first Canadian to lead a social democratic party in Parliament.

Nonetheless, both Canada and the United States have received millions of immigrants, on the whole successfully, in the course of their respective histories, although many instances of anti-immigrant prejudice and discrimination can be found in the histories of both countries. The two North American neighbours, along with Australia and New Zealand, differ from most of the world's sovereign states in that the vast majority of their people are descended from persons who arrived voluntarily from a different continent within the past 400 years. In addition, many families now established in Canada arrived by way of the United States and vice versa. In both countries, the great majority of the immigrants, or at least their children, eventually came to identify emotionally and politically with their new country while adopting most aspects of its prevailing culture. The Swedish film, *The Emigrants*, sensitively portrayed this process of integration as it operated in the mid-nineteenth-century United States. More recent experience, and Canadian experience, does not seem to have been much different, although some differences in the details vary from time to time and from place to place. Admittedly, immigrants who were not "white" (i.e., not European) faced considerably greater difficulties than those who were, but exclusionary policies made such immigrants a very small proportion of the total until the 1960s.

The result of this shared history is that most North Americans, most of the time, consider immigration to be "normal" and on the whole desirable, while most Europeans and Japanese still have great difficulty in coming to terms with it. In most European countries and in Japan, the national identity is based on a language that is named after the state (or vice versa) and on a population that is believed, perhaps falsely, to have shared a common ancestry and culture for at least a millennium and in the Japanese case for much longer. The title of President Kennedy's book, *A Nation of Immigrants*, indicates a collective self-perception that most Americans and most Canadians (although less so in Quebec than elsewhere) find acceptable. The common fact of being immigrant-derived communities is, along with liberal democracy, federalism, a large geographical space, and the predominance of English common law and the English language, an important characteristic shared by the two North American neighbours.

Admittedly, there are differences as well, which will be highlighted in the next chapter of this book. The relations of European settlers with the Aboriginal North American "Indians" were similar in both countries but not identical for various geographic, economic, military, and cultural reasons. The importation of African slaves played a gigantic role in the development of the United States, where at one time they and their descendants comprised about a fifth of the population. The tragic consequences of this fact have marked American history unto the third and fourth generation and beyond, as Abraham Lincoln noted in his second inaugural address, perhaps the greatest and most moving speech in the English language. Slavery existed in French Canada and for a short time in British Canada, but it was never of great importance, largely because Canada was not suited to the type of agriculture for which slave labour was useful.

If slavery, as I would argue, is the dominant fact in American history, the dominant fact in Canadian history is the conquest of a French-speaking colony by the British during the Seven Years' War. Language (French versus English) is the Canadian obsession in the same way that skin colour (African versus European) is the American obsession. Admittedly, portions of the United States were originally colonized by the Dutch, the French, or the Spanish before being conquered or purchased by Anglo-Americans, but the populations speaking a European language other than English were relatively small in relation to the Anglo-American population that assumed control over them. Except for Spanish, which has been reinforced by later waves of migration from the southern neighbours of the United States, the other European languages that were added to the American mixture in this way largely died out. In Canada, as noted above, the conquered French remained a majority of the population for several generations and have proudly retained their language to the present day, making it one of the country's two official languages and, in one province, the dominant language. This was largely the consequences of British policies toward the conquered French Canadians that have no parallel in American experience. These contrasting formative experiences, slavery in one country, conquest followed by indirect rule in the other, have influenced the responses of the two countries to other aspects of ethnic and cultural diversity.

Another contrast between the two countries concerns their political histories. The United States developed from a group of British colonies that collectively declared and successfully defended their independence from the British Crown. In its place they created a republic that they proudly declared to be a *novus ordo seclorum*, or a new order for the ages, and a model, supposedly, for other peoples to follow all over the world. Canada developed from a collection of British colonies, the largest of which by far had been a French colony, that chose to remain under the protection of the British Crown and to adopt a constitution "similar in principle to that of the United Kingdom." The meaning of this latter phrase was not without ambiguity, especially since it was drafted at a time when the British form of government was evolving rapidly, but it clearly and deliberately marked Canada as different from the United States. As will be explained subsequently in this book, monarchy and republicanism have different implications for the relations among ethnic and cultural groups. In addition, Canada's very gradual evolution toward formal independence from the United Kingdom had implications different from those of the abrupt declaration of independence in the United States, particularly for immigration policy and for concepts of citizenship.

Given these different circumstance, how did the United States and Canada deal with a problem shared by both: the need to populate half a continent and to attract the supply of labour and skills needed for economic growth? How did they respond to, and at times encourage, the desire of many non–North Americans to enter the land of opportunity and share in its resources? How did they deal with the diversity of language, culture, and religion that resulted from the process of mass migration? How did they classify and categorize the various elements of their respective populations at different times? And how were the respective national identities of the two countries defined and adapted to the changing ethnic, cultural, and religious composition of their respective populations?

This book attempts to answer these questions, although it is not a comprehensive history of ethnicity and immigration in either country, let alone in both. (In particular, it must be emphasized that its theme is ethnic diversity resulting from immigration and not ethnic diversity in general. Thus, the tragic legacy of contact between indigenous North Americans and European explorers and settlers is mentioned only in passing, as is the equally tragic legacy of the importation of African slaves.) There are a number of historical surveys of immigration to the United States[12] and of immigration to Canada.[13] There are also historical surveys of the migration experience of particular ethnic groups, which make reference to both Canada and the United States as host countries for migrants of the relevant group.[14] There is at least one book on the history of migration between Canada and the United States in both directions.[15] There is, however, a dearth of studies that explicitly compare the two countries in this regard, even though at least one book compares immigration policy in Canada and Australia.[16] It is hoped that the present book will help to fill that gap in the literature.

The methodology of the book is based on historical institutional-. ism and on the concept most closely and prominently associated with that school of social science – namely, path dependence.[17] Like other studies of this genre, it uses the term "institution" in the broad sense to include persisting patterns of behaviour and policy and not in the narrow sense that includes only formal institutions like parliaments and courts. An earlier book by this author used the same methodological framework to explore the development of nationalism in Ireland and Quebec.[18]

The term "path dependence" refers to a historical sequence of events that begins with a "contingent" event, or one that seems more or less accidental and not explicable in terms of any theory. The event causes a society to make choices about practices and institutions and thus sets in motion chains of events that have deterministic properties. Choices made at one point in time may persist merely because it is not worth the effort to change them (the illogical arrangement of letters on the conventional keyboard, beginning with QWERTY, is an often-cited example) or because they seem to close off the opportunity to make other choices. More typically, perhaps, they persist because they seem to have positive results for those who exercise power in the society. For as long as this seems to be the case, there is no incentive to change.

However, the theory is not totally deterministic. New contingent events or externally determined circumstances may alter the prevailing path in the same way that one billiard ball may alter the course of another one with which it collides. Alternatively, a prevailing path may be deliberately rejected because it was finally recognized as counterproductive, as in the way that both Germany and Japan adopted an exaggerated anti-militarism after the debacle of 1945.

The book therefore began with the hypothesis, which seems to be confirmed, that the responses of both the United States and Canada to immigration and ethnic diversity over the years were powerfully influenced by formative circumstances, as outlined above, that set them on particular paths. These formative circumstances are the subject of the next chapter. As the theory of path dependence would suggest, they largely predetermined patterns of policy and narrowed the range of possible choices that seemed desirable or even possible.

A second hypothesis, however, is that new events and circumstances encountered along the way modified these existing patterns from time to time so that the eventual outcomes could not have been fully predicted at the outset. This hypothesis also seems to be confirmed by the investigation. In particular, Canada and the United States to some extent influenced one another, given their proximity and their fairly intimate economic and social relationships, and they were also both influenced by shared events and circumstances, some of them external and some arising out of their cultural similarities, that produced a gradual convergence of their respective historical trajectories, especially in recent years. For example, World War II demonstrated the appalling consequences of racist theories and ideologies and led to a global commitment to human rights, in theory if not always in practice, and these circumstances affected both the United States and Canada. In other words, the contrast between melting pot and mosaic had considerable validity at the outset and thus retains a certain degree of credibility even today, but has in practice become much less pronounced than it used to be and may be in the process of disappearing entirely.

As noted above, the chapter immediately following this one outlines the formative events and circumstances in the history of the two neighbours up to about the middle of the nineteenth century, including geography, early patterns of settlement and economic activity, relations with the indigenous peoples, the contrasting experiences of slavery and conquest, and the contrasting choices of republican independence and monarchical dependence, which defined and differentiated the two societies after the American Revolution.

The next three chapters examine how the patterns of development and policy set in motion by these circumstances played themselves out in relation to three specific groups of immigrants that attracted considerable attention from the middle of the nineteenth century until the early decades of the twentieth. The choice of three ethnic groups out of the many that have contributed to the population of North America is not made arbitrarily but reflects the timing and circumstances of their arrival, the issues that they seemed to present for the two North American societies, and the impact of choices made at that time on further developments in policy. In each case, the relationship between the immigrant group and the host societies (Canada and the United States) extending to the present day will also be briefly examined.

Chapter 3 is devoted to the Irish and particularly to the Catholic Irish, because they were the first large group of immigrants whose religion seemed to challenge the ideological and cultural norms of Protestant Anglo-America. In fact, it has been suggested that they were the first large group who were regarded in North America as "immigrants" (a foreign element needing to be absorbed) rather than as "settlers" (people from an imperial country who move to the colonial hinterlands of that country). The massive Irish immigration of the 1840s, precipitated by the failures in three successive years of the potato crops on which most of Ireland's people depended, was also unusual if not unique in the number of immigrants, in absolute terms and relative to the size of the originating country's population, who crossed the Atlantic in a very short period of time. Finally, it exacerbated tensions between Catholic and Protestant that had very deep roots in English, and therefore in North American, history. The hostile response of many North Americans to the newly arrived Irish Catholics set the pattern and served as the prototype for anti-immigrant sentiments that greeted other groups of new arrivals in later years.

Chapter 4 looks at the Chinese, who played an important economic role in western North America but whose physical appearance, as well as their culture, caused many North Americans to doubt that they could or should be incorporated fully into the host society. The Chinese began to arrive in large numbers soon after the Irish, attracted to North America first by the discovery of gold in California and British Columbia and later by the need for labour to build transcontinental railways in the very thinly populated area west of the continental divide. As well as differing in language and culture, the Chinese looked different from North Americans of European ancestry. They also looked different from the non-Europeans with whom North Americans were most familiar: slaves or former slaves of African ancestry and the indigenous peoples of the North American continent. Finally, they were almost entirely non-Christian. However, they were the first but not the last large group of immigrants who shared these characteristics and in a sense paved the way for the others who followed them. As in the case of the Irish, the response to the Chinese set the pattern and served as the prototype for the response to other non-Western immigrants who came later.

Chapter 5 examines the response to Jewish immigrants from Europe whose arrival, like that of the Catholic Irish, raised religious issues for some North Americans but also tapped prejudices that had even deeper roots in European history than those that the Irish encountered. The presence of small numbers of Jews in North America pre-dated the American Revolution, but the arrival of large numbers of Jewish immigrants from eastern Europe really began in the 1880s and was largely a response to developments in the Russian Empire. Like the Irish and the Chinese before them, the immigrant Jews attracted some hostility from non-Jewish North Americans and were even greeted with mixed feelings by some of the western European Jews whose ancestors had arrived earlier. Their fate also became linked in various ways with the explosion of anti-Semitic sentiments in Europe during the first half of the twentieth century, culminating in the systematic mass murder of European Jews by the Nazis and with the foundation of the state of Israel, which was largely a response to that event.

Chapter 6 looks at a particular aspect of ethnic relations in North America that had an impact on more than one ethnic group – namely, the response to "enemy aliens" and other persons who shared the ethnic and cultural characteristics of enemy nations during the two world wars in the first half of the twentieth century. The best-known aspect of this phenomenon is the simultaneous internment of Japanese Americans and Japanese Canadians by the two federal governments after the Japanese attack on Pearl Harbor in December 1941. However, the experiences of German Americans and of German Canadians and Ukrainian Canadians during World War I are also of considerable interest.

Chapter 7 looks at the evolution of immigration policy in both countries during the twentieth century, including the very rigid exclusionary policies adopted by the United States (much more rigid and explicit than Canada's policies) during the interwar period and the movement in both countries toward more liberal policies after 1945, culminating in the elimination of racial discrimination, in theory at least, during the 1960s. The consequence of the latter development was greatly increased immigration from non-European sources in both countries just as the increasing prosperity of western Europe was causing immigration from traditional sources to taper off. This in turn led to a rapid increase in the number of Canadians and Americans with non-European and non-Aboriginal ancestry, people known in the official jargon of the Canadian state by the unfortunate label "visible minorities."

Chapter 8 is devoted to the increased politicization of language issues from the 1960s onwards, with movements toward English–French bilingualism in much of Canada, French unilingualism in Quebec, English unilingualism (in response to Hispanic immigration) in parts of the United States, and a certain degree of de facto English–Spanish bilingualism in the United States as a whole. Although the sources of these developments in Canada were largely unrelated to immigration, immigration to Quebec and the anxieties it aroused about the future of the French language had some impact on them. In the United States, immigration of Spanish-speaking people, particularly from Mexico, created anxiety among some Anglo-Americans but elicited a more pragmatic and flexible response among others.

Chapter 9 examines the real origins of "multiculturalism" in Canada and slightly later in the United States and may challenge some traditional interpretations. In Canada, the idea of multiculturalism arose from the resentment of some European ethnic minorities at what they considered excessive attention to French Canadians by the federal government. In the United States, there was a similar backlash by European ethnic minorities against what they viewed as excessive attention to African Americans. Government responses in both countries in the 1970s to these ethnic concerns were somewhat similar, but the idea of multiculturalism was eventually adopted by other (non-European) elements of the population, including African Americans, while the ethnic groups that had originally favoured it largely lost interest. In Quebec, the term "multiculturalism" remains unpopular, although the "interculturalism" adopted by that province's government seems little different from Canadian multiculturalism in practice.

Chapter 10 looks at the most recent challenge to the ethnic and religious harmony of the North American nations: the Islamophobia that was triggered largely by the events of 11 September 2001 and other incidents of terrorism by extremist Muslims in various parts of the world but also by increasing Muslim immigration to North America. It will be suggested that there are parallels between this anti-Muslim sentiment and the anti-Catholic sentiment that Irish immigrants faced a century and a half ago. At the same time, controversy has developed over the extent to which the state should accept and adapt to the religious practices associated with Islam and other minority religions. In North America as a whole, religion appears to be overtaking both skin colour and language in its importance as a political issue.

Chapter 11 concludes the book with a summary of the findings and their implications, an overview of the present, increasingly complex pattern of ethnic and religious diversity in North America, and some suggestions on what might lie in the future. As noted above, Canada and the United States originally differed to some extent in their general approaches to immigration and ethnic diversity, but it appears that they have tended to converge over time to the point where the similarities now outweigh the differences. Finally, while by no means minimizing the role that xenophobia and intolerance have played in the history of both North American nations, the book concludes on an optimistic note. Immigration has on the whole been good for the United States and Canada and good (most of the time) for the immigrants themselves, whatever difficulties they may have experienced along the way.

2

Setting the Patterns

Canada and the United States are both products of the exploration and settlement of the North American continent by peoples from northwestern Europe, a process that began about 1600. European explorers had visited the eastern shores of the continent before that date, and the cod fisheries of the Grand Banks had attracted many Europeans from about 1500 onwards. Several centuries before that date, the Vikings had settled for a while on the island of Newfoundland and possibly at other locations. Jacques Cartier had formally claimed a portion of the continent for the king of France in 1534. However, permanent settlement by Europeans, out of which Canada and the United States would eventually develop, is a product of the seventeenth century. Jamestown, Virginia, was founded by the English in 1607, and the French founded Quebec City a year later, in 1608. In 1620, the landing of a group of religious refugees from England at Plymouth, now in Massachusetts, marked the foundation of New England, and in 1626 the Dutch founded New Amsterdam (New York) at the southern tip of Manhattan Island.

These various groups of settlers encountered indigenous North American peoples, the so-called "Indians" of the eastern forests, who had reached by this time about the same level of material civilization and a similar way of life as their own ancestors had enjoyed when Julius Caesar encountered them almost seventeen centuries earlier. While their material achievements were less impressive than the civilizations of the Maya, the Aztec, and the Inca in what are now Mexico and Peru, the indigenous peoples of eastern North America had certainly developed agriculture and lived in extensive permanent settlements. The Haudenosaunee (Iroquois) in what is now upstate New

York also had a highly sophisticated political organization, which has been identified as a precursor of modern federalism.

The number of indigenous people living in eastern North America at the time when European settlement began is impossible to ascertain with any degree of accuracy, but they obviously outnumbered the Europeans for at least several decades after the beginning of European settlement, particularly in the northern regions that are now part of Canada. This fact, and their greater familiarity with the natural environment, gave them the upper hand, at least for a while, in relations with the new arrivals. Europeans attempted to coexist with the indigenous peoples and learned from them how to survive and thrive in a harsh environment that was subject to much greater extremes of hot and cold than western Europe.

In the fur trade, which was a major motive for European exploration and settlement in the territory that is now Quebec, Ontario, and the state of New York, indigenous people played an important part, and Europeans were well advised to collaborate with them. However, this fact also entangled the Europeans in already existing rivalries and conflicts among the indigenous nations themselves. Conversely, the indigenous peoples became entangled in commercial rivalries among the European nations, so the contacts between Europeans and indigenous North Americans were by no means uniformly peaceful. In areas where Europeans were primarily interested in agriculture, which tended to be further south as well as in New England, their interests naturally clashed with those of the people who already occupied the land, so violence was probably inevitable. This was increasingly the case as the Europeans became more numerous and more demanding.

The English proved to be considerably more successful than the French or the Dutch in exporting large numbers of their people to North America, even though England at that time had a considerably smaller population than that of France. This was partly because the French and the Dutch were particularly interested in the fur trade, for which a large settled agricultural population was not an asset and might be a liability. (For similar reasons, the English were very slow to settle Newfoundland, the first part of North America that they "discovered," because they envisaged it as a fishing station rather than an agricultural colony.) Also, the French, unlike the English, discouraged religious dissidents from settling in North America, thus reducing the pool of potential settlers.

However, it should also be noted that the English by 1700 had established eleven distinct colonies along the Atlantic coast of North America, from New Hampshire (1623) in the north to South Carolina (1670) in the south. Some of these colonies were initially private ventures while others were established by the Crown. The English also seized the Dutch colony of New Netherland, including its capital, New Amsterdam, from the Dutch in 1664, closing the gap between their northern and southern colonies. They gave both the captured colony and its principal city the name of New York. At the opposite extremities of the long seaboard, Nova Scotia (formerly the French colony of Acadia) and Georgia, which had been explored but not really settled by the Spanish, were added to the list of British possessions and settled by English-speaking people after the union of England and Scotland in 1707. In contrast, the Dutch established only one viable colony (New Netherland) and the French only two (Canada and Acadia), all of which were small in population and would eventually fall under the dominion of the British Crown. Neither the Dutch nor the French devoted as much effort to North American settlement as did the English. The Netherlands was a small country primarily interested in trade and with few people to export, while France was preoccupied with the European balance of power, as well as with seizing territory from its European neighbours, and could thus spare little attention for North America. Nonetheless, the French explored a huge part of the North American continent even though they did not settle it, as can be seen from the place names on a modern map of the continent as far west as the foothills of the Rocky Mountains and as far south as the Gulf of Mexico.

The French colony of Canada, centred around the city of Quebec, was initially a private venture, as were many of the English colonies to the south, but was brought under the direct control of the French Crown in 1663 by King Louis XIV after its progress under private management proved unsatisfactory. It remained under the direct rule of the French Crown for almost exactly a century before coming under British control during the Seven Years' War, which Americans refer to as the French and Indian War. British control was confirmed by the peace treaty signed in 1763, according to which the French, tired of their North American colony, retained the more profitable and more easily defended Caribbean islands of Guadeloupe and Martinique rather than Canada. This proved to be a wise decision for France, which retains ownership of those two islands up to the present.

During the century when Canada was governed by the French Crown, France was a centralized absolutist monarchy under the Bourbon dynasty during the exceptionally long reigns of Louis XIV and Louis XV. It had no functioning parliamentary institutions: the Estates General did not meet between 1614 and 1789. Government in the colony was also centralized and authoritarian, with power divided between the governor, whose main responsibility was to defend it from external threats, the intendant, who managed the economy, and the Catholic bishop. In accordance with the mercantilist doctrines popular at the time, the colony was closely attached to France economically as well as administratively. It also practised what was intended to be a North American version of European feudalism. Land was granted by the French Crown to lords (seigneurs) who in turn could lease it to tenants (*censitaires*). The tenants held the land on condition that they perform certain services for the seigneur, who in turn had certain obligations to the Crown. Most of the seigneurs were individual proprietors, while some lands were held in seigneurial tenure by religious orders. In practice, Canadian feudalism was a pale shadow of its European counterpart. The obligations imposed on the *censitaires* could not be too onerous; otherwise, they would simply escape into the surrounding forests to mingle with the indigenous peoples or participate in the fur trade. The seigneurs had no obvious function in a colony dominated by the army and the church and could hardly be considered a governing class. The elected officers of the militia, which was supposed to assist the French army in defending the colony from hostile neighbours both indigenous and European, were arguably more important, although the militia itself was so poorly trained as to be nearly useless.[1] Nonetheless, the seigneurial system long outlasted the transfer of the colony to British rule and would be abolished only in 1854, by which time many of the seigneurs would be English-speaking settlers.

The European settler population of Canada at the time when its ownership passed from the French to the British Empire was only about 60,000, compared to a total of about 1.5 million in the fourteen (including Nova Scotia) British colonies. The European population of New Netherland had been ethnically diverse from the outset, and the English colonies collectively included a variety of ethnic groups (including English, Irish, Scottish, German, and Dutch) and a variety of religious groups ranging from Quakers to Catholics. In contrast, French Canada was homogeneous in ethnicity and language (northern French) and in religion (Catholic), largely by deliberate design. Protestants were prohibited from migrating to the colony and had been largely expelled from France itself by 1685, with many of them finding their way to England or its colonies. There is some evidence, however, that the French intermarried with the indigenous peoples of North America to a much greater extent than did the English or the Dutch, partly because the fur trade brought settlers and indigenes together and partly because of a persistent shortage of European women in Canada. Also, the Catholic religious orders in the French colony converted many of the indigenous people to their faith, while the Protestant Dutch and English, without a comparable body of potential missionaries and being mainly in pursuit of economic gain, seem not to have made conversion a priority. Racism and the obsession with skin colour have generally been less prominent in the Catholic countries of Europe with languages and cultures derived from ancient Rome than in the northern parts of Europe where Roman civilization had less influence.

While France enjoyed political stability and continuity from the middle of the seventeenth century until the revolution that began in 1789, the history of England over the same period was considerably more complex. The execution of King Charles I in 1649 following the civil war between his supporters and those of Parliament was followed by the abolition of the monarchy and formation of a new regime under Lord Protector Oliver Cromwell. The restoration of the monarchy in 1660, two years after Cromwell's death, was followed by a so-called "Glorious Revolution" in 1688 in the course of which King James II was deposed and replaced by a dual monarchy under his daughter Mary and her husband, William of Orange. This event seems to have been provoked in large part by James's effort to establish a centralized absolutist monarchy on the French model, although his Catholic faith was certainly a factor as well.[2] His defeat led to England becoming a decentralized oligarchy in which the personal powers of the monarch were seriously curtailed, the bureaucracy was weak, and Parliament was effectively supreme, a tendency reinforced after the elector of Hanover, who could not speak English, inherited the English throne in 1714.

Meanwhile, England and Scotland, which had shared the same monarch since 1603 while remaining separate kingdoms, were combined in 1707 into a "United Kingdom" with one parliament, although the established churches (Anglican in England and Presbyterian in

Scotland) and the legal systems (common law in England and civil law in Scotland) remained distinct in the two parts of the United Kingdom, as they still do. Neither the realm nor the people can correctly be termed "British" before the union in 1707, although American writers in particular tend to use the term anachronistically with reference to the seventeenth century.[3] The "United Kingdom" also acquired the English dependency of Ireland, which the English had finally brought under their complete control in 1690 after several centuries of effort. Ireland remained a dependency with its own subordinate parliament until it was fully merged into the United Kingdom in 1801. Unlike Scotland, it was considered conquered territory and was forced to practise the same established form of religion (until 1869) and the same common law as England, even though most of its people were Catholic and a great many of them did not speak English.

Partly because of this complex history, the English (subsequently "British") colonies were less homogeneous, collectively and even individually, than French Canada, just as the "United Kingdom" itself was more diverse (especially in terms of religion) and less centralized than France. Some were ruled directly by the Crown, as New York was after its acquisition in 1664. Others had been granted to private proprietors. Massachusetts adhered to the rigid Calvinism of its founders, while neighbouring Rhode Island, founded by the Quaker Roger Williams, was an oasis of religious tolerance. Pennsylvania, founded by the prominent Quaker William Penn, became very diverse in both religion and ethnicity. Maryland was founded by Lord Baltimore, one of the rare Catholics among the English aristocracy, and Catholicism was more accepted there than elsewhere in the colonies.[4] New York, a mosaic of ethnic diversity even under Dutch rule, remained so under British rule.[5] The southern colonies imported African slaves, who soon became a large component of their populations. In contrast to French Canada, all of the English colonies had elected legislatures before the end of the seventeenth century, and even Nova Scotia (formerly Acadia) was granted one in 1758.

Diverse as Great Britain's North American empire was, Canada, after its acquisition in 1763, posed unique problems for British statecraft. The French settler population was much larger than that of Nova Scotia, from which most of the Acadians had been expelled in an early example of ethnic cleansing before the colony was granted a legislature. It was also much larger and much more homogeneous than the settler population of New Netherland had been in 1664.

France was England's traditional enemy, so the loyalty of the new subjects could not be taken for granted.

Most seriously of all, the French were almost entirely Catholic. Catholicism had been viewed in England for two centuries as a subversive conspiracy directed from Rome and had been largely driven underground in Great Britain and Ireland. The monarch's traditional title, "defender of the faith," was understood to refer to defence of the Church of England. Oliver Cromwell, who encouraged European Jews to settle in England, and John Locke, the philosopher who argued for religious toleration, both viewed Catholicism as uniquely dangerous and did not extend to it the same acceptance that they were willing to grant to other varieties of religious belief. The second half of Thomas Hobbes's *Leviathan* is largely devoted to denunciations of the Catholic Church. After the revolution of 1688, the English Parliament firmly declared that no Catholic, and no one married to a Catholic, could sit on the English throne. Anti-Catholicism was among the few common bonds that strengthened the artificial union between England and Scotland after 1707.[6] Events in 1715 and 1745 would show that there were still people, particularly in the Scottish Highlands, who were not reconciled to the United Kingdom's official Protestantism and who wished to see a Catholic member of the exiled Stuart dynasty on the British throne. While English attitudes were gradually becoming more flexible toward the end of the eighteenth century, Catholics would not be given full civil rights in the United Kingdom until 1829.

Nonetheless, the terms on which Quebec City, and later Montreal, surrendered to the British army included the promise that the practice of the Catholic faith would be permitted. The peace treaty of 1763 amended this concession to stipulate that it would be permitted "as far as the laws of Great Britain permit." The French population was obviously too large to be expelled as the Acadians had been or to be easily replaced by new settlers if expulsion had been feasible. Yet the laws of Great Britain did not permit Catholics to sit in Parliament or hold any political office. At the insistence of the few hundred English-speaking Protestant civilians who had arrived in Canada with the British army, the Royal Proclamation issued eight months after the peace treaty promised an elected legislative assembly such as existed in Great Britain's other North American colonies. However, no conscientious Catholic could sit in such a body because to do so would require taking an oath of allegiance to the Crown, which incorporated an explicit renunciation of Catholic doctrine. On the other hand, a Protestant legislature in an overwhelmingly Catholic country had not worked well in Ireland, where it would be abolished in 1801, and would make even less sense in Quebec, whose Protestant minority was proportionately much smaller than Ireland's.

The British waffled for more than a decade before finally implementing a solution to these problems. As early as 1764, the attorney general of England ruled that the right of Canadian Catholics to own land had survived the conquest and could only be terminated by an explicit act of Parliament.[7] The first British governor, James Murray, was a Scot whose two brothers had supported the cause of the exiled Catholic Stuarts in 1745.[8] Murray himself found French Canada's Catholic seigneurs, whose language he could speak, more congenial than the English-speaking Protestant merchants, most of them from New York, who noisily demanded an elected legislature dominated by themselves. Murray was recalled to England in 1764 because of the merchants' complaints about him but remained formally in office until 1768. His successor, Guy Carleton, an Irish Protestant, arrived with the idea that the French should be assimilated as rapidly as possible, but he quickly became more sympathetic to them and abandoned this idea.[9] In 1766, the British allowed a Catholic bishop appointed by the pope, Jean Olivier Briand, to take up residence in Quebec City, replacing the previous bishop, who had died in 1760 soon after the British captured the city. This event indicated that the idea of imposing Protestantism on the French Canadians would no longer be taken seriously, if it ever had been. Lord Shelburne, the secretary of the state for the colonies, even suggested that Catholics could be allowed to sit in a colonial legislature without renouncing their faith.[10]

Gradually, the British governing class were coming to the conclusion that Canada's civil society, such as it was, consisted mainly of the Catholic Church and that this exotic addition to the empire could only enjoy political and social stability if that fact were taken into account. The Catholic clergy were close to the common people, from whom many of them had sprung. The Catholic parish was the most important local institution in every village and the basis of what local government there was. French Canada's other elites, the French army officers, the bureaucrats, and most of the merchants, had returned to France after the conquest. Only the clergy remained to manage the colony in collaboration with the conquerors, who could thus retain as much control as they needed without extending the tentacles of the British administration into every parish and locality. The continuing unrest in Catholic Ireland suggested that it was not wise to try to govern a country while disparaging and persecuting the religion of most of its people, and Catholics comprised a much higher percentage of the population in Canada at that time than they did in Ireland.

The result was the Quebec Act, adopted by the British Parliament in 1774 and taking effect the following year. It owed its name to the fact that the Royal Proclamation of 1763 had changed Canada's name to the Province of Quebec, an innovation that lasted until the province was partitioned into Lower Canada and Upper Canada in 1791. The Quebec Act guaranteed the free exercise of the Catholic religion, the existence of a Catholic hierarchy in the province, and the right of the Catholic Church to collect tithes from the Catholic population. It also restored the system of French civil law that had existed before the British conquest, a concession that had been promised in the peace treaty of 1763 but not fully implemented in practice. British criminal law, however, would remain in force. An appointed council would be set up to advise the governor. Nothing was said explicitly about the French language, probably because in the absence of an elected legislature, there was no need to specify the language of legislative debates or of statutes.

Recent scholarship has undermined the traditional notion that the Quebec Act was designed to secure French Canadian support against the impending threat of a declaration of independence by the English-speaking Americans.[11] Rather, its essential features seem to have been more or less decided upon several years before it saw the light of day. Political instability in the United Kingdom and the obstinate anti-Catholic sentiments of King George III delayed the project for several years until the Tory prime minister, Lord North, was able to persuade the monarch to accept a measure first proposed by the Whigs, whom the king distrusted. The belated timing of the Quebec Act ensured that it would actually make the situation in the thirteen colonies worse for the British instead of better. The already restless Americans, most of whom were almost as hostile to Catholicism as King George, added the Quebec Act to the list of grievances that they expounded in their Declaration of Independence. Apart from its recognition of Catholicism and French law and its lack of any provision for an elected legislative assembly, the fact that the Quebec Act extended the boundaries of Canada, or "Quebec," into what is now the American midwest certainly did nothing to make the Americans happier.

In a brilliant essay on the origins of French Canadian nationalism, Hubert Guindon has argued that the Quebec Act was both an expression of British political ideas and an important contribution to the theory and practice of imperialism.[12] He suggested that by creating a regime for French Canada entirely different from that which existed in their English-speaking North American colonies, the British were implementing the notion that the political and civil rights of any group of people are the product of their peculiar history, culture, and circumstances rather than something that can be derived from universal principles and standards. Thus, the political regime suitable for one ethnic or national group is not necessarily suitable for another. Even where different populations are mingled on the same territory, they may enjoy different sets of rights, depending on their respective traditions and cultures. According to this view, efforts to force the same type of regime on all of humanity are doomed to futility or worse. Edmund Burke would later use this idea to distinguish between the traditional "rights of Englishmen," which he supported, and the universal "rights of man" proclaimed by the French revolutionaries, which he opposed. Burke supported the American Revolution, but not the French Revolution, because he viewed the Americans as English settlers who retained the "rights of Englishmen" even after settling on a different continent and who were fighting for the same principles as did the English revolutionaries of 1688.

Related to this theory, according to Guindon, is the idea of "indirect rule" as a technique of imperialism for which the Quebec Act was the prototype and which the British would later use in their Asian and African colonies. If the most effective and stable government for any group of people is one that accords with their own experience and traditions, the best way to rule a colony is by making use of its traditional and existing elites, who will govern it in the way to which it is accustomed. The imperial power retains ultimate control but does so in an unobtrusive way that keeps its own institutions and personnel and its military and economic objectives out of sight as much as possible – the iron fist in a velvet glove. Edward Gibbon, in the first chapter of *The Decline and Fall of the Roman Empire*, perhaps foreshadowed this insight with his celebrated observation that the various religious cults practised in that empire were all regarded by their followers as true, by the philosophers as false, and by the magistrates as useful.[13] People will not rebel if their traditions and beliefs are apparently respected, and the imperial power will therefore not have to govern them by force and fear.

In Canada, where the seigneurs were not really as important as they may have thought they were and the merchants were mainly English-speaking Protestants with little understanding of, and less regard for, the local population, the only elite that could possibly serve the purposes of indirect rule were the Catholic clergy. The clergy were also convenient partners for the British, since they shared their dislike of democracy and republicanism and would not demand an elected legislature. The British may have derived the idea less from political philosophy than from a belated reappraisal of the English experience in Ireland. Six centuries of efforts to subdue that country had failed to do so, because its predominant religion had been persecuted, its land confiscated and distributed among alien settlers, and its people subjected to invidious discrimination while English law and the English language had been imposed. The decision to try a different approach in French Canada would later be imitated to some extent in Ireland itself but much too late to undo the damage. In Asian and African colonies acquired subsequently, it would be used from the outset, as it had been in Canada, with somewhat happier results.

The idea that different groups of people should be treated differently from one another and provided with legal, political, and religious institutions appropriate to their peculiar needs and circumstances is the actual foundation of the Canadian mosaic. As well as being applied to the Catholic French Canadians, it would also, at least for a while, govern British policy toward the Aboriginal peoples of North America. The Royal Proclamation of 1763, which is still often cited by leaders of the First Nations, confirmed their possession of their ancestral lands, to the dismay of Anglo-Americans in the thirteen colonies, and provided that they could only be divested of those lands through a formal treaty with the Crown and not through surrender or sale to private individuals.

In the War of 1812, indigenous North Americans fought as independent allies of the British Crown, not as part of the British army. Like the Royal Proclamation half a century earlier, this practice infuriated the Americans, who hated and feared the native warriors and regarded a military alliance with "savages" as contrary to the laws of civilized warfare. (Northern Americans would later express the same view when the southern Confederacy, as a desperate measure, formed an alliance with some indigenous tribes in what is now the state of Oklahoma. The southerners, of course, regarded the enlistment of African Americans in the Union army as equally reprehensible.) During the War of 1812, the British vaguely promised their allies an indigenous buffer state between Canada and the American republic (a purpose for which the present state of Michigan would have been very well suited), but in the end they abandoned and betrayed their allies to reach a compromise peace with the Americans.

In Quebec and elsewhere in British North America, the mosaic was of course vertical, with British Protestants at the top, but that was perhaps inevitable. If different groups of people are treated as though they really are different, the corollary is perhaps that they are assigned different roles: the British to run the economy, the French to tend their farms and obey their clergy, and the indigenous peoples to hunt and fish in the northern forests. So it would be for most of Canadian history. The gamble is that people will care more about maintaining their traditional way of life than about achieving a theoretical equality with people different from themselves, and for most people most of the time, that may very well be true.

This approach to governing an empire is also related to monarchy as a form of government and to the unique institutional architecture of the United Kingdom itself. In the eighteenth century, all European states except Switzerland were monarchies, and most were complex patchworks of territory assembled through dynastic marriages, peace treaties, or conquests, with no regard for the ethnicity or the preferences of the inhabitants. In a monarchy, the essential relationship is a vertical one, between the subject and the monarch. Horizontal ties between subjects or groups of subjects are not as essential, nor is any real sense of community or common origin between subjects or groups of subjects. A loyal subject need not share the ethnic origin or even speak the language of other subjects or of the monarch. In the words of the Canadian historian W.L. Morton, "As America is united at the bottom by the covenant, Canada is united at the top by allegiance. Because Canada is a nation founded on allegiance and not on compact, there is no process of becoming Canadian akin to conversion, there is no pressure for uniformity, there is no Canadian way of life. Anyone, French, Irish, Ukrainian or Eskimo, can be a subject of the Queen and a citizen of Canada without in any way changing or ceasing to be himself."[14]

Relations between the monarch and the various peoples that owe allegiance to him or her need not be symmetrical, and relations among groups of subjects can be virtually non-existent apart from their common allegiance to the Crown. In the seventeenth century, England and Scotland shared the same monarch while being otherwise separate, just as the United Kingdom and Hanover did between 1714 and 1837 and as Canada, Australia, and New Zealand do today.

The United Kingdom formed in 1707 was, as it still is, a complex organism consisting of many parts, united primarily by their common allegiance to the Crown. The main innovation of that year was the merger of the English and Scottish parliaments, with the successor parliament meeting in Westminster, so that Scotland ceased to be an independent state even though it retained its distinct legal system and established religion. In addition to England and Scotland, the newly formed "British" state included, as it still does, the principality of Wales, united with England in medieval times but very different from it in language and culture, as well as the Isle of Man and the Channel Islands, which also retained their own peculiar institutions and cultures. Ireland, also a realm of the British Crown, was subordinate but separate until the abolition of its parliament in 1801 made it, in theory at least, fully a part of the United Kingdom. Even after 1801, Ireland's formal relationship with Westminster was different from that of Scotland, since it was governed by a lord lieutenant representing the Crown and had, unlike Scotland, a legal system and an established church based on the English model. The United Kingdom was and is, in other words, a multinational state. (Today its structure is even more complex than that just described, since Scotland, Wales, and Northern Ireland have elected assemblies that differ from one another in the extent of their powers.) As a multinational state not dedicated to symmetry or uniformity, the United Kingdom could easily accommodate and accept special arrangements for the French-Canadian subjects of the Crown, as represented by the Quebec Act. The Canadian "mosaic" that would develop later was fully compatible with, and in fact a logical consequence of, the theory and practice of British government.

One interesting consequence of the indirect rule and the vertical mosaic was that the census in British North America, and later in the Canadian federal state, always meticulously recorded the ethnic origins of the inhabitants, a practice that has become increasingly artificial and pointless in recent years as people of different origins intermarry and have children. Most of the censuses have also recorded the religions of the people, a practice that was significant for the state when Catholics paid tithes and later when public education was divided on sectarian lines, as happened in the nineteenth century. In contrast, the American state, which theoretically regarded ethnic distinctions among Caucasiáns as irrelevant and religion as a private matter in which the state should not interfere, contented itself with distinguishing people by race (indigenous North American, African, Asian, or Caucasian) until very recently. In 1980, the census added for the first time an ethnic-ancestry question similar to that used in Canada, a reflection of the growing influence of Canadian-style multiculturalism in the United States. Asking about a person's religion in the census was still prohibited by American law at the time of writing, and this is not likely to change any time soon, even though the preoccupation with religion in the United States probably exceeds that in any other Western democracy.

When the thirteen American colonies renounced their allegiance to the British Crown in 1776 and when their independence was grudgingly accepted by the British in 1783, they repudiated most of the British and British North American approach to ethnicity. Indeed, the distinctive arrangements made by the British for North American indigenous peoples, as represented by the Royal Proclamation of 1763, and for French-Canadian Catholics, as represented by the Quebec Act, were prominent among the issues that led the colonists to sever their ties with the British Crown in the first place. However, the relationship between the Declaration of Independence and what would later evolve into the so-called melting pot goes deeper than this. By repudiating the Crown and adopting a republican form of government, albeit one based in part on the writings of the English philosopher John Locke, the Americans were choosing a regime that would place a greater emphasis on the desirability of uniformity among the people.

This may seem paradoxical, since England had, and still has, an established church with bishops appointed by the state while the Constitution of the United States appears to prohibit any "establishment of religion." However, appearances in this case are somewhat deceiving. First, while England does have one established church, the United Kingdom has two: the Church of England and the Church of Scotland. Second, while the Constitution indeed prohibits an established church at the federal level, it says nothing about established churches in the individual states of the union, several of which existed in 1787 and some of which lasted well into the nineteenth century.

The more important consideration, however, is that a republic vests sovereign authority in the people of the state rather than in the Crown. Since this is so, a "people" must be deemed to exist, not just a collection of individuals owing allegiance. Monarchies have subjects, but republics have citizens. As citizens, the persons who live in a republic are expected to participate in its governance, not merely to obey its laws. "We, the people of the United States" are said to have given themselves a constitution, acting as the sovereign authority, and have therefore exercised a general will, as understood by Jean-Jacques Rousseau. They were expected to govern themselves collectively after the constitution came into effect. To do this effectively required a sense of community, a practice of participation, a shared discourse, and the ability to speak and understand one another's language, both literally and metaphorically. If they did not share common principles and beliefs, the republic would dissolve into "factions," a phenomenon greatly feared by the founding fathers of the United States.

These requirements explain the American concern with ideological conformity, which still exceeds that of most Western democracies. The infamous House of Representatives Committee on Un-American Activities, which existed from 1937 to 1969 and whose name seemed utterly bizarre to non-Americans, was an extreme manifestation of this concern, and the restrictive immigration policy established in the 1920s, discussed in a later chapter, was another. Yet even a liberal like Thomas Jefferson worried about un-American, or more precisely un-republican, ideas being imported into the United States by immigrants.[15] Because of the fear that un-republican ideas and practices might be contagious, the regime established by the Quebec Act, a measure based on decidedly un-republican principles, was considered as offensive and threatening a presence in America's neighbourhood as Cuba's communist regime would be two centuries later. The Declaration of Independence denounced the Quebec Act for "Abolishing the free System of English Laws in a neighbouring Province, establishing therein an Arbitrary government."

What has all this to do with ethnic and religious diversity? The Quebec Act may have suggested a relationship between cultural diversity and arbitrary government, particularly in a province where by far the most numerous ethnic group had not experienced or absorbed the liberal ideas of England's Glorious Revolution. Other unassimilated ethnic groups might also be potentially threatening, like the Dutch of New York or the much more numerous Germans of Pennsylvania, or "Pennsylvania Dutch" as they would be inaccurately described by later generations. The Germans, who managed to preserve their original language under generations of English and later American rule, were particularly suspect, because some of them were religious pacifists who refused to bear arms in defence of liberty, a decidedly un-American preference.[16] Benjamin Franklin, a resident of Pennsylvania although a New Englander by birth, was particularly hostile to the Pennsylvania Germans, whom he described as "Palatine Boors," and worried that they "will shortly be so numerous as to Germanize us instead of our Anglifying them." Franklin even alleged that most Germans and even Swedes had a "swarthy Complexion" in contrast to the English.[17] The fact that these minorities as well as the Highland Scots, another unassimilated ethnic group, were disproportionately numerous among the Loyalist refugees who fled from the revolution was an additional reason to regard them with suspicion. What could such people know about the "rights of Englishmen"? Admittedly, the Declaration of Independence declared that "all men" are created equal, and its author, Jefferson, would later become an enthusiast for the universalistic principles of the French Revolution. However, the philosophical origins of the declaration were clearly English and derived from the seventeenth-century struggles against the Stuart monarchs.

If a republic is believed to require a homogeneous people, the wish becomes the father to the thought. Michel de Crèvecoeur, a French immigrant who lived through the American Revolution, anticipated Israel Zangwill by claiming that "Here individuals are melted into a new race of men."[18] To say the least, this assessment was highly premature. In the second of the *Federalist Papers*, John Jay famously asserted that "Providence has been pleased to give this one connected country to one united people – a people descended from the same ancestors, speaking the same language, professing the same religion, attached to the same principles of government, very similar in their manners and customs."[19]

Even if one assumes, as Jay did, that indigenous peoples and enslaved Africans were not part of the "people," this was a considerable exaggeration. A modern study based on counting surnames has estimated that in Jay's own state of New York, only 44.2 per cent of the white population was of English ancestry in 1790. In Pennsylvania, North Carolina, South Carolina, and the then-new fourteenth state of Kentucky, the percentage was apparently even lower. New York still had a significant Dutch element in its population, which would subsequently contribute three presidents to the United States, as well as other minorities of which some dated from its days as a Dutch colony. In Pennsylvania, the Germans comprised a third of the population, outnumbering the English. The southern states had large Irish and Scottish populations not easily distinguished from one another in retrospect, since they often had similar surnames. Only the New England states, as the name of that region suggests, were overwhelmingly English.[20]

To oversimplify somewhat, the thirteen colonies that became the original states of the union divided neatly into three geographical clusters with different ethnic characteristics. The four New England colonies (Vermont and Maine were not recognized as separate entities in the colonial period but were admitted to the union in 1791 and 1820 respectively) were English, as noted above, with most of their people having migrated in the seventeenth century from the parts of England that supported the parliamentary cause in the English civil war of 1640–49. However, they differed from one another in religion, with the Calvinism of Massachusetts and the Quakerism of Rhode Island making a particularly sharp contrast. The middle states (New York, New Jersey, and Pennsylvania and to some extent their southern neighbours Delaware and Maryland) were ethnic and cultural mosaics including a variety of European origins. The states south of the Potomac had been settled mainly by people from Ireland, Scotland, and the northern and western parts of England that had supported King Charles I in the civil war. They also were distinguished by the fact that they contained very large numbers of slaves of African ancestry, whose presence was of course the result of involuntary rather than voluntary migration, although slavery existed in the other states as well.

According to Lawrence Fuchs, the most important colonies in each of the three regions (Massachusetts, Pennsylvania, and Virginia, respectively) were founded on different principles with respect to religious and ethnic diversity and continued to reflect those principles for some time after independence.[21] Massachusetts preferred to be, and was, homogeneous in terms of religion (Calvinist) and ethnicity (English), discouraging immigration that might undermine its distinct moral and ideological character and sense of community. Pennsylvania adopted a more pragmatic attitude, welcoming Europeans of any religion or ethnic background (even though Franklin grumbled about the Germans) and evolving into a multicultural mosaic. Virginia imported cheap labour, first in the form of white indentured servants and later in the form of African slaves, but did not allow such people to become full members of the community. According to Fuchs, the Pennsylvania approach ultimately prevailed in the United States as a whole, because it was the most suited to the country's needs for economic development and social harmony.

Daniel Elazar, on the other hand, has suggested that these three distinct approaches to migration and diversity gave rise to three distinct political cultures, which he called moralist (Massachusetts), individualist (Pennsylvania), and traditionalist (Virginia), and that all three have survived in different regions of the present-day United States.[22] As the frontier moved westward, the three political cultures were carried more or less in straight lines from the Atlantic all the way to the Pacific. The northern tier of states share the characteristics of the Massachusetts political culture, middle states like Illinois and Colorado resemble the political culture of Pennsylvania, and the sunbelt perpetuates the characteristics of colonial Virginia, presumably with Mexicans substituting for Africans as the exploited underclass. David Hackett Fischer has identified essentially the same political cultures, attributing them to early immigration from different parts of England. He also adds a fourth political culture in the upland regions of the South, which he attributes to migration from northern Ireland, northern England, and southwestern Scotland.[23]

Whatever else the Americans at the end of the eighteenth century were or were not, they were overwhelmingly Protestant – an admittedly broad category that ranges from Unitarians (like Thomas Jefferson) who denied the divinity of Jesus to Bible-thumping fundamentalists and from Episcopalians, an offshoot of the Church of England complete with bishops, to Quakers, who govern their "meetings" without benefit of clergy, let alone a hierarchy. By one estimate, there were only about 70,000 Catholics in the United States in 1807, which would make them about 1 per cent of the population.[24] Even England, and certainly Scotland, had a higher percentage of Catholics than that, and before the purchase of Louisiana in 1803, the number in the United States would have been significantly smaller. Protestantism, however defined, became associated with American nationalism, as it still is. The nomination of Catholics as major-party candidates for the presidency of the United States was highly controversial in 1928, the first time it occurred, and to a somewhat lesser extent even in 1960, the only occasion when a Catholic was elected.

In the assertion by John Jay as quoted above, the key phrase is perhaps "attached to the same principles of government." Although John Adams had earlier estimated that only about a third of the population had supported the revolution, a third were hostile, and a third were undecided or neutral, support for republican principles became a sort of civic religion after independence, a substitute for the nationwide established church that the Constitution prohibited. Those who had opposed independence, known to Americans as Tories and to Canadians as Loyalists, were harassed, intimidated, and deprived of their property during the war, and many thousands of them eventually departed for Canada, Nova Scotia, or other parts of the British Empire. The neutral and uncommitted presumably stayed and accepted the outcome, with most of them probably supporting the conservative Federalist Party of Adams and Alexander Hamilton when distinct political parties emerged in the 1790s.

Although Africans and indigenous peoples were denied most of the rights and privileges of American citizenship and although Catholics and certain groups of Europeans were viewed with suspicion by many Americans, the real litmus test for being an "American" was primarily ideological rather than ethnic. Precisely because it was not as ethnically homogeneous as Jay pretended it was, the new nation relied on ideology to bind together its diverse peoples. The corollary of this was that being American was viewed as a choice and not as an unavoidable consequence of ancestry or place of birth. The people as a whole had chosen to create an independent republic, and individuals who migrated to it, at least if they were of European ancestry, could make the same choice individually and be accepted as Americans by other Americans, at least in theory. Conversely, people not reconciled to the American ideology were free to leave, as the Loyalists and many so-called "late Loyalists" actually did. While native-born Americans did not always live up to this ideal in practice, this interpretation of citizenship as essentially voluntary made the United States the first civic nation. It provided a means by which the country could grow rapidly through immigration without threatening its essential unity. In fact, the only serious threat to the unity that emerged subsequently was between two groups of mainly native-born English-speaking Americans: those who supported slavery and those who opposed it.

The contrast between the American ideal of voluntary citizenship in a republic and the British concept, shared by most other European monarchies, of involuntary allegiance to the Crown was an important cause of the War of 1812. The British believed that anyone born a subject of the Crown remained so forever and could not abandon that status voluntarily. This meant that the "rights of Englishmen," such as they were, were carried by British subjects wherever they lived, in the colonies or elsewhere. But it also meant that the obligations of a British subject continued indefinitely as well, regardless of personal choice. The British had very grudgingly accepted, after the intervention of France in the War of Independence left them no choice, the collective decision of Americans to secede from the empire. They did not accept subsequent decisions by individual British subjects to do likewise.

A serious dispute between the United Kingdom and the United States arose over this issue of principle during the long war between the United Kingdom and France that followed the French Revolution. The British had traditionally resorted to kidnapping men in British seaports to recruit sailors for their navy, since the appalling conditions on British warships discouraged most men from joining voluntarily. With its human resources stretched to the limit by the war, the Royal Navy began to stop American merchant ships, looking for British-born crew members who could be seized and pressed into service. American-born crew members who, like most people in those days, could not prove their place of birth were not given the benefit of the doubt and were thus also in danger of being seized. Anyone who spoke English seemed to be fair game. American indignation over this practice, which threatened not only the life and liberty of individual Americans but the concept of voluntary citizenship on which the republic was based, eventually led to a declaration of war, although other grievances, such as British arming of indigenous peoples on the American frontier, also played a part.[25]

Although the War of 1812 began primarily because of events at sea, it was fought mainly in Canada, which as a consequence became much more distinct in sentiment from the United States. As noted above, American independence had led to an outflow of Loyalists from the United States, some of whom went to the Province of Quebec although the maritime colony of Nova Scotia received a larger number. In response to this influx of British subjects, both colonies were partitioned. A new colony of New Brunswick was carved out of Nova Scotia and given its own elected legislative assembly in 1784. Seven years later, the old Province of Quebec was divided into Lower Canada (present-day Quebec) and Upper Canada (present-day Ontario). Because of the Loyalist influx, Upper Canada's small settler population was mainly English-speaking and Protestant, while Lower Canada remained largely French-speaking and Catholic. Both were given elected legislative assemblies, the oath of allegiance having been modified so that conscientious Catholics could be elected to the Lower Canadian assembly and take their seats. The American and, to an even greater degree, the French revolutions had persuaded the British that radical republicanism was now a greater threat to their Crown and empire than the Catholic Church, which shared their fear and dislike of revolutionary France. Even in Ireland, the traditional British hostility to Catholicism gradually diminished, leading to more tolerant and liberal policies. Lacking this incentive for rapprochement with the Catholic Church, most Americans remained as anti-Catholic as ever.

The first lieutenant governor of Upper Canada, John Graves Simcoe, had tried to populate his sparsely settled domain by offering free land to settlers from the United States. As a result, large numbers of so-called "late Loyalists," motivated more by acquisitiveness than by ideology, moved there to join the much smaller number of genuine Loyalists who had arrived before 1791. The majority of Upper Canada's people when war broke out in 1812 were American-born, and there was considerable doubt as to which side they would support.[26] Lower Canada, where the Catholic clergy preached obedience to lawful authority and hostility to both the United States and revolutionary France, promised to be more reliable in support of the Crown. Perhaps for that reason, the Americans concentrated most of their military efforts, such as they were, on the Niagara frontier.

Some Upper Canadians, whether American-born or not, did support the invading American army at first, but the experience of invasion and occupation, as well as the failure of the Americans to indicate clearly that they intended to liberate and annex the colony, turned many against it.[27] In addition, there were enough genuine Loyalists to assist the British and their indigenous allies in repelling the invaders, whose politicians and generals proved to be singularly inept and whose highly decentralized federal regime was inadequate to wage a serious war of conquest. For example, Laura Secord, the Canadian heroine of the war, and Roger Sheaffe, who succeeded General Isaac Brock in command when the latter was killed at Queenston Heights, had both been born in Massachusetts.

While it may have originally resembled a civil war, as the American historian Alan Taylor has recently argued, the War of 1812, or perhaps more precisely the memory of it, produced the first stirrings of nationalism among English-speaking Canadians.[28] The war could be mythologized, with only a slight exaggeration of the truth, as one in which French Canadians and British Canadians had jointly resisted the invasion of their common enemy. (The highly significant role of their indigenous allies, who had done much of the fighting but received nothing in return for their efforts, was less frequently remembered.) Both Canadians and Americans could claim to have won the war, with the former contending that it forced the Americans to accept the permanence of a separate Canada while the latter argued that it forced the British to accept American independence. Neither side was entirely wrong in claiming to have won; only the indigenous peoples had clearly lost.

Memories of the war contributed to giving Canada's new nationalism an ideological character, the mirror image of the ideological republican nationalism in the United States. Canadian nationalism was "British" while American nationalism, even though many of its strongest proponents were of English ancestry, was anti-British almost by definition. It must be remembered that the artificial term "British" dated only from 1707 and had not really caught on in England where the ethnic label "English" was preferred and still is. Admiral Nelson had signalled at Trafalgar in 1805 that "England [not Britain] expects every man to do his duty." In Canada at least, and perhaps in Scotland and Ireland, "British" was less an ethnic than an ideological label. It meant loyal to the Crown. As time went on and Canada's institutions evolved, it eventually came to stand for the conviction that responsible parliamentary government under the Crown was a better form of government than the separation of executive and legislative powers as in the United States, that public opinion and party politics had no legitimate role in the administration of justice, and that "peace, order, and good government" mattered more than popular sovereignty.

Whether one agreed with it or not, this was a political philosophy not exclusive to any ethnic group and potentially acceptable to people of any origin. It could be shared by Canadians of different origins and even different languages, just as republican principles could unite the diverse peoples of the United States. The difference, as noted above, was that sharing an allegiance to a monarch required less homogeneity and consensus than participatory citizenship in a republic and was perhaps even reinforced by the absence of homogeneity. Immigrants from Great Britain to Canada did not really see themselves as immigrants but as British subjects who had carried their rights with them as they moved to a different part of the empire. People of other origins, who were regarded and who considered themselves as immigrants in the usual sense, did not share this heritage. However, if they retained their distinct characteristics and ways of life, they were less likely to be attracted by American republicanism, which promised "life, liberty, and the pursuit of happiness" in return for a greater degree of conformity than allegiance to the Crown required. In the words of Canadian sociologist S.D. Clark, "Assimilation in Canada meant an increasing conformity to American values of life and standards of behaviour. Efforts to check American influences in Canadian cultural life thus involved the strengthening of the supports of ethnic group loyalties."[29] First the French Canadians, then immigrants from the United Kingdom, and finally those from other parts of the world were encouraged to retain those loyalties for this reason. Persistent diversity reinforced the status quo and was a symptom of Canada's colonial status.

The War of 1812 also helped to associate the United States, as viewed by Canadians, with radical and left-wing ideas, however strange that seems today. Such ideas could be discredited by linking them with memories of the American army that had invaded Upper Canada during the war, a linkage that conservative forces in Canadian society naturally emphasized wherever possible and with considerable success. Thus, Upper Canada's pathetic rebellion in 1837 was easily discredited and suppressed, even though it responded to real and legitimate grievances against the ruling oligarchy and was actually led by a Scottish immigrant, not by an American. The much more serious rebellion in Lower Canada, where support for republican ideas was reinforced by the first stirrings of ethnic nationalism, was also unsuccessful, thanks in large part to the hostility of the Catholic hierarchy. Rebels in both colonies hoped for American support, but the administration of Martin Van Buren refused to risk another war against the British Empire by interfering in Canadian affairs.

Thus, as the nineteenth century wore on, the two North American neighbours developed distinct and to some extent mutually hostile personae based on ideological and political rather than ethnic and cultural differences, much as the two Korean states were to do in the second half of the twentieth century. Both political systems and both ideologies in North America could transcend ethnic differences and cleavages, which were always abundant on both sides of the Canadian–American border. However, the Canadian system, placing much less emphasis on popular sovereignty and political participation, required less ideological conformity than the American system and could easily accommodate two official languages, which the American system could not. It was also much more compatible with the conservative and authoritarian principles of the Catholic Church, which was convenient, because Catholics comprised about half of Canada's population.

The war in North America had ended in 1814 and the war in Europe, after Napoleon's final defeat at Waterloo, a year later. With peace restored in the North Atlantic world, travel across the Atlantic became easier, and transatlantic immigration to North America increased. While there was still migration in both directions across the Canadian–American border, the American-born percentage of Canada's population declined rapidly as unprecedentedly large numbers of immigrants arrived from across the Atlantic. Ireland, Scotland, and England, probably in that order of importance, contributed most of the new arrivals to British North America. By 1841, when Upper Canada and Lower Canada were reunited into one province as recommended by Lord Durham's report, their combined population was about a million, roughly half of whom were French Canadians. About half a million people lived in the four eastern colonies of Nova Scotia, New Brunswick, Prince Edward Island, and Newfoundland at the same date. Immigrants to British North America mainly went to Upper Canada, which had the greatest supply of unoccupied and fertile land, so by the 1850s it would surpass Lower Canada in the size of its population and would greatly surpass the four Atlantic colonies combined.

The United States drew most of its postwar immigrants from the same sources as did British North America but also acquired some from more exotic locations such as Germany and Sweden. The American census of 1840 counted more than 17,000,000 people in the United States. This ratio between the respective populations of British North America and the United States of America would not change much over the next century and a half. Immigrants to the United States tended to avoid the southern states where they would have to compete with slave labour and where there was little industrialization. New York, with only half as many people as Virginia and fewer people than North Carolina in 1790, had become by far the largest state as early as 1820, a position it would retain for a century and a half. New York had always been an ethnically diverse state and would continue to be so. In later years, the Statue of Liberty and the poem by Emma Lazarus inscribed on it would aptly symbolize New York's role in American history, even though the statue is, strictly speaking, in New Jersey.

In the decade after 1840, the United States greatly increased the size of its territory by attacking Mexico, provoking a war that Ulysses S. Grant, who fought in it as a young officer, later called "one of the most unjust ever waged by a stronger against a weaker nation."[30] The treaty of Guadeloupe Hidalgo, which ended the war in 1848, granted American citizenship to Mexicans who wished to stay in the surrendered territory. It also included attached protocols containing vague promises to protect the Spanish language and culture of the inhabitants, but the Americans claimed that the protocols were not part of the treaty itself and thus not legally binding.[31] The republic could not, or would not, easily accommodate another official language within its borders. It was also increasingly preoccupied with the growing sectional conflict over slavery, which the Missouri Compromise of 1820 had not resolved and which would culminate in civil war by 1861.

In British North America, the second half of the same decade saw the establishment of responsible government, meaning that colonial governors would henceforth be advised by cabinets whose members sat in the elected lower house of the legislature. In effect, this meant internal self-government under the Crown, with the politician at the head of the party that controlled the lower house becoming the real leader of the government while the queen's appointed representative was relegated, like the queen herself, to a largely ceremonial role. Nova Scotia in 1848 was the first colony to achieve this fundamental change in the nature of the regime, but the united Province of Canada followed within a few months and the other colonies a few years later.

In Canada, the former lower and upper sections, known officially since the union as Canada East and Canada West, retained distinct systems of law, civil law and common law, respectively, and separate political parties. Governments were jointly led, in effect, by co-leaders representing the two sections. The French language, which Lord Durham had hoped to suppress, received quasi-official recognition at the same time when Governor General Lord Elgin read part of the

Speech from the Throne in that language. Embittered by these reforms and by a law providing compensation for Canadians whose property had been destroyed by the British army during the recent rebellion, some of the English-speaking merchants in Canada East drew up a manifesto demanding annexation of the colony by the United States. While somewhat absurd, their gesture indicated an accurate assessment that the republic was less likely to respect French Canada's distinct language, culture, and religion than the British Crown.

While these events were taking place in North America, a tragedy on the other side of the Atlantic led to the dispatching to both Canada and the United States a larger volume of immigration within a short period of time than either country had previously experienced or imagined. The great majority of the new arrivals, many of them ill, starving, and destitute, were Catholics, and by no means all of them spoke English. As described in the next chapter, their arrival would test the ability of both Canada and the United States to absorb and accommodate a distinct ethnic and religious group within their borders.

3

The Irish

The English conquest and colonization of Ireland, a lengthy process that was finally completed during the so-called Glorious Revolution, was the prelude to, or perhaps the dress rehearsal for, their subsequent conquest and colonization of North America. It had begun in the twelfth century when England was ruled by the Norman-French Plantagenet dynasty. Somewhat ironically, Pope Adrian IV (who happened to be the only Englishman ever to sit on the throne of St Peter) had given his blessing to the project in 1155, and some semblance of Norman-English authority and control was established in Ireland by the end of the century. However, this first conquest did not firmly establish English rule in practice. A Scottish invasion, bubonic plague, and political turbulence in England itself all helped to weaken the authority of the conquerors. The Norman overlords sent to govern the country gradually "went native" and ceased to regard themselves (if they ever had) as English, leaving as their main legacy some surnames, such as Roche and Fitzgerald, that are now regarded as typically Irish. By the fifteenth century, effective English control of Ireland was confined to a small area around Dublin known as the Pale in much the same way as English control of North America two centuries later was confined to the Atlantic seaboard.

A second and more effective conquest began under Henry VIII, who proclaimed himself King of Ireland in 1541, and was largely completed by his daughter Elizabeth I. English common law was imposed on Ireland for the first time, and a Protestant "Church of Ireland," in communion with the Church of England and equally subordinate to the English Crown, became the official religion of the country. The English monarchy was by this time officially and militantly Protestant and hostile to the Catholic Church, while the Irish, including those with some Norman ancestry, remained almost entirely Catholic. In response to this problem, James I of England, who also occupied the Scottish throne as James VI, encouraged settlement by Scottish and English Protestants in the province of Ulster, the last of Ireland's four provinces to have been effectively subdued during the reign of Elizabeth and at that time the most thinly populated. Since many of these settlers were Presbyterians, a new element was added to the sectarian cleavages on the island of Ireland.

Colonization of the country and persecution of the Catholics were pursued more ruthlessly by Lord Protector Oliver Cromwell, who granted much Irish land to the officers in his army and hoped to remove the entire Catholic population to the area west of the Shannon River. Charles II allowed the Cromwellian settlers to keep their land, although most of them had opposed his father Charles I in the English civil war. The brief reign of James II, the younger brother of Charles II, raised some hopes of a Catholic revival, but his decisive defeat by his son-in-law William of Orange at the Battle of the Boyne on 12 July 1690 established the economic, social, and political domination of Ireland by the Protestant minority that would last for more than two centuries and in six northeastern counties (part of the old province of Ulster) for more than three.

Although Ireland had a rich cultural heritage and had been Christian for longer than England itself, the English did not regard it as a civilized country comparable to their other European neighbours, perhaps because it had lacked an effective central government prior to the conquest. Instead, they treated the supposedly primitive Irish much as they later treated the Aboriginal peoples of North America, if not worse. Unlike Scotland, which negotiated its union with England in 1707, Ireland was always considered a conquered colony, the first of many that the English would acquire over the next three centuries. The fact that most of the Irish were Catholic at a time when the English regarded Catholicism as a threatening international conspiracy provided another reason, or excuse, to treat them with contempt. As a result, their land was stolen, their traditions disregarded, their religion driven underground, their language discouraged, and they were subjected to invidious rules and prohibitions known as the Penal Laws. The resistance to English rule, such as it was, thus naturally had a sectarian character at first. Toward the end of the eighteenth century, when the English were beginning to relax their hostility to Catholicism, a more modern type of Irish patriots appeared, inspired by the American and French revolutions. Many of them were Protestants, and they dreamed of uniting the Catholics, Anglicans, and Presbyterians of Ireland in a non-sectarian republican movement, but this proved to be easier said than done.

Emigration from England's first overseas colony to its newer ones in North America began well before the American Declaration of Independence. Some went to the island of Newfoundland, although any permanent settlement there was discouraged until the end of the eighteenth century, or to Nova Scotia, but most went to Pennsylvania, Maryland, Virginia, and the Carolinas. Very few went to the New England states, and Upper and Lower Canada did not attract significant numbers until the nineteenth century.

It is estimated that only about 20 to 25 per cent of Irish immigrants to the thirteen colonies before 1776 were Catholics.[1] Kerby Miller has suggested that a surplus of men among the early arrivals led to intermarriage of Catholic men with Protestant women and that the second generation adopted the mother's faith in many cases.[2] Many of these early Irish settlers became Baptists or Methodists in America, since the decentralized organization of those sects and their emotional style of worship seemed to meet the spiritual needs of the American frontier. These early immigrants settled mainly in rural and highland areas of the southern colonies rather than in cities or on the seaboard where slave labour predominated. They also tended to blend easily with settlers from southern Scotland or northern England, so it is not entirely clear in retrospect who came from where. David Hackett Fischer, among others, has attributed to them some characteristics that persist to this day in the areas where they settled, including fundamentalist religion, violent feuds and rebellions, a taste for whisky, and even the building of log cabins, although the last of these traits was probably a natural and inevitable response to their new environment.[3] They also seem, not surprisingly, to have overwhelmingly supported the patriot cause during the American War of Independence. Ten American presidents, beginning with Andrew Jackson, who took office in 1829, were descended from this element of the population.[4]

After the War of 1812, British North America became a destination favoured by Irish emigrants. The Irish eventually became, and remained throughout the nineteenth century, the largest element in Upper Canada's population. Lower Canada also attracted Irish immigrants at this time, and Montreal's annual St Patrick's Day parade has been held continuously since 1824. The St Patrick's Society in Montreal was founded a decade later, in 1834. Both the parade and the society were non-sectarian institutions, supported by Irish Protestants as well as Irish Catholics.

Unlike those who had migrated to the American frontier during the previous century, many of these Irish immigrants were conservative and monarchist in their political orientation, which made colonial Canada more attractive to them than the republican United States. Many belonged to the official Church of Ireland, which had been established under the Tudors and was not disestablished in Ireland until 1869, and they remained Anglicans when they moved to Canada. Republicanism among Irish Protestants, relatively strong in the latter part of the eighteenth century, had been greatly weakened by the disastrous Irish rebellion of 1798, which was bloodily suppressed by a British army under the same Lord Cornwallis who had surrendered to the Americans at Yorktown in 1782. However, some of the Irish in Lower Canada are known to have supported the patriotes during the rebellion of 1837. One of the most prominent patriotes, Edmund Bailey O'Callaghan, had immigrated to Montreal from County Cork in 1823. He fled to New York State after the Lower Canadian rebellion and eventually became the director of the state's public archives in Albany.

Another new factor in Irish (and Canadian) politics was the Loyal Orange Order, a semi-secret anti-Catholic and anti-republican organization formed in County Armagh in 1795 under the influence of Protestant landlords. Originally restricted to members of the Church of Ireland, it subsequently began to admit Presbyterians and other Protestants, although Catholics and persons married to a Catholic were rigidly excluded. In British North America, where the first Orange Lodge was formed in Brockville in 1830, it admitted Protestants, particularly Scottish Presbyterians, who had no Irish ancestry at all. It also eventually had some branches or "lodges" in the United States where its appeal was purely sectarian and the monarchist sentiments of its founders were for obvious reasons not emphasized. However, it should be noted that even in Ireland its loyalty to the Crown has always been conditional on the Crown taking seriously its role as "defender of the faith" against Catholicism.

The involvement of Orangemen in sectarian violence was no longer acceptable to the British government once the republican threat in

Ireland and the external threat from republican France had disappeared. An effort was made to suppress the order in 1825, and it was
driven underground and theoretically disbanded, although not for
long, in 1836. These events encouraged many Orangemen to immigrate to Canada where, as noted above, the first Orange Lodge was
established in 1830. In Upper Canada, particularly in the area east of
Toronto, the Orange Order became a broadly based and politically
influential mass movement, combining anti-Americanism and political
conservatism with anti-Catholicism. As party politics developed, the
Orangemen became highly influential within the Conservative Party
although distrustful of the party's efforts, especially after Confederation,
to reach out to Catholic voters. They conducted annual parades on the
anniversary of the Battle of the Boyne in several Canadian cities well
into the twentieth century. In 1878, a planned Orange parade through
predominantly Catholic Montreal, which the order absurdly compared to "the entry of our Saviour into Jerusalem," threatened to pro-
voke violence, which was averted when the Liberal government called
out the militia prior to the event.[5] Peacekeeping operations by
Canadian soldiers are not a twentieth-century innovation, as is generally assumed.

Catholics were probably a minority of the Irish population in
North America, apart from Newfoundland, until at least the 1830s.
Ironically, their tendency to leave Ireland in large numbers seems to
have followed Catholic emancipation in 1829, which provided political opportunities for the small Catholic middle class but had little
direct impact on the rural tenants and farm labourers who made up
the great majority of Ireland's population. It has been estimated that
from 1825 until 1842, the British colonies in North American received
more Irish immigrants than did the United States.[6] Most Irish emigrants to Upper Canada were Protestant, but Catholics predominated
among the Irish who migrated to Lower Canada, New Brunswick,
Nova Scotia, Prince Edward Island, and Newfoundland. In predominantly Catholic Lower Canada, the Irish Catholics were generally
welcomed, and they intermarried extensively with the French population, as indicated by the many French-speaking Canadians today
who have Irish surnames. Apart from the obvious Ryans and O'Neills,
some "French" family names found in Quebec, such as Bourque,
Morin, and Sylvain, are modified versions of Irish names (Burke,
Moran, and Sullivan, respectively). In all four of the Atlantic colonies,
Irish immigration made Catholics the largest religious group, although

not a majority, by the middle of the nineteenth century. Catholics, mainly Irish, did become a majority in the seaport cities of Halifax, Saint John, and St John's, where many of them landed and stayed.

Catholics also seem to have predominated after about 1830 among Irish emigrants to the United States, perhaps because Irish Protestants were more attracted to Canada.[7] While Catholicism was familiar to, if not always admired by, British North Americans, it had been scarcely known before 1830 in the United States, except in Maryland and Louisiana. Americans were not inclined to welcome its increasingly conspicuous presence, partly because American political and religious thought, especially in Massachusetts but to some extent everywhere, was rooted in the anti-Catholic struggles of seventeenth-century England. Catholicism was also feared and resented because it was a universal creed that rivalled and clashed with the universal creed of American republicanism and because Catholics owed allegiance to a foreign potentate, the pope, who still ruled extensive territories in Italy. Therefore, it was felt that a loyal Catholic could not be a patriotic American. Samuel Morse, subsequently the inventor of the telegraph and the Morse code, warned that Catholic immigration was a threat to free institutions and even to the independence of the United States.

In the words of two American scholars, "The Irish were the first among the voluntary mass immigrant groups to confront intense antipathy."[8] Anti-Catholic and anti-Irish sentiment flared up in the United States and led to numerous violent incidents along the east coast, including the burning of churches, even before the Famine of 1845–47 produced a huge increase in Irish-Catholic immigration. For example, a mob in Boston burned down a Catholic convent in 1834. Ten years later, Philadelphia experienced an anti-Catholic riot that lasted four days and killed fourteen people. It took 4,000 soldiers to restore order in the city, whose name means the city of brotherly love.[9] Even in Canada, where Catholics had been generally accepted and were still a majority of the population, anti-Catholic agitation appeared in the 1840s.[10]

Protestant Irish Americans whose ancestors had arrived earlier, in most cases before the War of Independence, came to be referred to as "Scotch-Irish," a uniquely American label that probably first appeared in the 1830s.[11] Most scholars believe that they invented this label themselves to distinguish themselves from the Catholic Irish and perhaps to protect themselves from the growing anti-Catholic and anti-Irish violence. However, Andrew Greeley, a sociologist who has written extensively about Irish Americans and is also an ordained Catholic priest, has claimed that "they hated the label Scotch Irish which was affixed to them by their neighbors."[12] Whichever explanation for the term is true, the usual American practice, after about 1850, was to use the term "Irish" to refer exclusively to Catholics.

In Canada, where the census enumerated all Irish as such regardless of religion, this practice did not develop. The term "Scotch-Irish" was (and is) never used in Canada, and Irish-Canadian Protestants continued to label themselves as Irish. John Francis Maguire, an Irish member of the British Parliament who published a book about the Irish of North America in 1868, accused persons who called themselves "Scotch-Irish" of being ashamed of their ancestry and wrote that he had never heard the term during his travels in Canada, only in the United States.[13] A cross-tabulation of a sample of responses to the ethnic and religious questions in the Canadian census of 1941 indicated that about two-thirds of self-labelled Irish Canadians were Protestant, a ratio that seems to have remained fairly constant over many generations.

Ireland had endured many famines during its years as a colony and perhaps even before that, but the one that is universally designated as the Famine with an uppercase letter began in the autumn of 1845. A mysterious blight attacked the Irish potato crop, which had become the staple food source for most of the population because of its unparalleled ability to produce a large amount of relatively non-perishable food from a limited amount of land and labour. The disease made the potatoes turn black and become totally inedible within a few hours. It struck the crop again the following year. The response of two British governments, Whig in 1845 and Tory in 1846, was so inadequate as to create suspicion that the devastating effect on Ireland's population was the result of a deliberate conspiracy. Wall paintings can still be seen in parts of Ireland referring to the Famine as "the Irish Holocaust." While this is probably not the case, some Anglo-Irish landlords were not sorry to see the human population decline on their large estates, leaving space for more profitable livestock farming.[14]

Ireland continued to export food, although not of course potatoes, during the Famine. The import of American corn (known as maize in Great Britain and Ireland) was allowed on an emergency basis, but corn was not familiar to the Irish and not greatly appreciated. The

Corn Laws that protected British agriculture from foreign imports were repealed by the Tory government of Robert Peel, although more to reduce the cost of maintaining an industrial labour force in England than to help the Irish, but this important decision had little immediate effect. Public works projects were launched in Ireland as a pretext for feeding the people and were then replaced by soup kitchens when most of the victims of the Famine became too weak to perform manual labour. At their peak, the soup kitchens were feeding three million people. Private charitable initiatives, particularly by English Quakers, provided some help but not nearly enough to overcome the catastrophe.

More than one million Irish people died because of the Famine, some from actual starvation but many more because lack of food lowered their resistance to diseases like dysentery, cholera, and typhus. More than a million people emigrated from Ireland in a period of five years. The shortfall of births over what might have been expected in the absence of the Famine has been estimated at 416,000.[15] The Famine began a long period of continuous depopulation that no other country has experienced in modern times. Ireland's population of more than eight million in the census of 1841 declined to just over six and a half million (fewer than in 1821) a decade later and continued to fall to a low of just over four million by 1926. It has never returned to the level it attained before the Famine, and two of Ireland's four provinces have fewer people today than they had in 1841. The western part of Ireland, overwhelmingly Catholic and Irish-speaking, was the hardest hit by the disaster and still shows signs of it today. The eastern part of the country, including the major cities of Dublin and Belfast, suffered less, but by no means all Irish Protestants lived there, and Protestants were not spared the Famine's effects or the tendency to escape them through emigration. All three of the main religious groups in Ireland, Catholic, Anglican, and Presbyterian, experienced comparable declines in their numbers, which never returned to pre-Famine levels.

By no means all of the people who left Ireland during those years headed for North America, since England, Scotland, and Australia were other possible destinations, but a great many did. Quebec City was a major port of entry for Irish immigrants because it was used regularly by ships carrying timber to the United Kingdom. With no cargo to carry in the opposite direction, the timber ships filled their holds for the westbound journey by offering the cheapest available fares, albeit for a trip characterized by great danger and hardship. Many of the Irish who landed at Quebec remained in Canada, but a great many others proceeded, sooner or later, to the United States, which exercised no control in those days over migration across the border. Since US immigration data for this period exclude those who came by way of Canada, they seriously underestimate the actual extent of Irish immigration. Other people leaving Ireland and able to pay slightly higher fares travelled directly from Irish or British seaports to American seaports like Boston, New York, Philadelphia, and Baltimore. Only 9 per cent of the Irish who embarked for ports in the United States died en route, compared to 30 per cent of those who embarked for British North American ports, of which Quebec was by far the most important.[16]

Many of the Irish people who took passage to North America during the Famine were already suffering from infectious diseases, a fact that stretched the hospitality even of French-speaking Catholic Canadians to the breaking point. In addition to the thousands of immigrant deaths, many residents of Canada died from diseases brought by the immigrants, including the American-born mayor of Montreal, John Easton Mills, who succumbed to typhus in November 1847 after working as a volunteer nurse in the immigrant sheds. However, some Irish children orphaned by famine and disease were adopted by French-Canadian families and absorbed into the francophone population of what is now the province of Quebec. French-Canadian nuns and priests also did their best to help the new arrivals, with some of them losing their own lives to infectious diseases as a result. The quarantine station at Grosse Île, slightly downstream from Quebec City, had been established by the government of Lower Canada in 1832 and processed most of the immigrants who arrived during the Famine. It is now a national park containing an Irish monument, erected by the Ancient Order of Hibernians in 1909, and the unmarked graves of several thousand Irish people who died there. An even older monument in Montreal, usually known as the Irish Stone, marks the grave of 6,000 Famine victims who died in that city.

More than four million immigrants arrived at American seaports between 1840 and 1860, of which about 40 per cent were Irish. Between 1820, the first year in which the numbers of immigrant arrivals were recorded, and 1840, there had been only 743,000 arrivals from all sources.[17] (As noted above, those who crossed the border from Canada were not counted.) The great majority of them were presumably Catholic, and about one-third probably had Irish as their first language, although the lack of ethnic or linguistic data in the US census makes it impossible to be precise in this regard. In the United States, more than in Canada, the legitimate fear of infectious disease was reinforced by sectarianism and racism, which had already appeared before the Famine, as noted above. The situation was worst in Puritan Massachusetts, where Catholicism had been anathema since the founding of the colony more than two centuries previously. Despite this history, the state attracted a huge number of Irish-Catholic immigrants, either directly or by way of Quebec, and Boston eventually became the most Irish of North America's major cities. By 1885, Irish-Catholic children outnumbered Protestant children in Boston.[18]

However, opposition to the new arrivals was not based only on their religion, although religious and political anxieties may have given it a slightly more respectable appearance. Cartoonists like Thomas Nast depicted the Irish with ape-like faces, and some Americans even questioned whether they were really part of the white race. (The expression "black Irish" probably dates from this period.) Even in Canada, where skin colour was supposedly less of an obsession, Thomas D'Arcy McGee, who had thick lips and a fairly dark skin, was sometimes referred to by political opponents in Canada as "darky McGee."[19] McGee had originally emigrated from Ireland to the United States but left that country in 1857 because of its anti-Catholicism and moved to Canada, where he became one of the Fathers of Confederation.

In both parts of North America, people of real or imagined English ancestry began to call themselves "Anglo-Saxons" around the middle of the nineteenth century to distinguish themselves from Irish-speaking people presumed to be of Celtic ancestry.[20] The popularity of this label reflected the nineteenth-century view that race and language were closely associated and also suggested a kinship between "Anglo-Saxons" and Germans, whose languages are somewhat similar. In the United States, where Germany was the second-largest source of nineteenth-century immigrants after Ireland, most people believed that the Germans were more desirable and more easily assimilated than the Irish, even though about half of the Germans were also Catholic.[21] Finley Peter Dunne, a second-generation Irish American whose satirical comments on American life in the Roscommon accent of the fictitious Mr Dooley became popular in the 1890s, made fun of this belief with the statement "An Anglo-Saxon, Hinnissy, is a German that's forgot who was his parents."[22]

In the 1840s, a number of more or less clandestine organizations were formed in the United States to oppose immigration, particularly of Irish Catholics. The anti-Irish and anti-Catholic agitation of this era marked the revival of nativism, which had briefly appeared in the last years of the eighteenth century when conservative Americans were fearful of revolutionary France. Irish Catholics were the first specific ethnic immigrant group to be the target of intense antipathy by native-born Americans, but they would not be the last. After the Civil War, East Asians would become the primary target for several decades, as discussed in the next chapter of this book, and in the 1920s a generalized hostility to all immigrants would lead to major changes in immigration policy. More recently, immigrants from Latin America, particularly Mexicans, seem to have aroused the greatest anxiety and hostility, particularly in the southwestern region of the United States, which at one time was part of Mexico.

In 1849, a number of the anti-immigrant groups coalesced into the American Party, better known as the "Know Nothing Party" because its members initially made a practice of denying its existence. The Know Nothings were suspicious of all immigrants who were not English or Scottish Protestants, not only of the Irish. Like other new parties in Western democracies, this one was able to occupy a niche created by the problems of the existing parties. The Whigs, successors to the Federalists, were in decline and had won only two presidential elections, in both cases by narrow margins and with successful generals, William Henry Harrison in 1840 and Zachary Taylor in 1848, as candidates. Both presidents elected as Whigs died before completing their terms. The Democrats, dominant since the days of Jefferson, were bitterly divided over slavery. The Know Nothings quickly gained strength and at their peak in 1855 controlled the legislatures of Connecticut, Massachusetts, New Hampshire, Rhode Island, Maryland, and Kentucky, as well as having seventy-five representatives in Congress. The governor of Massachusetts was also a member of the party.[23]

Abraham Lincoln, a Whig at the time, was among the bitterest critics of the Know Nothings and wrote to a friend that he preferred the despotism of czarist Russia, which at least admitted its true character, to the hypocrisy of the Know Nothings, who pretended to support American ideals but betrayed them in practice.[24] (John Wilkes Booth, who later assassinated Lincoln, had been a Know Nothing member in Maryland.) In 1856, the American Party nominated Millard Fillmore, the Whig who had completed Zachary Taylor's term of office as president after the latter's death, as their presidential candidate, but he carried only the state of Maryland, with eight electoral votes. The party soon faded away, partly because it was divided on the issue of slavery, which increasingly dominated the political agenda.

The Civil War affected Irish-American Catholics in various ways. Most of them supported the Democratic Party, which was viewed as less hostile to immigrants and more open to cultural diversity than the Republican Party despite Lincoln's opposition to nativism. Some Irish-born Americans were hostile to African Americans, who ranked immediately below them on the vertical mosaic and, in northern states that had abolished slavery, competed directly with them for jobs. Resentment against a war whose aims included emancipation of the slaves contributed to the serious draft riots in New York in 1863 in which Irish immigrants played a large part and in which violence was directed against African Americans. The death toll in these riots has been estimated at more than 2,000. On the other hand, large numbers of Irish Catholics served in the Union army, which included some exclusively Irish units with Catholic chaplains, and their contribution to preserving the Union may have lessened the hostility that native-born Protestant Americans felt toward them. Thomas Meagher, who had been a prominent member of Young Ireland in the short-lived rebellion of 1848, attained the rank of brigadier general in the Union army.

Another veteran of Young Ireland and one of its most celebrated thinkers, John Mitchel, had also immigrated to the United States and was the only prominent Irish radical to support the Confederacy, but Mitchel was a Protestant from Ulster. There were some Irish-Catholic soldiers in the Confederate army, but their numbers were much smaller than those in the Union army because of the smaller proportion of immigrants in the southern population, and they were not organized into distinctively Irish units. Patrick Cleburne, an Irish-born Confederate general who was killed in battle near the end of the war, made the sensible suggestion that the Confederacy should imitate the Union by enlisting African Americans as soldiers, but little was done to pursue this idea.[25] Irish Protestants, the so-called Scotch-Irish, were of course very numerous in the Confederate army, since they comprised a large part of the white population in the South and were by no means unfamiliar with violence as a means of

settling disputes. General Thomas "Stonewall" Jackson, a descen-
dant of Ulster Presbyterians, ranks second only to Robert E. Lee in
the pantheon of Confederate heroes.

Canadian nativism in the 1840s and 1850s was much weaker in
its support and less extreme in its methods than its American counterpart. Many of the Irish Catholics who arrived at Quebec moved
on fairly promptly to the United States while others were absorbed
into the French-speaking community through adoption or intermarriage. Irish immigrants who stayed in Canada were more likely to
settle in rural areas than Irish immigrants in the United States and
were thus less conspicuous and less likely to be the target of discrimination and violence. The leading historian of Irish Canadians,
Donald Akenson, has noted that in Canada "neither the Irish Protestants nor the Irish Catholics were a segregated minority, either
geographically or socio-economically."[26]

In Canada East and in the Ottawa Valley, there was some conflict
between French and Irish, who competed in the market for unskilled
labour, but religion was obviously not an issue in most cases.
Relatively few Irish Catholics went to Canada West (now Ontario)
and even fewer stayed there, perhaps because of its reputation as a
stronghold of the Orange Order. It has been estimated that Toronto
was about 17 per cent Catholic in 1841, rising to 25 percent in 1848
when Irish immigration was at its peak but declining again to only
15 per cent by 1891.[27] Immigration from continental Europe to
Canada was very small in volume compared to that experienced by
the United States and attracted little attention. The Orange Order
itself was evolving, in Canada although not in Ireland, into a fairly
harmless fraternal organization, and few acts of violence in Canada
could be attributed to it. No one seems to have contemplated creating a new nativist movement, let alone a new political party.

The contrast between Canada and the United States is perhaps
most striking in relation to education, a subject that in modern times
has always been a preoccupation for the Catholic Church. In the
United States, one of the major complaints against Catholicism was
that its parochial schools, maintained entirely at its own expense,
were indoctrinating children with un-American ideas. Public schools
were unabashedly Protestant in their orientation and included prayers and Bible readings in the curriculum, but Protestantism was considered part of the American creed, not an alternative to it. Public
financial support for Catholic schools, which is the practice in many

Western democracies and even existed under British rule in Ireland, is still anathema to most Americans.

In Lower Canada (now Quebec), the tradition of indirect rule and the alliance between church and Crown worked to the benefit of all Catholics, not just those who spoke French. Catholic parochial schools, at that time serving a clientele that was almost entirely French-speaking, began to receive subsidies from the colonial government in 1829. In 1846, parallel systems of state-supported education, Protestant and Catholic, were established in Quebec City and Montreal, while in rural areas of what was now called Canada East, whichever religion was in the minority (Protestant in most areas but Catholic in some) could establish its own school board in addition to the one that served the dominant religious group. Two years later, some of the Catholic boards began to offer education in English for Irish-Catholic children.

In 1853, a system of state-supported Catholic schools and school boards was also established in Canada West (Ontario), although it was bitterly opposed by the Orangemen and the bill to establish it passed only with the aid of French-Canadian votes in the legislature of the united province. Despite some continuing Protestant opposition, the right of Ontario Catholics, who at the time were mainly Irish, to their own state-supported school system was entrenched in section 93 of the federal Constitution in 1867 and survives to the present day. In 1905, similar systems were established in the then-new provinces of Alberta and Saskatchewan, where they also continue to exist. In Quebec and in Newfoundland, the sectarian school boards were abolished in the 1990s through amendments to Canada's Constitution, with the apparent acquiescence of most Catholics.

The 1860s marked an important watershed in the history of both the United States and Canada, not least for their Irish immigrants. The Civil War and the abolition of slavery left the United States much stronger and more united than before. The British North America Act of 1867 launched another federal union in the northern half of the continent, which, like its American rival, reached from sea to sea after British Columbia joined it in 1871. As suggested above, the contribution of Irish Catholics to winning the Civil War may have helped somewhat to improve their image among Protestant Americans. In any event, they had become so numerous and politically influential in several American cities that politicians had an incentive to seek their votes by treating them with respect. The Irish themselves also began to play an active role in politics, as discussed below. In Canada, Irish Catholics were much less numerous, but one of them, Thomas D'Arcy McGee, had been a prominent Father of Confederation as well as a spokesman for Irish-Catholic Canadians before his assassination in April 1868. McGee was a former Irish republican whose disillusionment with the United States had turned him into a monarchist, and his eloquent speeches played a part in the development of Canadian nationalism.

However, a new issue had arisen that helped to make Irish Catholics suspect in the eyes of some Canadians, although it may have increased their popularity in the United States. The Irish Republican Brotherhood, better known as the Fenians, was a secret society formed in Dublin in 1858 and marked the re-emergence of organized republicanism in its most serious form since 1798. The brotherhood's program called for an independent Irish republic based on universal suffrage and the separation of church and state as well as land reform in rural Ireland.[28] The Catholic Church disapproved of the Fenians, as it did of secret societies in general, but they attracted considerable support in Catholic Ireland, particularly among the working class and lower middle class in urban areas. Unlike the United Irishmen of 1798, the Fenians seem to have attracted few Protestants to their ranks, although the movement was avowedly non-sectarian. Because the volume of emigration was still very large at this time, the movement spread rapidly to Great Britain, the United States, and Canada, particularly to the major cities.

The British government closed down the brotherhood's newspaper in 1865, transferred military units believed to be infiltrated by the movement out of Ireland, and suspended habeas corpus in Ireland for a period of three years. In the United States, the Fenians were tolerated, since they posed no threat to American interests and their program was fully compatible with American ideals. About 10,000 Fenians, according to one estimate, served in the Union army during the Civil War.

All Fenians favoured using military means to end British rule in Ireland, but the American wing of the movement differed among themselves on the strategy that should be used. One faction proposed to concentrate on conducting an uprising in Ireland itself, while another faction saw greater hope for success in an indirect approach. The latter planned to invade and occupy Canada, which they viewed as a weak link in the British Empire, and then perhaps offer to restore it to British rule in return for Ireland's freedom. The end of the American Civil War, and the demobilization of several thousand American Fenians with military training and experience, made the latter plan more plausible than it would have appeared in normal circumstances. Both approaches were tried, and although neither was successful at the time, Fenian activities in North America had a significant impact on the course of Canadian history. Their rather feeble efforts in Britain and Ireland, on the other hand, succeeded only in creating three martyrs who were hanged after the shooting of a policeman in Manchester.

Canada, New Brunswick, and Nova Scotia were at this time debating whether to establish a federal union, as they finally did in 1867. One motive for doing so, although not the only one, was the need to make British North America more defensible against attacks from the United States, which had become hostile because of British support for the southern Confederacy. The first Fenian raid, from Maine into New Brunswick in April 1866, persuaded many in that province that a military threat really existed, albeit not from the United States government, and probably tipped the scales in favour of Confederation. The episode may also have contributed to the provincial government's decision five years later to end public support for Catholic schools, which in New Brunswick at that time served a population that was predominantly Irish.[29]

Two months later, a much more formidable Fenian force crossed the Niagara River from Buffalo and defeated the Canadian militia in the Battle of Ridgeway. The Fenians then re-crossed the river into the United States rather than continuing on to Hamilton and Toronto where they might have met with further success. Another foray from Vermont in the direction of Montreal, a city containing many Fenian supporters, occurred six days later. Again the Fenians returned to the United States after two days, in this case without fighting a battle. Although the Canadian government and legislature, unlike those of the Maritime colonies, were already fully committed to the Confederation project, these events helped to solidify public opinion in its favour. Like the War of 1812, they also strengthened the still rather weak sentiment of Canadian nationalism.

The Canadian government, following the British example, suspended habeas corpus for a brief period. A number of captured Fenian invaders were placed on trial and convicted after the raids of June 1866. At the suggestion of the British government, none was executed, contrary to the advice of the Canadian minister of agriculture, Thomas D'Arcy McGee, a former Irish republican himself.[30] Although the Fenian threat, such as it was, was probably viewed by most Canadians as coming from outside the country, there were many Fenian supporters in Canada, particularly among the Irish working classes of Montreal and Quebec City. A Fenian resident of Montreal was tried, convicted, and executed for the assassination of McGee in 1868, although there is little or no evidence to suggest an organized conspiracy. In 1870, there were further Fenian raids on Quebec and one on Manitoba, where the Fenians may have hoped for support from Louis Riel's provisional government. However, by that time the movement was in decline, both in Ireland and in North America. Nonetheless, the Canadian federal government remained preoccupied by Fenian threats, whether real or imaginary, well into the 1880s, recruiting many spies and informers and also employing a private detective agency that provided it with regular reports.

Irish republicanism remained very strong and was naturally considered respectable in the United States, since that country was itself a republic and the product of a struggle for independence against British rule. Since American Irish Catholics were a numerous but relatively low-status group, discriminated against because of their ethnicity and religion, and since they lived in a country where republican ideals were officially encouraged, it was natural that their support for Irish republicanism remained strong and quite conspicuous, as indeed it still is to the present day. Eamon de Valera, who was born in New York although his Irish mother took him back to Ireland as a child, toured the United States in 1919 and 1920 to raise money for the republican cause with considerable success, although he failed to gain access to President Woodrow Wilson. The anti-British sentiments of Irish Americans were much less appreciated by the American Protestant establishment in the twentieth century than they had been in the nineteenth, since the United Kingdom had become an ally of the United States, but they were expressed nonetheless, and politicians were fully aware of them. They may have helped to delay the entry of the United States into both world wars, at least until the pro-British incumbent presidents had secured fresh electoral mandates in 1916 and 1940, respectively. There were allegations during the "troubles" in Northern Ireland after 1968 that Irish Americans contributed funds and even weapons to the armed struggle against British rule in that province. More recently, President

Bill Clinton played a constructive role in accelerating the peace process in Northern Ireland, particularly when he allowed Sinn Fein
leader Gerry Adams to visit the United States and welcomed him to
the White House despite the opposition of the State Department.
Clinton asserted in his memoirs that his interest in the politics of
Ireland was first aroused by his involvement in the politics of New
York State when he ran for president.[31]

The situation in Canada was quite different. Canada after 1867
was not a popular destination for Irish emigrants and lost a large
share of its own population to the United States. The number of
Canadians claiming Irish ancestry in the decennial census grew very
slowly for a century until 1971, after which it became possible to
claim more than one ethnic origin and the data became increasingly
meaningless. The majority of Irish Canadians were Protestants, while
Irish-Canadian Catholics tended to keep a rather low profile and to
profess, at least publicly, support for the monarchy and the British
connection, particularly in Ontario. Irish Catholics as well as Irish
Protestants joined the Canadian contingent in the South African war
of 1899–1902, a sordid imperial adventure even by the standards of
that era. In World War I, the Canadian army included more than twice
as many anglophone Catholics, of whom most were presumably Irish,
as French Canadians, even though the latter group of course made up
a much larger share of the total population. The Canadian branch of
the Ancient Order of Hibernians, a fraternal organization on both
sides of the Atlantic, separated from the American branch because of
the latter's opposition to fighting in a British war.[32]

Irish republicanism in Canada seems to have declined after the
Fenian raids, probably in part because Irish Canadians with republican sentiments were perfectly free to move to the United States,
which many did. Support for Irish "Home Rule," or what would now
be called devolution within the United Kingdom, became much stronger in Canada than republicanism, since it was more in harmony
with Canadian political principles and experience.[33] The Home Rule
movement was also the dominant force in the politics of Ireland itself
from 1880 until World War I. In addition to Irish Canadians, it
attracted considerable sympathy from French Canadians, who saw
parallels between Ireland's nationalism and their own. Charles
Stewart Parnell, the leader of the Home Rule movement in Ireland,
was enthusiastically welcomed to Montreal in 1880. Six years later, the
Legislative Assembly of Quebec voted unanimously to congratulate

Prime Minister Gladstone for introducing his Home Rule bill in the British Parliament.[34] Gladstone's second and improved Home Rule bill, which he introduced in 1893 after Parnell's death, owed much to the advice of Edward Blake, the former leader of Canada's Liberal Party and former premier of Ontario.[35] Blake at the time was an Irish nationalist member of the British Parliament, and his parents had been Irish Protestants who emigrated to Canada in 1832, a year before his birth. Both Irish Canadians and French Canadians continued to support Home Rule for Ireland despite the continued failure to achieve it by peaceful means. By the time most of Ireland obtained independence by means of armed struggle in 1922, most Irish Canadians were several generations removed from their Irish roots. In the words of the most complete, albeit unpublished, study of Canadian attitudes towards the Irish question, "the Irish in Canada were left somewhat bewildered by the new Ireland of Pearse and de Valera."[36] In recent years, however, a new organization, the Friends of Sinn Fein, has acquired considerable support in Canada, mainly but not exclusively from Irish-born immigrants.

One of the paradoxes of Irish life in North America is that while the Canadian Irish, both Catholic and Protestant, melted fairly inconspicuously into the population, the American Irish, or at least the Irish Catholics in major American cities, remained a conspicuous group who were largely segregated, geographically, socially, and politically, from the rest of the population. In other words, the conventional stereotypes of American melting pot and Canadian mosaic seem to have been reversed in the case of this ethnic group. One possible reason for this may be that anti-Catholicism in the United States was more pervasive, deeply rooted, and intense than in Canada, where Catholicism predated the British conquest and had enjoyed a certain quasi-official status and respectability at least since the Quebec Act. Since Irish Catholics were the first Catholics to have lived in the United States in large numbers, the unfamiliar and, in the opinion of many Americans, un-American faith came to be associated with Irishness and vice versa. In Canada, the Irish, regardless of their religious or political beliefs, arrived with the formal status of British subjects and were thus included among what John Porter has called the "charter groups" in Canadian society.[37] This is demonstrated by the fact that the Canadian census, until very recently, enumerated the Irish as a sub-group within the broader category of "British Isles origins" almost a century after most of Ireland became a sovereign state.

Another factor may have been the much greater size of American cities in the middle of the nineteenth century and their continuing rapid growth in industry and population over the next several decades. The Industrial Revolution was well underway in the United States during the peak years of Irish immigration, while in Canada it had barely started. In 1850, seven American cities were more than twice as large as Montreal, the largest Canadian city, and they included the eastern seaports where many immigrants landed: Boston, New York, Philadelphia, and Boston. New York, which then included only Manhattan Island, had more than ten times the population of Montreal. Many Irish immigrants settled in these four American cities, where many jobs were available for those lacking skills or capital, or in inland cities like Buffalo and Chicago. Most of them were segregated, much as African Americans in the same cities are today, in densely populated low-income neighbourhoods that were regarded by other Americans as dangerous and unattractive places to live in or even visit. Apart from Montreal's Griffintown and perhaps Toronto's Cabbagetown, both very small by American standards, such Irish ghettoes were not really found in Canadian cities. Tim Pat Coogan, a prominent writer in Ireland, has suggested that the Catholic clergy encouraged Irish Americans to stay in predominantly Irish neighbourhoods rather than mingling with the rest of the population, but he presents no evidence for this.[38]

Another important difference between the United States and Canada was that in the United States the Catholic Church was, and for a very long time remained, an essentially Irish-American institution, while in Canada the church was and is dominated by French Canadians. The reason for the contrast is fairly simple. Canada in its origins was both Catholic and French, and a Catholic Church with a French-speaking clergy and predominantly French-speaking members was in place when the British arrived. Catholics who arrived later as immigrants, including the Highland Scots and the Irish, were fitted into this framework, as were the significant number of indigenous people who adopted the Catholic faith, but even today a majority of Canadian Catholics, practising or otherwise, are of French ancestry.

In the United States, where there were very few Catholics before large-scale immigration from Ireland began, the number of Catholic priests tripled, from 480 to 1,500, during the Famine decade of the 1840s.[39] Presumably, the great majority of these new priests were Irish. A majority of Catholics were of Irish ancestry for many decades and probably until the massive immigration of Spanish-speaking Catholics from Mexico and Central America in recent years. Clergy of Irish ancestry built the American Catholic Church into a major institution, just as clergy of French ancestry, in an earlier period, made the Catholic Church an important force in Canadian life. Major Catholic educational institutions in the United States, such as Fordham University in New York and the University of Notre Dame in Indiana, retain an Irish ambience to the present day. In both countries, the first predominantly Catholic ethnic group to arrive in large numbers was able to fashion the church in its own image.

As non-Irish Catholics entered the United States in increasingly large numbers, they exerted some resistance to the Irish domination of the hierarchy. The Irish-American clergy were viewed by some of their fellow Catholics as rigidly conservative, hostile to people of other religions, and partial to ethnic nationalism, characteristics by no means unknown among the French Canadian clergy in the same period. Ethnic conflicts within Canadian Catholicism were mainly between the French and Irish over the status of the French language outside of Quebec. Ontario's notorious Regulation XVII, which prohibited French as a language of instruction in the public (including Catholic) schools in 1912, was supported by the Irish-Catholic clergy in that province, particularly Bishop Michael Fallon of London, whose diocese included very few francophones. It was bitterly and understandingly resented by French Canadians in both Ontario and Quebec.

The role of the Irish in American politics and their gradual ascent, in George Reedy's words, "from the ward to the White House" has inspired a considerable volume of writing.[40] American party politics has usually had more to do with sectional and ethnic conflicts and cleavages than with class, particularly since the presidential election of 1840 when the age of Jacksonian democracy, represented by incumbent president Martin van Buren, was ended by the successful populist campaign of the conservative Whig candidate, General William Henry Harrison, a wealthy Virginia slaveholder who claimed to have been born in a log cabin. As the country drifted toward the Civil War, the Democrats became increasingly the party of the South while the Whig Party and its successor, the Republican Party, were stronger in the northern states. Civil War and Reconstruction reinforced this sectional contrast, which lasted until the civil rights legislation of the 1960s alienated white southern voters from a Democratic

Party that they viewed as excessively "liberal" in the American sense of the word.

With both parties dominated by Protestants of British ancestry and generally anti-Catholic views in their respective sections, Irish-Catholic immigrants in northern cities during the nineteenth century turned to the Democratic Party, the minority party in their section of the country, and gradually took it over. Their loyalty to it has lasted to the present day despite the ascent of most Irish Catholics into the middle class. The process began at the local level where municipal elections, in contrast to those in Canada, were contested under the same party labels that were used in the higher levels of government. As a vulnerable, poverty-stricken, and generally despised minority, the Irish immigrants in the large cities turned for help to municipal governments, which were more easily influenced than those at higher levels. In a highly decentralized political system where the central government until the twentieth century did little more than issue the currency and deliver the mail, municipal government controlled most of the patronage that was accessible to the immigrants and likely to influence their prospects in life. Succeeding waves of immigrants to the same cities from eastern and southern Europe would eventually realize the same fact and act accordingly, following in the footsteps of the post-Famine Irish.

The "Irish political machine" remained a celebrated institution in American folklore long after it was generally acknowledged to have disappeared for all practical purposes. Its reputation may have been enhanced and prolonged by the Hollywood film *The Last Hurrah* in which the great Irish-American actor Spencer Tracy portrayed a central character loosely based on a spectacularly corrupt former mayor of Boston, James Michael Curley, who was still living when the film was released in 1958. In fact, the most powerful, long-lasting, and notorious urban political machine, New York's Tammany Hall, was founded by Dutch Americans and British Americans in 1786 as an explicitly nativist organization, its most celebrated nineteenth-century leader, William "Boss" Tweed, was from Scotland, and its last boss of any significance, Carmine di Sapio, was an Italian American.

It is undeniably true, however, that from the end of the Civil War until the middle of the twentieth century a disproportionately large number of local politicians in large American cities outside of the South were Irish Catholics, as were a disproportionate number of municipal government employees. According to Stephen Erie, 30 per cent of municipal employees in the fourteen largest American cities in 1900 were Irish, compared to only 20 per cent of the entire labour force.[41] In New York City, where only 6 per cent of employed Irish people worked in the public sector in 1900, nearly a quarter of them did by 1930.[42] This fondness for the public sector may be a common characteristic of ethnic groups that are not faring well in the market economy, but the distribution of jobs and benefits by politicians of Irish ancestry was probably also a factor.

Boston, the most Irish of large North American cities, was the classic instance of Irish domination of local politics, where it began first and lasted longest. However, its local politics were usually characterized by factionalism rather than by a single centralized machine such as existed for a time in other cities. Stephen Erie, in his study of Irish urban machines, has suggested that the Irish domination of local government and politics began before the end of the nineteenth century in New York, Jersey City, and San Francisco as well as in Boston, while in Chicago and Pittsburgh it did not appear until about 1930, roughly the same time at which it ended in multicultural New York. San Francisco's Irish machine lasted only about a decade, from the 1870s until the 1880s. In Boston, Irish control ended only with the reform of the Democratic Party in the 1950s.[43]

Tom Garvin, an Irish political scientist, has suggested that Irish-American immigrants acquired their political skills before leaving Ireland, particularly by participating in the mass movement founded by Daniel O'Connell. (After his original goal of Catholic emancipation was achieved in 1829, O'Connell directed his efforts toward repeal of the Act of Union, which had abolished Ireland's parliament in 1801.) George Reedy has attributed the Irish-American penchant for politics to the informal networks of influence and participation that existed in Irish villages under British rule.[44] Three other historians of American ethnicity, in their jointly authored book, have suggested that membership in a hierarchical church gave the Irish a talent for organization, but this theory does not seem particularly persuasive.[45] It seems more likely that the Irish success in municipal politics in the United States was caused by the fact that they happened to arrive at a time of rapid urbanization, by their geographical concentration in certain cities and neighbourhoods, and by the "glass ceiling" that confronted them at higher levels of government where white Protestants clearly had an advantage.

Two areas of the public sector that have had a particularly Irish flavour in the United States, and even in Canada, are the police and the firefighters, particularly the latter. It has been suggested that Irish police personnel were deliberately recruited on the theory that they could best deal with criminals who were also, for many years, disproportionately Irish. The term "paddy wagon," still applied to the vehicles that carry arrested persons to the local jail in North American cities, has been attributed to the ethnicity of their drivers or, alternatively and perhaps more credibly, to that of their occupants. Noel Ignatiev has also suggested that the recruitment of Irish policemen, at a time when African-American policemen were still unknown, was an important milestone in the improving status of the Irish in American society. By entrusting Irish cops with a part of the state's coercive power, white Protestant America was empowering them to fight back against anti-Catholic violence and also implicitly accepting them as allies of the dominant ethnic group in American society.[46]

Firefighting was originally a volunteer activity in both the United States and Canada and was taken over in some cities by various gangs of predominantly Irish residents for whom it was perhaps as much an opportunity for social networking as for community service. At times, rival groups of volunteer firemen competed for control of the water needed to put out fires, a phenomenon depicted in the recent film *Gangs of New York*, which is set in the time of the Civil War.[47] The same phenomenon occurred in Montreal, where Irish, British, and French squads of volunteer firefighters "often resorted to bribes, fistfights and dirty tricks, like slashing the competition's hose."[48] In 1857, young Irish Catholics in Montreal attacked Irish-Protestant firemen who were putting out a fire, and one of the firefighters was shot.[49] When firefighting in major cities became a full-time professional activity, those who had been volunteer firefighters were the logical persons to be hired. According to a recent oral history of the Irish in Montreal, about half of the personnel in the fire department of that predominantly French-speaking city were Irish in the early part of the twentieth century, and there were many Irish policemen, in contrast to the second half of the century when only French Canadians were hired.[50] In Toronto in about the same period, the police and fire departments were dominated by Irish Protestants, specifically Orangemen, but there were some Irish-Catholic personnel as well.[51]

Although policing and firefighting seemed to be Irish specialties on both sides of the border, the phenomenon of the urban Irish political machine never really appeared in Canadian cities to a significant degree. Probably the closest Canadian approximation to the colourful

Irish machine politician of American folklore, one who appeared relatively late in Canadian and North American history, was Frank Hanley, an independent member of Quebec's Legislative Assembly from 1948 to 1970 and of Montreal's municipal council for an even longer period.[52] Hanley received clandestine support from the Union Nationale, the conservative Quebec nationalist party founded by Maurice Duplessis, but the decline and fall of that party, the election of reform mayor Jean Drapeau, and the destruction of Griffintown, his political base, by a major highway project eventually sealed his fate. Even at the peak of his influence, he never really enjoyed the power of his counterparts in the northeastern United States.

There were several reasons for the failure to develop urban Irish political machines on the American model in Canada. Since Irish immigration to Canada tapered off rapidly after the 1850s and since Canada was not a predominantly urban country until the twentieth century, Canadian cities had fewer unassimilated Irish residents than the cities of the northern United States. Those whom they had were less concentrated in particular neighbourhoods that might have served as the base for a political machine; Hanley's Griffintown was an exception, but its population declined as the Irish moved elsewhere and were not replaced by new arrivals. The Canadian Irish were more divided by religion than the American Irish, and they did not support one political party with the consistency and enthusiasm that marked Irish-American support for the Democrats. Canadian municipal governments were and are formally non-partisan and have no ties to the federal government, which rigidly abstains from interference in municipal affairs, so they cannot distribute federal largesse or have much influence over how it is spent. They are also regarded in Canadian law as "creatures of the province" and thus enjoy far less autonomy than their American counterparts.

Finally, the glass ceiling that barred Catholics from higher political office in the United States did not exist in Canada, thanks to the "charter group" status of the French Canadians. In Ontario, the most Protestant of the four original provinces, the first premier after Confederation was a Scottish Catholic, John Sandfield Macdonald. John Thompson became the first Catholic prime minister of Canada in 1892 and had previously served for a short time as premier of Nova Scotia. In Quebec of course, the great majority of political office-holders at all levels were Catholics. Only one Protestant, a

French-born Huguenot named Henri Joly de Lotbinière, has ever headed a major political party in the province.

Irish Canadians, both Protestant and Catholic, played prominent roles in Canadian federal and provincial politics from the nineteenth century onwards. From 1867 onwards, it was considered obligatory to have at least one Irish Catholic in the federal cabinet at all times. Louis St-Laurent, Liberal prime minister from 1948 to 1957, had an Irish mother and was as fluent in English as in French. Irish Protestants in Canada tend to be Conservatives and Irish Catholics to be Liberals, except in Newfoundland where it is usually the other way around because the Liberals sponsored, and the Catholic clergy opposed, the province's union with Canada. However, many Irish-Canadian politicians were exceptions to the rule. Robert Baldwin, the co-leader of the first responsible government in central Canada, and Edward Blake, the minister of justice who established the Supreme Court of Canada and later helped to draft Gladstone's second Home Rule bill, were Liberals and the sons of Protestant Irish immigrants. Thomas D'Arcy McGee, an Irish-born Catholic, ended his Canadian political career as a Conservative, although he had begun it as a Liberal. In more recent history, Lester Pearson, the last Protestant to serve as a Liberal prime minister of Canada, had Irish ancestors, while Brian Mulroney, a Catholic whose ancestors came from County Carlow, led a Conservative government as prime minister for nearly nine years.

Despite their political success at various levels, the descendants of the Irish Catholics who came to North America in the middle decades of the nineteenth century remained an economically and socially disadvantaged group for several generations on both sides of the border. Prominence in sports and entertainment provided upward mobility for a few, as it does for some African Americans today, but not for many.[53] The efforts of the so-called "lace curtain Irish" to rise into the middle class were often psychologically painful. "What will the neighbours think?" has been described as the mantra of Irish Americans who sought respectability with varying degrees of success.[54] George McManus's *Bringing Up Father*, a comic strip that began in 1913 and remained popular for more than half a century, depicted the conflict between Jiggs, a shanty Irish immigrant who yearned for corned beef and cabbage, and his bossy and socially ambitious wife, Maggie, who insisted on dragging him to the opera.

However, the economic, educational, and social status of Catholic Irish Americans rose rapidly during the twentieth century, particularly after 1945. Although the idea of an association between Protestantism and material success is an old one, going back at least to Max Weber, recent data indicate that the Catholic Irish have become one of the most affluent and successful ethnic groups in the United States and that the Protestant Irish, a large number of whom still live in the rural South, have lagged behind.[55] The greater tendency of nineteenth-century Catholics to settle in the urban areas of what would later be called the Boston–Washington corridor proved to be an advantage for their descendants in the long run.

As discussed above, Irish Catholics were for many years viewed with some suspicion by other North Americans for reasons that were mainly religious in the United States and mainly political in Canada. Prejudice against them seems to have lasted longer in the United States than in Canada, where they were much less numerous and conspicuous. It is also easier to change, or conceal, your political opinions than your religion, particularly if religion is taken seriously. It is interesting that as late as 1926, Joseph P. Kennedy, a graduate of Harvard who was already a millionaire at the time, moved his family from his native city of Boston to New York to escape from anti-Irish and anti-Catholic prejudice.[56] Three and a half decades later, the inauguration of his son, John F. Kennedy, to the presidency of the United States marked a symbolic turning point in the rise of Irish-Catholic Americans to complete acceptance and respectability.

In both Canada and the United States, anti-Irish prejudice probably declined in part because newer groups of immigrants, especially from southern Europe, replaced the Irish near the bottom of the socio-economic ladder. In the United States, an even more important factor was the massive migration of African Americans from the rural South to the northern American cities where Irish immigrants had previously settled, a phenomenon that became noticeable and significant in the first half of the twentieth century. Like the nineteenth-century Irish before them, the African Americans came from a rural environment where they had worked mainly as unskilled labourers on estates owned by a different ethnic group. Both groups had difficulty at first in adapting to an urban environment where they faced prejudice and discrimination as well as a job market requiring more education and training than they possessed. Many of the unflattering stereotypes that are applied to African Americans today were applied to Irish Americans in the past. However, the arrival of large numbers of African Americans in northern cities made the ethnic differences between Catholic Irish and Protestant English or Scottish Americans appear less significant and contributed to the Irish being accepted, finally, as fully "white."

By 1985, when President Ronald Reagan and Prime Minister Brian Mulroney sang "When Irish Eyes Are Smiling" at their "Shamrock Summit" meeting in Quebec City, there could be no doubt that the Irish on both sides of the border had arrived in every sense of the word. Today, when almost everyone in North America claims to have Irish ancestry, at least on 17 March, and when a conference on Irish unity organized by the Friends of Sinn Fein can receive a congratulatory message from the minister of citizenship, immigration and multiculturalism in a Conservative Canadian government, it is hard to imagine the hardship and prejudice that Irish North Americans faced in the not too distant past.[57] One can hope that all other immigrant groups will eventually travel along the same road. Yet other groups have faced even more serious obstacles to success on this continent than the Irish, and some still do. One such group, the Chinese, is the subject of the next chapter.

4

The Chinese

The Chinese were the first non-European ethnic group to come to North America in large numbers as voluntary immigrants. However, they encountered societies that were already divided racially between Aboriginal peoples and settlers and, particularly in the United States, between settlers of European ancestry and the descendants of African slaves. These existing social and ethnic differences influenced the ways in which the host societies responded to the Chinese and also the response of the Chinese themselves to their new environment. Although they represented one of the world's oldest and most highly developed civilizations, the Chinese were looked down upon in North America, because North Americans of European ancestry were accustomed to looking down upon all persons whose skin colour or "race" differed from their own. It is unlikely that many of the Chinese realized prior to their arrival in North America that the host societies were already racially divided and had long histories of conflict and misunderstanding between peoples of different ethnicity, particularly, but not exclusively, between Caucasians and non-Caucasians.

Another characteristic of the Chinese experience in North America that differed from that of earlier immigrants was that the Chinese, until very recent times, arrived almost exclusively on the Pacific coast of North America rather than on the more developed and thickly populated Atlantic side of the continent. Unlike the states and provinces that received most of the earlier settlers such as the Irish, California and British Columbia were immature, thinly populated, and scarcely developed frontier societies at the time when the Chinese influx began. Their remoteness and the small size of their populations made them particularly fearful of being overwhelmed by immigration from an alien country whose human resources appeared almost unlimited. As such, they represented difficult environments even for settlers more familiar than the Chinese were with the culture, religion, and language of the host society.

In his history of attitudes towards East Asians in British Columbia, W. Peter Ward has commented that "the history of west coast race relations suggests that the Canadian commitment to multiculturalism has been tenuous at best."[1] Whatever definition of the ambiguous term "multiculturalism" one chooses to adopt, this is a fair assessment. It could be observed with equal justice that the presumed American commitment to a "melting pot" has also been tenuous as far as the Chinese are concerned. The idea of the melting pot is that a person of any race, colour, or creed is capable of becoming an American and being treated as such if he or she accepts the principles of the Constitution and the Declaration of Independence. Chinese immigrants in the United States, or would-be immigrants to that country, were made aware, at least until very recent times, that this optimistic assumption applied only to Europeans, certainly not to themselves.

The governments of both the United States and Canada made it particularly difficult for Chinese women to enter their respective countries in what was clearly a deliberate effort to prevent any natural increase of the Chinese-origin population. While the manual labour of Chinese men was considered useful for specific purposes, those admitted were viewed as sojourners rather than permanent residents, and the formation of families was effectively discouraged. Chinese immigrant men, deliberately deprived of female companionship, were then frequently accused of a penchant for consorting with prostitutes or of endangering the virtue of Caucasian women. No one in nineteenth-century North America seems to have recognized that such tendencies, if they existed, were a natural consequence of official policy.

Despite its distance, both geographical and cultural, from North America, China had been visited by two categories of Americans in the decades after the United States became an independent nation: traders in tea, silk, and spices on the one hand and Protestant missionaries on the other. Unfortunately, neither group formed a favourable impression of the Chinese people, who were regarded by the traders as cruel, cowardly, dishonest, backward, and generally bizarre.[2] The Chinese also displayed little or no enthusiasm for the Christian faith, a fact that did not endear them to the missionaries. The impressions of these American observers, communicated to their fellow Americans through letters and newspaper accounts of their activities, contributed to a racist mindset that was to prove very long-lasting. Dislike of the Chinese was mingled with contempt, since China at this time had neither an effective central government nor an effective army. Despite China's vast size and population and its impressive cultural achievements, the authority exercised by the central government of China had declined drastically since the heyday of the Chinese empire, as had China's power and influence in the world. The first opium war of 1839–42, when the British attacked China and seized the important seaport of Hong Kong, revealed that the country was too weak and helpless to defend itself against much smaller but more technologically advanced opponents. The British fought a second opium war against China in 1856–60. In both wars, the British goal was to continue to sell opium from India in China, where the importation and use of the drug was prohibited. Although the United Kingdom and some other Western nations exchanged ambassadors with China, for most practical purposes it had ceased to be taken seriously as a factor in international relations. The century following the first opium war is referred to in China as the Century of Humiliation.

Nonetheless, it was very soon after this nadir of China's fortunes that Chinese people first appeared on the Pacific coast of North America. They were drawn there by poverty at home and by the attraction of gold, which was discovered in California in 1849 and led to an influx of fortune-seekers from many sources. (Further "gold rushes" in Australia, British Columbia, and Yukon would shape the history of the Pacific Rim over the next half century.) The Chinese came almost entirely from the southern part of China and spoke the Cantonese dialect. As the gold rush petered out, and because their participation in it was limited by a discriminatory tax and the hostility of white miners, most found other sources of employment. The Chinese laundry, a stereotypical occupation in both the United States and Canada, was seen by some as a niche in the economy that required little capital, skill, or education but provided a service that was much in demand.[3]

California, which the United States had acquired from Mexico in its aggressive war against that country in 1845–48, must have seemed almost as distant and exotic to most Americans in those days as China itself. The ostensible reason for its acquisition was the so-called Bear Flag Revolt of 1846 in which a handful of US citizens residing in California imitated their compatriots in Texas a decade earlier by rebelling against Mexican rule and proclaiming themselves a "republic." Fortunately for them, the California "republic" was occupied almost immediately by American military forces and formally ceded to the United States in 1848. Two years later, it became a state of the union, with a population of less than 100,000, ranking twenty-ninth in size among the thirty-one states. Communication by rail with the rest of the United States was not established, however, until 1869 when the Union Pacific Railroad and the California-based Central Pacific, both chartered by the Lincoln administration during the Civil War, united their tracks at Promontory Point in the territory of Utah. Since the Panama Canal was not constructed until after the turn of the century, California in its first two decades of statehood was extremely isolated.

It was to this new, small, and rather primitive community that the Chinese came after the beginning of the gold rush, preceded by the unfavourable reputation that the traders and missionaries had bestowed on them. Only a few Chinese came at first, but in 1852 no less than 20,000 of them arrived in California, a number equivalent to about a fifth of the state's existing population.[4] By 1882, about 250,000 Chinese had migrated to California.[5] It was perhaps almost inevitable that they would be resented by the state's white working class, primarily of Irish and German ancestry, since the Chinese worked hard and accepted very low wages. However, the effect of economic rivalry and competition was reinforced by a generalized resentment against persons of non-European ancestry, which had characterized the United States since before the Declaration of Independence.

There were at least two reasons for this. In the first place, the Aboriginal peoples of North America had been hated and feared by most Anglo-Americans since the beginnings of English settlement in the thirteen colonies. This pervasive sentiment had followed the advance of the American frontier across the continent, an advance that was marked by frequent violent clashes between the settlers and the original inhabitants of the land until almost the end of the nineteenth century. Second, the long and tragic history of slavery in the United States made "race" a constant preoccupation, both before and after the Civil War that ended slavery but left the political and social status of African Americans very much in question. The Chinese, also a minority conspicuous for their physical characteristics, added another piece to the complicated puzzle of "race," particularly in

California and some other western states and territories where they were the most numerous of the three racial minorities. Resentment traditionally directed against the other two groups, indigenous peoples and African Americans, were easily transferred to them, although their situation was in fact quite different. State and local politicians at times deliberately catered to such sentiments.

Before the Civil War, the federal government, facing the crisis over slavery, had little time for the distinct concerns of California, a small and remote state that had little political influence in Washington. The state made up for this apparent neglect by adopting a series of anti-Chinese measures. A discriminatory tax against Chinese gold miners was imposed in 1852, which, as already noted, was a year of massive Chinese immigration, and lasted until 1870.[6] In 1854, a new law prevented Chinese from testifying in California courts against white people, leaving them totally defenceless against white violence and persecution.[7] In 1855, the state imposed a head tax on every Chinese who entered California.[8] In 1880, after the Civil War and Reconstruction, California adopted an anti-miscegenation law that was modelled after those directed against African Americans in other states but which explicitly mentioned "Mongolians."[9] Measures like these, as well as much unofficial discrimination and harassment, did not end the migration of Chinese to California, where many employers welcomed them as a cheap and docile supply of labour. Between 1850 and 1882, about 330,000 Chinese immigrants entered the United States, but of these some 150,000 returned to China during the same period.[10] There were only 105,465 Chinese in the United States in 1880.[11] Almost all of the Chinese admitted to the United States were men; the scarcity of women explains why few Chinese families were formed, or babies born, and also largely explains why so many of the migrants returned to their native country.

As early as 1859, Chinese labourers were employed on a small local railroad in California, the San Francisco and Marysville. The "transcontinental" railroad, built to connect Omaha, Nebraska, with Sacramento, California, was a joint project by two companies, the eastern-based Union Pacific and the California-based Central Pacific. The location where they joined to create a continuous rail link between east and west would be determined by the speed at which they progressed, a fact that created an incentive for each company to work as quickly as possible. The Central Pacific (later called Southern Pacific), California's largest enterprise, had managed to lay only fifty-five miles of track by the end of 1865. In that year, it began to employ Chinese labour, because its largely Irish labour force was threatening to strike for higher wages.[12] The Chinese worked hard and gave little trouble to management, so eventually they took over about 90 per cent of the construction jobs on the Central Pacific.[13] Most of its main line through the Sierras from Sacramento to Promontory Point, a distance of 681 miles, was built in 1868 and 1869, almost entirely by Chinese labour. About 12,000 Chinese were working on the Central Pacific in 1867, two years before its main line was completed. Charles Crocker, one of the four partners who controlled the railroad, praised the Chinese as good workers.[14] The working-class whites with whom they competed for a limited supply of jobs tended to be less charitable in their sentiments. Ethnic animosity and rivalry between the Chinese working on the Central Pacific and the mainly Irish labour force of the Union Pacific probably speeded up the pace of construction on both railroads, and the last spike was driven in May 1869.

Canada's early experience with Chinese migrants was very similar to that of the United States. British Columbia, which at that time belonged to the Hudson's Bay Company, had experienced a gold rush beginning in 1857, eight years after the gold rush began in California. It was freed from the company's control and organized as a British Crown colony a year after the gold rush began, just as California had become an American state a year after the beginning of its gold rush. In 1866, the Crown colony of British Columbia (the mainland) was united with the slightly older colony of Vancouver Island, which had a much larger white population. The name British Columbia was retained, but the seat of government was moved to the island's capital city of Victoria, where it remains to the present day. In 1871, British Columbia was united, by its own wish, with the Dominion of Canada, becoming the sixth, and in population the fifth largest, province.

Even after its union with Vancouver Island, and certainly before that event, British Columbia was a society in which white settlers were greatly outnumbered by Aboriginal people. In fact, as late as 1881, ten years after it joined Canada, Caucasians amounted to only about a third of its population, with Aboriginals still comprising a slight majority and the Chinese comprising most of the remainder.[15] The sense of being a small minority in a place very distant from central Canada, and even more distant from their ancestral homelands in the United Kingdom, made white British Columbians fearful of being overwhelmed by an alien ethnic group like the Chinese, who arrived in considerable numbers soon after the gold rush. Lord Dufferin, the witty and urbane Irish landlord who was Canada's governor general from 1872 to 1878, described white British Columbians as having "the vulgar xenophobia of the English middle class."[16]

The terms of union on which British Columbia joined the Canadian federation included the construction of a transcontinental railway from Montreal to the Pacific coast. Like its American counterpart, this project, which British Columbians greatly desired, soon involved the recruitment of Chinese labour, which British Columbians desired not at all. In its early years as a province, British Columbia's rather tempestuous relations with the federal government were dominated by two somewhat inconsistent issues: demands that the Canadian Pacific Railway be completed more promptly and complaints about the presence of the Chinese.[17]

Traditionally, the Chinese role in building the CPR was neglected by Canadian writers, but in recent years there has been a pronounced reaction against that approach, including the construction of a large and conspicuous monument in downtown Toronto, to the point where many younger Canadians may now believe that the Chinese built the entire railway from coast to coast. In fact, they were employed only on the section from Eagle Pass (Craigellachie) to the Pacific coast, about 338 miles, and they had nothing to do with the most spectacular and rugged section of the railway, between Calgary and Revelstoke. At the peak of construction in the early 1880s, about 6,500 Chinese and 2,500 Caucasians were at work on the CPR west of Eagle Pass. The use of Chinese labour was the initiative of Andrew Onderdonk, an American contractor who had been hired to build the section of the line west of Kamloops at the behest of the federal government even before the Canadian Pacific Railway Company was given its charter in 1881. Onderdonk was familiar with Chinese labour because he had worked in California. In September 1885, he announced that all his labourers, regardless of race, would be discharged, since the contract was completed. According to the railway's official historian and archivist, many of the Chinese were subsequently offered permanent jobs on the CPR.[18]

In both countries, a serious movement to restrict further Chinese immigration began even before their respective transcontinental railways were completed but was resisted by the railway companies and by the two federal governments for as long as Chinese labour was needed. In Canada, support for the movement was confined to British Columbia, the only province with a significant Chinese population. In the United States, support for anti-immigration measures was more widespread, because many Chinese moved from California into neighbouring states and territories. For example, in 1870 they comprised 29 per cent of the population of Idaho, which was not yet a state.[19] There were even efforts in the southern states to replace African-American slave labour with Chinese after the abolition of slavery.[20] Some Chinese were also used as strike-breakers in the industrial states of the northeast.[21] However, the majority of Chinese immigrants still lived in California, where a referendum in 1879 produced a majority of more than 99 per cent in favour of excluding all further Chinese immigration.[22]

The Democratic Party in California used anti-Chinese agitation, as its counterparts in other states used anti-African agitation, to mobilize the white working class against the dominant Republicans and also to discourage the rise of more radical forms of working-class protest.[23] However, anti-Chinese sentiments were not confined to California. Organized labour throughout the United States was hostile to the Chinese, even though a large proportion of its members and leaders were Irish immigrants who had themselves been the targets of xenophobic and racist sentiments before the Civil War. Most newspaper editorialists and politicians of both major parties expressed the view that the Chinese were incapable of assimilation and that they were thus not acceptable as potential citizens of the United States. A corollary of this assumption was that they should not be welcomed as permanent residents. A bill to make them eligible for naturalization was defeated in the Senate in 1870, with majorities in all regions voting against it.[24]

In 1879, a bill prohibiting any ship from carrying more than fifteen "Mongolians" to an American port passed in both houses of Congress but was vetoed by Republican President Rutherford B. Hayes on the grounds that it was contrary to a treaty between the United States and China that had been signed in 1868.[25] Although this treaty had guaranteed unlimited freedom of immigration, it was amended in 1880 to allow the United States to restrict Chinese immigration. (This was the same year in which California prohibited marriages between Chinese and Caucasians.) In 1882, a year of high unemployment in which the number of Chinese immigrant arrivals reached an unprecedented level, Congress adopted, and Republican President Chester A. Arthur signed, the Chinese Exclusion Act.[26] Although initially it was supposed to remain in effect for only ten years, it was renewed in 1892 and made permanent in 1902.[27] The impact of this measure was that the Chinese ethnic population of the United States declined by more than 40 per cent between 1880 and 1920.[28] The scope of the Chinese Exclusion Act was extended to Hawaii after that country was annexed by the United States in 1898.

The act was directed primarily against Chinese labourers, the intent being to make it impossible for them to enter the United States even temporarily. Officials of the Chinese government, merchants, teachers, students, and tourists, as well as their wives and dependent children, were allowed to enter the United States but not to settle there permanently. A directive issued by the Department of Commerce and Labor in 1905 reminded immigration officers of these provisions of the law and warned them as follows: "While laborers must be strictly excluded, the law must be enforced without harshness, and unnecessary inconvenience or annoyance must not be caused such persons as are entitled to enter the United States. Chinese persons whose appearance or situation clearly indicates that they do not belong to the class of laborers must be treated with the same consideration extended to members of any other nationality, and they are not under any circumstances to be subjected to unnecessary surveillance."[29]

Another directive, in 1911, ordered that Chinese persons who claimed to belong to one of the exempt categories should be allowed to proceed to their destination in the United States on payment of a bond of not less than $2,000, pending the final determination of their status.[30]

There were very few loopholes by which Chinese could hope to enter the United States as permanent residents. The most important was a provision in the act that persons of Chinese ancestry who had been born in the United States could sponsor their Chinese wives and children as immigrants. Owing to the scarcity of Chinese women in the United States and the California statute prohibiting mixed marriages, some Chinese Americans travelled to China to seek wives in that country. The San Francisco earthquake of 1906 destroyed many birth records, permitting some Chinese people to claim without supporting evidence that they had been born in the United States and were thus eligible to make use of this loophole.[31] Criticism of United States immigration policy by Hong Kong newspapers in

1910 contributed to somewhat less rigid enforcement of the Chinese Exclusion Act over the next few years.[32] However, there was only a very thin trickle of Chinese migration to the United States during the years it remained in force. Particularly after China abolished the Manchu monarchy and declared itself a republic in 1911, the United States tended to regard it as a useful counterweight to Imperialist Japan, but this sentiment had little impact on immigration policy.

In Canada, where the Chinese issue attracted little attention outside of British Columbia, that province tried to take matters into its own hands by imposing a direct tax on all Chinese residents in 1878 and by adopting statutes to restrict Chinese immigration in 1884 and 1885. A message from the British Columbia legislature to the federal government alleged that the last of these measures was necessary "to prevent the province from being completely overrun."[33] All three statutes were promptly disallowed. The use of this federal power was motivated mainly by the need to complete the CPR and in part by representations from the Chinese embassy in London to the British government, which was then responsible for Canada's external relations.[34]

However, in 1885, with the railway close to completion, the federal government adopted its own act to restrict Chinese immigration, three years after a statute with the same purpose had been adopted by the United States. The Canadian statute, known as the Chinese Immigration Act, imposed rigid requirements of quarantine on Chinese immigrants, limited the number of Chinese that could be carried to Canada on any ship, and established the infamous "head tax" of $50 (equivalent to about $2,000 today) that was imposed on each Chinese entering Canada.[35] This measure did not, however, satisfy the government of British Columbia, which in 1891 urged that the head tax be increased to $100.[36] Part of the motive for this suggestion may have been the fact that revenues from the head tax were shared equally between the two levels of government. British Columbia, like most of the provinces in those days, was chronically short of revenue. Wilfrid Laurier's Liberal government increased the head tax to $100 in 1900 and then to $500 three years later, a level at which it remained until it was abolished.[37]

Unlike the American statute, the Canadian measure, including the head tax, did not significantly reduce the level of Chinese immigration. While onerous and invidious, the head tax was apparently set at a low enough level that many prospective immigrants were willing and able to pay it, even after 1903. British Columbia had three times as many residents of Chinese ancestry in 1931 as it had forty years earlier. However, as a percentage of British Columbia's population, the Chinese declined from 9.1 to 3.9 per cent over the same period, since the Caucasian population, starting from a very small base, grew even faster.[38] Only after the onset of the Great Depression did the Chinese population begin to decline, in British Columbia and in Canada as a whole.

Hostility to Chinese immigration remained strong in both countries throughout the first half of the twentieth century. The two main themes of the anti-Chinese discourse were, first, the conviction that the Chinese were too culturally and racially alien to be capable of transformation into Americans or Canadians and, second, the contrast between China's vast population and the rather small Caucasian populations on the Pacific coast of North America. Because of this disparity in population, many people feared that the Pacific coast states and British Columbia risked being "overrun" by Chinese immigrants. Other themes of the anti-Chinese discourse were the belief that the Chinese carried contagious diseases and their alleged threat to the virtue of Caucasian women. They were also accused, more accurately, of being fond of gambling, which was still considered a sin by many Protestant North Americans, and of opium-smoking, which was considered even worse. (Probably few North Americans knew or cared that the latter habit had been introduced to China by the British.) The same anti-Chinese sentiments, based on similar assumptions, were being expressed in Australia and New Zealand during the same period, and those two countries also had rigidly exclusionist policies, which lasted even longer than those of the United States and Canada.

Those Chinese who had managed to enter the United States demonstrated their commitment to the American way of life in at least one important respect. As Americans are wont to do, they resorted to litigation in the courts in an effort to defend or enlarge their "rights" under American law and the Constitution.[39] This strategy seems to have been adopted after earlier efforts to achieve their objectives through lobbying had made little progress at either the state or federal level of government. While few, if any, American judges supported either racial equality or Chinese immigration in principle, they were willing to use loopholes in the law to benefit individual litigants. Seeing an individual Chinese litigant seeking redress in court apparently prompted judges to be more humane and flexible in interpreting the law, whatever their views about Chinese in general.[40]

The Chinese Exclusion Act of 1882 seems to have actually benefitted Chinese litigants, because it required interpretation by federally appointed judges rather than by the less sympathetic, and in most cases elected, judges of California and other states. One important loophole in the Chinese Exclusion Act was the provision that Chinese labourers who could prove that they had resided in the United States before 1880, the date on which the treaty between China and the United States was amended to permit restrictive measures, could return to China for a visit and then be readmitted. If they left the United States temporarily after 1882, they were supposed to get a certificate at the time of their temporary departure that could be used to gain re-entry when they returned. In 1884, Congress amended the act to make these certificates obligatory, but the Supreme Court ruled in *Chew Heong v. United States* that those who had left temporarily before the certificates became available could re-enter without one. However, in 1888 an act of Congress abolished the right of return for Chinese labourers after a temporary departure and annulled the certificates already issued.[41]

These acts were upheld by the Supreme Court a year later. Nonetheless, between 1882 and 1891 more than 7,000 petitions were filed in the federal court at San Francisco against decisions to exclude Chinese from entering the United States, and more than 85 per cent of these petitions were successful. Even after 1891, when the almost simultaneous deaths of two sympathetic federal judges suggested that the chances of success would diminish, the rate of success remained surprisingly high until 1905. In an effort to reduce the amount of litigation, Congress provided in 1894 that a decision to exclude an alien, whether Chinese or otherwise, from entering the United States at a port of entry could not be appealed to the courts. However, the Supreme Court ruled in 1898 that this provision could not apply to persons born in the United States and that anyone claiming to have been born in the United States must be given the benefit of the doubt. This proved to be a short-lived victory, since in 1905 the Supreme Court ruled in *United States v. Ju Toy* that a decision to exclude was final even if the petitioner claimed to be a citizen. Ju Toy, who had probably been born in the United States, was deported, a decision that led to a boycott of American goods in China, and few petitions were successful after that date. In 1922, the Supreme Court ruled that persons known to be United States citizens and facing deportation had a constitutional right to a judicial hearing, but this affected relatively few Chinese Americans.[42]

Even in Canada, where the Constitution contained no bill of rights and litigation was a less popular pastime than in the United States, the judiciary were occasionally helpful, relying on a strict interpretation of the division of powers between the federal and provincial levels of government. In *Union Colliery v. Bryden*, the Judicial Committee of the Privy Council struck down a British Columbia statute that prohibited the employment of Chinese in underground coal mines.[43] Lord Watson, although he is generally remembered by Canadian constitutional scholars as a supporter of provincial autonomy, declared that this measure was ultra vires because it was directed specifically against Chinese and therefore trespassed on the federal jurisdiction over naturalization and aliens. However, the same tribunal ruled four years later in *Cunningham v. Tomey Homma* that British Columbia could exclude certain races from voting in provincial elections because the control of its own electoral process was a provincial responsibility.[44] The litigant in this case was Japanese, but the decision had implications also for Chinese Canadians, who were not allowed to vote in British Columbia's provincial elections until 1947.

In Canada, the striking down of provincial legislation by the courts was of less significance, generally speaking, than its disallowance by the federal government, a power that could be exercised on any grounds within a year of the statute being adopted. During the fifteen years when Wilfrid Laurier was prime minister of Canada (1896 to 1911), this power was used a total of twenty-nine times against all nine provinces. In fourteen of those instances, or almost half, the disallowed statute was a British Columbia measure directed specifically against East Asians. Six of the disallowed British Columbia statutes were entitled An Act to Regulate Immigration into British Columbia while the other eight imposed discriminatory labour regulations on East Asians.[45] In contrast to the earlier British Columbia statutes disallowed by John A. Macdonald's government, the measures disallowed by Laurier's government were directed against Japanese as well as Chinese. Protests from the Japanese government, which was an ally of the British Empire after 1902, contributed to many of the disallowances. However, the Chinese were by far the largest Asian ethnic group in British Columbia throughout this period and were the targets of most of the anti-Asian sentiment in the province. Apart from diplomatic considerations, a moderate view on the question of Asian immigration suited the interests of big business, which generally welcomed cheap Asian labour, at least in moderate quantities.

Despite the numerous disallowances, Laurier himself had no wish to see more Chinese immigration. In a private letter, he wrote in 1899 that "For my part, I have very little hope of any good coming to this country from Asiatic immigration of any kind."[46] Similar sentiments, if not worse, existed throughout the political spectrum. Robert Borden, the Conservative who succeeded the Liberal Laurier as prime minister of Canada in 1911, was even more adamant in his views and stated publicly in 1907 that "British Columbia must remain a British and Canadian province, inhabited and dominated by men in whose veins runs the blood of those great pioneering races which built up and developed not only Western, but Eastern Canada."[47] Henry Herbert Stevens, later a Conservative cabinet minister and the first and only leader of the short-lived Reconstruction Party, was Vancouver's leading anti-Asian spokesman in 1914.[48] Even James S. Woodsworth, the founding father of Canadian social democracy, warned in 1911 of Asian "hordes" taking over British Columbia and criticized the Chinese in particular for allegedly mistreating their wives, although he acknowledged that they seemed to love their children.[49]

Like its American counterpart, Canadian organized labour was hostile to Asian immigration beginning in the 1870s and for at least half a century afterwards. The Trades and Labour Congress of Canada (TLC) voted unanimously in 1898 to add the exclusion of Chinese immigrants to its program. The program was amended so that the term "Chinese" was replaced by "Orientals" in 1909 to cover the Japanese and by "Asians" in 1911 so that immigrants from India would also be identified as undesirable.[50] "Hindus," a term then used incorrectly in North America for all South Asians regardless of their religion, were also a particular source of concern for Woodsworth in his book on immigration, published the same year. Lobbying by the TLC between 1911 and 1914 led to laws in Ontario, Manitoba, and Saskatchewan that prohibited Asian-owned businesses from employing Caucasian women.[51] The validity of the Saskatchewan statute was upheld by the Supreme Court of Canada.[52] The Trades and Labour Congress continued its anti-Chinese agitation after World War I, arguing that the head tax had been ineffective in preventing Chinese immigration and should be replaced by a policy of total exclusion.[53]

The Canadian head tax was finally abolished by Mackenzie King's Liberal government in 1923 and replaced by a new Chinese Immigration Act. In the parliamentary debate on the new measure, the prime minister stated that the head tax was invidious and inconsistent with Christian principles. At the same time, he described the head tax as an ineffective way of restricting Chinese immigration, a goal that his government continued to support.[54] Under the new legislation, most Chinese would be excluded from entering Canada, but Chinese who were merchants or students would receive preferential treatment. The government hoped that this provision would contribute to maintaining good relations with China, which was beneficial to Canada's political and economic interests. According to Mackenzie King, the Chinese government understood and accepted Canada's wish to restrict Chinese immigration but was offended by the "indignity" of the head tax.

Although the effect of the new policy was to make Chinese immigration more difficult and less likely than before, it was denounced in the House of Commons by a former federal cabinet minister and future Conservative premier of British Columbia, Simon Fraser Tolmie, for being not restrictive enough. Raising the familiar spectre of hordes of Asians overrunning his underpopulated province, Tolmie absurdly claimed that the number of African Americans living in the United States was twenty-five times as large as it had been at the end of the Civil War, although in fact it had slightly more than doubled. Adding irrelevance to absurdity, he asserted that "Surely that is enough to make Canadians sit up and take notice of this Asiatic question."[55] Thomas G. McBride, a Progressive Party member from northern British Columbia and a native of Ireland, stated, "I do not think orientals should be allowed into this country under any conditions." In support of this position, he argued that "if the good Lord had intended orientals and white people to live in the same country he would not have put the Pacific Ocean between them." McBride accused both Chinese and Japanese of favouring polygamy, which he claimed was legal in both countries.[56]

A more thoughtful contribution to the parliamentary debate came from James S. Woodsworth, the newly elected leader of the small Labour group in the House of Commons. Although Woodsworth continued to doubt whether Canadians were "prepared at the present time to receive more orientals than we have," his views had become more liberal since the publication of his book on immigration a decade earlier. He denounced the hypocrisy of accusing Chinese immigrants of sexual immorality while not allowing them to bring their wives into Canada. Woodsworth also lamented the "immense amount of prejudice towards the orientals" in Parliament and elsewhere. He urged Canadians to try to overcome such prejudices and also to recognize that "there are a great many more things in common between the different races than things which separate us, and the apparent divergences are not so great as sometimes we imagine."[57]

By the 1930s, the Chinese ethnic populations of both the United States and Canada were declining as a result of the highly restrictive immigration policies of both countries, and animosity toward the Chinese was also declining. On the Pacific coast of North America, another Asian ethnic group, the Japanese, was assuming the place previously occupied by the Chinese as a target of animosity and prejudice, with consequences that will be discussed in a subsequent chapter. Japanese imperialism was increasingly viewed as a threat to Western interests in East Asia and the Pacific. Imperial Japan's annexation of Manchuria in 1931, and its invasion of China proper in 1937, caused many North Americans to sympathize with China, which was viewed, albeit inaccurately, as a democratic and pro-Western republic under the leadership of General Chiang Kai-Shek. On the other hand, immigration from any source was unwelcome during the Depression when unemployment in both the United States and Canada reached unprecedented levels. A Canadian order-in-council in 1930 prohibited any Asian person from entering the country.

After the Japanese attack on Pearl Harbor in December 1941, both the United States and Canada were allies of Nationalist China in the war against the Empire of Japan, which was the principal ally of Nazi Germany. President Roosevelt, despite British scepticism and Soviet indifference, envisaged Nationalist China as one of the four major powers that would jointly govern the postwar world. In response to these dramatic developments, and as a gesture of support to its embattled ally, the United States finally repealed the Chinese Exclusion Act in 1943. In the circumstances of wartime, this gesture had few if any immediate practical implications for immigration policy. Although immigration from China was no longer completely excluded, it was, like immigration from every other country outside the Western Hemisphere, subject to a quota, which corresponded roughly to the relative size of the ethnic group as a proportion of the existing population of the United States. The Chinese quota was set at the very low level of 105 immigrants per year. Despite this, more than 11,000 Chinese immigrants were admitted to the United States between 1945 and 1952. The vast majority were the wives of United States citizens, who were not subject to the quota.[58]

Canada followed in the footsteps of the United States but not until after the end of the war. In December 1946, the cabinet discussed the question of Chinese immigration. In January 1947, Prime Minister Mackenzie King promised the Chinese ambassador that the Chinese Immigration Act, which his first government had enacted almost a quarter of a century earlier, would be repealed.[59] In February, his government introduced a bill that, along with some fairly minor changes in immigration policy, would carry out this promise. The minister introducing the bill, J.A. Glen, indicated that the existing statute was widely regarded as discriminatory, that it singled out a country that had been Canada's ally in the recent war, and that it imposed hardships on Canadian citizens of Chinese origin. The latter group were said to number 8,749, or about one-quarter of the Chinese ethnic population residing in Canada. Under the new law, they would be allowed, like other Canadian citizens, to bring their wives and children into Canada.[60] However, their status still differed from that of European immigrants, who could sponsor their wives and children as immigrants even before acquiring Canadian citizenship. This anomaly lasted for another twenty years. After 1950, female Chinese-Canadian citizens were allowed to sponsor their husbands as immigrants in the same way that male Chinese Canadians could sponsor their wives.[61]

During the parliamentary debate in 1947, members of all parties expressed sympathy for the Chinese Canadians and appreciation for China's role in the recent war. Future prime minister John Diefenbaker, a strong supporter of civil rights and civil liberties, accused the government of hypocrisy, since the new law did not completely remove racial discrimination against persons of Chinese ancestry.[62] However, J.L. Gibson, an Independent Liberal from British Columbia, worried that as many as 120,000 dependent wives and children might become eligible for admission to Canada and alleged that "As a matter of fact, the Chinese have had a poor record from the point of view of assimilation in this country."[63] James Sinclair, a British Columbia Liberal and subsequently the father-in-law of Pierre Elliott Trudeau, probably spoke for most British Columbians when he said that the people of his province were prepared to give citizenship rights to the "orientals" already in Canada but did not want any more "oriental" immigration apart from the families of these men.[64]

In the same year that the Chinese Immigration Act was repealed, British Columbia became the last province to give Chinese Canadians the right to vote in provincial elections. By doing so, it also gave them the right to practise law or pharmacy in the province.[65] The very rapid growth of British Columbia's Caucasian population after the war, and the very small number of Chinese immigrants who entered Canada under the terms of the 1947 legislation, probably lessened the province's traditional anxiety about being overwhelmed by Asian immigrants.

In both Canada and the United States, overt discrimination against Chinese and other Asians remained a feature of immigration law until the 1960s. During the postwar years of rapid economic and demographic growth, the Chinese communities on both sides of the border dwindled in size and became less conspicuous. In some North American cities, the traditional Chinese ghettoes or "Chinatowns" became smaller or even disappeared under the impact of urban renewal projects. A few of them, in New York, San Francisco, Vancouver, and Montreal, survived and became tourist attractions, particularly as Chinese food and artifacts grew in popularity. The percentage of Chinese Americans and Chinese Canadians who lived in Chinatowns declined. Those who remained there were largely elderly and poor, while Chinese who lived elsewhere in North America generally prospered.[66] North American Chinatowns were also disrupted to some extent by conflict between pro-communists and pro-nationalists, although the latter generally retained the upper hand.

The communist takeover of mainland China in 1949, shortly followed by the Korean War in which Chinese troops fought against Canadians and Americans, gave China a less benign image than it had enjoyed in the previous decade. It also raised some legitimate anxieties that Chinese immigration, such as it was, might be a cover for communist espionage. On the other hand, the new Chinese regime imitated its Russian prototype in preventing the emigration of its own people, a practice that paradoxically reinforced the impact of restrictive immigration policies in North America. Both the United States and Canada continued to recognize the Nationalist *ancien régime*, whose effective jurisdiction was now confined to the island of Taiwan (formerly part of the Japanese Empire) and the tiny islands of Quemoy and Matsu, as China's legitimate government. Residents of Taiwan continued to enter North America in significant numbers, particularly as students. Canada also had a sort of special relationship with Hong Kong, a British possession to which Canadian soldiers had been sent on an ill-advised, controversial, and generally hopeless mission, which few of them survived, in 1941.

In addition to the absurdly low immigration quota that China had been given in 1943, American immigration law contained another discriminatory feature after 1952. The McCarran-Walter Act, which Congress adopted in 1952 by overriding President Harry Truman's veto, included an overtly racist provision known, rather oddly, as the "Asian-Pacific triangle." It provided that prospective immigrants from outside the Asia-Pacific region whose ancestry was more than half Asian or Pacific Islander could not benefit from the quotas assigned to the countries where they actually lived but would have to enter under the quota of the country where their ancestors had lived. For example, a partly Chinese person living in the United Kingdom would have to compete with residents of China or Taiwan for one of the 105 places assigned to Chinese immigrants each year rather than entering under the much larger British quota.

Refugees from China's communist regime continued to reach North America, although in fairly modest numbers, by way of Hong Kong, which provided an avenue of escape similar to that which West Berlin provided in the eastern part of Germany. In Canada, the population of Chinese ancestry nearly doubled between 1951 and 1961 after two decades of decline. There was a notable improvement in the sex ratio, with women increasing from 22 per cent to 39 per cent of the total population. The Chinese-Canadian population was also less concentrated in British Columbia than before, with nearly 60 per cent of them living in other provinces. In 1957, a young Vancouver lawyer, Douglas Jung, became the first Chinese Canadian elected to the House of Commons.

In 1960, Canada granted an amnesty to illegal Chinese immigrants, but it also launched a controversial police investigation into fraudulent immigration from Hong Kong, which dragged on for two years, found only a handful of miscreants, and greatly antagonized the Chinese-Canadian community. Douglas Jung opposed the investigation, although he was a member of the governing Progressive Conservative Party. However, Minister of Justice Davie Fulton, a British Columbian, was strongly committed to the investigation. This affair contributed to Jung's loss of his Vancouver riding (which had a large Chinese-Canadian population) in 1962. The downtown Toronto riding held by future governor general Roland Michener was also lost by the Progressive Conservatives, apparently for the same reason. Meanwhile, President Kennedy, disregarding the quota system, admitted 14,000 Chinese immigrants into the United States by executive action soon after taking office in 1961.[67] Despite this action, the Chinese ethnic population remained proportionately smaller in the United States than in Canada.

As will be discussed in chapter 7, the 1960s saw the final removal of racial and ethnic criteria from the immigration laws of both Canada and the United States. More recently, as China has become a capitalist country in all but name, it has relaxed the strict control of emigration that is characteristic of communist regimes. One result of these developments has been a remarkable increase in the population of Chinese ancestry, particularly in Canada. The number of Canadian residents claiming Chinese ancestry more than doubled in the 1960s and continued to grow at roughly the same pace until the end of the century. By 2006, the number of persons claiming Chinese as their only ethnic origin in the Canadian census reached 1,135,370, while another 211,145 claimed to be of partially Chinese ancestry. The traditional imbalance between the sexes, a consequence of the virtual exclusion of Chinese women from Canada for many years, was negligible by 1981. By 1991, there were actually more females than males among the Chinese-Canadian population. Also, by 1981 Ontario had more residents of Chinese ancestry than British Columbia, and this gap continued to widen in later years. However, British Columbia still has the highest percentage of Chinese in its population of any North American state or province, about 10 per cent.

By 2001, the census metropolitan area of Toronto had more residents of Chinese ancestry than that of Vancouver, although the Chinese still formed a much higher percentage of Vancouver's population. Almost 12 per cent of Canada's foreign-born population in that year had been born in China, Hong Kong, or Taiwan, and indeed the number of Canadian residents born in those countries slightly exceeded the number born in Great Britain and Ireland. The People's Republic of China was also the largest source of new immigrants admitted to Canada in 2000, providing almost one sixth of the total number admitted.[68]

American data concerning ethnicity are less complete and less reliable, but there was significant growth there as well. China, including Hong Kong and Taiwan, was the source of 202,500 immigrants

admitted to the United States between 1971 and 1981, 451,800
admitted between 1981 and 1991, and 605,000 admitted between
1991 and 2001.[69] New York's Chinatown had a population of about
150,000 in 2005, which was ten times its population in 1965, the
year that racial discrimination was removed from American immigration law.[70] The Asian American Studies Center at the University
of California in Los Angeles (UCLA) estimated that in 2009 there
were 3.8 million persons of Chinese ancestry in the United States, or
about three times as many as there were in Canada at the same date,
and that 2.6 million persons over the age of five spoke Chinese at
home.[71] Since the total population of the United States is about nine
times larger than that of Canada, the Chinese are clearly a much
larger percentage of Canada's population. This has probably been
the case since the early 1880s when the passage of the Chinese
Exclusion Act in the United States coincided with the construction of
the Canadian Pacific Railway. While China, including Hong Kong, is
now the largest source of immigrants to Canada, with India close
behind, Mexico is by far the largest source of immigrants entering
the United States and contributes several times as many immigrants
to that country as China.[72]

In both the United States and Canada, people of Chinese origin
appear to have fared relatively well in recent years, although not
spectacularly so. In the United States, Asian Americans, including
Chinese, are sometimes referred to as a "model minority" in contrast
to African Americans and Mexican Americans, the two large ethnic
groups that have continued to lag behind the rest of the population
in socio-economic status. Unfortunately, the United States since
1980 includes most data relating to Chinese Americans in the
broader category of "Asian Americans," making the data less useful.
However, students of Chinese origin, both American-born and otherwise, are overrepresented in American universities, particularly in
California, and tend to outrank Caucasians in academic achievement, particularly in mathematics and science. On the other hand,
Chinese Americans have slightly lower incomes than non-Chinese
Americans with equivalent levels of education.[73]

In Canada, where the available data are more useful, persons of
Chinese origin are far more likely to have a university degree, and
particularly a post-graduate degree, than the population as a whole.
This is probably in part because well over half of them were born
outside of Canada and because the immigrant selection process gives

a substantial preference to persons having a degree. However, Canadian-born Chinese, like their American counterparts, are somewhat overrepresented among the students at universities. On the other hand, persons of Chinese origin in Canada have somewhat lower than average incomes and somewhat higher than average levels of unemployment, circumstances which may also be in part at least a function of the high percentage of immigrants in that population. The income gap is particularly pronounced for women and for elderly persons, particularly the latter. About 70 per cent of Chinese Canadians over the age of sixty-five are estimated to live in poverty.[74]

In both countries, many persons of Chinese origin are successful entrepreneurs, although perhaps not as many in fact as in popular belief. A great many people with wealth and entrepreneurial skills left Hong Kong for other countries, and particularly for Canada, immediately prior to the British withdrawal from the colony in 1997. This phenomenon led to complaints, particularly in Vancouver, that Chinese immigrants were building "monster houses" and driving up real estate prices, which for geographical reasons were already exceptionally high in that city. More recently, there have been expressions of concern in British Columbia about the increasing prominence of the Chinese language. While these expressions of Sinophobia are troubling, they are far milder than those in the first half of the twentieth century. Also in contrast to those of earlier times, anti-Chinese sentiments nowadays are not encouraged or echoed by politicians at any level of government.

Persons of Chinese origin in North America have not been particularly prominent in electoral politics, although San Francisco has elected a Chinese-American mayor. As of 2012, there appears to be no one of Chinese ancestry in the United States Senate. There is only one Chinese American in the House of Representatives, Representative Judy Chu, a Democrat from California. In Canada, the appointed Senate contains one person of Chinese origin, Vivienne Poy, a Liberal from Ontario. In the House of Commons there are five Chinese Canadians: Michael Chong, Olivia Chow, Ted Hsu, Chungsen Leung, and Alice Wong. All represent Ontario ridings except Wong, who is from British Columbia. Three are members of the Conservative Party while Chow is a New Democrat and Hsu is a Liberal. Michael Chong briefly held a minor portfolio in Stephen Harper's cabinet but resigned because he disagreed with the decision to recognize the Québécois as a nation within Canada. Raymond Chan, former MP for Richmond, BC, which has a large Chinese population, was a minister in the previous Liberal government.

The best-known Chinese Canadian is undoubtedly Adrienne Poy Clarkson, who arrived in Canada from Hong Kong as a child, had a successful career in the media, and then served as a very popular and effective governor general of Canada from 1999 to 2005, the first person of non-European ancestry to hold that office. Clarkson is also the sister-in-law of Senator Vivienne Poy. Two Chinese Canadians have represented the Crown at the provincial level as lieutenant governor: David See-Chai Lam in British Columbia from 1988 to 1995 and Norman Kwong in Alberta from 2005 to 2011. Kwong had been a professional football player with the Calgary Stampeders and the Edmonton Eskimos for a total of thirteen seasons.

If legislative bodies were exactly representative of the populations they represent, which of course they rarely are, there would be six Chinese Americans in the House of Representatives and twelve Chinese Canadians in the House of Commons. The failure to attain these numbers is perhaps in part because so many Chinese North Americans are recent arrivals and in part because of the absence of democratic traditions in China itself, including Hong Kong. The fact that Canada has come much closer to attaining these numbers than the United States probably reflects the enormous financial cost of running for office in the United States. This is partly a function of the large size of congressional districts, which have an average population of about 700,000 compared to about 110,000 in a Canadian parliamentary constituency, but also of the fact that primary elections are used to select the candidates in American congressional elections.

Although Canada's notorious Chinese head tax disappeared almost a century ago, it has regrettably lingered on as a political issue until recent times. The practice of governments apologizing or providing financial compensation for the sins of their predecessors began with the efforts of postwar Germany (although not the communist-ruled part of it) to make amends to Jews for the Holocaust. Appropriate as it was in that particular instance, the increasing popularity of the practice, especially in English-speaking countries, has been much more questionable. Prior to the federal election of 1984, the Chinese Canadian National Council began to demand an apology for the head tax and financial compensation for those who had paid it or for their descendants. The council also considered complaining to the United Nations, an organization that did not exist until more than two decades after the tax was abolished. The council's demand came despite the fact that no one had been forced to come to Canada, that an estimated 81,000 people had paid the tax voluntarily, and that central Canada's pre-Confederation government had for a short period imposed a head tax on all immigrants regardless of ethnic origin. Discussions on the issue dragged on for ten years through several governments until in 1994 the Liberal minister of multiculturalism, Sheila Finestone, apologized on behalf of the Canadian state but said there would be no financial compensation.[75] The council reacted angrily to this announcement and persisted for another decade. In 2006, Prime Minister Stephen Harper issued another apology, accompanied this time by a promise of financial compensation but only for payers of the tax who were still alive. Cheques of $20,000 each were distributed the following year.[76]

It would be naive to pretend that racist sentiments against the Chinese have entirely disappeared in North America, but they have undoubtedly declined. A recent study of immigrants in New York City asserts that "Asians are no longer the target of virulent racism," at least in that city.[77] Given China's economic achievements in recent years and the large number of Chinese doctors and scientists in North American, it would be hard for even the most dim-witted of North Americans to persuade themselves that the Chinese are racially inferior. The fact that most Chinese Canadians (and probably most Chinese Americans) have no religious affiliation protects them from certain kinds of prejudice. A survey conducted for Multiculturalism and Citizenship Canada in 1991 indicated that Canadians are much more likely to feel "comfortable" with Chinese than with West Indians, Muslims, South Asians, Arabs, or Sikhs.[78] There has been considerable intermarriage between East Asians and Caucasians in North America, with Adrienne Clarkson and Olivia Chow being prominent examples. Although 34 per cent of Chinese Canadians claimed in a 2001 survey to have experienced discrimination, the corollary is that at least 66 per cent had not.[79]

Unlike the Irish, who were discussed in the previous chapter, and the Jews, discussed in the next chapter, the Chinese are likely to form an increasingly large proportion of North America's population in the coming years. Their birth and fertility rates are relatively low, but China is a huge reservoir of potential immigrants, and it will be many years before its standard of living reaches the level at which migration to North America ceases to be attractive to at least some of its people. Unless either a hot or cold war breaks out between the People's Republic and its North American neighbours, immigration is likely to continue at a fairly high level.

At one time, this prospect would have caused fear and anger among native-born North Americans as much lower levels of Chinese immigration did in earlier times. However, the present wave of Chinese immigration seems to be reasonably well received. Chinese immigrants tend to be peaceful, law-abiding, well-educated, and hardworking, and their family life appears to be more stable than that of most North Americans. Their settlement in the United States and Canada will give those countries increased access to trade and investment opportunities in the huge and rapidly growing Chinese economy. More North Americans are travelling to China than ever before, and the economic and cultural achievements of that country are increasingly admired. There will be occasional friction along the way, but the integration of Chinese immigrants into the societies of Canada and the United States appears to be proceeding smoothly and will probably continue to do so. Certainly it is far more successful than anyone would have anticipated fifty or a hundred years ago.

5

The Jews

Hostility to Jews is a phenomenon with very deep roots in Western culture. Anti-Jewish comments occur in the dialogue of Chaucer's *Canterbury Tales*. Shakespeare devoted an entire play, *The Merchant of Venice*, to the subject of anti-Semitism. Jews were expelled from England long before Shakespeare's time, so it is unlikely that he ever encountered one, although Oliver Cromwell allowed them to return a few decades after Shakespeare's death. While anti-Semitism is nowadays associated with unemployed and intellectually challenged losers who paint graffiti on walls and overturn gravestones, it must sadly be conceded that some of the most gifted and otherwise distinguished persons in European and North American history (religious leaders, statesmen, soldiers, entrepreneurs, artists, poets, and composers, among others) were anti-Semites, at least to some degree. It is not unfair to say that among non-Jewish Europeans and North Americans born before the twentieth century, some degree of anti-Semitism was almost universal.

The reasons for this unattractive but singularly durable obsession have still not been clearly explained or understood. Some passages in the Christian scriptures, particularly in the Gospel of John, appear to be anti-Semitic, although it is possible that the term "Jews" in those passages had a narrower meaning than it does today. Although it is self-evident that Jesus, Peter, Paul, and the other major figures in the Christian narrative were Jewish, anti-Semitism has infected all the principal branches of Christianity, particularly Roman Catholicism and Eastern Orthodoxy, however illogical and regrettable that may be.

Anti-Semitism has also been attributed to the role of Jews in medieval Europe as money-lenders, a niche in the economy that they had to fill because "usury" was considered a sin by medieval Christians, as it still is today by Muslims. The reliance of dynastic European empires on Jewish money-lenders may also have turned some nationalist opponents of those empires into anti-Semites. Nineteenth-century racial theories that equated language with ancestry and the general obsession with such issues that grew out of the theories of Charles Darwin and Gregor Mendel also played a role. The term "Semitic," derived from the name of one of Noah's three sons in the Book of Genesis, actually refers to a group of languages that includes Arabic as well as Hebrew, and the term "anti-Semitism" in its modern sense was apparently first used in the 1870s.

The brutal right-wing European anti-Semitism that became powerful in the first half of the twentieth century culminated in the Nazi genocide of 1941–45, although its precursors appeared in Russia and France before it became significant in Germany. It was largely inspired by anti-communism and also, particularly in France, by anti-liberalism. The Dreyfus case, in which a Jewish officer in the French army was unjustly accused of being a German spy, became a cause célèbre in France at the turn of the century and polarized opinion in that country between the republican left and the reactionary right. The link between anti-communism and anti-Semitism was not accidental; Karl Marx was the grandson of a rabbi, and Jews played a disproportionately large role in the Russian Revolution, an event that (not entirely without reason) frightened many Europeans out of their senses. Yet communists themselves, especially after 1945, were not immune to the disease of anti-Semitism. Soviet leader Nikita Khrushchev allegedly blamed the anti-communist Hungarian rebellion of 1956 on "too many Jews in a small country." If the quote is authentic, this was an insensitive remark less than a dozen years after the mass murder of Hungarian Jews by the Nazis and an ironic one, since Hungary's first and short-lived communist government had been headed by a Jew, Bela Kun.

For many European Jews, North America offered the promise of an escape from Europe's problems, with the European penchant for anti-Semitism heading the list. It was an American-born Jewish woman, Emma Lazarus, who wrote the famous lines inscribed on the base of the Statue of Liberty:[1]

"Give me your tired, your poor,
Your huddled masses yearning to breathe free,
The wretched refuse of your teeming shore.

Send these, the homeless, tempest-tost to me,
I lift my lamp beside the golden door!"

Immigrating to North America was a rational decision for the vast majority of the many Jews who made the journey. They, or at least their descendants, were almost certainly better off as a result. Yet despite the promise of Emma Lazarus's poem, neither the United States nor Canada was always open to the Jews who would have liked to go there. For those who did make the journey, North American anti-Semitism, although by no means as virulent as the European variety, often reared its ugly head. It is only in recent times that Jews have been fully accepted as equals in every walk of North American life on both sides of the border.

The first Jews in what is now the United States were apparently twenty-three Sephardic Jewish refugees from Brazil who arrived at the Dutch colony of New Amsterdam in 1654.[2] The Dutch republic was, like Cromwell's England, one of the few European countries where Jews were welcome at that time. The founder of the colony, Peter Stuyvesant, was reluctant to admit them but was overruled by his sponsors. Massachusetts, considered a bastion of liberalism in modern times but an intolerant theocracy in its early days, did not welcome Jews until after the Declaration of Independence.[3] Canada's first Jewish settler was apparently a merchant named Aaron Hart, probably born in New York, who followed the British army into the conquered colony during the Seven Years' War and later settled in Trois Rivières.[4] His son Ezekiel Hart was elected to the legislative assembly of Lower Canada in 1807 but could not take his seat because only Christians could swear the necessary oath of allegiance.

In neither the United States nor Canada were these earliest pioneers of Jewish settlement followed by a large number of their kin, at least not immediately. By one estimate, there were only 1,350 Jews (0.03 per cent of the population) in the United States in 1790, and the Jewish community was no larger in proportion to the total size of the population forty years later.[5] The Canadian census of 1881 counted only 2,443 Jews, or about 0.06 per cent of Canada's population. By that time, the United States had about one hundred times as many Jews as Canada, but Jews were still only about one-half of 1 per cent of the American population.

The Jewish population of the United States began to grow rapidly after 1830, however, and continued to do so for about a century. Jews as a percentage of the total population of the United States reached its peak in 1940, when they comprised 3.65 per cent of the total.[6] By that date, about 30 per cent of all the Jews in the world lived in the United States. A decade later, following the genocide in Europe, that figure would increase to more than 43 per cent, since the number of Jews living outside the United States had declined drastically.[7]

Most of the Jews who came to the United States between 1830 and 1880 were from Germany and particularly from Wurttemberg, a mainly Protestant state in southwestern Germany with a fairly strong liberal tradition.[8] (A much more recent emigrant from Wurttemberg to the United States was Albert Einstein.) They were Ashkenazi, a Jewish word that literally means "German," the type of Jews found in central and eastern Europe. Ashkenazi are distinct from the Sephardic Jews of Spain, Portugal, and other Mediterranean countries, many of whom had settled in England, France, or the Netherlands and who had provided most of the early Jewish immigrants to the United States.

In Wurttemberg and in most other German states, Jews were largely assimilated and ranked reasonably high in socio-economic status. Both before and after entering the United States, they tended to be regarded, and to regard themselves, as Germans who practised a different religion from other Germans rather than as a distinct ethnic group.[9] The southwestern part of Germany contributed a disproportionate share of the huge German migration, non-Jewish as well as Jewish, to the United States in the middle decades of the nineteenth century. Jews were a part, but only a small part, of this massive migration. Like the other German immigrants of that era, many of them settled in the middle west, especially in the so-called "German triangle" (Cincinnati–St Louis–Milwaukee). The eastern seaports of New York, Philadelphia, and Baltimore also attracted many of them.

Like the Catholic Irish, the Jewish Germans in the United States were a mainly urban population. But unlike Catholic Irish immigrants in the nineteenth century, a large proportion of the Jewish German immigrants could be considered middle class. Some became rich, particularly in retailing, where the names Macy's, Gimbel's, Filene's, Neiman-Marcus, Bloomingdale's and Sak's Fifth Avenue testified to the important Jewish presence. Levi's, the manufacturer of denim blue jeans that was founded in San Francisco during the California gold rush, was also a Jewish contribution to the culture and economy of the United States. German Jews in the United States were generally prominent in the garment industry. Russian Jews who arrived later often worked in clothing factories owned by German-Jewish entrepreneurs.

As time went on, Jewish entrepreneurship extended in other directions. The banking and investment firm Goldman Sachs was founded in 1869 by two Jewish immigrants. Adolph Ochs, the son of Jewish immigrants from Bavaria, took over the *New York Times* in 1896 and quickly made it the most respected newspaper in the United States. When motion pictures became a major industry, all four of the principal Hollywood studios, Columbia, Metro-Goldwyn-Mayer, 20th Century Fox, and Warner Brothers, were founded and for many years controlled by Jews.

Some of the institutional framework of Jewish life in the United States also dates from the middle decades of the nineteenth century. B'nai Brith, which eventually spread to Canada, Europe, and Palestine and included Sigmund Freud among its members, was originally an American organization, established in 1843. Its offshoots, the student organization Hillel (named for a rabbi who lived shortly before the time of Jesus) and the Anti-Defamation League, which was formed in response to the lynching of a Jewish man in Georgia, were products of the twentieth century.[10] The Hebrew Emigrant Aid Society, which provided financial assistance to Jewish refugees, dates from 1870.[11] Reform Judaism, which is roughly a counterpart of the Unitarian persuasion among Protestants, was established by assimilated Jews in Germany and carried to the United States. Cincinnati, Ohio, one of the most German cities in the United States, became its global centre after the Union of American Hebrew Congregations was established there in 1873.[12] Reform Jews traditionally have regarded themselves as a religious rather than an ethnic group and have been lukewarm at best towards Jewish ethnic nationalism. Conservative Judaism, a compromise between Orthodoxy and Reform, was invented in the United States. The United States is the only country in which most religious Jews are either Conservative or Reform.

Jews participated in American politics as well. Louis Levin, a congressman from Pennsylvania, represented the Know Nothing Party.[13] The short-lived Confederate States of America was probably the first country in the world to have a Jewish attorney general in the person of Judah P. Benjamin. After the collapse of the Confederacy, Benjamin moved to England where he became a practising attorney and on several occasions represented Canadian litigants, including provincial governments, in their appeals to the Judicial Committee of the Privy Council. He represented the losing side in one of the most important Judicial Committee rulings on the division of legislative powers in Canada's Constitution, *Citizens' Insurance v. Parsons*.

While the mid-century wave of German-Jewish immigration had an important impact on the United States, it had practically no impact on Canada. Immigrants from Germany in the nineteenth century tended to avoid Canada, which received very few of them before 1945, and this was particularly true of German Jews. The 2,443 Jews who lived in Canada in 1881 would have been mainly Sephardic Jews, and they or their ancestors would probably have arrived by way of the United Kingdom or the United States. Like American Jews at the time, they tended to be more affluent than the general population, but their very small numbers prevented them from having much visible influence on Canadian society during the nineteenth century.

Jewish life in North America was fundamentally transformed, and the numbers of North American Jews greatly increased, by the growth of European anti-Semitism after about 1880. Although not unique to czarist Russia, this trend was particularly pronounced in that empire, which was then home to more than half the Jewish population of the world. The assassination in 1881 of the liberal czar Alexander II, who had abolished serfdom twenty years earlier, unleashed reactionary forces and contributed to a wave of anti-Semitism. This included pogroms, or anti-Semitic riots and massacres encouraged by the authorities of both church and state. A pogrom at Kishinev at Easter 1903 resulted in the deaths of forty-nine Jews and the injuring of another 500, as well as extensive damage to Jewish property.[14] This episode attracted particular attention in the United States. Some Russian Jews responded to these developments by embracing Marxism, while others saw the Zionist movement, which began in 1896, as a better solution to their problems.

The response of many Russian Jews, however, was to emigrate, as depicted in the final scene of the popular Broadway musical, *Fiddler on the Roof*. Many of them went to other European countries, particularly the dual monarchy of Austria-Hungary, which already had a large Jewish population. Unfortunately, the result was to stimulate anti-Semitism in the places where they settled, particularly since Russian Jews tended to be much more conspicuous than the largely assimilated Jews of Germany and Austria. Vienna, in which the young

Adolf Hitler spent his formative years, became a particular hotbed of working-class and lower-middle-class anti-Semitism prior to 1914.

The luckier, or perhaps more astute, Russian-Jewish refugees went all the way to North America, a decision for which their children and grandchildren had good reason to be grateful in later years. About two million Jewish immigrants entered the United States in the years from 1881 to 1914, comprising about 10 per cent of all immigrant arrivals during those years. In 1906, the peak year for Jewish immigration, 153,748 Jews arrived at American ports, comprising 14 per cent of all immigrants who arrived in that year.[15] In contrast to other European immigrants during that period, the overwhelming majority of the Jewish immigrants remained permanently in the United States, since they had no homelands to which they had any desire to return. A Jewish-American writer in the 1920s suggested that Jews were more determined than other immigrants to become fully "American" for the same reason.[16] By 1900, there were one million, and by 1910 two million, Jews living in the United States.

This period also saw the beginning of large-scale Jewish immigration into Canada, when Sir John A. Macdonald encouraged the migration of Russian Jews to western Canada, particularly Manitoba, in the 1880s.[17] Although it was hoped that they, like most other settlers in the west, would become farmers, very few persisted with this occupation. As in the United States, Jewish immigration, and immigration in general, peaked in the first decade of the twentieth century. By 1901, Canada was home to 16,493 Jews, and by 1911 it had 76,199, who comprised almost 1 per cent of Canada's population. Most were from the Russian Empire, which then included Poland, or from Romania, which had gained its independence from Turkey in 1878 and was also pervaded by anti-Semitism. Most settled in Montreal, Toronto, or Winnipeg, with Montreal alone being home to about half of Canada's Jewish population.

This large influx of eastern European Jews was not particularly welcomed by the established Jewish communities, which were mainly German Ashkenazi in the United States while in Canada the very small Jewish community was largely Sephardic and from a variety of sources. Unlike the established North American Jews, whom they soon outnumbered, the Russians were generally poor, unskilled, poorly educated, and conspicuous by their different speech, appearance, and behaviour. Coming from cities, they ranked somewhat higher in socio-economic status than the rural peasants from Italy and the Slavic countries who were emigrating at the same time but far lower than their fellow Jews who had arrived earlier. They had little in common with the established and largely assimilated Jews from Germany and elsewhere and even less with the rest of North America's population. As in central Europe, although to a lesser extent, their arrival stimulated anti-Semitism from which all Jews potentially would suffer. They also imposed much greater demands on the established institutions of the Jewish community, including synagogues, schools, and charitable organizations. New institutions that were formed at this time included the American Jewish Committee in 1906 and the somewhat more radical and less elitist American Jewish Congress in 1916. In the United States, German Jews and Russian Jews, although both Ashkenazi, mingled little and remained largely separate groups until the 1930s when the Nazi threat brought them together.[18] Religious differences helped to keep them apart, since most of the Germans were Reform and most of the Russians were Orthodox.

As they had done in eastern Europe, the newly arrived Jews tended to congregate, partly by necessity and partly by choice, in particular neighbourhoods, which became seriously overcrowded. By far the largest and most celebrated of these neighbourhoods was the Lower East Side of Manhattan, from which the growing Jewish population eventually spilled over the river into neighbouring Brooklyn, annexed by New York City in 1898. Although three-quarters of New York's Jews lived on the Lower East Side in 1892, less than one quarter lived there in 1916.[19] New York City by 1905 had a Jewish population estimated at 672,000, or nearly half of all the Jews in the United States.[20] In Montreal, the main centre of Canadian Jewry, most of the Jewish population lived in a small area along the parallel streets of St Laurent and St Urbain, which run perpendicular to the river. After World War I, this area was normally represented by a Jewish member in both the Quebec legislature and the federal Parliament. (It had the dubious distinction, in 1943, of electing the only communist ever to serve in the latter institution.) In Winnipeg, the Jews were concentrated in the north end near the CPR station, which had been the point of arrival in the city for most of them.

Although an American Jewish historian has written that "anti-Semitism never became rooted in the political tradition of American society,"[21] it was not entirely absent. In 1877, a German-Jewish banker named Joseph Seligman was refused as a guest at a hotel in Saratoga Springs, New York, in what was perhaps the first such incident in American history.[22] Reflecting the popular theories at the time that associated "race" with language, an American law professor, John Wigmore, alleged that Jews were not really "white," in contrast to Persians and "pure Hindus."[23] (Sanskrit is classified as an "Aryan" language, and the swastika was originally a Hindu symbol representing the sun.) Paradoxically, Jews may have been more accepted in the racist and backward southern states than in other parts of North America, since they were obviously not African and the African-American "threat" dominated the southern agenda.[24]

On the other hand, presidents Theodore Roosevelt and Woodrow Wilson were both sympathetic to Jews. Roosevelt's enthusiasm for Israel Zangwill's play The Melting Pot has already been mentioned. He sent a very sympathetic message to the Jewish community in 1905 to commemorate the two hundred and fiftieth anniversary of the arrival of the first Jewish settlers in New Amsterdam.[25] In the following year, he appointed Oscar Straus as secretary of commerce and labor in his cabinet; Straus had been one of the founders of the American Jewish Committee and was its president at the time of his appointment.[26] President Wilson appointed Louis D. Brandeis as the first Jewish justice of the Supreme Court in 1916. Jewish hostility to czarist Russia may have been a factor in Wilson's decision not to enter World War I until after the czarist regime collapsed. By 1920, there were eleven Jews in the House of Representatives, a representation that was almost proportional to their share of the population.[27] Almost half a century would pass before Canadian Jews attained a similar level of political influence, although Henry Nathan, a British-born Conservative from British Columbia, had been the first Jew elected to the House of Commons in 1871. Admittedly, the Jewish community in Canada was, and still is, much smaller in proportion to the size of the country's population.

World War I, however, led to increased anti-Semitism in the United States and other allied countries, probably in part because Jews and Germans were still regarded as overlapping categories and were closely associated in the popular imagination.[28] Jews in both Europe and North America had good reason to be pro-German, as most of them were, for as long as czarist Russia was fighting on the side of Britain and France. When a character in John Buchan's novel Greenmantle, which was published during the war, said that "The

Jew is behind most German enterprises," he was expressing a fairly common view at the time, although Mordecai Richler's assertion that Buchan himself was an anti-Semite remains unproven.

Support from the German government enabled Lenin and his Bolshevik faction to seize power in Russia in November 1917. The new Russian regime, in which Jews like the charismatic Leon Trotsky were prominent, was at first considered a German puppet. It also provided another (and somewhat more plausible) pretext for anti-Semitism than the theory that Germany itself was under Jewish control. After the armistice in November 1918, the fear and hatred of the English-speaking world was directed almost exclusively at revolutionary Russia. The fact that the short-lived postwar communist governments in Hungary and Bavaria were both headed by Jews reinforced the impression that Jewishness and communism were closely associated. In April 1920, J. Edgar Hoover, then a special assistant to the attorney general of the United States and later the director of the FBI for four decades, sent a letter to the commissioner of immigration enclosing what he called "the list of bolshevik commissioners and officials, giving the real name, the alias and the nationality of each." According to Hoover, the list contained two ethnic Russians (Lenin and his wife), three ethnic Germans, and forty Jews.[29] Josef Stalin, an ethnic Georgian, failed to make the list, a rather remarkable oversight.

An even more prominent anti-Semite than Hoover was the most influential industrialist in the United States, Henry Ford, who began to disseminate anti-Jewish propaganda in 1920. He continued to do so until 1927 when the threat of a lawsuit and a Jewish boycott of his cars persuaded him to desist and issue an apology.[30] Ford's propaganda was part of a general climate of intolerance and xenophobia, sentiments that usually lead to anti-Semitism. The restrictive immigration laws of the 1920s, discussed in chapter 7, were mainly directed against Jews and Italians, two groups that had been particularly prominent among immigrants in the decade before the war. The resurrected Ku Klux Klan of the 1920s differed from its post–Civil War namesake in that it was not confined to the southern states and not exclusively focused on hatred of African Americans. It spread throughout the middle west and even as far north as the Canadian prairies, and it was violently opposed to Jews and Catholics as well as to the descendants of slaves.

However, the anti-Semitism of the 1920s was not confined to the rednecks derided by urban sophisticates like H.L. Mencken. It appeared also among the well-educated and the affluent, who barred Jews from their social clubs and excluded them from living or buying property in high-status neighbourhoods. The growing number of Jews entering universities also became targets of discrimination. By the 1920s, Jews comprised about 20 per cent of the students at Harvard, about 40 per cent at Columbia, and about 80 per cent at Hunter College and the City College of New York. In response to this situation, Harvard, considered the most prestigious university in the United States, imposed a quota on the number of Jews who could be admitted.[31]

The same practice was instituted at McGill University, which liked to consider itself the "Harvard of the north" and was located not far from the neighbourhood where almost half of Canada's Jews lived. By the early 1920s, Jews comprised 25 per cent of the students in McGill's faculty of arts, 15 per cent in medicine, and a remarkable 40 per cent in law. As McGill's official historian was to write half a century later, "The university, liberal as its tradition might be, was not ready for such a sudden change in its constituency." Quotas were imposed in the faculties of medicine and law, while Jewish applicants to the faculty of arts were required to have higher marks than other applicants in order to be admitted. By 1939, Jews comprised only 12.1 per cent of the students in arts, 12.8 per cent in medicine, and 15 per cent in law. Soon afterwards, while Canada was at war with an overtly anti-Semitic regime in Germany, representations from the Jewish community succeeded in having these restrictive practices permanently abandoned.[32]

During the 1920s, Canada admitted about 50,000 Jewish immigrants, approximately one-seventh the number admitted to the United States.[33] Since the total population of the United States was about twelve times larger than that of Canada and the Jewish population about forty times larger, this was a substantial number. Canada's somewhat more liberal immigration policy in relation to the United States benefitted other groups of Europeans, such as Finns and Ukrainians, to an even greater extent than it did the Jews. Only about 4 per cent of all immigrants admitted by Canada during the decade were Jewish, compared to about 8 per cent of those admitted by the United States.[34] Although persons of British ancestry remained firmly in control of Canada, the country was becoming more diverse than ever before in terms of both ethnic culture and political ideology.

Canadian Jews obviously had a much slower start than American Jews in their efforts to gain economic power, but some progress was made. As in the United States, the clothing industry in Montreal and Winnipeg, including the production of fur garments, was largely dominated by Jewish capital and Jewish labour. In Montreal, the Steinbergs established the first Canadian-owned chain of supermarkets, and Jewish entrepreneurs prospered in other types of retailing as well, such as Freiman's department store in Ottawa. The most important and most celebrated of Jewish fortunes in Canada, however, was that of the Bronfmans, who profited greatly from the American experiment of imposing a constitutional ban on alcoholic beverages between 1919 and 1933. Beginning as bootleggers in southern Saskatchewan, they built one of the largest distilling companies in the Western Hemisphere, which was able to serve the American market openly and legally after prohibition ended. The family patriarch Samuel Bronfman, after he moved to Montreal, was president of the Canadian Jewish Congress from 1939 to 1961.

Unlike other immigrants, Canada's Jewish immigrants continued to favour Montreal as a place to settle, and this preference involved them willy nilly in Canada's perennial conflict between the British and the French, a conflict of which the country's largest city was the principal battleground. Neither of the principal ethnic groups was particularly sympathetic to the Jews, most of whom lived along the unofficial border between the anglophone west end and the francophone east end of the city. In Quebec's sectarian system of education, the Jews were arbitrarily classified as Protestants and excluded from the Catholic system, which meant that their children adopted English rather than French as their primary working language. In 1912, the Judicial Committee of the Privy Council ruled that this arrangement violated the constitutional right of Protestants to manage their own system, so Jews could not sit on the school boards to which they paid their taxes and that required their children to participate in Protestant hymns and prayers. Jewish discontent increased over the next two decades, and the provincial government considered, but eventually abandoned, the idea of creating a third school system for the exclusive use of the Jews.[35]

Anti-Semitism was widespread among the francophone population of Quebec in the 1930s and was openly catered to by some politicians as well as by the nationalist daily newspaper *Le Devoir*. The priest and historian Lionel Groulx, French Canada's most important public intellectual in the interwar period, helped to give anti-Semitism an undeserved legitimacy. One of its more subtle aspects was a bias in favour of small independent grocery stores (as opposed to the Steinberg supermarkets) to which the provincial government gave a competitive advantage by allowing them to sell beer.

British Protestant prejudice against Jews also was significant in Montreal and elsewhere in Canada. Kate Foster's book *Our Canadian Mosaic*, published in 1926, distinguished "semitic" people from "pure Aryans" and alleged that "Jews are readily identified the world over by their distinct facial characteristics."[36] In August 1933, a serious riot broke out at Toronto's Christie Pits baseball field when a swastika was displayed during a game in which a largely Jewish team participated. McGill University's quotas on Jewish students prompted many Montreal Jews to become fluent in French and to study law, medicine, or pharmacy in that language at l'Université de Montréal. Executive positions in Canada's major financial institutions were reserved for British Protestants. Montreal Jews who became affluent tended to live in Outremont, the stronghold of the francophone bourgeoisie, which was conveniently close to Montreal's Jewish neighbourhood, rather than in the British enclave of Westmount. However, Samuel Bronfman, who was wealthy enough to break down almost any barrier, did live in Westmount.

Most American Jews were Republicans during the era of Theodore Roosevelt, including ten of the eleven Jewish congressmen at the time of his death. In the 1920s, after Roosevelt's death, the Republican Party became increasingly the voice of Anglo-Saxon Protestant nativism, except in the southern states where it was then virtually non-existent. The increasingly Democratic orientation of Jewish voters, particularly in New York, was reinforced by two liberal Democratic governors of that state, Alfred E. Smith and Franklin Delano Roosevelt, who after serving as governor became the Democratic candidates for the presidency in 1928 and 1932, respectively. When Franklin Roosevelt was elected president for the first of four terms, Herbert Lehman, who was Jewish, followed him as the Democratic governor of New York. Subsequently, in 1950, Lehman became the first Jewish United States senator.

During Franklin Roosevelt's long presidency, Jews enjoyed unusual influence in Washington. In part this was because the president came from the state that had by far the largest number of Jews but also because Roosevelt was a liberal who liked and admired Jewish people. Two of New York's most important labour unions, the Amalgamated Clothing Workers and the International Ladies' Garment Workers, were largely Jewish organizations and assisted Roosevelt's rise to the presidency. Henry Morgenthau, Jr, Roosevelt's friend and Hyde Park neighbour, served as secretary of the treasury for all but the first year of the administration and was the first Jew to hold that office. (Harry Dexter White, the actual author of the infamous Morgenthau Plan for the de-industrialization of Germany, was also Jewish; he was subsequently revealed as a Soviet agent.) Roosevelt appointed Felix Frankfurter to the Supreme Court in 1939, replacing Louis Brandeis. About 15 per cent of Roosevelt's high-level appointments were Jewish, which was approximately four times the percentage of Jews in the total population of the United States.[37]

An important issue that confronted both the American and Canadian governments in the 1930s was how to respond to the increasingly virulent anti-Semitism of Nazi Germany and in particular whether to admit German and other European Jews who wished to escape from the Nazis by immigrating to North America. Both governments have been criticized after the fact for not doing enough in this regard, and with hindsight it is certainly regrettable that both didn't do more. However, the record of the United States in regard to this issue, as might be expected given its much larger and more influential Jewish population, was much better than that of Canada. Between 1 July 1933 (five months after Hitler became chancellor of Germany) and 30 June 1942 (six months after Germany declared war on the United States), 161,051 Jews were admitted as immigrants to the United States, and they comprised more than one-third of all the immigrants admitted from all sources during those years. In 1939 and 1940, Jews made up more than half of all immigrants admitted, the only years in American history when this was the case.[38] Canada in contrast admitted only a handful.

In assessing the performance of both governments, which particularly in Canada remains a sensitive and controversial topic, a few things should be borne in mind. First, although Nazi anti-Semitism was hardly a secret, scarcely anyone imagined in the 1930s that the Nazis would actually attempt to exterminate the entire Jewish population of Europe and come dangerously close to succeeding. Indeed, no proof has ever been found that the Nazis themselves planned to do so that far in advance; it is more likely that the genocide was a by-product of the unsuccessful attempt to conquer the Soviet Union in 1941–45.[39] Second, even if all potential Jewish refugees from Germany and Austria had been admitted to North America before the war, the genocide would not have been prevented, since fewer than 10 per cent of the nearly six million victims were living in Germany or Austria at the time. Third, public opinion in North America was hostile to any form of immigration during the Depression; in fact, even a slight majority of American Jews, as well as the major Jewish-American organizations, opposed admitting Jewish refugees from Europe.[40] So did 77 per cent of all Americans in late 1938, although 94 per cent said in the same poll that they disapproved of Germany's anti-Semitic policies.[41] Fourth, immigration laws in the United States were very rigid, and it is highly unlikely that any effort by President Roosevelt could have persuaded Congress to change them. The last caveat, however, does not apply to Canada, where there is no separation of legislative and executive powers and where the immigration laws left much greater scope for discretionary initiative on the part of public servants or the cabinet.

Of the letters that Roosevelt received from American citizens on Jewish immigration and related subjects before the war and even during the war, more seem to have come from anti-Semites than from Jews or people sympathetic to Jews, although there were some in the latter category and some that cannot be easily classified. (Among the odder items was a proposal from an Ohio man that the president should offer to buy British Columbia from King George VI, who was visiting the United States at the time, and turn the province into a Jewish homeland.)[42]

Roosevelt nonetheless made clear his opposition to the Nazis and their policies and did what he could to help their victims enter the United States, as shown by the data on immigration cited above. After Germany annexed Austria in March 1938, he tried to help Jews escape from that country. He took the initiative to organize an international conference on Jewish refugees at Evian, although the conference in July 1938 achieved very little and some writers have questioned Roosevelt's sincerity in proposing it. Following the so-called *Kristallnacht*, a nationwide pogrom organized by the Nazi government on 9 November 1938, he withdrew his ambassador from Berlin. After Britain and France declared war on Germany in September 1939, the immigration quotas allocated to various European countries in the American immigration law were used almost exclusively to admit Jewish applicants from the countries concerned.[43]

Much notoriety has been attached to the voyage of the steamship St Louis, which was the subject of a television drama half a century after it occurred. It is true that this vessel carrying 936 Jewish refugees was not allowed to land them in the United States in June 1939. However, the president did persuade Britain, France, Belgium, and the Netherlands to take many of the passengers (he did not waste time trying to persuade Canada), and more than 75 per cent of the passengers on the ship were still alive when the European war ended six years later.[44]

In a book defending Roosevelt's record on the question of Jewish immigration, Robert N. Rosen has suggested that the president detested anti-Semitism and was determined to destroy the Nazi regime by going to war against it. However, this goal required him to proceed carefully in the face of American public opinion that was highly isolationist, somewhat anti-Semitic, and definitely hostile to immigration. Too much zeal on behalf of Jewish refugees might threaten Roosevelt's long-term objective, which was presumably shared by most Jewish people. It is a matter of record that Roosevelt concealed his goal of going to war against Germany, and even lied about it, until after he had been elected to an unprecedented third term in November 1940. Perhaps his deviousness was justified, and it can be said in his defence that the United States admitted more Jewish immigrants during his term of office than any other country. According to a leading historian of Nazi Germany, about one-third of the Jews who left that country prior to the invasion of Poland went to the United States.[45] Furthermore, American negotiations with Hungary in 1944, when that country was preparing to defect from the Axis, may have saved about one-third of Hungary's Jews.[46]

Canada's record in relation to Jewish refugees is less easily excused than that of the United States. Between 1933 and 1945, the years when Hitler was in power, Canada admitted only about 5,000 Jewish immigrants: one-third as many as Australia, one-tenth as many as Argentina, one-fourteenth as many as the United Kingdom, and less than one-thirtieth as many as the United States. As Irving Abella and Harold Troper assert in what is perhaps the definitive book on the subject, "That record is arguably the worst of all possible refugee-receiving states."[47] This has led some observers to suspect that Prime Minister William Lyon Mackenzie King was anti-Semitic. The fact that he met Hitler in Berlin in 1937 has even been used to suggest that King was pro-Nazi, although he used the occasion to warn Hitler that Canada would fight alongside Britain in any war against Germany. Judging by King's account, neither he nor Hitler mentioned the Jewish question during this meeting.

An examination of King's famous diary, which can now be searched on-line, lends some support, but not much, to the accusation of anti-Semitism. One thing about Jews that seemed to bother him, especially in the 1920s, was the possibility of Jews buying land near his country estate of Kingsmere. The diary refers to this issue on 11 April, 15 May, and 14 August 1927 and again on 2 May 1929. On 2 June 1935, however, he was sceptical about a rumour that Jews were going to buy some land near Kingsmere and suggested that someone had started the rumour to persuade King to buy the land himself. On 10 February 1937, he feared that Jews might take over Sandy Hill, the part of Ottawa where he lived when Parliament was in session. There is a more ambiguous reference to Jews buying land at Kingsmere on 8 March 1943.

A more serious issue that concerned King occasionally was the influence of Jews in the Roosevelt administration and the possibility that some of them might be communists. On 9 August 1936, King mentioned "the association of the Jews with Russian Sovietism" and "The association of Roosevelt with Jewish influence etc." However, he added, "My own view is that there are good as well as bad Jews, and it is wrong to indict a nation or a race." On 16 March 1937, King wrote, "I do not like the extent to which the Jewish influence is honeycombing American social and industrial movements." On 18 November 1938, "one can see wherein the atmosphere around the President is very strong as to Jewish influence." On 20 February 1946, after Roosevelt's death and the postwar revelations about Soviet espionage, King wrote, "I am coming to feel that the democratic [sic] party have allowed themselves to be too greatly controlled by the Jews and Jewish influence and that Russia has sympathizers in high and influential places to a much greater number than has been believed. Indeed I used to feel that even with Franklin Roosevelt, he was perhaps trusting Russia far too much, sympathizing of course with the mass of the people."

On the other hand, the diary contains many favourable references to Jews whom King knew personally. For example, on 5 March 1925 King noted that Sam Jacobs, a Jewish Liberal MP from Montreal, was elected to the Rideau Club after being nominated by King himself. He said that Jacobs was only the second Jew to become a member of the club. On 12 May 1926, he was very favourably impressed by his meeting with eighteen-year-old Carl Goldenberg, who later in life became a distinguished constitutional lawyer and a Liberal senator. Five years later, on 4 June 1931, he invited Goldenberg to dinner and was still very impressed with him. The diary contains numerous favourable comments about A.J. Freiman, the owner of a department store in Ottawa, and about his wife Lillian, who were Liberal supporters as well as prominent in the Zionist movement. On 27 August 1936, Mackenzie King wrote that at a cabinet meeting "I put forth the necessity of recognizing some member of the Jewish community on some boards" and suggested Mrs Freiman as an appointee. "The suggestion met with pretty general approval." On 16 June 1937, King described the Jewish director of a museum bookstore in London as "one of the most interesting men I have yet met." On 6 December 1938, he expressed satisfaction that David Croll, a Jewish Liberal, was elected mayor of Windsor, Ontario. Croll had been dismissed from the provincial cabinet for his pro-labour views by Premier Mitchell Hepburn, whom King considered to be an anti-Semite as well as a generally bad character. On 2 July 1940, King contemplated appointing Sam Factor, a Jewish MP from Toronto, to his cabinet but was dissuaded by his French-Canadian ministers. On 7 November 1940, he described Factor, who had just joined the air force and was actually 48 years old, as "a splendid young fellow." Five years later, he appointed Factor as a judge. There would be no Jews in the federal cabinet until after Pierre Trudeau became prime minister in 1968.

King also made comments critical of Nazi anti-Semitism. On 23 April 1933, less than three months after Hitler became chancellor, he praised a sermon about the Jews that included "a protest against Hitler's action." On 28 March 1938, he said there was "much I cannot abide in Nazism," including "oppression of Jews." On 12 November 1938, a few days after *Kristallnacht*: "The sorrows which the Jews have to bear at this time are almost beyond comprehension." Two days later, he called Germany and Japan "gangster nations" and added, "The treatment of the Jews by the Germans discloses how quickly feeling may come to the point where war against these forces will be irresistible." On the same day, he mentioned that Mrs Freiman called (again) to discuss the fate of Jews in

Germany and concluded, "I feel we must do something as a country to admit some of these refugees." On 11 June 1944, referring to the fate of the Jews in Europe, he wrote, "I must say when one listens to accounts of their persecutions, one cannot have any human sympathies without being prepared to do much on their behalf."

The fact remains, however, that Canada had done very little. On 29 March 1938, King wrote in his diary that Roosevelt's appeal to Canada and other nations to admit Austrian and German Jews after the *Anschluss* raised "a very difficult question ... I fear that we would have riots if we agreed to a policy that admitted numbers of Jews." On 23 November 1938, he met a delegation of Jewish Canadians who urged him to admit 10,000 refugees. King expressed sympathy but also referred to Canada's high rate of unemployment and pointed out that "we had to consider the constituencies and the views of those who are supporting the government," a comment that is probably a subtle reference to anti-Semitism in Quebec. The following day, he wrote that he had urged his cabinet to adopt a more liberal policy toward Jewish refugees but added, "I did not get any real response from this appeal, most of those present fearing the political consequences of any help to the Jews." Early in 1943, the United States government proposed another international conference on the Jewish refugee problem and suggested Ottawa as the site. Canada, which had not been consulted, was angered and embarrassed by the suggestion. In the end, the conference was held in Bermuda, and Canada did not take part.[48]

Abella and Troper suggest that the person who contributed most to Canada's failure to help Jewish refugees was Frederick C. Blair, who from 1935 to 1943 was the director of the Immigration Branch in the Department of Mines and Resources and the person who ultimately decided who would be admitted to Canada. Blair was clearly a convinced anti-Semite. On the other hand, he could have been overruled or dismissed by a prime minister who was willing to take political risks. Mackenzie King, as suggested above, was not really an anti-Semite by the standards of his time, but he was a very cautious politician who preferred consensus to confrontation. In particular, he was obsessed with the need to maintain Canadian unity between anglophones and francophones in the event of war, as Robert Borden's government had conspicuously failed to do during World War I. It is not clear whether King's Quebec ministers were themselves anti-Semitic, but they believed that most French Canadians

were, and they persuaded King that openness to Jewish immigration
would be politically suicidal in Quebec, particularly after Maurice
Duplessis became premier of that province in 1936. Like Roosevelt,
King felt that he had to be devious, but he achieved considerably less
on behalf of Jewish refugees than Roosevelt did.

After the war, many Canadians and Americans remained reluctant
to admit more Jewish immigrants. A Canadian poll in 1946 that
asked for views on various ethnic groups as potential immigrants
found that the least popular groups were the Jews and the Japanese.[49]
In the same year, an American poll found that 72 per cent of respondents opposed President Truman's efforts to admit more refugees
from Europe, including Jews.[50] Nonetheless, many survivors of the
Nazi genocide did immigrate to North America during the postwar
decade. In Canada, the total size of the Jewish community increased
substantially as a result of this postwar immigration. In the United
States, where the existing Jewish population was much larger and
the number of immigrants proportionately smaller, the demographic
impact was fairly slight.

In both countries, the Jewish community after 1945 matured and
became more self-confident, more united, and, at least in the
Canadian case, more influential. The distinction between Jews whose
ancestors had come from western or central Europe before 1880 and
those who had come from eastern Europe after 1880 no longer
seemed important in the light of the Nazi experience. The descendants of the post-1880 Russian Jews were increasingly well-educated
and affluent on both sides of the border. They were also spreading
more widely across the continent as the traditionally Jewish neighbourhoods in North American cities were abandoned by their Jewish
residents and in some cases occupied by new waves of non-Jewish
immigrants.

As the true dimensions of the Nazi genocide finally penetrated the
consciousness of postwar North Americans, anti-Semitism even in its
more subtle forms ceased to be respectable or widely accepted. The
tacit agreements that had kept Jews out of many residential neighbourhoods gradually disappeared. Increasingly, it was fashionable to
be pro-Jewish rather than anti-Jewish. The popularity of postwar
Jewish writers like Saul Bellow, Norman Mailer, Mordecai Richler,
Philip Roth, Leon Uris, and Herman Wouk was perhaps both a cause
and a consequence of this shift in attitudes. So was the growing
prominence of Jewish academics, many of whom had been refugees

from Nazism before the war, and their influence on generations of students. The Christian churches, particularly the older Protestant denominations with roots in England or Scotland, began to question their traditional tolerance of anti-Semitism and to seek a dialogue with religious Jews. The adjective "Judeo-Christian," unknown before the war, was increasingly used to convey the idea that Judaism, as well as Christianity, was a part of the spiritual heritage that contributed to North American liberalism and democracy. Some of this ecumenical discourse glossed over the real differences between the two faiths, and some religious Jews had misgivings about it, but at least it was well-intentioned.

Zionism also became popular among non-Jewish North Americans after 1948. The idea of a Jewish national homeland in Palestine had been endorsed by a joint resolution of the United States Congress as early as 1922, but some of those who voted for it may have seen it as a way to reduce the Jewish population of the United States in the same way that some nineteenth-century Americans had favoured sending freed slaves to Africa. The Nazi genocide seemed to strengthen the argument for a Jewish homeland outside of Europe, and President Roosevelt endorsed the idea in 1944.[51] However, it was opposed by some Americans, often stigmatized as "isolationists," who accurately foresaw that it would impose new commitments on the United States that would not be directly related to its national interests. There had also been misgivings about the idea of introducing possibly radical or even pro-communist European Jews into the Middle East, a region rich in oil where British influence was still predominant.

In the end, however, the governments of both the United States and Canada supported the partition of Palestine and the creation of the state of Israel, although the British government did not. Many non-Jews, as well as many Jews, saw that event as a way of making partial amends for what the Nazis had done to the Jews of Europe. Israel's defence of its newly won independence against much larger (although poorly armed and poorly organized) opponents was widely admired in North America, especially given the well-known fact that many Egyptians and Iraqis, as well as the Muslim Grand Mufti of Jerusalem, had supported Nazi Germany before and during the war. Canada's most effective wartime fighter pilot, Buzz Beurling, volunteered to fight for Israel, although he was not Jewish. The fact that the creation of Israel involved the displacement of several hundred thousand Palestinians from their homes and the deliberate murder of some of them was not widely known or understood at the time, although it would be later.

The idea that there was an association between Jews and communism disappeared rapidly after 1948. This idea had not been entirely without foundation. Although communists were always a small minority among North American (and European) Jews, the communist movement in the United States had included a disproportionate number of Jews, particularly in New York. Jewish voters in Canada had sent a Jewish communist from Montreal, Fred Rose, to the federal Parliament in 1943. Another Jewish communist, J.B. Salsberg, was elected to the Ontario legislature in 1945 and remained there for ten years. When massive Soviet espionage in North America was revealed soon after the war, Fred Rose and, more famously, Julius and Ethel Rosenberg were among those involved.

At a time when the Soviet army was driving the Nazis out of eastern and central Europe, a certain amount of Jewish pro-communist sentiment was understandable. However, such sentiment evaporated quickly after 1945. Jewish influence in the Soviet regime, although significant in its early years, had been greatly reduced by the expulsion of Trotsky in 1928 and by Stalin's purges of the Communist Party's ranks in the 1930s. The Soviet Union, perhaps hoping to drive a wedge between the United Kingdom and the United States, had nonetheless voted for the partition of Palestine in 1947. In the following years, however, Stalin's regime became not only anti-Zionist but increasingly anti-Semitic, with its propaganda denouncing Soviet Jews as "rootless cosmopolitans" and agents of the United States. Some prominent Jewish communists were purged in the Soviet satellite states of central Europe. Israel, always sympathetic to the United States, became increasingly dependent on that country for weapons and subsidies and increasingly aligned with the United States in the cold war, although it remained theoretically neutral.

Partly in response to these developments, and partly because of their rising socio-economic status, North American Jews became overwhelmingly anti-communist and in some cases militantly so. The so-called neo-conservative movement that arose in the United States in the 1970s and continued past the turn of the century included many Jewish intellectuals, some of whom had been pro-communist in their youth. To some degree, it was a reaction against the "new left" of the 1960s, which was actually more anarchist than Marxist and in which many Jewish university students participated.

Militant anti-communism was part of a process by which Jews became increasingly integrated, although not totally assimilated, into North American life. In both countries, Jews became the most highly educated and most affluent ethnic group, although in Quebec as late as 1961 their average income was below that of persons of British ancestry. (It was, however, far above the average income of French Canadians.[52]) Despite their relative affluence, most Jews continued to vote for the Democratic Party in the United States and for the Liberal Party in Canada and to play a more prominent part in those parties than in the Republican and Conservative parties. However, support for Jews, and particularly for Israel, was and is a matter of bipartisan consensus in both countries. In Canada, the Conservative prime ministers John Diefenbaker, Joe Clark, Brian Mulroney, and Stephen Harper all surpassed the Liberals in their public and lavish expressions of enthusiasm for Israel. Clark, by promising to move the Canadian embassy from Tel Aviv to Jerusalem, created a diplomatic embarrassment for Canada that was only ended by the electoral defeat of his government within a year of its taking office.

Jews continued to hold high public offices in the United States, to a greater extent than before the war. Michael Blumenthal and Robert Rubin were secretaries of the treasury under Democratic presidents Carter and Clinton, respectively. Edward H. Levi was attorney general under Republican president Ford. Henry Kissinger, a former refugee from pre-war Germany, was President Nixon's national security advisor and then secretary of state under both Nixon and Ford. He was largely responsible for the rapprochement between China and the United States. Madeleine Albright, who apparently only discovered her Jewish ancestry after taking office, was secretary of state under Clinton. Joe Lieberman was the Democratic candidate for vice-president in 2000. Alan Greenspan was chairman of the Federal Reserve from 1987 until 2006 and was then succeeded by another Jewish American, Ben Bernanke.

However, the prominence of Jews in Canadian public life after 1960 was more unusual and, given the relatively small size of Canada's Jewish population, more surprising. Louis Rasminsky was appointed chairman of the Bank of Canada by Prime Minister Diefenbaker in 1962. Prime Minister Pierre Trudeau appointed Canada's first two Jewish federal cabinet ministers, Herb Gray in 1969 and Barney Danson in 1974. Trudeau also appointed Bora Laskin to the Supreme Court of Canada in 1970 and then made him chief justice in 1973. Irwin Cotler, a past-president of the Canadian Jewish Congress and an internationally known authority on human rights, was Canada's minister of justice in Paul Martin's government from 2003 to 2006. As of 2012, there were four Jews sitting simultaneously on the nine-member Supreme Court (Rosalie Abella, Morris Fish, Michael Moldaver, and Marshall Rothstein), a record unlikely ever to be surpassed in any country apart from Israel. David Barrett of the New Democratic Party of British Columbia became the first Jewish premier of a Canadian province in 1972. David Lewis, who had emigrated from Poland as a child, headed the federal wing of the same party from 1971 to 1974. His son, Stephen Lewis, was the leader of the Ontario NDP from 1970 to 1978 and later became Canada's ambassador to the United Nations. Simon Reisman negotiated Canada's free trade agreement with the United States, and Allan Gotlieb was Canada's ambassador to the United States at the time of the negotiations. Probably neither was amused when the president of the AFL-CIO insisted on referring to the proposed agreement as the *Anschluss*.[53]

Canadian Jews also played a very prominent part in the Canadian nationalism, not unmixed with anti-Americanism, that flourished during and after the war in Vietnam. Herb Gray, a Liberal, was the minister who presided over the drafting of a critical report on American direct investment in Canada. Eddie Goodman, a Progressive Conservative, was one of the principal founders of the Committee for an Independent Canada. Jim Laxer, whose father was Jewish although his mother was not, was the candidate of the nationalist Waffle faction for the leadership of the New Democratic Party in 1971. Mel Hurtig, the Edmonton-based publisher, was a tireless advocate of Canadian nationalism, at first within the Liberal Party and later as the leader of the National Party of Canada, which he founded.

One reason why all this was possible was the rapid decline of traditional anti-Semitism in Quebec after the Quiet Revolution. Fear of Quebec's reaction had previously inhibited any public expression of sympathy for Jews by federal politicians, especially Liberals, but by the 1960s this was no longer the case. Premier Robert Bourassa, a Liberal, appointed Quebec's first Jewish provincial cabinet minister, Victor Goldbloom, in 1970. Goldbloom remained a minister until the provincial Liberals were defeated in 1976 and was later appointed Canada's commissioner of official languages by Brian Mulroney's Conservative government in 1991, serving until 1999. Meanwhile,

Bourassa, after returning to office, appointed Herbert Marx, a bilingual product of the old Jewish neighbourhood described in Mordecai
Richler's novels, as Quebec's minister of justice in 1985.

A Jewish sociologist who has lived in both countries has suggested
that Canadian Jews are more isolated, partly by choice, from
Canadian society than American Jews are isolated from American
society.[54] If this is so, it is largely because Canada's Jewish community contains a much larger proportion of people born outside the
country than does the Jewish community in the United States. This
reflects Canada's somewhat more liberal immigration policies in the
two decades after World War II. In addition, many of Canada's
immigrant Jews are from North Africa and speak French more fluently than English. Naturally, most of these North African Jews have
settled in Montreal, while many of the English-speaking European
Jews who formerly lived in that city have moved to other parts of
Canada, particularly Toronto.

Another sociologist has suggested that "In America today, the
boundary between Jew and non-Jew is not a clear one."[55] American
Jews are more likely to marry non-Jews than their counterparts in
Canada. From 1966 to 1972, almost one-third of marriages involving American Jews were exogenous, or "mixed," compared to only
about one-eighth of marriages involving Canadian Jews. Jews in the
United States are much less likely (51 per cent) to say that most of
their close friends are Jewish than Jews in Canada (78 per cent),
according to a survey conducted in 1990. American Jews are less
likely to read a Jewish newspaper (33 per cent as opposed to 60 per
cent), to have visited Israel (35 per cent as opposed to 66 per cent),
and to observe Jewish religious rituals than Canadian Jews.[56] These
facts, as well as the small volume of recent Jewish immigration to the
United States, has aroused fears among American Jews that the
American Jewish community may eventually disappear with barely
a trace into the general population. Israel Zangwill's dream of the
"melting pot" may thus be in the process of becoming reality in the
case of his own ethnic group, although not in the case of African
Americans, Asian Americans, or Hispanic Americans.

So far at least, this seems less of a possibility in Canada. Interestingly,
the Canadian concept of "multiculturalism" was greeted enthusiastically by Canadian Jews. Two Jewish ministers have held the multiculturalism portfolio in Canadian governments, the Conservative
Gerry Weiner from 1988 to 1991 and the Liberal Sheila Finestone

from 1993 to 1996. American Jews, in contrast to some other American ethnic groups, have shown little interest in the idea.

Despite these contrasts, it has been suggested that Canadian and American Jews are converging with one another in some ways. Reform and Conservative Judaism, traditionally regarded as American innovations by Canadian Jews, have rapidly gained ground in Canada at the expense of Orthodox Judaism. The fact that the centre of gravity in Canadian Judaism is now in Toronto rather than Montreal has contributed to this trend. On the other hand, American Jews are increasingly likely to enrol their children in Jewish day schools and to regard their Jewishness as an ethnic rather than a religious identity, characteristics traditionally associated more with Canadian Jews.[57]

In the 1960s, American Jews faced a crisis in their relations with the increasingly militant African-American community. Traditionally, Jews had given great support to the African-American struggle for civil rights. Martin Luther King relied heavily on the advice of a Jewish friend and advisor, Stanley Levison, whose previous association with the Communist Party of the United States provided the pretext for the surveillance of King by J. Edgar Hoover of the FBI. More than half of the white volunteers who worked for civil rights during the Mississippi "freedom summer" of 1964 were Jewish.[58] Two young Jews, Andrew Goodman and Michael Schwerner, were murdered, along with an African-American companion, by the Ku Klux Klan during that summer. However, within a few years of these events, some of the more radical and nationalist elements in the African-American community developed anti-Semitic tendencies, claiming that Jewish landlords and small business proprietors exploited African Americans in New York and other cities. To many Jews, these accusations appeared to be, as they were, alarmingly similar to those used by anti-Semites in central and eastern Europe prior to World War II. The fact that some young Jews active in the "new left" sympathized with the black nationalists who made the accusations was particularly disturbing to older Jews who had traditionally lent their support to civil rights and other liberal causes.

The increasing affluence and influence of North American Jews, and their evolution from victims into the targets of other victims, have been paralleled to some extent by the changing fortunes, and changing image, of Israel. After two successful wars in 1967 and 1973, that country became the dominant military power in the

Middle East and was more closely tied than ever to the United States, which gives more economic and military aid to Israel than to any other country. The democratic socialism that had prevailed during the early years of the state disappeared for all practical purposes as a variety of conservative parties and factions, some of them religiously based, gained strength at the expense of the secular and socialist Labour Party. Israel also controlled the entire territory of the former British mandate of Palestine after 1967 and began to colonize the newly acquired land with Jewish settlers, particularly after the collapse of communism permitted many Jews to emigrate from the former Soviet Union. By the turn of the century, about half a million Israeli Jews were living on land acquired by their state in 1967, regardless of the wishes or needs of the original inhabitants.

Despite or perhaps because of these developments, the American and Canadian governments continued to give Israel almost unconditional support, as did most (although not all) of the Jewish population in both the United States and Canada. Some of Israel's former admirers in North America, however, became increasingly dubious about the Jewish state and supportive of the Palestinians, who attracted the same kind of sympathy from left-leaning people that the beleaguered Jewish settlers had enjoyed in 1948. After Israel's unexpectedly decisive victory in 1967, as one historian of American Jewry wryly commented, "The Christian community redirected its love to groups more in need of it."[59] This was also true in Canada, where many Jews were outraged soon after the 1967 war by some pro-Palestinian editorials in the *United Church Observer*, the official publication of Canada's largest Protestant denomination.[60]

The Muslim population of North America is growing rapidly, and in Canada Muslims already outnumber Jews. By no means all North American Muslims are of Arabic descent, but many are, and even those who are not tend to sympathize with the Palestinians. As will be discussed in a subsequent chapter, Muslims, and especially Arab Muslims, in North America face much of the same prejudice and discrimination today that the Jews (and before them the Irish) experienced in earlier times. Nonetheless, North American Muslims are likely to become more affluent and influential, as well as more numerous, with the passage of time. As this occurs, their sentiments and interests will eventually exert some influence on the domestic and also on the foreign policies of North American governments.

Their status as victims, both at home and overseas, will in the long run win them more allies and supporters among liberal-minded people in both the United States and Canada.

In response to this threat, North American Jews constantly evoke the memories of the Nazi genocide or, as it has become fashionable in recent years to call it, the "Holocaust." It is only since 1967 that this event has been incorporated into the "civil religion" of North American Jews, and it has also become the central legitimizing myth of the state of Israel.[61] Holocaust museums have been opened in Washington, DC, and in Toronto, and the government of Canada is helping to fund a Museum of Human Rights in Winnipeg that will apparently be mainly devoted to commemorating the same event. The purpose, of course, is to remind other North Americans of the fact that Jews once faced the most extreme kind of persecution, far worse than what is experienced by Palestinians and other Muslims today. Those memories, however, are a fading asset in terms of appealing for sympathy from populations who are increasingly of non-European ancestry, most of whom were born long after World War II.

6

Ethnic Minorities in Wartime

Winston Churchill, by his own admission, disliked studying Latin in school and never acquired much knowledge of the language, but one Latin expression apparently was lodged in his memory and remained there until late in life. The expression, *inter arma silent leges*, means that the laws are silent in the midst of war. In his memoirs of World War II, Churchill rather glibly used this aphorism to excuse the invasion and conquest of neutral Iran, which he and Josef Stalin jointly planned and executed in the summer of 1941.[1] The lasting consequences of that event, it might be argued, include the animosity between Iran and the Western world that persists more than seven decades later.

North America's wartime leaders, in contrast to Churchill and Stalin, lived thousands of miles away from the battlefields of both world wars and never were in any danger of personal injury or death from enemy action. Nonetheless, the laws and the normal standards of civilized behaviour were largely ignored on this continent as well, and the consequences were experienced by members of certain ethnic minorities in both Canada and the United States. What happened in World War II is fairly well known, in its broad outlines if not in its details, and many who experienced it are still alive. World War I, now almost a century past, has largely receded from memory or common knowledge, apart from the celebrated Canadian poem *In Flanders Fields*, which conveys nothing of the ugliness of that unnecessary and pointless conflict. However, ethnic minorities in North America suffered during that war as well, and the events of the two wars can now be seen as part of a common pattern. Neither Canada's claim to be a tolerant multicultural mosaic nor the proud American boast that theirs is a government, as John Adams put it, of laws and not of men receives much support from a contemplation of these events.

In World War I, both countries were at war with Germany and with the dual monarchy of Austria-Hungary, Canada from the outset of the war in 1914 and the United States from 1917. As part of the British Empire, Canada was also automatically at war with the Ottoman Empire and Bulgaria, although the United States did not declare war on these countries. In World War II, the Axis alliance consisted of Germany, Italy, and Japan, supported by Hungary and Romania, and both Canada and the United States were eventually at war with all of these countries. Canada made an independent declaration of war on Germany in 1939 and on Italy in 1940, while the United States remained neutral, at least in theory, until after Pearl Harbor was attacked on 7 December 1941. The United States also declared war on Bulgaria, although Canada did not, and Canada declared war on Finland, although the United States did not. In both wars of course, Germany was the most powerful opponent and accounted for the great majority of Canadian and American casualties.

Prior to World War I, the influence of Germany and its culture on the United States was enormous. Even at the time when American independence was achieved, about one-third of Pennsylvania's population was of German origin, and there were significant German minorities in Maryland, New Jersey, and New York. The ancestors of the so-called Pennsylvania "Dutch" (Deutsch) were viewed with disfavour by Benjamin Franklin, as noted in chapter 2, but the German strain in American culture would receive significant reinforcement in later years. From 1820, when the United States began to collect statistics on immigration, until the outbreak of war almost a century later, Germany contributed about five and a half million immigrants to the United States, more than any other country.[2] Admittedly, some of these immigrants may have been members of Germany's ethnic and linguistic minorities, but on the other hand a large, and probably larger, number of immigrants were ethnic Germans from outside of Germany's boundaries, who were counted according to their previous place of residence rather than according to ethnicity and language. Germans (from Germany) comprised more than a third of immigrants entering the United States between 1850 and 1870 and more than a quarter between 1870 and 1890.

The German-American vote may have been decisive in electing Abraham Lincoln president in 1860.[3] German voters in St Louis were also decisive in keeping the large and strategically vital slave-owning state of Missouri within the Union, even though most rural Missourians probably favoured the Confederacy. Sources within this German immigrant community, incidentally, provided most of the information that Karl Marx and Friedrich Engels used in their extensive writings on the Civil War. By one estimate, about 30 per cent of the soldiers who fought for the Union in the Civil War were of German ancestry, including about 10 per cent of German birth.[4]

The total volume of German immigration to the United States actually reached its peak in the 1880s, when almost one and a half million immigrants arrived from Germany.[5] Thereafter it declined sharply, probably because of increasing industrialization and prosperity in Germany, and the number of arrivals from Germany was overtaken by immigrants of other nationalities, particularly Italians and Russian Jews. However, even in the decennial census of 2000, only the third American census in which a question on ethnicity was included, more Americans still claimed German ethnic origin than any other, including English and Irish. Self-reported German ethnicity predominates in a huge section of middle America, extending from the Alleghenies to the Rockies and from the Canadian border to the Ohio River. German is the most frequently reported ethnic origin in twenty-two of the fifty states, including every state in the northern half of the country apart from the six New England states and Utah.

In spite of these facts, little overt evidence of German culture is evident in the United States today to a superficial observer, apart from the strong national preference for lager beer over the ale that is preferred by beer-drinkers in England and Ireland. Even the formerly ubiquitous hot dog, allegedly invented at a baseball field in the once very German city of St Louis, is gradually declining in popularity owing to a growing tendency to prefer healthier forms of nourishment. German Americans in the course of two world wars learned to keep a low profile to the point where nowadays they are virtually indistinguishable from the rest of the population.

Prior to 1914, however, things were very different. Eight midwestern states allowed the use of German as the language of instruction in their public schools. When Illinois in 1889 and Wisconsin in 1890 attempted to reverse this policy, strong opposition from German-American voters soon forced them to repeal the laws requiring instruction in English and to maintain the status quo.[6] Many churches also conducted services of worship in German. By one estimate, there were forty-nine monthly, 433 weekly, and seventy daily German-language periodicals in the United States just prior to World War I.[7] It would not be an exaggeration to say that German was the unofficial second language of the United States, occupying much the same position that Spanish does today.

On 6 October 1883, German Americans commemorated what was alleged to be the bicentennial of German settlement in North America, and the anniversary was celebrated for the next thirty years as "German Day," complete with parades and other festivities.[8] The largest ethnic organization in the United States at that time was the Deutsch-Amerikanischer Nationalbund (National Federation of German-Americans) with a membership variously estimated at between two and three million.[9] It apparently managed to bridge the gap between Catholic Germans, mainly from southern and western Germany, and Lutheran Germans, mainly from the north and east, a cleavage that had important political consequences within Germany itself.

Even Americans who were not of German ancestry paid tribute to the importance and prestige of German culture in those years. Knowledge of German as a second language was considered almost essential for a highly educated person, and German was the foreign language most frequently taught in American high schools, colleges, and universities. New American universities were founded, and old ones were reformed, to resemble the German universities, which were then the best in the world, and to diverge sharply from the English model of post-secondary education. American scholars, particularly in the social sciences, had often studied in Germany and developed a Germanic style of writing, complete with copious footnotes, of which some traces still survive.

The German imprint on Canada, however, was considerably less important. Germans had played an important role in the settlement of Nova Scotia in the middle of the eighteenth century when General Cornwallis imported a number of them to stimulate development in a colony that had been rather slow in getting off the ground. Many Loyalists who moved from Pennsylvania and other states to Upper Canada were of German ancestry.[10] However, Canada attracted very few immigrants from Germany in the nineteenth century, in contrast to the huge numbers who entered the United States, so the process of assimilation for most German Canadians had been in progress for well over a century.[11]

Since the Canadian census, unlike the American, always enumerated people by ethnicity, the fifth largest ethnic group (after the French, English, Irish, and Scottish) were "Germans," but most of them were the descendants either of eighteenth-century settlers or of more recent arrivals from the German-speaking minorities in various parts of central and eastern Europe. Many in the latter category belonged to religious sects such as the Mennonites and Hutterites, which tended to isolate themselves from the rest of the population, whether German or otherwise. A large number of western Canada's "Germans" were actually midwestern Americans who had moved to what are now Saskatchewan and Alberta in search of free land after the closing of the American frontier in 1890. Although the American census had not recorded their ethnicity when they lived in the United States, the Canadian census required them to specify an ethnic origin, and "American" was not a permissible category.

These assorted groups of "Germans," all relatively small and scattered across a vast country, had little in common with one another and little obvious impact on Canadian life outside of a few enclaves like Lunenberg (Nova Scotia) and Berlin (Ontario), where elements of their German heritage survived. Canadian education at all levels was much more influenced by England and especially Scotland than by Germany.

The outbreak of war in 1914 had serious consequences for German Canadians and also for German Americans. International law recognizes the legitimacy of interning people who are citizens or subjects of a state against which war has been formally declared. To avoid internment, some German citizens residing in Canada returned home in 1914, often for the purpose of joining the German army. The most subsequently famous of these was a young resident of Ottawa, Joachim Ribbentrop (he added the "von" later), who eventually became the foreign minister of the Third Reich and a principal defendant at the Nuremberg tribunal. The number of German residents who failed to escape and were interned in Canada during World War I totalled 1,192, but the number of "Austrians" interned in Canada during the war was much higher, at 5,954.[12] The great majority of these "Austrians" were actually ethnic Ukrainians, whose fate will be discussed later in this chapter. After the United States entered the war in 1917, it interned about 1,200 Germans and German Americans immediately and about another 5,100 before the end of the war. These numbers were relatively small compared to the 45,000 German internees in the United Kingdom, which rounded up everyone who had been born in an enemy country.[13] Such a policy would obviously have been impractical in the United States where the German-born population was in excess of two million.

However, internment, which affected relatively few people and in the case of German internees was conducted in a fairly civilized manner, was only the tip of a very large iceberg. What was more striking, and more unprecedented, was the hatred and hostility directed against every trace of German culture or heritage and against everyone who displayed evidence thereof, including persons who had been born in North America and had never seen Germany in their lives. This phenomenon became apparent in Canada almost as soon as the war began and in the United States, despite that country's neutrality until April 1917, not long afterwards. In the words of one historian, "The war precipitated a violent, hysterical, concerted movement to eradicate everything German from American civilization."[14]

Prior to the war, most English-speaking Protestant people in both the British Empire and the United States had regarded the Germans as a kindred people having much in common with themselves, as suggested by the popularity of the term "Anglo-Saxon." Once the war began, this belief was quickly abandoned. "Anglo-Celtic" replaced "Anglo-Saxon" as the preferred label in both Canada and the United States.[15] "After 1915 little more was heard in the United States about the origins of liberty in the forests of Germany."[16] In 1918, the revised edition of Madison Grant's influential racist book, *The Passing of the Great Race*, classified the Germans as "Alpine" and thus distinct from the "Nordic" people of England, the Netherlands, and Scandinavia.[17]

In both Canada and the United States, the anti-German sentiment seems to have built up to a climax in 1917 when Russia's October Revolution, which many people attributed to German influence, brought about a major reinforcement of North American paranoia and xenophobia. Frustration at the growing number of casualties, and at the prolongation of a war that had originally been expected to last only a few months, contributed to the trend as well. The influence of very effective British propaganda, which invented many fictitious German "atrocities" and exaggerated the significance of real events like the violation of Belgian neutrality, the sinking of merchant vessels by submarines, and the rather pathetic raids on British cities by German Zeppelins, should also not be discounted. As Otto von Bismarck had allegedly predicted, the fact that the United States and

England shared a common language had an important influence on the history of the twentieth century.

In Canada, the War Measures Act, which permitted arbitrary actions by the government and overrode both the common law protections of civil liberties and the normal distribution of legislative powers between Parliament and the provincial legislatures, was adopted soon after the outbreak of the war. In 1917, the Wartime Elections Act disenfranchised Canadians of "enemy" origins, including those who had been naturalized as British subjects within the preceding fifteen years. This provision of the act, as well as its selective enfranchisement of women who had a son or husband serving in the army, helped to elect conscriptionist candidates (almost entirely of British ancestry) in the ethnically mixed Prairie provinces. In September 1918, when the war was almost over, the Canadian government finally banned all German-language publications, apparently because it feared that they would be targets of violence when Canadian veterans returned from Europe.[18] The ban lasted until 1920.[19]

Apart from these federal initiatives, there were many local expressions of Germanophobia. One historian has suggested that this sentiment was especially strong in British Columbia.[20] If so, this fact foreshadowed the fate of Japanese Canadians in World War II a generation later and also gave credence to Lord Dufferin's comment on the people of that province, quoted in chapter 4 of this book. In 1915, the sinking of the Lusitania, a British ocean liner on its way from New York to Southampton, caused anti-German riots in Victoria, Calgary, and Montreal. (The ship was actually carrying some Canadian soldiers on their way to the western front, a fact that was kept secret and not widely known at the time.) In Winnipeg, where there had been some rioting and anti-German vandalism in 1914, German schools, churches, and bookstores were searched by the police in 1915 and again in 1917.[21] In Ontario, the city of Berlin, the birthplace of William Lyon Mackenzie King but also the major centre of German culture in the province, was renamed as Kitchener in memory of the recently deceased British minister of war and former general, whose image appeared on recruiting posters throughout the empire. This decision, which has never been reversed, followed from two referenda, the first on the abolition of the city's original name and the second, conducted immediately after Kitchener's death, on the choice of its new name.[22]

In the United States, Germanophobia was probably no more extreme than in Canada, but it had a much greater effect on more people and on the future development of the country, because the size of the ethnic German population and the influence of German culture on American life were so much greater than in Canada. Anti-German sentiment became apparent long before the United States entered the war, since Americans of British origin, especially the Ivy League elites of the eastern seaboard, supported the British cause from the very beginning of hostilities in Europe. The sinking of the *Lusitania* in April 1915, a few days after its departure from New York with many American passengers on board, reinforced this tendency. The United States might have entered the war at that time, as former President Theodore Roosevelt urged, but President Wilson, although pro-British himself, knew that sentiment in the country was divided along ethnic lines and prudently waited until after his re-election in November 1916.

Nonetheless, the offensive against every trace of German culture in the United States did not wait for the formal declaration of war. Some aspects of it were absurd, like the proposals to outlaw dachshunds and the (temporary) renaming of sauerkraut as "liberty cabbage." German shepherd dogs became "Alsatians" in reference to the disputed territory of Alsace-Lorraine, a name that is still used for them in the United Kingdom. German classical music also became unpopular in some circles.[23] It is interesting, however, that Bismarck, the capital of North Dakota, managed to keep its original name, in contrast to Berlin, Ontario. The reason for the contrast is probably the fact that North Dakota was a predominantly German and Scandinavian state where there was little enthusiasm for the war, while sentiment in Ontario, where most of the people were of British ancestry, was aggressively imperialist and pro-British.

More serious than these semantic controversies was the attack on German-language schools, German-language periodicals, and churches that conducted some or all of their services in German. By 1918, these public manifestations of German culture had virtually disappeared from the United States. The governor of Iowa, a state with a large German-American population, issued a proclamation prohibiting the use of any language other than English in schools, churches, conversations in public places, and even on the telephone.[24] The Deutsch-Amerikanischer Nationalbund, which had supported Germany during the war for as long as the United States was officially neutral and had campaigned against President Wilson in 1916, was investigated by a Senate committee and then dissolved itself in 1918.[25]

Although they were the largest ethnic group in the United States, with the possible exception of the English, German Americans became an invisible minority to protect themselves from the rising hatred and hostility. Before the war, they had been among the strongest and most effective opponents of the "melting pot" concept that was then gaining in popularity and had preserved their own culture with considerable success. Indeed, one historian implies that they had gone too far in resisting assimilation and had thus attracted the hostility that overwhelmed them during the war.[26] After 1917, they made every effort to blend in and become nearly indistinguishable from other Americans, and this change proved to be permanent. Almost the only overt evidence of their existence that survived, at least for a while, was their voting behaviour. In the elections of 1940 and 1944, most of the midwestern and prairie states with large German-American populations voted against pro-British President Franklin Roosevelt, who had carried every state except Maine and Vermont in 1936.

The war greatly increased the popularity of the "melting pot" concept, which had been invented only a few years earlier. Pressure to conform with American values and cultural patterns, whatever they might be, was directed particularly against Germans as the largest and most unpopular non-English-speaking ethnic group but also against other groups considered to be of dubious reliability. In the words of one historian, the new ideology of 100 per cent Americanism rose to a frenzy after the United States declared war in April 1917, while another says that "The war unleashed a frenzy of anti-foreign feeling."[27] President Wilson, although his party derived much of its support in the northern states from unassimilated minorities like the Irish, Italians, and Jews, began to compete with his long-time rival Theodore Roosevelt in his enthusiasm for assimilation and the melting pot. The Russian Revolution, which occurred in the same year the United States entered the war, provided another incentive, or excuse, to "Americanize" the immigrant population as rapidly and aggressively as possible.

Another development that was a consequence, at least in part, of Germanophobia was the prohibition of alcoholic beverages.[28] Beer in particular was considered a German invention, and the German fondness for this beverage had attracted the disapproval of Anglo-Celtic North Americans, particularly the Baptists, Methodists, and Presbyterians, for some time before the war. Like the alleged Chinese fondness for opium and the Irish taste for whisky, German beer-drinking was considered un-American as well as socially undesirable. The Canada Temperance Act had provided for prohibition by local option since 1878, as every student of Canadian constitutional law is aware. The war, and the War Measures Act, gave a major impetus to the movement for prohibition, and by 1918 alcoholic beverages were legally unobtainable in practically the entire country outside of Quebec. The United States went further by writing prohibition into the Constitution in 1919, a disastrous experiment that lasted until 1933 when the Eighteenth Amendment was repealed by the Twenty-First Amendment.

In Canada, the ethnic group that probably suffered the most from prejudice and discrimination attributable to World War I were the Ukrainians, most of whom were recent arrivals from the Austro-Hungarian Empire. Canada was automatically at war with that empire in August 1914, unlike the United States, which did not declare war on it until December 1917, eight months after their declaration of war against Germany.

Although Canada's first Ukrainian settler is said to have arrived in 1891, the recruitment of Ukrainians as immigrants to the Canadian prairies had really begun under the Laurier Liberal government of 1896–1911. Laurier's first minister of the interior, Clifford Sifton, famously defined the ideal immigrant as "a stalwart peasant in a sheepskin coat, born on the soil, whose forefathers have been farmers for ten generations, with a stout wife and half a dozen children."[29] The Ukrainians seemed to fit this description, and their experience as peasants in central Europe prepared them for the hardships of pioneer life on the prairies, as well as for the physical labour that largely built the Canadian Northern and Grand Trunk Pacific railways between Winnipeg and Edmonton. Almost all of the Ukrainians who came to Canada before 1914 were from the Austrian part of Austria-Hungary. Ethnic Ukrainians from Hungary and from the Russian Empire seemed to prefer the United States. Practically all of the Ukrainians who came to Canada were peasants who had worked on the estates of Polish or German-Austrian landowners.[30]

In the Canadian census they were not designated officially as Ukrainians until 1921 when Ukraine had briefly achieved independence after the collapse of the Austro-Hungarian and Russian empires. In the census of 1901, they were referred to as Galicians, after the Austrian province (which was transferred to Poland after the war) from which most of them came. At that time, they numbered only 5,682 in all of Canada. By 1911, their reported numbers in the census had increased to 72,963, designated either as Galicians, Ruthenians, or Bukovinians. (A footnote in the census explained that ten years earlier all three of these groups had been enumerated as Galicians.) By 1921, when the Ukrainian label first appeared, the census counted 106,721 Ukrainians. Almost half of them were still labelled as Bukovinians, Galicians, or Ruthenians, which the 1921 census regarded as subcategories of Ukrainian.[31] It is possible that a few more were enumerated as "Russian" or "Polish" in that census, given the numerous changes of European boundaries following the war.

Whatever they were called, most Ukrainians in Canada had been born as subjects of the Austrian emperor and were thus considered "enemy aliens" after August 1914. It is important to note, however, that they had been unpopular with many of their Canadian neighbours even before the outbreak of war. Sifton's favourable impression of them was hardly typical. British Protestants, who still comprised slightly more than half the population of the Prairie provinces, disliked the religion of the mainly Catholic Ukrainians, and some feared that they would unite with French Canadians to control the country, however improbable that may seem. They also tended to believe that "illiterate and uneducated fugitives from autocratic empires" could not become good citizens of a democratic Canada, particularly if they continued to speak a language other than English.[32] With few skills and little knowledge of the country or its language, Ukrainians who did not acquire land to farm were easily exploited. In 1907, the Austrian consul in Ottawa issued a formal protest against the treatment of Austro-Hungarian nationals employed in railway construction.[33] When war broke out in 1914, many Ukrainians in Canada were unemployed, since a recession had begun a year earlier.

The circumstances in which the war began proved to be particularly unfortunate for Ukrainians in Canada. Following the assassination of Archduke Franz Ferdinand at Sarajevo in June 1914, the young spiritual leader of the Ukrainian Catholics in Canada, Bishop Nykyta Budka, celebrated a requiem mass for the deceased. About a month later, as war between Austria and Russia was clearly imminent, Budka, who had been in Canada for less than two years, also issued a pastoral letter urging Ukrainian men of military age to return home and fight against the Russians. Most Ukrainians, like their Polish and Jewish neighbours in central Europe, regarded the Austrian emperor, with good reason, far more favourably than they regarded the Russian czar. Since the British Empire was not yet at war, Budka's suggestion was entirely proper although perhaps indiscreet. On 6 August, after the United Kingdom had declared war on Germany and Austria-Hungary, he issued a new pastoral letter retracting his earlier one and stating that Ukrainians in Canada should support their new country, which was now at war. However, the damage done by the earlier pastoral letter was not easily repaired.[34]

The Borden government soon began to take steps against the Ukrainians, who were the largest group of unnaturalized enemy aliens in Canada. Although the Canadian government had originally inclined toward letting them escape to the United States, pressure from the British government led to a reversal of this policy.[35] Five hundred members of the Royal Northwest Mounted Police were deployed along the border to prevent them from escaping to Europe via the United States.[36] A public notice was issued in September stating that enemy aliens who did not try to return to Europe and did nothing hostile to Canada had nothing to fear.[37] However, in October 1914 an order-in-council issued under the authority of the War Measures Act gave the government power to intern any enemy alien who aroused suspicion for any reason. Internments began soon afterwards, with young men, particularly the unemployed, being the most likely to be interned. Any attempt to cross the border into the United States was automatically grounds for internment, although most of those making the attempt were merely going there in search of employment, as Canadians had done for generations past. Some were interned for attempting to join the Canadian army, an action that one might have assumed would be welcomed by a government that was desperately seeking military manpower.

About two-thirds of all the nearly 9,000 enemy aliens interned in Canada during the war were from Austria-Hungary, and the majority of these were ethnic Ukrainians. A list of interned persons of apparently Ukrainian ancestry compiled long after the event by the Ukrainian Canadian Civil Liberties Association includes about 5,200 names.[38] In contrast to the far less numerous German internees, who were mainly middle-class and well-educated, the generally poor and illiterate Ukrainians were harshly treated. Concentration camps in remote locations were established all over Canada to house them, with some of the most notorious camps located in the Banff, Yoho, and Jasper national parks in the Rocky Mountains.

Canada was apparently the only belligerent country in 1914–18 that forced interned enemy aliens to work, a practice that was in violation of international law. They were paid twenty-five cents a day for hard physical labour.[39] An order-in-council issued in June 1915 made the remarkable suggestion that unemployed Ukrainians were being interned for their own protection, presumably from the wrath of native-born Canadians who believed that every able-bodied man should be either employed or in the army.[40] As time went on, however, many were released, since the Canadian economy increasingly suffered from a shortage of labour and the type of work performed in internment camps was not deemed essential. The Jasper camp was closed in August 1916 and the one at Banff in July 1917.[41] However, many Ukrainians remained in confinement until after the armistice, and the last of the camps did not close until February 1920. Ukrainian-language newspapers were suppressed in 1917, possibly in response to the Russian Revolution.[42]

Ukrainians and other people from Austria-Hungary were treated much better in the United States than in Canada, perhaps because they were a less conspicuous minority and perhaps also because they were less likely to be unemployed. Also, the United States declared war on Austria-Hungary very belatedly and seems never to have taken that country very seriously as an opponent. The number of Ukrainians in the United States during World War I is very difficult to estimate accurately, since the US census did not collect data on ethnicity and US immigration records referred only to country of origin. However, the total number of Ukrainians was certainly much larger in the United States than in Canada. A book published in 1937 estimated the number of Ukrainian Americans at that date at 700,000.[43] If that number is fairly accurate, it cannot have been much less twenty years earlier, given the highly restrictive immigration policy adopted after the war.

As in Canada, the term "Ukrainian" was not always used, even by the immigrants themselves. Most referred to themselves when they arrived in the United States as "Rusyn" or Ruthenian, which was sometimes incorrectly translated by American immigration officials as Russian.[44] After arriving, some began to call themselves Ukrainian, Russian, Hungarian, Polish, or Slovakian.[45] Since there was little unoccupied farmland in the United States after 1890 and since the country was industrializing rapidly, they were typically employed in mining and manufacturing. Most settled in the industrialized states of New Jersey, New York, and Pennsylvania where the ethnic diversity of the working class was widely accepted and taken for granted.[46] Very few were interned during the period of less than a year when the United States was at war with Austria-Hungary. This probably was, at least in part, because most of them were doing work deemed essential to the war effort. Insofar as they were regarded with suspicion, this was more because of the Russian Revolution than because their former homeland happened to be at war with the United States.

World War II, which is conventionally dated from September 1939 although some would say that it began two years earlier or two years later, was in some ways a sequel to the earlier war but in other ways different. Once again the English-speaking world was at war with Germany, although Germany this time was allied with two major powers, Italy and Japan, and one minor power, Romania, which had fought against it in the earlier war. Japan's involvement was particularly important, since it exposed North America to what was, in effect, a war on two widely separated fronts, across the Atlantic and across the Pacific. Once again Canada officially went to war more than two years earlier than the United States, although the sympathy of the "neutral" US administration for the British and Canadian war effort was even more obvious in the second war than in the first. Once again the Canadian and American governments committed actions against portions of their own populations that would have seemed unthinkable in peace-time, although in the second war the war crimes committed by their enemies were admittedly much worse.

World War II, at least in its European dimension, had an ideological character that distinguished it from World War I. Particularly after Germany attacked the Soviet Union in June 1941, it was widely portrayed as a struggle between right and left rather than a struggle between ethnic nations. Radicals, who had generally opposed the Canadian and American war efforts in the first war, supported them enthusiastically in the second, at least after June 1941 and in some cases even before. Because of the ideological aspect of the war, less emphasis was placed on promoting hatred of the enemy nation's culture, partly because this was less necessary to maintain popular enthusiasm and partly because appeals to ethnic hatred and prejudice characterized the Nazi ideology of the enemy (which in fact consisted of little else) and thus seemed unworthy of those who were fighting on the side of the angels. For example, the British Broadcasting Corporation used the opening notes of Beethoven's Fifth Symphony as a symbol of "victory" during World War II, although Beethoven was a German, and the service of thanksgiving at London's St Paul's Cathedral in 1945 featured a German Lutheran hymn, "Now Thank We All Our God." These things would have been unthinkable in the earlier war.

Partly for this reason and partly because German Americans and the much smaller number of German Canadians had learned from bitter experience in World War I to make themselves inconspicuous, there was much less cultural Germanophobia in North America during the second round of the struggle. Very few Germans had migrated to North America during the interwar years, and the German cultural presence in Canada and the United States was simply too insignificant and invisible to attract much hostility. While there was a small pro-Nazi element in both countries, its bizarre ideology did not represent the sentiments of more than a tiny fraction of German Americans and German Canadians. There were no attacks against German dogs, German food, or German classical music. Even the northern Ontario hamlet of Swastika managed to retain its peculiar name.

In the words of a German historian, "The treatment of German Canadians in World War II differed significantly from World War I ... The Canadian government recognized that World War II was a war of ideologies rather than of national loyalties."[47] However, when Canada declared war on Germany in 1939, the War Measures Act was again brought into effect. Germans and later Italians naturalized after 1 September 1929 (ten years before the war began in Europe) were considered enemy aliens. Internments began during the brief interval between the British declaration of war and that of Canada a week later. Only 847 persons of German ancestry were interned (out of nearly half a million), either because they retained their German citizenship, were members of pro-Nazi organizations, or both.[48] Given the scarcity of immigrants during the Depression, practically all of these persons had entered Canada before the Nazis gained control of the German state.

When Italy entered the war in June 1940, there were more internments. Although support for Hitler among German Canadians was extremely rare, support for Mussolini among Italian Canadians, many of whom had emigrated after Mussolini took power in 1922, was much more widespread. It is important to remember that Mussolini, until he entered the war, was considered quite respectable in the English-speaking world as an anti-communist who had "made the trains run on time" and ended the cold war between the Italian state and the Catholic Church. Even Winston Churchill publicly referred to the inventor of fascism as "a great man" as late as December 1940.[49] North Americans of Italian ancestry were even more likely to admire the leader who had apparently raised Italy's power and prestige to a level not seen since the Renaissance.

The RCMP kept fascist activity in Canada under surveillance, and an internal report of the Department of Justice estimated that there were about 3,500 fascists in an Italian-Canadian community that then numbered about 115,000. Between 500 and 600 of them were interned in 1940, along with ninety-nine Italian merchant seamen whose ships were still in Canadian ports at the time. At least one-third of the internees lived in Montreal, where admiration for the fascist regime that had recognized the independence of the Vatican was by no means confined to persons of Italian origin. The internees, who included some of the leading figures in the Italian-Canadian community, were treated reasonably well, and about two-thirds had apparently been released by the summer of 1942.[50] An Italian-Canadian historian who studied this episode concluded that "Canada's internment of Italian-Canadian fascists was sound and necessary."[51]

A more questionable initiative by the Canadian government in 1940 required persons of either German or Italian "racial origin" to register. Future prime minister John Diefenbaker, whose paternal ancestors had emigrated from Germany in the eighteenth century, noted during a parliamentary discussion of the regulations that most people listed in the census as being of German origin had, like himself, no connection with Germany.[52] Subsequently, a new order-in-council modified the earlier one so that only those of German or Italian birth had to register, including those born in Austria and the Sudetenland, territories that had become part of *Grossdeutschland* before the war. About 82,500 people registered before the requirement to do so was eliminated at the end of 1942.[53]

The situation in the United States was somewhat similar after that country went to war with Germany and Italy in December 1941. There were some ethnic and immigrant organizations that caused concern to the FBI and the administration, particularly the German-American Bund, whose membership the Department of Justice estimated at 8,500 in 1938. Most were immigrants who had arrived since 1918.[54] The House of Representatives Committee on Un-American Activities, which became notorious during the cold war for its anti-communist witch hunt, had actually been formed in 1938 to investigate Nazis and fascists in the United States, most of whom were of German or Italian origin, respectively.[55] As in Canada, Mussolini had been considered more respectable than Hitler during the 1930s, at least by persons with conservative views, regardless of their ethnicity. Roosevelt's rhetorical reference in June 1940 to Italy stabbing France in the back with a dagger sounded like an ethnic slur. Probably because of this, his support among Italian Americans in New York City fell to only 42.2 per cent in the presidential election of 1940, compared to 78.7 per cent in 1936.[56]

On the day of the Pearl Harbor attack, the president issued proclamations 2525, 2526, and 2527, which dealt, respectively, with Japanese, German, and Italian enemy aliens. The first of these proclamations noted that Japan had perpetrated an "invasion" upon the territory of the United States. The other two stated that "an invasion of predatory incursion is threatened upon the territory of the United States" by Germany and Italy, respectively. (Neither Germany nor Italy was yet at war with the United States.) The proclamations prohibited enemy aliens from doing certain things, including travelling by airplane, entering or leaving Alaska, Puerto Rico, or the Virgin Islands, and possessing certain items, such as firearms, short wave radios, or cameras. All were warned that they might be liable to detention. Subsequently, pressure was put on Latin American countries to send their German, Italian, and Japanese residents to the United States for internment, and most of them did so, apart from pro-fascist Argentina. By the end of the war, 10,905 German nationals living in the United States had been interned as enemy aliens.[57] Estimates of how many Italians suffered the same fate vary widely, but the number was apparently smaller. On 12 October 1942 (Columbus Day), the attorney general of the United States, Francis Biddle, announced that Italian nationals would no longer be considered enemy aliens, although Italy would remain at war with the United States until July of the following year. Italians were also allowed to resume commercial fishing on the Pacific coast, where 80 per cent of commercial fishermen before the war had been Italian.[58] Among them was the father of New York Yankees outfielder Joe DiMaggio, perhaps the most celebrated athlete in the United States at the time.

The simultaneous war in the Pacific against Germany's principal ally, Japan, had a very different character from the European war, less ideological and more an old-fashioned struggle between nations defined by ethnicity and race. Despite its army's dismal record of war crimes against their fellow Asians, Imperial Japan was not a totalitarian dictatorship like Nazi Germany. It was a monarchy with some pluralistic features, similar to the Germany and Austria-Hungary of World War I. North American radicals had little interest in the Pacific war, since the Soviet Union was not involved in it until a few days before it ended. Indeed, the Japanese could claim, whether sincerely or not, that they were fighting to free Asia from Western colonialism and racism, an argument that might have had some appeal to radicals and to African Americans. Elijah Muhammed, the leader of the Black Muslims, was interned as a Japanese sympathizer during the war.[59] Ideological arguments for fighting against Japan were thus not very effective. Instead, the war inflamed a racial animosity against the Japanese that had long existed in North America, particularly on the west coast, with shameful consequences that belied the claim of both North American nations to be fighting for freedom, democracy, and racial equality.

Anti-Japanese sentiment on the west coast of North America in some ways resembled the anti-Chinese sentiment described in chapter 4, so both can be regarded as aspects of a generalized dislike of "Orientals." However, the circumstances of the two Asian groups, in North America and the world, were not identical. China throughout the nineteenth century and well into the twentieth was weak and helpless, lacking an effective central government. Japan was a more compact and homogeneous country that began to construct a modern centralized state on the Western model in the 1860s, almost simultaneously with Canada's Confederation and the end of the American Civil War. By the end of the century, it was generally recognized as a rising major power with significant military and naval capabilities. The treaty of alliance between Japan and the United Kingdom in 1902 reflected this perception, which was reinforced by Japan's victory over Russia in the war of 1904–05. The hostility that Japanese immigrants faced in North America was thus mingled with respect, which was not accorded to the Chinese.

The circumstances of the two migrations were also different. Until 1885, the Japanese government prevented its people from leaving Japan, so their migration to North America began somewhat later than that of the Chinese.[60] When this policy was abandoned and the Japanese began to migrate, most of them were, or at least hoped to be, farmers, fishermen, or entrepreneurs rather than unskilled labourers like the Chinese who had worked on the transcontinental railways. Also, the Japanese migration was reasonably balanced between men and women, in contrast to the Chinese, so Japanese families were established in North America. This contributed to the fact that most Japanese immigrants were both willing and able to remain permanently, while most of the Chinese were sojourners who eventually returned to China.

Harold Innis suggested that the influence of the women and the demands of family life were the reasons that most Japanese immigrants remained on the coast while the Chinese were more likely to move inland.[61] However, this contrast may also reflect the fact that the Japanese were a maritime people with a particular penchant for commercial fishing as an occupation. In any event, a study of Japanese Canadians published in 1937 noted that about 95 per cent of them lived in British Columbia, mostly on the coast, compared to only about 60 per cent of Chinese Canadians.[62]

Unlike the Chinese, the Japanese did not compete with, or lower the wages of, unskilled labour, and their numbers were still insignificant when hostility to them became apparent. Economic competition does not seem to explain the prejudice that they aroused.[63] The hostile stereotypes of the two groups also differed. Chinese who came to North America were often alleged to be dirty, disease-ridden, ignorant, and addicted to opium, gambling, and prostitution. These characteristics could not plausibly be attributed to the Japanese, who were more likely to be resented for their work ethic, high levels of achievement, and tendency to form a cohesive community that looked after its members, the same characteristics that were often attributed to the Jews. The Japanese also adapted to Western culture much more readily than the Chinese, and most became Christians, but this unfortunately did not lessen the racism they experienced.

After 1905, when Japan had demonstrated its ability to defeat a European great power both on land and at sea, respect for the Japanese was mingled with fear. The Pacific coast, like Australia, was an isolated and thinly populated outpost of an English-speaking world that was centred on the North Atlantic, thousands of miles away. The settlement of Japanese families with allegedly high birthrates seemed threatening in a way that the almost entirely male Chinese immigration was not.[64] Some people even viewed Japanese immigration as part of a plot to colonize the Pacific coast as a prelude to its conquest and annexation. In Canada, such fears were alleviated somewhat by the alliance between Japan and the United

Kingdom, which actually removed any possibility of a German threat to British Columbia in World War I, but the British terminated the alliance in 1922, largely because of American pressure. In the 1930s, when Japan began to conquer China and moved toward an alignment with Nazi Germany and fascist Italy, it was increasingly regarded as aggressive and dangerous by both North American nations. When Canada declared war on Germany in 1939, Japanese Canadians were not allowed to join the army.

Outright exclusion of Japanese immigrants, or overtly racist measures like the Chinese head tax, ran the risk of offending an increasingly important and influential nation-state so were not often resorted to. The United States finally took this step in 1924, but Canada never did. Both Canada and the United States sought instead to limit the volume of Japanese immigration by treaties or non-binding "gentleman's agreements" with the Japanese government. The latter were particularly important in Canada, which lacked the independent authority to make treaties until the 1920s. Mackenzie King as a civil servant, as Laurier's minister of labour, and finally as prime minister after 1921 was involved in some of these.

Japanese who managed to immigrate to North America were subject to various kinds of discrimination. Persons born in Japan could not be naturalized in the United States until 1952. California prevented them from owning land after 1913 and from leasing it after 1920.[65] For forty years after 1905, at least one anti-Japanese bill was introduced at each annual session of the California legislature.[66] In British Columbia, persons of Japanese ancestry could not vote, a policy upheld by the Judicial Committee of the Privy Council in 1903.[67] The CCF (predecessor of the NDP) endured much criticism in the 1930s and 1940s for its courageous opposition to this policy. The Judicial Committee did, however, strike down in 1930 federal efforts to restrict the number of commercial fishing licences issued to Japanese Canadians.[68]

War with Japan affected the United States and Canada in somewhat different ways. The Roosevelt administration had committed a series of overtly hostile acts against Germany since the president's re-election in November 1940, and it steadfastly pursued a "Germany first" strategy after Germany declared war on the United States in support of its Japanese ally. This strategy ensured that Germany would be defeated before the final assault on Japan and also meant that the majority of American casualties would be suffered in the

European theatre of war. However, most Americans regarded the attack on Pearl Harbor as the real cause of the war and the "Japs" as the primary enemy. After the war, they would rightly celebrate the defeat of Japan as an American achievement to which other nations had contributed relatively little, while in Europe the laurels had to be shared with the United Kingdom and, even worse, the Soviet Union. It is probably significant that the three most important and success-ful American novels of World War II, James Jones's *From Here to Eternity*, Norman Mailer's *The Naked and the Dead*, and Herman Wouk's *The Caine Mutiny*, are all set in the Pacific theatre.

In Canada, which had declared war on Germany in September 1939, the defeat of the Nazis and the rescue of the United Kingdom from the threat of Nazi invasion were almost universally regarded as the primary objectives of the war. Canada's war effort, with the sup-port of a general consensus of the population east of the Rocky Mountains, was directed almost exclusively toward Europe and the North Atlantic, apart from the tragic and pointless expedition to Hong Kong in 1941. The attack on Pearl Harbor was probably wel-comed in Canada, since it brought the United States into the war, far more than it was resented.

British Columbia, however, was the exception to the rule. Fear of Japan and hostility toward Japanese immigrants had been growing before the war in that isolated province with its population of only about 800,000. Such sentiments were understandably reinforced by the attack on Pearl Harbor and the rapid expansion of the Japanese Empire, which soon stretched from Burma to the Aleutian Islands. After much of the American Pacific fleet was put out of action, the threat of a Japanese invasion seemed real to many British Columbians. To calm their anxieties, the federal government even provided an armoured train, which patrolled the Canadian National Railways line between Terrace and Prince Rupert for more than a year but never saw any action.[69] Canada declared war on Japan almost immediately after the attack on Pearl Harbor, and within days British Columbia politicians were clamouring for the removal of Japanese Canadians from the province.

In the United States, action against the Japanese population on the Pacific coast had been contemplated and planned by various agencies of the federal government even before the outbreak of war. The com-mander of US naval forces on the west coast had expressed concern about them as long before as 1922.[70] The War Department, which was responsible for the US Army but not the navy, began to gather data on Japanese Americans at least as early as 1938 and did not distinguish between those born in Japan and their American-born children.[71] The Office of Naval Intelligence broke into the Japanese consulate in Los Angeles in search of incriminating documents but apparently found that Japan did not trust the Japanese Americans and would not use them as agents.[72] However, between April and July 1941 the War Department and the Department of Justice jointly prepared a plan to deal with the presumed security threat from Japanese Americans. In October, the FBI raided the offices of some Japanese organizations in California. Attorney General Francis Biddle had some qualms about incarcerating or relocating persons of Japanese ancestry who had been born in the United States, but his misgivings were not shared by the War Department, the FBI, or President Roosevelt.

Hawaii, which at that time was a territory rather than a state, posed a particular problem because of its vulnerability to attack but also because persons of Japanese ancestry comprised about 40 per cent of its population. Many of them, or their parents, had settled in Hawaii when it was an independent kingdom that imposed few restrictions on immigration. After the Pearl Harbor attack, the secretary of the navy, Frank Knox, wanted to remove all Japanese from at least the main island of Oahu, where Pearl Harbor was located, and the cabinet and the president supported this idea. However, the territorial government and even the army officer in command of the troops there opposed this action on the grounds that it was impractical and would create a severe shortage of labour. Selective internments did take place in Hawaii, as they did elsewhere, and Japanese-language schools were closed, but there was never any general evacuation of Japanese from the islands, even though Hawaii was placed under martial law.

On the mainland, where the Japanese were a small minority, they were more vulnerable. The attack on Pearl Harbor, the first serious foreign attack on the United States since the battle of New Orleans in 1814, produced panic and hysteria on the Pacific coast, along with exaggerated fears of Japanese espionage. One headline at the time solemnly proclaimed, "Caps on Japanese Tomato Plants Point to Air Base."[73] California's attorney general, Earl Warren, who would later be renowned as a civil libertarian after President Eisenhower appointed him chief justice of the United States, was convinced that the threat of espionage justified removing the Japanese Americans, whether American-born or not, from his state.[74]

Initially, Japanese in the coastal states were merely encouraged to move farther east. Pressure for more decisive action quickly mounted, although even J. Edgar Hoover of the F B I attributed the pressure for compulsory evacuation to "public hysteria."[75] The senior army officer on the west coast, General DeWitt, was strongly in favour of evacuation, and the Justice Department reluctantly agreed. On 11 February 1942, President Roosevelt directed the War Department to do whatever it thought necessary, including the removal of American citizens. Two days later, a congressional delegation from the west coast states recommended total evacuation of Japanese from those states. Executive Order 9066, signed by the president on 19 February, began the process of evacuation, although it made no mention of incarcerating those evacuated. The evacuation was carried out by the army after Congress confirmed the executive order with legislation on 21 March, which the president signed ten days later. Originally, it was hoped that the Japanese could be released once they were moved inland, but the governors of the states to which they were sent refused to accept this, fearful that the Japanese would settle there permanently. Concentration camps surrounded by barbed wire and patrolled by armed guards were established by an agency called the War Relocation Authority, mainly on the deserts and prairies of the western interior. By 6 June 1942, a total of 93,754 persons of wholly or partly Japanese ancestry, many of them born in the United States, had been shipped there, and eventually the number incarcerated in the camps reached 118,803.[76] During the course of the war, seven inmates were killed by gunfire, possibly while attempting to escape.

As the tide of war began to turn against Japan in 1943, conditions in the camps were somewhat relaxed. Many inmates of the camps, especially younger American-born persons who had demonstrated their loyalty to the United States, were allowed to leave them either to attend university or to join the army. The army formed a Japanese-American military unit of three battalions, the 442nd Regimental Combat Team, which fought with great distinction in the European theatre. In February 1944, the War Relocation Authority and the camps were transferred from the War Department to the Department of the Interior.

In December 1944, three cases arising out of the relocation were decided by the Supreme Court of the United States. The Court upheld the constitutionality of the evacuation, with three justices dissenting, but ruled that the continuing confinement of loyal American citizens was unconstitutional.[77] A few days prior to this, the secretary of war had secretly advised President Roosevelt that the exclusion of Japanese from the west coast was no longer a military necessity. At the beginning of 1945, the Japanese Americans were allowed to return to the west coast, but many chose not to. After the war ended, 4,724 were relocated to Japan at their own request while many more settled in other parts of the United States. In 1950, only 58 per cent of Japanese in the continental United States were living in California, Oregon, or Washington, compared to 88.5 per cent before the war.[78] The War Relocation Authority formally ceased to exist on 30 June 1946.

Canada's actions toward the Japanese on the Pacific coast were similar to those of the United States, on a smaller scale, in some respects better, but in some respects worse. Even before Japan entered the war, Japanese Canadians had not been allowed to join the Canadian armed forces. In June 1940, the Canadian army prepared plans for evacuating Japanese from the immediate vicinity of strategic locations such as air bases. In August 1941, the officer commanding Canada's only Pacific naval base, at Esquimalt, asked for authority to seize Japanese-owned fishing boats in the event that Japan entered the war. The Permanent Joint Board on Defence, a Canadian–American advisory body formed after the fall of France, suggested in November that the two countries should co-ordinate their efforts against their respective Japanese minorities.[79] Most British Columbia politicians, apart from members of the CCF, favoured evacuation of the entire Japanese population from their province in the event of war with Japan.

The RCMP had found no evidence of a credible threat of espionage or subversive activity among the Japanese Canadians, although this did not necessarily prove that none existed. The army and navy head-quarters in Ottawa were not convinced that a Japanese invasion was a realistic possibility but thought removal of the Japanese Canadians from the coast might be necessary to reassure the rest of the population. Two British Columbians in the Department of External Affairs, Henry Angus and Hugh Keenleyside, opposed a wholesale evacuation. The department's undersecretary, Norman Robertson, who was also from British Columbia, told the American ambassador on the day after Pearl Harbor was attacked that the government hoped not to have to intern all the Japanese Canadians but that public pressure to do so might be irresistible.[80] This proved to be an accurate assessment.

On the day Pearl Harbor was attacked, the Canadian cabinet met. According to Mackenzie King's diary on 7 December, it discussed the desirability of "counselling against any anti-Japanese demonstration in BC and expressing the government's belief in the loyalty of Japanese nationals and Canadian-born Japanese in BC." The prime minister broadcast a statement to this effect on the following day.[81] However, the Royal Canadian Navy seized all west coast fishing boats owned by persons of Japanese ancestry, whether naturalized or not.[82] These boats would never be returned to their rightful owners, and no compensation was ever paid for them. Instead, they were sold to white fishermen in the early part of 1942, with the federal government taking the proceeds.

On 14 January 1942, the Canadian government announced that Japanese-born men of military age would be removed from certain strategic areas along the coast. It also prohibited "persons of Japanese race" from owning, operating, or working on fishing boats. This announcement was not enough to satisfy the white people of British Columbia, particularly since only about one hundred persons of Japanese ancestry were actually relocated over the next six weeks. President Roosevelt's Executive Order 9066, issued on 19 February, made the pressure on the Canadian government irresistible, at least for a politician as sensitive to the nuances of public opinion as Mackenzie King.

On 24 February, five days after Executive Order 9066, Mackenzie King announced that all persons of Japanese ancestry would be relocated away from the area of British Columbia between the Cascade Mountains and the Pacific coast as well as from all the offshore islands. According to figures provided by the government a year later, the population of Japanese ancestry in British Columbia in February 1942 was 21,975, of which only 6,084 were Canadian-born and 6,497 were naturalized.[83] No legislation was required, in contrast to the American situation, because the War Measures Act gave the government the power to take such action by order-in-council, a fact that was confirmed by the Judicial Committee of the Privy Council in 1946.

Those who were married to persons of other ethnic origins, and the children of such marriages, were not evacuated. Automobiles and trucks belonging to the Japanese Canadians were seized without compensation as the fishing boats had been two months earlier. The evacuation proceeded at a leisurely pace and was not completed until the end of October, although any credible threat of invasion had disappeared after the battle of Midway in June. There were no visible signs of opposition from any part of the Canadian public, in British Columbia or elsewhere.

The majority of those evacuated were placed in internment camps, whose population numbered 12,177 in the spring of 1943.[84] These camps, many of them in the Rocky Mountains or the foothills, were considerably more pleasant in both their physical setting and their amenities than the American camps and were not surrounded by barbed wire. Even Ken Adachi, a Japanese Canadian who wrote what is perhaps the definitive book on the subject, conceded that "on the whole, life in the interior camps was not unbearable."[85] They may even have protected their inmates from the racist violence to which they would almost certainly have been exposed in Vancouver and Victoria. However, none of this excused or made more acceptable the confiscation of property, an action that had no counterpart in the United States. In Adachi's words, "The Canadian policy on property, from beginning to end, fell far short of the American record in almost every respect."[86] This contrast probably reflects the fact that property rights are guaranteed in the Fifth Amendment to the United States Constitution. Even today there is no such guarantee in the Canadian Charter of Rights and Freedoms, and obviously there was none in 1942, four decades before the Charter existed.

Although inmates born in Japan were kept in the camps for the duration of the war, the Canadian-born were supposed to be held only temporarily until they could be dispersed across the country. The reluctance of the provinces and municipalities to accept them delayed the implementation of this plan, but many were eventually sent elsewhere, particularly to work on farms, where they replaced the young men who had joined the armed forces. (Japanese Canadians themselves were not allowed to enlist until 1945 when the war was almost over.) According to Adachi's account, the sugar beet farms in southern Alberta provided the worst working conditions, comparable almost to slavery.[87] The more fortunate evacuees went further east, some as far as the Niagara region of Ontario.

On 4 August 1944, Mackenzie King informed the House of Commons of the government's plans for Japanese Canadians after the war. He stated that allowing them to be concentrated almost exclusively in British Columbia, as they had been before the war, would not be in the best interest either of that province or of the Japanese themselves. He also admitted that "no person of Japanese race born in

Canada has been charged with any act of sabotage or disloyalty during the years of war." However, those who were found to be "disloyal," whether Canadian-born or not, would be sent to Japan. The remainder would be distributed as widely as possible throughout Canada. Also, no further immigration from Japan would be allowed.[88]

This policy was largely implemented after the war. The deportation of Canadian-born or naturalized persons to Japan was contested by civil liberties groups but was upheld by the Judicial Committee of the Privy Council. The number sent to Japan, either because they were considered "disloyal" or because they had expressed the wish to go there, was proportionately much larger in Canada than in the United States.[89] In contrast to the situation in the United States, very few Japanese Canadians returned to the west coast, where most of the public and the politicians remained extremely hostile to them. Most of the Japanese Canadians found new homes in other provinces, particularly Ontario. The first postwar census, in 1951, showed that only one-third of Japanese Canadians lived in British Columbia, where practically all of them had lived before the war.[90]

Examining the record of both Canada and the United States, it is apparent that in both countries the Japanese were singled out for discriminatory treatment and persecution to an extent not experienced by any other "enemy" ethnic group in either of the world wars. There was no other ethnic group of which the majority, in both countries, were subject to compulsory relocation and incarceration. Even the Ukrainian Canadians interned in World War I amounted to less than ten per cent of that ethnic group's population. The internment of Italian Canadians in World War II involved only a few hundred people, most of them known sympathizers with fascism, from a population of more than 100,000, although these facts did not prevent Prime Minister Brian Mulroney from issuing an inappropriate apology for their internment in 1990.[91]

As extenuating circumstances, it may be argued that the Japanese were unusually concentrated in a particular region of both countries and that Japanese naval power made the threat of an amphibious invasion of that region at least faintly plausible, which the threat of a German, Italian, or Austro-Hungarian invasion of North America never was in either world war. However, it is hard to escape the conclusion that the Japanese were singled out for reasons that had more to do with racism than with national security. The fact that Japanese Americans living in Hawaii, more than half of the total number, were spared the fate of their counterparts on the mainland tends to confirm this hypothesis.

Neither Canada nor the United States emerged with much credit from this episode, although opinions may differ on which government's behaviour was worse. The United States incarcerated its Japanese minority under much worse conditions than Canada did. On the other hand, Japanese Americans were allowed to demonstrate their loyalty by joining the army, which many did, and they were not deprived of their property without compensation, as the Japanese Canadians were. Canada did not distinguish between persons of Japanese ancestry who were citizens and those who were non-citizens as clearly as did the United States, perhaps in part because Canadian citizenship did not, strictly speaking, exist until 1947. Before that time, Canadian-born persons were simply British subjects. The contrast may also suggest that English-speaking Canadians still tended to define their identity in terms of "British" ethnicity rather than in terms of political principles and ideology. However, persons whose ancestry was only partly Japanese were generally spared incarceration in Canada but not in the United States.

In the last analysis, Japanese Americans and Japanese Canadians suffered their fate because public opinion, particularly in California and British Columbia, was hostile to them and wanted them out of the way. The war provided an excuse for west-coast people to display the hatred and prejudice against the Japanese that had long existed in their region. This fact does not absolve either federal government from responsibility for what happened, unless one assumes that democratic governments should always do what is popular rather than what is morally justifiable.

7

Immigration Policy:
The Rise and Fall of Nativism

In the aftermath of World War I, most Americans were disillusioned with the world outside their own borders and inclined to reject it, insofar as this was possible. The "war to end war" and to "make the world safe for democracy," as President Wilson had called it, had failed to accomplish either of these goals and had left much of Europe and the Middle East in turmoil. Civil wars in Ireland and Finland, a Russian invasion of Poland, radical movements in Germany and Hungary, boundary disputes everywhere, and ethnic cleansing in the new Turkish republic seemed to be all that the victorious powers had to show for their triumph on the battlefields. The Bolshevik regime was winning control of Europe's largest country and was far more threatening to American ideals than the enemy against which Americans had recently fought in France. At home, the high hopes with which the Wilson administration had begun ended with an ailing president trying in vain to win support for the League of Nations while his attorney general, Mitchell Palmer, conducted a ferocious witch hunt for suspected radicals, assisted by the young J. Edgar Hoover. The "Red Scare," as it was called, reinforced the desire of many Americans to exclude Europeans (particularly Jews and Italians) and their radical ideologies.

Rejecting Wilson's legacy, Americans chose as their new president in 1920 the Republican candidate Warren G. Harding, an amiable nonentity from small-town Ohio who might have stepped out of a Sinclair Lewis novel. Harding promised a return to "normalcy," a word he invented, and Americans outside of the solidly Democratic South gave him almost two-thirds of their votes. His share of the overall popular vote in the country was 60.3 per cent, the largest percentage ever received by a Republican presidential candidate and one slightly exceeded only twice by Democrats, in 1936 and 1964. "Normalcy" and isolationism returned, along with a level of political corruption matched by few previous administrations and exceeded by none. The Americans who chose Harding as their leader, as well as the southern Democrats who voted for his main opponent, wanted their country to be white, Protestant, English-speaking, inward-looking, and conservative, as they vaguely imagined it had been in some half-remembered past.

The rejection of foreign influences, from the League of Nations to Scotch whisky, French wine, and German beer, also included a rejection of the social changes wrought by more than half a century of largely unrestricted European immigration. The war seemed to suggest that the melting pot extolled by Israel Zangwill and Theodore Roosevelt before the war had not worked. The Germans, Italians, Poles, Irish, and Jews who had helped the country to triple the size of its population since the Civil War had retained their ancestral customs, beliefs, and identities rather than becoming "unhyphenated Americans." So, for that matter, had the British Americans, whose economic power, social prestige, and enthusiasm for the British cause had forced the United States to enter the war despite the misgivings of most of their fellow Americans. Despite its vast increase in wealth and power, America seemed in danger of losing its soul, or so at least many Americans believed.

The concept of the melting pot, it must be remembered, had been the product of American optimism. It was based on the belief that human nature was malleable enough that anyone, or at least any European, could become an American by abandoning European ways and adopting American ideals and that those ideals were universally applicable. If these assumptions were wrong and the assimilation of immigrants into a common pattern of undifferentiated "Americanism" was an unrealistic goal, there were two possible responses. One was to recognize that the country must remain pluralistic and heterogeneous forever and to celebrate the diversity that immigration had brought to it. The second was to close the door to most immigrants before further damage was done and to ensure that any future immigrants would be selected so as to restore the country's original cultural and political characteristics or at least to prevent any further deviation from them.

The first option, similar to what would later be called multiculturalism, had little appeal or influence at the time, but it is worth mentioning because it foreshadowed developments that would take place much later, in Canada as well as in the United States. It was largely the work of two young intellectuals, Horace Kallen and Randolph Bourne, who wrote during World War I. Kallen was the son of a German rabbi and had emigrated with his parents as a child. Bourne was a native-born American of English ancestry and the grandson of a Congregational minister. Both noted the failure of the melting pot during the war and asserted that the United States was fated to remain a pluralistic nation. Both asserted that this was not a bad thing, since the country was enriched by having a multiplicity of cultures.

Kallen suggested that the "Americanism" extolled by nativists was really a thinly disguised recipe for Anglo-Saxon predominance and that "there is a marked tendency in the United States for the industrial and social stratification to follow ethnic lines."[1] But a "democracy of nationalities" was possible if the dominant classes, mainly of English ancestry, were willing to accept it. The Scandinavians in Minnesota, the Germans in Wisconsin, and the Irish in Massachusetts and New York had remained distinct and gave distinctive characteristics to their respective states. Thus "the United States are in the process of becoming a federal state not merely as a union of geographical and administrative unities, but also as a cooperation of cultural diversities."[2]

According to Bourne, the war had shocked Americans by revealing the failure of the melting pot. "The truth is that no more tenacious cultural allegiance to the mother country has been shown by any alien nation than by the ruling class of Anglo-Saxon descendants in these American States."[3] However, the persistence of cultural allegiance was not necessarily a bad thing. "The failure of the melting pot, far from closing the great American democratic experiment, means that it has only just begun ... America is already the world federation in miniature."[4] Perhaps Americans should even accept the possibility of some kind of dual citizenship. Accepting and encouraging diversity would produce a more dynamic and successful country. The parts of the United States where most recent immigrants had settled had prospered, while the South, which most immigrants had avoided since the Civil War, remained "an English colony, stagnant and complacent, having progressed culturally scarcely beyond the early Victorian era."[5]

The ideas of Kallen and Bourne had little influence at the time they were presented, because they were too radically different from the traditional ideal of a homogeneous nation that repudiated its European past to embrace a new and distinctive "American way of life." Few Americans were willing to take a chance on the encouragement of multiculturalism, but few still believed that the assimilation of immigrants from a variety of cultures was really possible. The more popular solution, therefore, was to reduce or even eliminate immigration from sources deemed too alien to be successfully assimilated, a category that included not only Asians but many Europeans as well. This preference was reinforced by the belief that the United States no longer needed more people from any source. The population of the United States had surpassed 106,000,000 by 1920, more than the combined populations of Germany and France. The American frontier had been closed for a generation, and most immigrants since 1890 had congregated in the large cities, places that many conservative Americans viewed with suspicion for a variety of reasons.

Restrictions on immigration from southern and eastern Europe had been suggested by some Americans since the 1890s, when immigration from those sources, particularly Italians and Jews, increased rapidly. Henry Cabot Lodge of Massachusetts, who would lead the fight against the League of Nations as a Republican senator after World War I, was among the first to propose a literacy test for immigrants as a means of achieving this objective. Several bills providing for such a test were adopted by Congress between 1897 and 1917 but fell victim to presidential vetoes.[6] However, the last veto, by President Wilson, was overridden by a two-thirds vote in both houses of Congress. In 1920, the House of Representatives actually voted by an overwhelming margin to admit no immigrants at all during the following year, a suggestion that was wisely rejected by the Senate.[7] Republican Senator William Dillingham of Vermont then proposed a quota system for immigrants, which was adopted by Congress and signed by President Harding.

The quota system did not apply to independent countries of the Western Hemisphere (including Canada) or to the Philippines, which had been an American colony since the Spanish-American War. Immigrants from China were already totally excluded from entering the United States, as noted in chapter 4, and those from Japan soon would be. Thus, it affected mainly immigration from Europe. Each European country was assigned an annual quota equal to 3 per cent of the number of people born in that country who had resided in the United States in 1910. If all the quotas were filled, this would allow for about 350,000 European immigrants each year, but if there were not enough British, German, or Irish immigrants to fill the fairly large quotas assigned to those nations, the total number would be fewer, since unused portions of the quotas could not be transferred to other nations.[8]

The idea, of course, was to limit any further change in the ethnic composition of the United States and to preserve the dominant position of supposedly superior people whose ancestors came from northwestern Europe. However, since a large part of the immigration to which conservative Americans objected had taken place between 1890 and 1910, a quota system based on the 1910 census did not go far enough to satisfy them. In 1924, the Dillingham Act was replaced by a new version of the quota system known as the Johnson-Reed Act, which based the quotas on the census of 1890. In 1929, this act was amended to base the quotas on the census of 1920, but the Depression that began in that year reduced immigration to extremely low levels in any event.[9] With various modifications, the quota system would last until 1965.

Canada adopted a somewhat different and more liberal approach to immigration in the 1920s, not because Canadians were more liberal than Americans in their attitudes toward ethnic minorities but because the circumstances of the country were different. In contrast to Americans, Canadians viewed their country as underpopulated, and with good reason. Canada had only 8.8 million inhabitants in the census year 1921, or less than one-twelfth the population of the United States. In fact, New York State alone had more people than all of Canada, as it would continue to do until the 1950s. In 1871, in the first census after Confederation, Canada had counted almost one-tenth as many inhabitants as the United States. In the half-century after its first census (1790–1840), the United States had grown from just under four million people to seventeen million. In the half-century after its first census (1871–1921), Canada had grown from just under four million to less than nine million.

The main reason for this poor demographic performance was the steady outward migration of Canadians toward the United States. There were effectively no limits on immigration from Canada to the United States, and this continued to be the case after 1921, since Western Hemisphere countries were exempted from the American quota system. There was also no reason to worry about the portability of government pensions or health insurance, since neither existed at the time. For Canadians without a criminal record, moving to the United States was as easy as moving to another province. More than 2.2 million Canadian residents moved to the United States between 1820 and 1914, and the exodus continued in the 1920s.

One view expressed at the time, notably by the Canadian historian Arthur Lower, was that immigration contributed to this problem by increasing the supply of labour in Canada, lowering the level of wages and thus making Canada less attractive to its own people and encouraging them to leave for the United States.[10] Since there was no conclusive evidence to support this theory, the Canadian government continued to encourage immigration. The United States itself had been an important source for a brief period when Alberta and Saskatchewan were being settled in the Laurier era but provided hardly any immigrants after 1914. British immigrants were preferred, and the Canadian immigration regulations reflected this preference, but their arrival in sufficient numbers to replace the loss to the United States could not be guaranteed. The United States offered a fairly large quota for British immigrants, while Australia, New Zealand, South Africa, and even Kenya and Rhodesia provided alternative destinations within the empire. The first two in particular offered less culture shock for British immigrants, as well as milder winters, than Canada could provide.

Canada therefore had to look further afield if it were to attract as many people as it seemed to need. A particularly strong influence pushing it in this direction was that of the transcontinental railway companies, Canadian Pacific and Canadian National, which were the two largest enterprises and employers in the country. Both wanted more people in Canada, and particularly in western Canada, to provide passenger and freight traffic for their overextended networks. The Canadian Pacific had an additional incentive in that its ships could carry immigrants across the Atlantic Ocean. While Canadian Pacific was profitable, Canadian National did not earn enough to pay the interest on its enormous debts, and since it was a Crown corporation, any shortfall in its revenue had to be made up by the federal government. The result of these circumstances was that in 1925 Mackenzie King's government signed an agreement with both railway companies that allowed the companies to select immigrants from central and eastern Europe.[11] Over the next six years, until the

Depression and the election of a Conservative government led to the cancellation of the agreement, 185,000 Europeans arrived under these auspices, comprising about half of Canada's total immigration from continental Europe.[12]

The countries targeted by the railway agreement were Estonia, Latvia, Lithuania, Poland, Czechoslovakia, Austria, Hungary, Germany, Yugoslavia, Romania, and Russia. Finland was excluded, probably because the people who wanted to leave that country after it broke free from Russian domination were mainly communists. (Finns and Ukrainians in fact provided most of the support base for Canada's small communist party throughout the Stalinist era.) Ethnic Russians and Romanians were also excluded, for less obvious reasons, although ethnic minorities from those two countries were welcomed.[13]

The result of Canada's openness to central and eastern European immigration after World War I was that Canada became more ethnically diverse and to some extent more politically radical than it was before the war, in contrast to the United States. People of British or Irish ancestry ceased to be a majority of the population during the 1930s. (The Canadian census did not stop including the Irish in a category called "British Isles origins" until 2001, eighty years after the peace treaty that recognized southern Ireland's independence.) It was also during the interwar period that the idea of the "Canadian mosaic" was invented and popularized by people like Kate Foster, John Murray Gibbon, and Governor General Lord Tweedsmuir. However, immigration from continental Europe was by no means universally welcomed. The railway agreement in particular was opposed by prominent Conservative politicians, the United Grain Growers, the Trades and Labour Congress, and, more surprisingly, the United Church.[14]

The Great Depression, followed by World War II, greatly reduced the flow of immigrants to North America for a decade and a half. Immigration was largely removed from the political agenda, apart from the question of Jewish refugees attempting to escape from the Nazis. As noted in chapter 5, the Canadian response to this question was shamefully mean-spirited. The American response was significantly more generous, although perhaps not as generous as it should have been. The aftermath of World War II produced a new wave of refugees, this time fleeing from communism or from the chaotic conditions that had left many central and eastern Europeans, the so-called "displaced persons," with no state in which they were both willing and able to live. Even in western Europe, where conditions were much better, many people were disillusioned with their native lands, unimpressed by the centre-left governments that took office after the war, and attracted by the greater freedom and prosperity that North America seemed to offer. At the same time, the economies of the United States and Canada were growing rapidly, creating a demand for labour that displaced or disillusioned Europeans could possibly fill. However, most Europeans found it much easier to enter Canada as immigrants than to enter the United States, which still retained the quota system. The major exception to this rule was Ireland, which had a very large immigration quota in relation to the size of its population.

Although not immediately apparent at the end of the war, another new factor loomed on the horizon. The Nazi debacle had discredited racist theories and ideologies and made it increasingly difficult to justify the fact that immigration to North America was a privilege effectively reserved for "white" people of European heritage. Paradoxically, the temporary success of Nazi Germany's principal ally, Imperial Japan, had also discredited the view that Europeans were a superior race and had fatally undermined European colonial regimes in South and Southeast Asia. Post-colonial states like India, Pakistan, and Indonesia had emerged as important players in international relations, potentially perhaps holding the balance of power in the global conflict between the American-led and Soviet-led blocs. Racist immigration policies exposed the hypocrisy of American and Canadian claims to stand for democracy and freedom.

Despite all of these circumstances, the US Congress remained committed to the quota system, and there was little change in immigration policy for twenty years after the war. In 1948, President Harry Truman in two separate messages to Congress urged the removal of ethnic and racial barriers to naturalization and also to the admission of "displaced persons" from Europe. The response was not favourable. In 1952, Congress adopted the McCarran-Walter Act, which made incremental changes to immigration and naturalization policies but retained the quota system in a slightly modified form. The McCarran-Walter Act also included an overtly racist concept known, rather obscurely, as the "Asia-Pacific triangle." This provided that prospective immigrants living outside of Asia and the Pacific islands whose ancestry was half or more Asian or Pacific Islander could not benefit from the quotas assigned to the countries where they actually lived but would have to be included in the very small quotas assigned to the countries where their ancestors had lived. (The Arab countries, Iran, Israel, Turkey, and the Asian portions of the Soviet Union were not included as part of Asia.) President Truman vetoed the bill, mainly on the grounds that the quota system was "insulting to large numbers of our finest citizens, irritating to our allies abroad, and foreign to our purposes and ideals," but his veto was easily overridden by two-thirds majorities in both houses of Congress.[15] One future president, John F. Kennedy, took Truman's side on this issue, but three others (Lyndon B. Johnson, Richard M. Nixon, and Gerald R. Ford) voted with the majority to override his veto.[16]

A Gallup Poll in 1955 suggested that most Americans knew nothing about the contents of the McCarran-Walter Act but that the minority who did know about it were inclined to favour a more liberal policy.[17] The quota system was becoming increasingly unworkable, because the large quotas assigned to Britain, Germany, and Ireland exceeded the number of prospective immigrants from those countries while countries where there was significant demand for immigration visas developed long waiting lists because of the very small quotas they were assigned. Ad hoc measures to benefit refugees, particularly refugees from Hungary after the rebellion of 1956, reduced the pressure for change to some extent.

John F. Kennedy had repeatedly called for immigration reform before being elected president and had introduced several immigration bills while serving in the Senate. In 1957, one of his bills became law; it provided for the admission of more than 60,000 backlogged applications and provided that persons admitted as refugees would no longer be counted against the future quotas of the countries from which they came.[18] In 1958, the future president published a pamphlet celebrating the multicultural origins of Americans and making the case for reform.[19] (During his presidency, he would expand the pamphlet into a book, which was published shortly after his death.) In 1959, while still a senator, he introduced a plan to eliminate the quota system entirely.[20]

Soon after taking office as president, Kennedy promised the American Committee on Italian Migration (ACIM), an interest group composed largely of Italian Americans, that he would support legislation to reallocate unused immigration quotas to countries such as Italy whose quotas were inadequate to deal with the number of outstanding applications.[21] However, he failed to mention immigration in any of his State of the Union messages in 1961, 1962, and 1963.

In January 1963, he was asked about immigration reform at a press conference and indicated merely that his administration would introduce legislation to redistribute unused quotas. In June, he repeated this promise at a symposium sponsored by the ACIM.[22]

The Justice Department, which administered immigration policy, proposed to reduce the national quotas by 10 per cent each year for five years and redistribute the additional visas thus made available on a basis of first come, first served with no ethnic discrimination. The State Department disliked this proposal, because it would actually reduce immigration from NATO allies in northern and western Europe. Their own measure would redistribute only the unused portions of the quotas (mainly from Britain, Ireland, and Germany) to countries where there was actual demand for them, would exempt newly independent Jamaica and Trinidad-Tobago from the quota system, and would repeal the invidious "Asia Pacific triangle" provisions. An alternative proposal, suggested by Democratic Congressman Emmanuel Celler of New York, would have abolished the quota system entirely. Celler had first been elected to the House of Representatives in 1922, when John F. Kennedy was five years old, and had voted against the quota system when it was introduced in 1924. Abba Schwartz of the State Department, a determined advocate of immigration reform within the administration, appeared to sympathize with the Celler proposal, since he included it, along with the department's own proposal, in a message to the White House in June 1963.[23] Secretary of State Dean Rusk, reflecting the attitudes of the Deep South from whence he came, was less enthusiastic about reform and reportedly defended the quota system in private on the grounds that "we are an Anglo-Saxon country."[24]

In July 1963, Kennedy sent his immigration proposal to Congress, stating that "The use of a national origins system is without basis in either logic or reason" and describing the quota system as an anachronism.[25] He suggested reducing existing quota allocations by 20 per cent a year for five years, a compromise between the more cautious approach favoured by the Department of Justice and Celler's plan to abolish the quotas immediately. In place of the quota system, preference would be given to prospective immigrants with skills that would benefit the US economy, to relatives of persons already residing in the United States, and to others on the basis of first come, first served. No more than 10 per cent of immigrants in any year could be from a single country. The Asia-Pacific triangle provisions would be abolished, and Jamaica and Trinidad-Tobago would be exempt from the quota system.

A file of newspaper editorials collected by Abba Schwartz suggests that the administration's proposal was favourably received in the northeastern states but less so in the midwestern and western states, while editorial comments from the southern states were predominantly hostile.[26] The executive council of the AFL-CIO issued a statement warmly supportive of the president's proposal, a significant development, since Samuel Gompers, the founder of the AFL, had supported the quota system when it was introduced.[27] However, like much else in his legislative program, Kennedy's immigration bill was not acted upon by Congress before his assassination on 22 November 1963.

Although President Lyndon Johnson, like most politicians from the southern states, had shown little or no previous interest in immigration reform, he took up the cause and met with representatives of pro-reform groups in January 1964.[28] The immigration bill that he submitted to Congress soon afterwards was almost identical to Kennedy's, but it made little progress in 1964. By 1965, the election of a much more liberal Congress, and the overwhelming mandate given to Johnson in his electoral victory over Barry Goldwater, seemed to improve the prospects for immigration reform. The administration reintroduced its bill with only slight changes.[29] Congressman Michael Feighan of Ohio, the chairman of the immigration subcommittee in the lower house and a major obstacle to reform, indicated a willingness to put some water in his wine by publicly supporting the end of the quota system, a suggestion that he had previously opposed. However, his price for this concession was that an overall ceiling on immigration, albeit a higher one than before, should apply to the entire world, including the Western Hemisphere.[30] This suggestion was opposed by the State Department, which feared that it would be resented by Latin American governments and peoples and would thus interfere with US foreign policy objectives. The continuing popularity of Fidel Castro in much of the region, and Johnson's invasion of the Dominican Republic earlier in the year, made the possible Latin American reaction a major source of concern. No one seems to have worried about the response of Canadians, although Canada was still at that time the largest source of Western Hemisphere immigrants to the United States.

In an effort to move the debate over immigration reform outside of Congress, the Johnson administration encouraged the formation of a National Committee for Immigration Reform, which represented a large, although not entirely representative, section of elite opinion. A number of prominent businessmen, mostly based in New York, joined it, as did former presidents Harry Truman and Dwight Eisenhower, retired generals Carl Spaatz and Alfred Gruenther, Father Theodore Hesburgh of the University of Notre Dame, classical musicians Leonard Bernstein and Yehudi Menuhin, and Dr Jonas Salk, the inventor of the polio vaccine. More to the point, politically speaking, the committee recruited some of the most prominent spokesmen for organized labour: George Meany of the AFL-CIO, I.W. Abel of the steelworkers, Walter Reuther of the auto workers, and David Dubinsky of the garment workers.[31]

Despite this initiative, a Harris poll published in May indicated that only 24 per cent of Americans favoured increasing immigration while 58 per cent were opposed. Support for immigration was particularly low among Protestants (18 per cent) and southerners (12 per cent) but was higher among Catholics (33 per cent), Jews (41 per cent), and residents of the northeastern states (37 per cent). The most popular sources of immigrants were, in order, Canada, Britain, Scandinavia, Germany, and Ireland. Immigrants from Asia, the Middle East, and Mexico ranked near the bottom. The only mildly encouraging finding, from the administration's point of view, was that 36 per cent of those polled favoured selecting immigrants on the basis of their skills and education, compared with 29 per cent who favoured selecting them on the basis of nationality; the remainder expressed no preference or were not sure of their opinions.[32] However, in July another poll, by the Gallup organization, found a bare majority (50 per cent) in favour of replacing the quota system with a system of selection based on skills. Only 7 per cent of respondents thought the number of immigrants should be increased while 32 per cent thought it should be reduced.[33]

Feighan's subcommittee finally reported the bill toward the end of July, with no ceiling on immigration from the Western Hemisphere.[34] Instead, there was a provision that no single country could supply more than 20,000 immigrants to the United States in any calendar year in addition to an overall annual limit of 170,000 immigrants from countries outside the Western Hemisphere. At the last moment, Feighan tried to reinsert the ceiling on immigration from the Western

Hemisphere, but he was outvoted and accepted defeat on this issue. The national origin quotas would be phased out over a three-year period. The bill then went to the Judiciary Committee of the House of Representatives where it faced a new amendment that would give the secretary of labor the authority to prevent admission of agricultural workers. This threatened to prevent adoption of the bill by Congress for another year, but the administration persuaded Andrew Biemiller, the AFL-CIO's lobbyist on Capitol Hill, to use his influence against the amendment.[35] The Judiciary Committee reported the bill, without the amendment, in early August. On 25 August, the House of Representatives passed the bill by a vote of 318 to 95, with 19 members not voting.[36]

In a message to the Speaker of the House of Representatives, President Johnson expressed the hope that both houses of Congress would act speedily and without "crippling amendments" on the immigration bill, which he said was more demanding of passage "in terms of decency and equity" than any other piece of legislation on the agenda.[37] However, it soon became apparent that the issue of placing a ceiling on immigration from the Western Hemisphere was far from extinct and that the administration would have to accept a compromise on this issue before the Senate Judiciary Committee would report the bill. Senate Minority Leader Everett Dirksen of Illinois was particularly insistent that a limit on Western Hemisphere immigration would be the price for his support of the bill. After consultations between the attorney general and the State Department, the latter reluctantly, and "as a last resort," accepted the idea of an overall limit on immigration from all sources, including the Western Hemisphere.[38] Nonetheless, the debate in the full Senate extended over five sitting days, compared to only two days in the House of Representatives.

On 22 September, exactly four weeks after the bill had passed in the lower house, the Senate approved it by a vote of 76 to 18, with six members not voting.[39] Most of the leading Republicans in both houses supported the bill, including future president Gerald R. Ford. The last-ditch opposition in both houses consisted mainly of right-wing legislators from the former Confederate states, most of whom in 1965 still wore the Democratic Party label.

The final version of the bill differed in certain respects from the one that the Johnson administration had submitted to Congress.[40] There would be an annual limit of 120,000 immigrants from the independent nations of the Western Hemisphere in addition to the annual limit of 170,000 from the rest of the world, no more than 20,000 of whom could be from any single country. The limit on Western Hemisphere immigration would take effect on 1 July 1968 unless Congress enacted otherwise prior to that date. The national origins quotas would be eliminated completely on 1 July 1968 rather than gradually over a period of five years as the administration had originally suggested. In selecting immigrants, priority would be given to close relatives of persons already residing in the United States rather than to persons selected on the basis of their skills and occupations. The secretary of labor would be given some authority to regulate and restrict immigration, in addition to the authority given to the attorney general, a provision that the administration had resisted because the Department of Labor was more sensitive to the protectionist instincts of American workers. The final version of the bill also provided for a commission to review the question of Western Hemisphere immigration and report its findings by 1968; the commission would include five members of the House of Representatives appointed by the Speaker, five senators appointed by the president of the Senate (Vice-President Hubert Humphrey), and five other persons appointed by President Johnson.

Johnson finally signed the long-awaited bill in a ceremony held at the Statue of Liberty on 3 October 1965. There had been some debate about the choice of a site that would be both symbolically appropriate and convenient in other respects. Plymouth (Massachusetts) and Jamestown (Virginia) were rejected because of their Anglo-Saxon associations.[41] Ellis Island, where millions of immigrants had arrived before the imposition of the quota system, was apparently the president's first choice but was rejected because the facilities there were in a derelict state. (Only later was it reopened as a museum.) The decisive argument for the Statue of Liberty was probably a reminder to Johnson that his hero, Franklin D. Roosevelt, had been the last president to visit the statue while in office.[42]

As anticipated, the new legislation had an immediate effect on the geographical distribution of immigrants to the United States, although the overall level of immigration remained so low in relation to the size of the US population that this effect was at first scarcely noticeable to most Americans. Comparing the winter of 1965–66 with the same time period a year earlier, the number of immigrant visas issued in Ireland fell from 1,036 to 82, in Britain from 4,108 to 2,192, in the Federal Republic of Germany from

3,813 to 515, and in Canada from 9,691 to 2,652. On the other hand, the number of visas issued to Italians rose from 1,744 to 12,058 so that Italy replaced Canada as the principal source of immigrants to the United States.[43]

The sequel to the adoption of the new legislation was the establishment and report of the fifteen-member select committee on Western Hemisphere immigration, as provided for in the statute. The majority of the committee members approved a report recommending the postponement until 1969 of the imposition of the annual ceiling of 120,000 on Western Hemisphere immigration. This recommendation was approved by the House of Representatives but not voted upon in the Senate, largely at the insistence of Minority Leader Dirksen, so the committee's report had no effect.[44] In 1976, Congress amended the legislation to provide that the limit of 20,000 immigrants per annum from any one country be applied to Western Hemisphere countries (i.e., Mexico) as well as to those in other parts of the world. Two years later, a further amendment replaced the separate annual limits for the two hemispheres with a single limit of 290,000 immigrants from all parts of the world, but this limit has been honoured more in the breach than in the observance owing to the many exceptions and loopholes in the statute.[45]

Supporters of immigration reform in the Truman-Eisenhower-Kennedy-Johnson era had assumed, or at least asserted, that the total volume of immigration would not increase significantly and the principal beneficiaries of reform would be prospective immigrants from European countries such as Italy and Greece. Neither prediction proved accurate. Between 1971 and 1980, the United States admitted 4,493,314 immigrants, the largest total for any decade since before the imposition of the quota system, and only 17.8 per cent of them were from Europe. In the following decade, the total number of immigrants rose to 7,338,062, which was about equal to the total number admitted in the four decades between 1931 and 1970. Only 10.4 per cent of the immigrants admitted between 1981 and 1990 were from Europe. The percentage of US residents born outside of the country, which had reached an all-time low of 4.7 per cent at the time of the 1970 census, rose to 10.4 per cent by 2000, the highest percentage in any census since 1930.[46] The United States was becoming a multiracial and multicultural country, a development that has gained increasing acceptance with the passage of time.

In contrast to the United States, Canadian immigration policy was largely made by executive or administrative rule-making rather than by statute law. In the aftermath of World War II, Canadian officials seriously considered instituting a quota system on the American model, designed to maintain the same proportional distribution of ethnic groups in Canada's population that already existed. An undated cabinet document, almost certainly drafted in 1947 and labelled "Confidential," proposed such a measure and outlined how it would work.[47] British and American immigrants, as well as the spouses and unmarried children of Canadian citizens, would be admitted regardless of the quota, with the explicit proviso that "British" referred only to the United Kingdom itself and not to its non-white colonies and dominions. (Curiously, nothing was said about excluding African Americans, probably because few of them were expected to be interested in moving to Canada.) Immigration from other sources would be fixed at a maximum level of 40,000 per year, distributed among the countries of the world in accordance with the proportions of various non-British ethnic groups in the entire population according to the 1941 census.

Unlike the American quota system, which gave a free pass to immigrants from the Western Hemisphere, the proposed Canadian version would have imposed quotas on Latin American countries. The rationale for this was that if immigrants from Latin American countries were not subject to quotas, it would be difficult to justify assigning a quota to France. Since almost one-third of Canadians in 1941 were of French ancestry, the quota for France would of course be very large and far in excess of the number of French people who were likely to be interested in moving to Canada. The advantage of this fact, according to the anonymous author of the document, was that the large French quota would not come close to being filled but its existence would make the quotas assigned to other European nations much smaller than they would be if France were to be excluded from the calculation. Thus, the goal of keeping the country "British" would be facilitated without the need to say so. With the French quota amounting to 24,588 out of 40,000, according to the author's calculation, other quotas would range from 3,280 for Germany and 2,804 for the Soviet Union down to 520 for all of Asia and 156 for "Negroes" from all of Africa. (The latter figure was based on the fact that Canada contained 22,174 persons of African ancestry in 1941, very few of whom, of course, had ever seen Africa.)

A quota system was not adopted, but Mackenzie King's policy statement on immigration, delivered to the House of Commons in 1947, stated explicitly that the government had no intention of presiding over a significant change in the ethnic or racial composition of Canada's population. Nonetheless, King conceded that Canada's population was still too small and that immigrants were needed.[48] Even that view was apparently contested by his minister of labour, Humphrey Mitchell, who complained a year later about British immigrants coming to Canada when there were no jobs awaiting them on their arrival.[49]

Canada had traditionally given preference to immigrants from English-speaking countries, but in 1948 France, the mother country for 30 per cent of Canada's population, was belatedly added to the preferred list. This rather overdue reform raised two sensitive issues: whether Algeria was really part of "Metropolitan France," as France claimed it was, and whether it would risk admitting too many "subversive elements," given the fact that about a quarter of the French electorate supported the communist party. The latter issue particularly worried the secretary of state for external affairs, Lester B. Pearson. As for the Algerian issue, Minister of Justice and soon-to-be prime minister Louis St Laurent suggested that avoiding the term "Metropolitan" and using the phrase "born in France" would suffice to keep out any Algerians.[50]

An order-in-council adopted by the St Laurent government in 1950 outlined the main parameters of Canada's immigration policy, which were essentially repeated in a new Immigration Act two years later. Preference would be given to citizens of the United Kingdom, Ireland, Australia, New Zealand, South Africa, the United States, and France. Consideration would also be given to anyone else who could satisfy the responsible minister that he or she would be suitable to Canadian conditions and "not undesirable owing to his peculiar customs, habits, modes of life, methods of holding property," or probable inability to adapt to Canadian ways. The reference to methods of holding property was designed to exclude members of religious sects, such as the Hutterites, who believed in collective farming, a practice resented by Canadian prairie farmers and one that in 1942 had been the target of the last provincial statute ever disallowed by the federal government. The order-in-council also explicitly provided "that the provisions hereinabove set out shall not apply to immigrants of any Asiatic race."[51]

Although these provisions appear somewhat restrictive, Canada's experience with immigration in the years following the war actually diverged sharply from that of the United States. Not being constrained by a quota system, the Canadian government could admit as many immigrants as were needed in a thinly populated country with a rapidly growing economy. During the 1940s, Canada admitted 491,321 immigrants, almost half as many as the 1,035,039 immigrants admitted by the United States. During the 1950s, Canada admitted 1,574,841 immigrants, more than three-fifths the number of 2,515,479 admitted by the United States. In 1957 alone, Canada welcomed 282,164 immigrants, the largest number since 1913 and a number that has never subsequently been exceeded. Even in the 1960s, the decade in which the United States finally abandoned the quota system, the Canadian total intake of 1,409,627 was more than 40 per cent of the American total intake of 3,321,677.[52]

Overall in those three decades, Canada admitted slightly more than half the number of immigrants who entered the United States, a country with about ten times Canada's population. The result was that the percentage of Canadian residents who had been born outside of Canada remained stable at about 15 per cent in the postwar years, in contrast to the United States where the percentage of residents born outside the country declined from 8.8 per cent in 1940 to 6.9 in 1950, 5.5 in 1960, and an all-time low of 4.7 per cent in 1970.[53] The absolute number of foreign-born people in Canada increased from about two million to about three million between 1940 and 1970, while the absolute number of foreign-born residents in the United States declined from about 11.5 million to about 9.5 million. It was during this period that the alleged contrast between a homogeneous American "melting pot" and a pluralistic Canadian "mosaic" appeared most plausible and became engraved on the Canadian imagination. Toronto, which in the 1940s had reminded some observers of Belfast, had become almost as ethnically diverse as New York by 1970.

However, Canada's immigrants in the postwar years had one thing in common with its native-born population: they were almost entirely of European ancestry. "Asiatics," whatever that might mean, were virtually excluded. The repeal of the Chinese Exclusion Act in 1947 raised fears in official Ottawa that the country might face an influx of the wives and children of Chinese Canadians.[54] This did not really happen, partly because the communist victory in the Chinese civil war made it difficult for people to leave that country. A memorandum to the cabinet in 1948 noted that Lebanese, Syrian, and Armenian

Canadians resented being classified as "Asiatics" and insisted they were "of Aryan stock," a rather unfortunate choice of terminology. Also, a certain Dr Pandia had submitted a request that "East Indians," of which he was one, should be allowed to sponsor their relatives as immigrants, a privilege enjoyed by European Canadians.[55] The few Canadian citizens of Chinese ancestry had this privilege after 1947, but when an organization representing them requested that non-naturalized Chinese be given the same privilege, the director of immigration expressed concern that this would lead to other non-naturalized "Asiatics," including Japanese, demanding it for themselves.[56]

When India, Pakistan, and Ceylon (Sri Lanka) became independent nations and members of the Commonwealth, Canada signed agreements with all three granting them annual immigrant quotas of 300, one hundred, and fifty persons, respectively. Previously, persons from those countries had been almost entirely excluded. In 1956, a new set of immigration regulations established a hierarchy of source countries, with the white Commonwealth, France, Ireland, and the United States in the first and most preferred category, the rest of Europe in the second, and Egypt, Israel, Lebanon, Turkey, and Latin America in the third. Immigrants from countries in the third category could be admitted only if they had close relatives in Canada, while India, Pakistan, and Ceylon retained their small quotas. Immigration from the rest of Asia and Africa remained almost impossible.[57]

In 1957, John Diefenbaker defeated the governing Liberals and formed a Progressive Conservative government. Diefenbaker was a Red Tory maverick, to the left of his own party and sometimes even of the Liberals. Having grown up with a German name on the prairies, he was sensitive to any kind of racial or ethnic discrimination. He was also a strong supporter of the multiracial Commonwealth, of which Ghana became the first black-ruled member in the same year that Diefenbaker became prime minister. In 1947, he had pointed out that the Liberal government's racist immigration policy probably violated Canada's obligations as a member of the United Nations, and in 1955 he criticized the Liberal minister of immigration, J.W. Pickersgill, who had said that a Canadian-born baby was more likely than an immigrant to become a good Canadian.[58] Diefenbaker was also proud of the fact that the first-ever Chinese-Canadian MP, Vancouver lawyer Douglas Jung, was a newly elected member of his party.

Immediately after taking office, Diefenbaker attended a conference of Commonwealth prime ministers at which immigration was apparently discussed in private conversations. Diefenbaker reported to cabinet that the prime ministers of Asian and African Commonwealth countries would not demand wholesale admission of their nationals to Canada, provided that the barriers to their admission were not based on the criterion of race.[59] Some incremental changes in immigration policy were made by order-in-council. Immigrants admitted under the small annual quotas allowed to the Commonwealth countries of South Asia (India, Pakistan, and Ceylon) were allowed to bring in their dependents, who would not be counted as part of the quotas.[60] Pleas from the South Asian community in Canada for an increase in the quotas were turned down, although 398 persons who had already applied for landed-immigrant status without success were admitted by order-in-council.[61]

There was more hesitation about changing the regulations that applied to Chinese and Japanese immigrants, partly because China was a communist country that had recently been at war against Canadian troops in Korea. On the other hand, the government was under some pressure from the Chinese-Canadian community and from Douglas Jung to liberalize the regulations. A cabinet committee headed by Ellen Fairclough, the minister of citizenship and immigration, proposed only that Chinese and Japanese immigrants be allowed to bring in their married as well as unmarried children under the age of twenty-one, but the cabinet deferred action on this recommendation.[62]

Immigration from the Commonwealth Caribbean was also considered by the cabinet. Most of the immigrants from that source were either female domestic servants admitted under a special program or relatives of persons already in Canada. A quota system like that for the South Asian countries was considered, but after discussions with the government of the newly created West Indies Federation, which was still a British dependency, the idea was abandoned on the grounds that it would be unnecessarily restrictive. A cabinet document noted that in 1958, for the first time, more than half of the immigrants from the West Indies had been of African ancestry and that the number of Afro-Caribbean immigrants had increased steadily from 122 in 1954 to 661 four years later.[63]

These changes attracted less attention than an ill-advised decision in March 1959 to restrict the categories of relatives who could be sponsored as immigrants by Canadian citizens who had emigrated from Europe, the Western Hemisphere, or selected countries of the Middle East. Egypt, which Progressive Conservatives considered a hostile country since the Suez crisis of 1956, was removed from the preferred category, and the siblings or married children of naturalized Canadians from any country could no longer be sponsored.[64] The latter change caused an outcry in Canada's ethnic communities, disturbed the newly elected Progressive Conservative government in Manitoba, and embarrassed the Italian ambassador, who had not been able to inform his government of the changes before they were leaked to the media. The cabinet therefore limited the damage by rescinding the new regulations only five weeks after they had been adopted.[65]

Later in 1959, the Diefenbaker government considered introducing a completely new immigration act, which was promised in the Speech from the Throne the following year. A first draft was prepared by D.H. Christie, the legal advisor to the deputy minister of citizenship and immigration. The proposed act would have given immigrants from all Europe access to Canada on the same terms already enjoyed by the British and the French. For the rest of the world, it recommended a quota system, with the quotas for each country to be established by order-in-council. In contrast to the American model, the quotas would not be based on ethnic origin but on a more vague and subjective criterion: "the likelihood of the prospective immigrants becoming readily integrated and assuming the duties and responsibilities of Canadian citizens." This language was borrowed from the Immigration Act of 1952, except that the bar would be lowered significantly by substituting "integrated" for "assimilated."[66]

The Department of External Affairs indicated its disapproval of this draft on several grounds. Establishing quotas for individual countries would be "a complicated and delicate task," and there would be constant pressure to revise them. Favouring Europe would give most communist countries preference over members of the Commonwealth, including even Australia and New Zealand. It also was unclear whether "Europe" would include Turkey (a NATO ally), Algeria (technically part of France), or Cyprus (a British dependency). Finally, the proposal appeared likely to make Canadian immigration policy more rigid when the United States (in 1952) had moved at least slightly in the opposite direction.[67]

The government remained torn between the view that at least the appearance of racial discrimination in immigration policy must be eliminated for the sake of Canada's reputation and the suspicion that this might not be popular with Canadian voters. As the director of immigration advised in early 1961, "there is no general desire amongst the Canadian public at large to increase – or at least increase substantially – the proportion of coloured or Asiatic persons in the immigration flow ... Canadians generally prefer to see those of their own ethnic origins come in as immigrants."[68]

By the fall of 1961, it was evident that any changes in immigration policy would take the form of new regulations under the existing act rather than a new statute. In October, Fairclough submitted new draft regulations to the cabinet, along with a memorandum noting that Canada's immigration policy was being criticized on the grounds that it discriminated on racial grounds and admitting that "There is no doubt that this criticism is to some extent justified."[69] This problem, she indicated, could be removed by changing the regulations, particularly regulation 20, which outlined the grounds on which immigrants could be excluded. She proposed to remove from regulation 20 any reference to geographical origin while substituting references to education, training, and skills. Another regulation provided that immigrants would be tested for literacy, although literacy could be in their own language rather than in English or French. Furthermore, the range of relatives who could be sponsored by Canadian citizens or landed immigrants would be the same regardless of race or geographical origin.

The proposed new regulations did not escape criticism. The citizenship branch of Fairclough's department disapproved of literacy tests, noting that they were probably unnecessary and could potentially be administered in a discriminatory way and that such a test had been adopted by the US Congress only by overriding President Wilson's veto in 1917.[70] Several of the government's supporters in the House of Commons also disliked the idea, and it was dropped from the final version of the regulations at the suggestion of the deputy minister.

On the other hand, the director of immigration was still worried about admitting "unassimilable immigrants." He asked, "How do we avoid the impression that we are suddenly going to accept large numbers of other races, but without giving the impression that the new regulations are meaningless?" He suggested that to resolve this dilemma the government should make clear that it would still discriminate on geographical grounds although not explicitly on racial grounds. In effect, this was an argument to maintain the status quo while pretending to change it.[71]

Some Progressive Conservative members of Parliament noted that the proposed uniform regulations for sponsoring close relatives regardless of race would actually narrow the range of relatives who could be sponsored by European-born Canadians or landed immigrants. Yet allowing the same sponsorship privileges to non-Europeans was considered unthinkable even by the relatively liberal deputy minister, George Davidson.[72] In response to this problem, a change was made so that Canadians from Europe and the Western Hemisphere as well as those from Egypt, Israel, and Lebanon would continue to retain the same sponsorship privileges as before, privileges that were not extended to Canadians from other parts of the world. Fairclough informed the cabinet on 18 January 1962 that this was "the only part of the Regulations where any element of preferential treatment or discrimination in favour of European and Western Hemisphere countries remains." She added that rather than taking existing privileges away from those countries, "It is considered preferable to move the less favoured groups forward, by progressive stages, to a position where they will eventually be on a basis of complete equality with the more favoured groups."[73] The revised regulations were approved by cabinet on the same day.

In reply to a query from Diefenbaker, Fairclough had assured him in November 1961 that the new regulations would indeed "provide for all applications to be dealt with on the basis of exactly the same criteria without discrimination on grounds of race, colour, ethnic origin or on any other grounds." She added that the government's next task would be to ensure that there would be no valid grounds for accusations of discrimination in the application or administration of the regulations."[74] In her statement to Parliament announcing the new regulations, Fairclough asserted that "This means that any suitably qualified person, from any part of the world, can be considered for immigration to Canada entirely on his own merit, without regard to his race, colour, national origin or the country from which he comes." She predicted that the chief beneficiaries of the changes would be "Asians, Africans, and nationals of Middle Eastern countries." She added that the special quota agreements with India, Pakistan, and Ceylon would no longer be necessary but would remain in effect pending discussions with those countries.[75]

There matters rested until March 1964, when René Tremblay, the minister of immigration in Lester Pearson's Liberal government, proposed a reformulation of immigration policy with two objectives: to match the policy with Canada's economic needs and to eliminate discrimination in sponsorship privileges between different groups of

Canadian citizens. A list of specific proposals for actions toward these ends was approved by cabinet with apparently little debate.[76] Later in the year, Tremblay proposed an amendment to the regulations allowing the sponsorship of male fiancés of Canadian citizens regardless of their country of origin. (Female fiancées could already be sponsored regardless of origin.) An additional amendment would broaden the list of relatives who could be sponsored by any Canadian citizen.[77] The cabinet approved these changes almost immediately.[78]

Following the 1965 election, Jean Marchand took over the Department of Citizenship and Immigration at the same time it was announced that it would become the Department of Manpower and Immigration. A White Paper on Immigration, approved by cabinet and published in October 1966, was more a defence of existing policy than a blueprint for innovation. It affirmed that immigration was desirable but emphasized the need for immigrants with skills that would contribute to Canada's urban and industrial economy. It also noted that Europe's increasing prosperity was making it harder to attract desirable immigrants from that continent and that "immigrants of the quality required by Canada are relatively scarce." However, it promised that "More will be done to maintain and improve international relations by removing the last vestiges of discrimination from immigration legislation and regulations." In particular, the rules regarding sponsorship as immigrants by relatives already in Canada would finally be made completely uniform for all parts of the world. To avoid an excessive number of sponsored immigrants (a category that already comprised about 40 per cent of all immigrants, according to the White Paper), it recommended that the right to sponsor relatives should henceforth be limited to immigrants who had lived in Canada for at least five years and had acquired Canadian citizenship. Landed immigrants already in Canada when the White Paper was tabled would retain their existing privileges in this regard for six years.[79]

The White Paper was referred to a parliamentary joint committee, which considered it from November 1966 until May 1967. Since the document inspired little enthusiasm on the part of either the committee or the various individuals and groups that appeared before it, Marchand asked his deputy minister, Tom Kent, to develop a more comprehensive and innovative proposal for immigration reform with the help of some senior officials in the department. The result was the invention of the point system, whereby each potential immigrant would be evaluated according to a number of numerically weighted criteria such as education, work experience, and knowledge of official languages.[80] It was hoped that this system would finally lay to rest the ghost of "any discrimination by reason of race, colour or religion," a goal that Marchand had emphasized in a memorandum to cabinet shortly after the joint parliamentary committee began its operations.[81]

Although Marchand, like previous ministers, had suggested proceeding by way of amendments to the Immigration Act and had introduced amendments to cabinet in March 1967, the point system was actually introduced in the form of regulations, which the cabinet approved in August of that year. This procedure avoided the need for a potentially controversial debate in the House of Commons, where the Liberals did not have a majority and a party hostile to immigration, Social Credit, held the balance of power. There was little controversy about it in cabinet, where most of the discussion of the new regulations revolved around concerns that communists or persons with criminal records might be admitted. During this discussion, Prime Minister Pearson rather oddly indicated that communist party members from countries with strong communist parties, such as France or Italy, would be admissible while British or American communists would not be.[82] Apparently his view of French communists had mellowed since 1948.

The regulations took effect in October 1967, but a completely new Immigration Act, replacing that of 1952 and incorporating the point system, was not adopted by Parliament until 1976, when Pierre Trudeau was prime minister and almost two decades after the Diefenbaker government had begun to consider the idea. The new statute was largely the work of Robert Andras, minister of manpower and immigration from 1972 to 1976.[83]

Although racial, ethnic, and religious discrimination was thus ended and replaced by a system based on objective criteria, changes in the geographical and ethnic pattern of Canadian immigration took place only gradually. In 1968, about 77 per cent of Canada's immigrants still came from Europe or the United States.[84] Thereafter, the percentage of Canada's immigrants from those traditional sources declined steadily. As the White Paper had anticipated, this trend was probably as much because of the declining interest in moving to Canada on the part of Europeans and Americans as because of the change in policy. The number of immigrants admitted from Asia exceeded the number arriving from Europe for the first time in 1979, about a decade after the same thing happened in the United States.[85]

The fact that the United States and Canada eliminated racial discrimination from their immigration policies during the same decade was more than coincidental, not because one country influenced the other but because both were responding to social and cultural changes in North America and in the world. (It is somewhat ironic that Kennedy and Diefenbaker, who notoriously disliked one another, were both instrumental in promoting the cause of immigration reform and for similar reasons.) One reason that immigration reform eventually succeeded was that existing policy seemed increasingly incongruous with the formal commitment of both countries to racial equality, as represented in Canada by Diefenbaker's Bill of Rights and in the United States by the Civil Rights Act of 1964.

Both countries had previously entrenched ethnic and racial discrimination in their immigration policies, although in somewhat different ways and for somewhat different reasons. Both had made entry exceedingly difficult for most persons of non-European ancestry, but this was qualified in the United States by the exclusion of Western Hemisphere immigrants from the quota system and in Canada (much less significantly) by certain limited special arrangements for Commonwealth countries. Both had sought to perpetuate the distribution of ethnic origins in their respective populations that existed at an earlier time, but in Canada this was done by explicitly favouring residents of specific countries (English-speaking countries and, after 1948, France) while in the United States it was done by assigning quotas to Eastern Hemisphere nations based on US census data, a practice that looked more impartial in form even if it was not so in fact. These existing and familiar patterns of policy created path dependence that was not easily overcome. The quota system survived for decades despite its increasing unworkability, its absurdity, and its incongruity with the myth of the "melting pot." Canada's preference for the "charter groups" (British and French) is still perpetuated more subtly by the point system, which gives a significant advantage to those who can speak one of the two official languages.

In both the United States and Canada, the most significant motives for removing racial and ethnic criteria from immigration policy were two in number. First was the question of international reputation, particularly important for the United States as the leader of the anti-Soviet camp in the cold war but also significant for Canada as a middle power that sought respect and influence in the United Nations and the Commonwealth. The second motive was the desire to appease ethnic groups within the country's existing population that either wished to sponsor relatives and former neighbours as immigrants or simply saw existing policies as invidious. Italian Americans seem to have been particularly important and influential in this regard. In Canada, the small Chinese community, and Douglas Jung in particular, seems to have had some influence on the Diefenbaker government.

In the 1960s, neither the United States nor Canada expected, or wanted, a major increase in the volume of immigration, but such an increase did take place later on in the United States, which admitted almost three times as many immigrants between 1981 and 1990 as it had done between 1951 and 1960. Canada, on the other hand, actually admitted fewer immigrants between 1981 and 1990 than it had done in any decade since the 1940s. Only in the 1990s did immigration to Canada increase dramatically to attain an average level of more than 200,000 immigrant arrivals each year.[86] Today, the volume of immigration in relation to the size of the existing population remains greater in Canada than in the United States, but the disparity between the two countries in this regard is much less than it was previously.

In both countries, of course, the most visible change has been the declining importance of Europe as a source of immigration, the result of declining European birth rates and rising European living standards, and the dramatic increase in immigration from Asia. In the United States, immigration from Asia in the 1980s was greater than the total immigration from all sources in the 1950s, and the number of Asian immigrants had increased eighteen-fold over the same period of time.[87] Immigration from Hispanic America to both the United States and Canada has also increased, although less dramatically. The changes in immigration policy that took place in the 1960s facilitated these developments but were not the only or even the primary cause of them.

8

The Politics of Language

The politics of language has not played a large part in the history of the United States, at least until recently. From the beginnings of colonial settlement in Massachusetts and Virginia, the hegemonic position of English was taken for granted. In contrast to Bolivia, Ecuador, and Peru, no indigenous language was spoken by enough people at the time of European settlement to play a significant part in shaping the culture and society of the new nation. The European languages that preceded English in different parts of what became the United States – Dutch in New York, Swedish in Delaware, and French in Louisiana – were soon overwhelmed by the influx of English-speaking settlers, although Louisiana remained officially bilingual until the Civil War.[1] (Spanish in New Mexico, a late addition to the territory of the United States, was a partial exception, as will be discussed below.) Most immigrants to the United States, if they did not come from an English-speaking country, quickly learned at least some English and relegated their original language to private use so that by the third generation it was virtually extinct among their descendants. The Irish language, for example, seems to have left no traces whatever in the United States, although it is almost certain that a large percentage of the Irish immigrants who arrived in the 1840s could speak it, probably more fluently than they spoke English.

As described in chapter 6, German was the "foreign" language that had the greatest impact on the United States until it fell victim to the Germanophobia of World War I. It benefitted from some particular circumstances: its prestige as one of the major European languages, the very large volume of German immigration in the nineteenth century, the fact that German had already established roots, particularly in Pennsylvania, before the Declaration of Independence, and the preference of non-Jewish Germans for settling in rural areas, in some of which they comprised the majority of the population. The Continental Congress translated some documents into German during the War of Independence, although a motion to translate federal statutes into German was rejected in 1795. There were proposals to translate some federal documents into German in 1835 and again in 1862.[2] However, the ease with which German language and culture succumbed to the Germanophobic onslaught unleashed by World War I suggests that it was more vulnerable than it appeared and would probably have suffered a similar although more gradual fate even if the war had not taken place. Only Nebraska considered it necessary to respond to the German "threat" by specifying in its constitution that English was its official language, which it did in 1920. A Nebraska law making it a crime to use German as the language of instruction in a private school was struck down by the Supreme Court of the United States in 1923.[3] Also in 1923, Illinois adopted a bill (although without amending its constitution) that made "American" its official language. The bill was introduced by an Irish-American legislator, and the choice of label was apparently intended as an anti-British gesture.[4]

The recent history of language politics in the United States, of course, has been dominated by the alleged threat of Spanish and is closely linked to anxieties about immigration, particularly immigration from Mexico. Whatever one may think of the anti-Spanish agitation, it cannot be denied that the presence of the Spanish language on the territory of the United States, particularly in the states that share a border with Mexico, has expanded significantly in recent decades and is increasingly conspicuous. The fact that the language is spoken by one hundred million people on the other side of the border obviously is an asset shared by no other minority language in the United States. Arguably, this represents a new situation in American experience, one whose outcome is not easily predictable on the basis of past history.

In contrast to the situation of the United States, the politics of language has been an important theme – some would say the most important theme – in Canada's history. The competition between English and French in Canada resulted not from immigration subsequent to the founding of the Canadian state but from the transfer of the country from French to British rule in the eighteenth century. For reasons that were partly demographic and partly political, the French language easily survived that event and was spoken by more Canadians than those who spoke English until about the middle of the nineteenth century. Even today it is the first language of, and the language mainly used by, almost a quarter of Canada's population and by an overwhelming majority of the population in Canada's second largest province.

It might seem, therefore, that the politics of language in the two neighbouring North American countries represents two phenomena so distinct that they can hardly be compared with one another. In fact, this is not really so. Admittedly, Quebec, as a mainly French-speaking province in a mainly English-speaking federation, has no real equivalent in the United States. However, in some other parts of Canada, French was in some sense an "immigrant" language (as it also was in the New England states) that was brought by migrants from Quebec and whose arrival was at times greeted with hostility and suspicion. In Lower Canada (Quebec) itself, English could also be viewed initially as an "immigrant" language, although one of a special kind since it was the language of the conquerors. More to the point, perhaps, Quebec's response to more recent immigrants, whose first language is neither English nor French, can be compared with the response of Americans to the immigration of Spanish-speaking people, although the circumstances are not exactly the same. Rightly or wrongly, the reaction of the host society in both cases has been influenced by anxiety over the future of its own language.

Since the politics of language has a longer and more complex history in Canada than in the United States, it is perhaps appropriate to begin this chapter with a discussion of the Canadian case. As was noted near the beginning of this book, the British decision to rule Canada indirectly in collaboration with the Catholic clergy and the seigneurs, and to retain the French legal system, was an event that has shaped the course of Canadian history up to the present day. While the Quebec Act did not explicitly mention the French language, indirect rule was conducive to the continuing use of that language, which was also facilitated by the fact that many of the British governing class were able to read and speak it. Indirect rule also led to public education, when it began early in the nineteenth century, being left in the hands of the Catholic clergy. Since all of the Catholic clergy and members of Catholic religious orders were francophones at that time, they naturally taught in their own language, which was thus perpetuated with the tacit approval of the colonial regime.

The survival of French in Canada was also assisted by demographic factors. Relatively few anglophones migrated to Canada, particularly to Lower Canada, in part because most considered the United States a more attractive destination. Also, French Canadians had higher birth and fertility rates than the anglophones who did settle in Canada. Although not reinforced at all through immigration, and losing some of its people through emigration to the United States, the francophone population increased from about 60,000 at the time of the conquest to about a million a century later, indicating that it doubled about every twenty-five years. The reasons for this rapid increase are not entirely clear, since the population of France grew very slowly during the same period of time, but the abundance of land in Canada, the system of seigneurial tenure, and the influence of the Catholic Church may all have contributed to the result. In any event, Lower Canada, which was created by the partition of the colony in 1791, remained, as it still is, a society where about four-fifths of the population had French as their mother tongue. The partition helped to steer most British and Irish immigrants towards neighbouring Upper Canada (Ontario) where the English language, Protestant religion, and English common law prevailed.

French also acquired a foothold in other parts of what would become the Dominion of Canada after 1867. On the western prairies, intermarriage between French men involved in the fur trade and Aboriginal women produced a distinct people known as Métis, most of whom spoke the French language. Acadia, which corresponds roughly with the present provinces of New Brunswick, Nova Scotia, and Prince Edward Island, had been colonized by the French simultaneously with their colonization of Canada and had a population of more than 10,000 French-speaking Acadians in 1755. At that date, most of them were expelled by the British, who had acquired Acadia in 1713 by the Treaty of Utrecht, but after the conclusion of the Seven Years' War they were allowed to return, since they were no longer considered a military threat. Many did so, and the French population of Acadia numbered about 8,000 in 1800.[5] With birth and fertility rates similar to those of French Canadians in Quebec, that population increased to 139,006 by 1901, but this number fell far short of being a majority in the three provinces, which had a combined total population of 893,953 according to the 1901 census.

The francophones of Lower Canada never faced the trauma of expulsion, but their time of greatest crisis followed the unsuccessful rebellion against British colonial rule in 1837–38. Lord Durham was sent by the British government in 1838 to govern the colony, which had been placed under military rule, and to analyze its problems. Although some people of Irish or British ancestry had joined the rebellion and some French Canadians, including the higher clergy, had opposed it, Durham chose to view the rebellion as an ethnic struggle or, as he put it, "two nations warring in the bosom of a single state." As a radical, by the standards of his time and place, Durham admired the United States, which he contrasted with the apparently backward condition of Canada. He also had little regard for the culture of the French Canadians, to whom he referred as a people with no history. He proposed reuniting Upper and Lower Canada, discouraging the use of the French language, and, when the French Canadians had been assimilated or at least overwhelmed by subsequent immigration, granting responsible government. Durham's comments and recommendations made him the bête noir of French Canada, as he has remained right up to the present day.

Durham spent only six months in Canada before he resigned, and his prescription was followed only in part. The two colonies were united, but responsible government was granted in 1848 without waiting for the French Canadians to be either assimilated or overwhelmed, which they showed no sign of becoming. Responsible government in fact required cooperation between politicians of both language groups, which strengthened the bargaining position of the French, who were still a slight majority of the population in the united Province of Canada. The governor, Lord Elgin, who ironically was married to Durham's daughter, appointed a francophone first minister, Louis-Hippolyte Lafontaine, to head the first responsible government in 1848 and read part of the Speech from the Throne in French. The following year, he signed a controversial bill to compensate French Canadians whose property had been damaged or destroyed by the British army during the rebellion. Thereafter until 1867, the united province had a consociational regime involving both language groups, and the two languages were roughly equal in status.

In 1867, the British North America Act gave Canada a federal constitution, re-established the boundary between Upper and Lower Canada (known henceforth as Ontario and Quebec), and added two new provinces, Nova Scotia and New Brunswick, with others to be added later. Quebec, whose francophone majority and anglophone minority were both ably represented in the negotiations that led to this outcome, would be a bilingual province with education and public services, such as they were, available in both languages. In the other provinces, whose small francophone minorities were not represented, English would be the only official language. At the federal level, section 133 provided that federal statutes would be printed in both English and French and that either language could be used in Parliament or in any courts that Parliament would subsequently establish. The federal government would be located in Ottawa, part of the unilingual province of Ontario.

These provisions established a *modus vivendi* between the two language groups but not for long. In 1869, Canada added more than five million square kilometres to its area by purchasing Rupert's Land and the North-West Territory from the Hudson's Bay Company, but Canada's authority and control over this vast domain was not securely established until the completion of the Canadian Pacific Railway from Montreal to the Pacific coast in November 1885. In the meantime, the newly acquired territory, whose small population included a substantial number of French-speaking Métis, became a source of conflict between anglophones and francophones. The Métis leader, Louis Riel, established a provisional government at Fort Garry (now Winnipeg) and in 1870 forced the federal government to create the bilingual province of Manitoba, about half of whose population at the time were francophones, in a small portion of the former Rupert's Land. As in Quebec, the two languages enjoyed equal status in the legislature and courts of Manitoba, guaranteed by the Manitoba Act, which in effect served as the new province's constitution.[6]

Official bilingualism in Manitoba did not last long after the completion of the Canadian Pacific in November 1885, which facilitated the rapid colonization of Manitoba, and later of the territories further west, by English-speaking settlers. Almost simultaneously with the completion of the railway, Louis Riel was executed after he led a rebellion in 1885 on behalf of the Métis in what is now the province of Saskatchewan. Within a few years, the francophones had been reduced to a small minority in Manitoba and in western Canada as a whole, although the omission of the customary ethnic question from the census of 1891 makes it difficult to be more precise. In 1890, the Manitoba government, now securely in the hands of English-speaking settlers from Ontario, amended the Manitoba Act to remove the official status of the French language and to abolish the Catholic school system, which the Manitoba Act had also

provided.[7] It could do these things because the British North America
Act allowed the provinces to amend their own constitutions, except
with regard to the office of lieutenant governor, by a simple act of
the legislature.

Although the federal minister of justice, John Thompson, predicted
that the abolition of bilingualism in Manitoba would be successfully
challenged in court, this did not happen until almost a century later.[8]
With increasing immigration over the next two decades, Manitoba
would become an ethnic mosaic in which the French were only one
minority among many, with no special rights or privileges. Meanwhile,
the issue of Catholic schools, until it was finally resolved by a compromise in 1896, attracted far more attention in Manitoba and elsewhere than the issue of language rights.

The same issues of language and religion arose again in the vast
area between Manitoba and British Columbia, which was part of the
North-West Territories until 1905. Like Manitoba, this territory
included a significant number of French-speaking and Catholic Métis.
The North-West Territories Act of 1875 had provided for Catholic
separate schools, and in 1877 an amendment to the act gave the
English and French languages equal status in the legislature and courts
of the territories.[9] However, another amendment, adopted shortly
after the death of Prime Minister Macdonald in 1891, provided that
the North-West Territories legislature could abolish official bilingualism after the next territorial election, which it promptly did.[10] Another
territorial ordinance, in 1901, retained separate Catholic schools but
required them to teach the same curriculum as the public schools.[11]

These events stimulated Quebec's interest in the newly acquired
western territories and particularly in their French-speaking minorities, of whose existence most people in Quebec had scarcely been
aware in 1867.[12] Some French Canadians in Quebec began to argue
for a truly bilingual Canada in which the French language would
enjoy equal status with English from coast to coast, not only in
Quebec. Henri Bourassa, subsequently the founder of the daily newspaper *Le Devoir*, became a thoughtful and eloquent spokesman for
this point of view after 1896, when he was first elected to Parliament.
Bourassa challenged French Canadians in Quebec to view the whole
of Canada as their country, and he challenged English-speaking
Canadians to recognize that a bilingual and bicultural Canada would
be more secure than a unilingual Canada against the threat of cultural and political absorption by the United States. However, his

appeal to anglophone Canada fell on deaf ears, and even in Quebec his influence declined after World War I as the province became increasingly inward-looking.

In 1905, the great surge of immigration that would transform Canada into a multicultural country had just begun, and the North-West Territories were attracting large numbers of settlers. Prime Minister Wilfrid Laurier, a French Canadian Catholic from Quebec, introduced legislation to create two new provinces, Alberta and Saskatchewan, between Manitoba and British Columbia. Bilingualism in the west was no longer acceptable to English-speaking Canadians, and Laurier made no effort to restore it. He did insist on retaining Catholic separate schools in the two new provinces, thus provoking the resignation of his western lieutenant and minister of the interior, the same Clifford Sifton who encouraged the immigration of "men in sheepskin coats." Before entering federal politics, Sifton had been a minister in the Manitoba government that abolished both bilingualism and sectarian schools in that province. As a compromise, Laurier agreed that the ordinance of 1901, requiring Catholic schools to teach the curriculum of the public schools, would remain in force, but that concession came too late to prevent Sifton's resignation.[13] As had been true in the case of Manitoba a decade earlier, the religious issue overshadowed the language issue. An amendment by an opposition member from Quebec to make the new provinces bilingual was easily defeated.[14] Separate schools, however, survive in Alberta and Saskatchewan to the present day.

Anglophone Canada, which had apparently accepted the idea of a bilingual Manitoba in 1870 and bilingual territories in 1877, was in a different and more militant frame of mind a generation later and now insisted that English must predominate everywhere, except possibly in Quebec. There were several reasons for this development. Chauvinistic ethnic nationalism and imperialism were on the rise in Europe and also in the United States. Anglophone Canadians, most of whom identified more strongly with the British Empire than with their own country, were not immune to this tendency. Laurier's government had encouraged it in 1898 by issuing a postage stamp depicting a map of the world on which the lands of the British Empire were painted red and with the slogan "We hold a vaster empire than has been." Closer to home, there was anxiety and resentment among anglophones about the demographic progress of French Canadians in Quebec, where six predominantly English-speaking counties had become predominantly French-speaking since 1867, and even in eastern Ontario, where the counties of Prescott and Russell had experienced the same transformation.[15] In western Canada, this anxiety about the English language was reinforced by the growing volume of immigration from continental Europe, with or without sheepskin coats.

To many anglophone Canadians who worried about such matters, it seemed that if Canada was to remain a British dominion in fact as well as in form, it must defend the English language against inroads by any potential rivals, whether French or otherwise. If the Protestant faith, which the British monarch was supposed to defend, could also be protected against inroads by other faiths, particularly by Catholicism, so much the better. Prior to his death in 1896, the principal spokesman for such ideas was D'Alton McCarthy, a Protestant who had emigrated from Ireland with his parents as a child. As a Conservative M P until he resigned from the party in 1893, McCarthy was a thorn in the side of John A. Macdonald and his successor, John Thompson, both of whom preferred a more conciliatory approach to French Canadians and other minorities. McCarthy's views were not unlike those of Lord Durham and also resembled those of contemporary nativists in the United States such as Henry Cabot Lodge.

Those who favoured a more British and more Protestant Canada viewed Manitoba, Saskatchewan, and Alberta, which were erroneously expected to contain the majority of Canada's people by the middle of the twentieth century, as the battlegrounds where Canada's future would be decided. In fact, few French Canadians actually moved to the western provinces, so they could only credibly be viewed as a threat in those provinces if they were associated with other minorities who were arriving from Europe. On the other hand, those European immigrants might be more easily persuaded to assimilate, or at least integrate, into anglophone Canada if they could be assured that the French language enjoyed no special privileges.

The situation was somewhat different in Ontario, Canada's most populous province but one whose population grew quite slowly between 1881 and 1911. People of French ancestry had comprised about 5 per cent of Ontario's population in 1871, rising to about 8 per cent in 1911, and eventually reaching a peak of just under 10 per cent in 1941. Some of this was the result of natural increase, but much of it represented the movement of French Canadians from Quebec to nearby parts of northern and eastern Ontario. In contrast to the western provinces, those areas were close enough to facilitate visiting friends and relatives back home. The mining, smelting, and forest industries of northern Ontario, a rapidly growing region in those days, also provided jobs at somewhat higher wages than were available in Quebec.

These developments opened a new front in Canada's linguistic war. In 1912, Ontario's Conservative government imposed Regulation XVII, which prohibited the use of French as the language of instruction beyond the second grade in any tax-supported school. The measure, which applied to the Catholic separate school system as well as to the mainstream system, was enthusiastically supported by Ontario's Catholic bishops, who were mainly of Irish ancestry. In 1916, the pope issued an encyclical urging francophones in Ontario to accept the regulation but to try to ensure that it be implemented in a liberal and flexible manner.[16] From the viewpoint of francophone Quebec, which was further alienated from Canada by the imposition of military conscription in World War I, Regulation XVII overshadowed even the Durham report and the fate of Louis Riel as a source of hurt and indignation. The regulation was abolished in 1927, but the effective revival of French-language education in Ontario did not take place until much later.

In New Brunswick, where out-migration caused the anglophone population to grow very slowly, Acadians increased from less than one-sixth of the population in 1871 to more than one-third in 1941. French was widely spoken in the northern and eastern parts of the province, while the southern and western counties were almost entirely English-speaking. Although the French language had no official status in the province, this geographical distribution and the relatively large size of the Acadian population made the language less vulnerable to assimilation in New Brunswick than it was in Ontario, Nova Scotia, or Prince Edward Island.

Lacking official encouragement from either level of government, the use of the French language outside of Quebec gradually declined after World War I. The number of persons claiming French as their ethnic origin continued to increase absolutely and in the 1930s, when there was practically no immigration, even relatively, but increasingly they lived and worked in English. A few French-Canadian nationalists still dreamed in the interwar period that "the revenge of the cradle" (a reference to their higher birthrate) would eventually make Canada a predominantly French-speaking country. A few anglophone

Canadians still worried about this prospect, strange as it may seem. However, all such prognostications were in the realm of fantasy, as the amateur demographer Richard Joy convincingly demonstrated in a book entitled *Languages in Conflict*.[17] His data suggested that the French language was viable only in Quebec and perhaps in the parts of Ontario and New Brunswick that were close to Quebec.

By the 1950s, linguistic issues had almost disappeared from Canadian politics, provincial as well as federal. In Quebec, French was almost universally spoken outside of Montreal, and in the rest of Canada English was almost universally spoken outside of the border zones of Ontario and New Brunswick. In Montreal, the only place where the two linguistic communities seemed equally viable, they appeared to have established a stable if not particularly cordial equilibrium. The French-Canadian birthrate, still significantly higher than that of anglophone Canada, counterbalanced the ability of the latter to reinforce itself through immigration in Quebec and in Canada as a whole. Neither linguistic community feared that the other was making progress at its expense.

In September 1959, the death of Maurice Duplessis, the conservative nationalist premier who had ruled Quebec without serious challenge since 1944, unleashed forces of social and political change in Quebec that had been gaining strength for some time. What came to be called the Quiet Revolution had begun as a movement of opposition to Duplessis's old-fashioned and arbitrary style of government, a movement largely inspired by Catholic social thought. However, it quickly acquired overtones of anti-clericalism and neo-nationalism that challenged the whole basis of Quebec's political order since 1867, or perhaps since 1774. The province's Liberal government, riding a tiger over which it had little control, fought an election in November 1962 on the nationalist slogan "*maîtres chez nous*" but found itself challenged by more radical elements, some of which aspired to make Quebec a sovereign state outside the Canadian federation.

For some French Canadians in Quebec, Henri Bourassa's old dream of a truly bilingual Canada was still more appealing than the prospect of separation. One such person was André Laurendeau, a cultural nationalist and the editor-in-chief of *Le Devoir*. On 20 January 1962, the paper published an editorial by Laurendeau urging the federal government to establish a royal commission that would find out what Canadians thought of bilingualism, examine the experience of other countries with more than one language, and study the status of

French within the federal public service.[18] Prime Minister Diefenbaker rejected the idea, but Lester Pearson, the leader of the Liberal opposition, endorsed it. When Pearson became prime minister in 1963, the Royal Commission on Bilingualism and Biculturalism was quickly established. Laurendeau was appointed co-chairman with Davidson Dunton, a university president and former journalist who had grown up in Montreal's anglophone community.[19]

The royal commission remained in existence for seven years and performed all three of the tasks Laurendeau suggested for it, although Laurendeau died in 1968 before its work was completed. It eventually produced a multi-volume report and more than one hundred recommendations. Among them were that the federal government, Ontario, and New Brunswick should all declare French an official language, that any county or district with an official language minority (i.e., English in Quebec or French elsewhere) exceeding 10 per cent of its population be declared a bilingual district where services would be provided in both languages, that public education in both languages be made available in bilingual districts and in all major cities, that units operating in French be established in the federal public service, and that French become the principal language of work in Quebec's private sector.

Although based on a solid program of research, these suggestions were not warmly received, even in Quebec. Few Canadians outside of Quebec, apart from francophones, took bilingualism seriously or favoured efforts to make it more meaningful, a fact that was made painfully obvious during the royal commission's public hearings across the country. Canadians whose origins were neither British nor French, as will be discussed in the next chapter, were offended by the term "biculturalism" and its implications. Provincial governments disliked the idea of school systems, which were already divided on sectarian lines in five of the ten provinces, being further divided on linguistic lines. Federal public servants, who were mainly unilingual anglophones, feared for their jobs. Quebec anglophones had no wish to see French become the principal language of the private sector in Quebec, and their representative on the royal commission, the law professor and poet Frank R. Scott, dissented from that recommendation.

In Quebec, from which the idea of the royal commission had come, its recommendations received a less favourable response than they might have done a few decades earlier. Most of the recommendations were viewed as irrelevant to the state-building project of the Quiet

Revolution and as oriented more toward the francophone minorities in other provinces than toward the francophone majority in Quebec. The bilingual districts and other measures to protect official-language minorities would strengthen Quebec's anglophone minority, which many people in Quebec viewed as having too many rights and privileges already. The royal commission seemed to assume that the French language was as secure within Quebec as English was elsewhere, an assumption that many Quebec francophones considered questionable. In 1968, while the royal commission was still at work, Quebec established its own commission on the status of the French language in Quebec, headed by Jean-Denis Gendron, to produce recommendations more suited to Quebec's needs.

In short, Henri Bourassa's dream of a bilingual Canada was no longer at the top of Quebec's agenda. In defining the issue between Quebec and Canada as a linguistic issue, the royal commission had sidestepped the problem of Quebec's desire for more autonomy that would allow it to build its own society with as little federal interference as possible. However, Pierre Elliott Trudeau, who succeeded Pearson as prime minister in April 1968, shared the royal commission's belief that a more bilingual Canada was not only intrinsically desirable but would lessen the attraction of a more autonomous Quebec. Throughout his long term of office, which lasted until 1984 with one brief intermission, bilingualism remained one of his government's main priorities, even if his popularity suffered as a result.

Efforts to increase the number and prominence of francophones in the federal public service, which had begun under Pearson, continued under Trudeau. Courses to make anglophone public servants fluent in French were established, and French-language units were established throughout the public service. In 1969, an Official Languages Act was adopted, which made the two languages equal in status in areas of federal jurisdiction and established a commissioner of official languages to monitor the progress of bilingualism.[20] The various holders of this office, which by tradition alternates between an anglophone and a francophone, have interpreted their mandate broadly and have not hesitated to criticize provincial governments, including that of Quebec. The Official Languages Act was supported by all parties in Parliament but opposed by a dissident group of mainly western Progressive Conservatives, including John Diefenbaker, who was still a member of Parliament although no longer the leader of his party.

The idea of establishing bilingual districts was seriously considered for several years but eventually abandoned.[21] Trudeau tried to make

Ontario agree to become officially bilingual but was never successful, although New Brunswick eventually agreed to do so. Quebec's decision in 1974 to make French its only official language, insofar as the British North America Act allowed this, eliminated any possibility of French becoming an official language in Ontario, but Ontario's government did place bilingual signs on the highways and began to provide some public services in French. In 1979, a decision by the Supreme Court of Canada forced Manitoba to restore the official bilingualism that it had abolished in 1890, although the francophone minority there had dwindled to about 5 per cent of the population in terms of mother tongue and about 3 per cent in terms of those actually speaking the language at home.[22] In 1982, the Canadian Charter of Rights and Freedoms entrenched much of the Official Languages Act, as well as the analogous legislation in New Brunswick, in Canada's Constitution. It also required every province to make primary and secondary education in both official languages available "where numbers warrant" and guaranteed the right of official-language-minority persons to choose such education for their children. The Supreme Court of Canada subsequently ruled that official-language-minority schools must be administered by the official-language community they served.[23]

Anglophone Canadians grumbled over most of these measures, particularly if they were federal public servants or lived in one of the western provinces. The Liberals lost a third of their parliamentary seats in the 1972 election, largely because of bilingualism, although their strength in Quebec held firm. Minor political parties hostile to bilingualism emerged at the provincial level in Alberta and New Brunswick. In 1977, a retired Canadian naval officer, J.V. Andrew, published a book alleging that Trudeau and "a half-dozen likeminded associates" were plotting to make Canada an entirely French-speaking country. The author suggested that encouraging Quebec to separate from Canada might be the only way to prevent the plot from succeeding. The tone of his argument is perhaps best conveyed by a sentence that begins on the very first page: "In the ten years from 1968 to 1978, without firing a shot, Mr. Trudeau will have taken more of the earth's surface for his race [sic] than did Napoleon, Alexander the Great, and all the Roman emperors combined."[24] The modestly priced book was widely sold in convenience stores and went through several printings.

However, there was and is no real evidence to suggest that the English language was in any serious danger, except possibly in Quebec.

Outside of New Brunswick and the Ottawa metropolitan area, the French-language minorities, which are now organized in a pressure group called La Fédération des francophones hors Québec, remained very weak and their future questionable, despite the best efforts of the federal government and the Supreme Court to keep them alive. In most of Canada's major urban areas, French is less widely spoken than Chinese. In every province, including even Quebec, the percentage of people having French as a mother tongue, or speaking it at home, was slightly lower in 2006 than it had been in 1981.

Language issues remained controversial in Quebec long after the fuss had died down elsewhere. For almost a century after Confederation, the demographic predominance of the French language in Quebec was taken for granted, even though English was associated with higher socio-economic status. However, many Quebeckers became convinced as early as the 1960s that the French language was in danger, particularly in Montreal where about a third of the population had a mother tongue other than French. The traditionally high birthrate of Quebec francophones declined suddenly as the birth control pill became available and as the province became more secular and socially liberal. Anxiety was also fuelled by the increasing number of European immigrants to Montreal, most of whom adopted English rather than French as their new language and educated their children in English. Some demographers alleged that Montreal would become a predominantly English-speaking city, as it had been for a brief period in the middle of the nineteenth century, unless immigrant children were forced into French schools and unless the use of English was restricted in the private sector of the economy.

These concerns, which the Royal Commission on Bilingualism and Biculturalism largely ignored, boiled over in 1967 when a nationalist faction gained control of the Catholic school board in the Montreal suburb of St-Léonard and demanded that all education there be in French. Italian immigrants, who made up about half of St-Léonard's population, insisted that it continue to be at least partly in English. This dispute led to the appointment of the Gendron Commission and then to the Official Language Act of 1974 (not to be confused with the federal Official Languages Act), which made French Quebec's official language, restricted the entry of immigrant children into English schools, and required firms holding government contracts to demonstrate that they encouraged the use of French in their operations.[25] After the nationalist Parti Québécois defeated the Quebec

Liberals and took office in 1976, they introduced a much stronger and more comprehensive language bill known as the Charter of the French Language, which became law in 1977.[26]

Quebec anglophones were indignant at both of these measures and responded variously by forming pressure groups, seeking redress through the courts, and leaving the province, which suffered a net loss of 100,000 anglophones between 1976 and 1981. An English-rights organization called Alliance Québec, mainly funded by the federal government, was formed in 1982 and existed for more than two decades, and the militant but short-lived Equality Party elected four anglophone members to the Quebec National Assembly in 1989. Most Quebec francophones welcomed the language laws, but the concerns that had led to their adoption did not entirely disappear, particularly since several provisions of the Charter of the French Language were struck down by the Supreme Court of Canada. The provisions for minority-language education rights in the Canadian Charter of Rights and Freedoms in fact clashed directly, and deliberately, with the provisions of the Charter of the French Language, which allowed an English education only for children whose parents had themselves received an English education in Quebec. Efforts by Quebec's government to restrict the plethora of English-language advertising on the streets of Montreal were also declared unconstitutional by the Supreme Court on the grounds that they interfered with freedom of expression.[27] The federal government's commitment to bilingualism was clearly a double-edged sword for Quebec francophones, who could never forget that their language was numerically weak in Canada and North America even if it was numerically strong in Quebec.

Language controversies in Quebec have been closely related to immigration, although not quite as closely as in the United States. In the rest of Canada, the link between language issues and immigration has been much weaker, although not entirely absent. In both parts of Canada, however, the history of controversy over language reveals that people are easily aroused by a perceived threat to the predominance of their own language where that predominance has previously been taken for granted. Whether the threat is real or only apparent and whether it comes primarily from compatriots or from recent immigrants is not always obvious but in any event makes little difference to the strength of the emotions aroused. An examination of the American response to the growing use of Spanish in the United States lends additional support to both of these generalizations.

The French language in Canada has been weakened by its isolation in the Western Hemisphere, where the remaining French possessions have a total population of less than a million. Haiti, with a population about equal to that of Quebec, has French as an official language, but the dialect spoken by most of its people is unintelligible to speakers of standard French. In contrast, the Spanish language in the United States benefits from the fact that Spanish is spoken by almost as many people in the Western Hemisphere as English is. Furthermore, Spanish-speaking America has in recent years been the most important source of immigration into the United States.

The history of the Spanish language in what is now the territory of the United States extends back even further than the history of the French language in Canada. Florida was first explored by the Spanish, who established the city of St Augustine there in 1565, and remained a Spanish possession until it was ceded to the United States in 1819. The states of Arizona, California, Colorado, Nevada, New Mexico, Texas, and Utah, together comprising more than a quarter of the land area of the United States, were originally part of Mexico, which was conquered by Spain in 1519–21 and became independent three centuries later. Santa Fe, the capital of New Mexico, was established as a Spanish settlement in 1608, the same year that Samuel de Champlain founded the city of Quebec.

English-speaking Americans began to settle in Texas after Mexico achieved its independence. Their resistance to Mexican rule led to the celebrated siege and capture of the Alamo and eventually to the secession of Texas, which became an independent English-speaking republic in 1836 and a state within the American federation nine years later. In 1846, the United States attacked Mexico, beginning a war that lasted for two years and resulted in about half of Mexico's remaining territory becoming part of the United States. However, the Mexican population of the ceded territory was only about 80,000 in 1848.[28] Mexico's total population was between six and seven million. The treaty of Guadeloupe Hidalgo, which ended the war and transferred control of the territory, promised the inhabitants a choice between American and Mexican citizenship. Those who chose to become Americans – the vast majority – were promised all the rights enjoyed by other Americans but were given no guarantees regarding their language.[29]

In 1854, some additional territory, known as the Gadsden Purchase, was acquired by another treaty with Mexico so as to facilitate the building of a railroad from New Orleans to the Pacific, a project that was not actually undertaken until after the Civil War. It now forms the southern part of Arizona and New Mexico. Most of the territory acquired from Mexico was organized fairly promptly into states of the union. Arizona and New Mexico, which were slow to establish English-speaking majorities, had to wait until 1912 and were the last of the contiguous 48 states to be established. New Mexico, which was about 40 per cent Spanish-speaking when it became a state, adopted a constitution that prohibited making knowledge of English a requirement for the franchise.[30] It continued to publish its statutes in both languages until 1949.[31] The percentage of New Mexico's residents who are Spanish-speaking and of Mexican ancestry has been fairly stable over a century of statehood. In contrast to other states with large Spanish-speaking populations, New Mexico's Spanish-speaking population is mainly descended from people who resided there before it became a state rather than from recent immigrants.

The brief and successful war with Spain in 1898 added the subtropical Caribbean island of Puerto Rico to the possessions of the United States. Unlike the territories acquired from Mexico, it was already densely populated and thus has remained almost entirely Spanish-speaking. For this reason, it has never been fully incorporated into the United States as either a state or a territory but has the unique status of a quasi-dependent "Commonwealth" with both Spanish and English as official languages. However, its residents are free to migrate to the United States whenever they wish to do so, and the number of Puerto Ricans residing in the United States (principally in New York) is more than half as large as the number who still live on the island. Since Puerto Rico is not foreign territory, they are not officially counted as immigrants.

The establishment of a boundary between Mexico and the southwestern United States did not end migration across the border, both legal and otherwise. However, it appears that the volume of migration was very low prior to 1900, when it is estimated that only 103,000 Mexican-born persons were residing permanently in the United States, or about 1 per cent of the total foreign-born population at that time.[32] In the following decade, Mexican immigrants represented only 0.6 per cent of new arrivals for a total of 49,642 persons. Between 1911 and 1920, Mexican immigration rose sharply to 210,004 over the entire decade, probably because World War I reduced immigration from Europe. Like other Western Hemisphere countries, Mexico was exempted from the national-origin quotas that were imposed on immigration from European countries after World War I, with the result that it provided nearly half a million immigrants between 1921 and 1930, or 11.2 per cent of total immigration.[33]

Over the next two decades, Mexican immigration was very small in volume, but it began to increase in 1943 when Congress introduced a program to admit large numbers of temporary workers in response to the wartime shortage of labour.[34] Some of these temporary workers decided to stay, and the program continued in existence until 1964, just prior to the major reform of US immigration policy described in the previous chapter of this book. From 1951 to 1960, Mexico accounted for 11.9 per cent of all immigrants, from 1961 to 1970 it provided 13.7 per cent of the total, and from 1971 to 1980 it provided 14.2 per cent. The decade from 1981 to 1990 was marked by an unprecedented level of Mexican immigration, with arrivals totaling 1,655,843, an increase of more than a million above the volume in the preceding decade. Mexican immigrants accounted for 22.6 per cent of all immigrants during those years.[35]

A smaller but still significant influx of Spanish-speaking people into the United States consisted of refugees from the Cuban revolution that brought Fidel Castro to power in 1959. Most of these refugees settled in Florida. In contrast to the typical Mexican immigrant, the Cubans tended to be persons of high socio-economic status and politically conservative, not surprisingly since they were fleeing from a left-wing revolution. It is largely because of their political influence that the United States has never normalized its relations with Cuba. In 1980, there was another influx of Cubans when the Castro regime allowed more than 100,000 of its people to immigrate to the United States. In contrast to those who arrived soon after the revolution, these Cubans tended to be of lower socio-economic status.

Between 1952 and 1980, US immigration law provided that only persons fleeing from communist regimes could be considered refugees. Nonetheless, about 400,000 persons fled from the Dominican Republic to the United States after the democratically elected president of that country was overthrown in 1963, only two years after the end of Rafael Trujillo's brutal dictatorship.[36] After the US Congress broadened the definition of a refugee in 1980, victims of civil wars and right-wing regimes in Central America began to arrive in the United States in large numbers. For example, the number of people from El Salvador living in the United States increased from 94,000 in 1980 to more than a million in 2000. The Reagan administration welcomed right-wing refugees from the Sandinista regime in Nicaragua but was suspicious of left-wing refugees from Guatemala and El Salvador and confined many of them in detention centres. Others found refuge in churches that were sympathetic to their cause.[37] The Dominican Republic has continued to be a major source of immigrants in recent years, although for economic rather than political reasons.

In response to all these demographic developments, the US census began to collect more data relating to language and ethnicity. Mother tongue, a category first used by the Canadian census in 1901, was introduced to the US census in 1960 and used again in 1970. Also in 1970, the term "Hispanic," divided into several sub-categories like Mexican, Puerto Rican, and so forth, was used for the first time in the United States census. Its precise official meaning has been redefined several times since it was introduced, but essentially it means someone whose ancestral origins are in a Spanish-speaking country. In 1980, the US census abandoned the mother tongue category and replaced it with language spoken at home, a category that Canada had introduced in 1971 following the adoption of the Official Languages Act. In 1980, the US census also introduced a general question on ethnic ancestry, which the Canadian census has always had except in 1891.[38] As noted in the next chapter, this innovation came largely in response to the growing popularity of ethnic labels among Americans of European descent.

Data from the Census Bureau come with the appropriate caveat that "Hispanic" persons may be of any race, but most Americans seem to ignore this. In the popular discourse of the American media and the general population, "Hispanics" are often treated as a mutually exclusive racial category analogous to European Americans, African Americans, or Asian Americans, even though they may be any of the above. After the 2000 census, it was announced that "Hispanics" had replaced African Americans as the largest "minority" in the United States. Despite this alleged revelation, "Hispanics" are a completely artificial category. They may or may not speak Spanish on an everyday basis or even at all. A middle-class Cuban refugee is probably of European ancestry, while an immigrant from the Dominican Republic or a Puerto Rican who moves to the mainland is almost certain to have African ancestors. Most Mexicans are of mixed ancestry, partly European and partly indigenous like the Métis of the Canadian prairies. Despite this fact, of which most

Mexicans are proud, Mexicans have been counted as "white" in the US census, except in 1930 when "Mexican" was considered, absurdly, to be a distinct race.[39] Few Americans of European ancestry, however, really regard Mexicans as "white."

In any event, all "Hispanics," whether they actually speak Spanish or not, are lumped together by the census, and in popular discourse, to form an essentially meaningless category. The term "Latino," which was more commonly used before "Hispanic" was invented by the Census Bureau, is still often used to describe athletes and entertainers but lacks official status. In contrast to "Hispanic," the term "Latino" includes Brazilians but excludes people from Spain. Neither term, incidentally, is popular with the people to whom it ostensibly refers, who quite sensibly prefer to be known as Cuban Americans, Mexican Americans, or whatever.[40]

Mexican Americans are by far the most important of the ethnic groups subsumed under the "Hispanic" label and the target for most of the hostility and anxiety that the growing "Hispanic" population has inspired. Since Mexico is by far the largest Spanish-speaking country in the world in population, this is not particularly surprising. According to the Census Bureau, slightly less than forty million foreign-born persons resided in the United States in 2010. Of these more than half had been born in Latin America or the Caribbean, and Mexico alone accounted for 11,711,000, or 29.3 per cent of the foreign-born population. More residents of the United States were born in Mexico than were born in all of Asia, and the Mexican-born constituted more than twice as many as the combined total of those who were born in Europe, Canada, Australia, or New Zealand.[41] In 1970, by way of contrast, there were only 759,000 Mexican-born persons in the United States.[42] In addition to those actually born in Mexico, millions of other Americans are of Mexican ancestry and are thus "Hispanics," whether they can speak Spanish or not.

The census data on language are also interesting, are probably more meaningful and accurate, and show a similar trend. In 1960, Spanish was estimated to be the mother tongue of 3,335,961 residents of the United States, about 10 per cent fewer than had Italian as their mother tongue and only slightly more than the number whose mother tongue was German. In 1970, Spanish was clearly in first place among non-English mother tongues, with a population of 7,823,583.[43] In 1980, the first census year in which the language spoken at home was enumerated, just over twenty-three million people spoke a language other than English at home, and the language spoken at home was Spanish in 11,116,194 of these cases, or almost half. The number speaking Spanish at home increased to more than seventeen million in 1990, more than twenty-eight million in 2000, and almost thirty-five million in 2007.[44] All of these data on language spoken at home exclude persons less than five years of age, unlike the data on mother tongue collected earlier. Since 1990, the total number speaking Spanish at home has exceeded the combined total for all other languages, apart from English. It is also significant that the number of persons speaking Spanish at home far exceeds the number born in a Spanish-speaking country, which indicates that to some degree at least the language is being passed on to the second generation.

Although people who speak Spanish at home are found in every state of the union, about two-thirds of them reside in the southwestern states that were previously part of Mexico. In 2010, people speaking Spanish at home comprised 43 per cent of the population in New Mexico, almost 35 per cent in both California and Texas (the two most populous states in the union), 28 per cent in Arizona, 19 per cent in Nevada, 12 per cent in Colorado, and almost 10 per cent in Utah. Other states with 10 per cent or more of their populations speaking Spanish at home are Florida, New York, New Jersey, Illinois, and Rhode Island.[45] In Florida, the Cubans are the largest Spanish-speaking group, while in New York and New Jersey that position is occupied by the Puerto Ricans. In all of the other states listed above, the Mexicans are the largest group and in most cases the overwhelming majority.[46]

As early as the 1960s, the growing presence of Spanish-speaking people in the United States began to have an impact on public policy. According to Juan Gonzalez, a historian and former Puerto Rican activist, John F. Kennedy was "the first US president to address the concerns of Latinos within the American family."[47] The Mexican-American vote was decisive in carrying Texas, New Mexico, and possibly Nevada for Kennedy in the close presidential election of 1960. Apart from Hawaii, those were the only states he won in the western half of the country. In 1965, an amendment to the Voting Rights Act sponsored by Senator Robert Kennedy provided that the right to vote was not dependent on knowledge of English, a provision of particular relevance in Puerto Rico.[48] Robert Kennedy also supported the efforts by Cesar Chavez to win collective bargaining rights for Mexican-American farmworkers in California. The

Mexican-American vote in that state was almost certainly decisive in enabling Robert Kennedy to win its presidential primary on 4 June 1968, the day of his assassination.

That same year, 1968, was also when President Lyndon Johnson signed the Bilingual Education Act, a measure introduced the previous year by Senator Ralph Yarborough of Texas. The purpose of the act was to improve the academic performance of school children with limited English-speaking ability (LESA) by providing federal funding for innovative programs to address their special needs in school districts with average incomes below the national average. Although few could argue with this objective, the title of the act, and some of the testimony of witnesses who lobbied in its favour, disturbed some Americans who saw it as part of a trend to downgrade the importance of English, a reaction not unlike the response of some Canadians to the Official Languages Act a year later.[49]

Children who spoke Spanish were the principal, but not the only, intended beneficiaries of the Bilingual Education Act. In 1974, the Supreme Court decided the case of *Lau v. Nichols* in which counsel for a group of Chinese-speaking children in the San Francisco public school system argued that the system was denying them the right to an adequate education and thus violating their rights under the Civil Rights Act of 1964.[50] The court ruled that since the state required students to master the English language, it was discriminating against the Chinese children by not giving them the means to do so. The effect, rather than the intent, must be used as the criterion to determine whether discrimination exists.

This judicial decision contributed in 1974 to major amendments to the Bilingual Education Act, some of which were sponsored by Democratic senators Edward Kennedy of Massachusetts and Alan Cranston of California, and to a considerable increase in the funding made available to implement it. An Office of Bilingual Education was established within the Department of Health, Education and Welfare, eligibility for funding was no longer restricted to low-income school districts, more reliance was placed on using the mother tongue of LESA students as a medium of instruction, and retention of the child's original language and culture was treated for the first time as a positive benefit in the legislation. To ensure that LESA children would still be integrated into American society, the amendments provided that they would be mingled with other children in art, music, and physical education classes, where language proficiency was not an issue, and that a limited number of non-LESA children would be included in the bilingual classes. Further amendments in 1978 required the teachers in bilingual programs to be bilingual themselves, emphasized the involvement of parents in the management of programs, and made limited ability to read and write English (and not merely to speak it) grounds for including a child in a bilingual program.[51]

The increasing numbers of children in bilingual education, as well as the fact that the census in 1980 for the first time collected data on the language spoken at home, led to growing anxiety about the future of English, particularly in the southwestern states that bordered on Mexico. This anxiety in turn led to the emergence of a movement to make English the official language of the United States, something that had not previously been considered necessary.

In August 1982, Republican Senator Samuel Hayakawa of California, who had been born in Canada to Japanese parents but confessed that he could not speak Japanese, introduced the idea in the form of an amendment to an immigration bill. Speaking in favour of his amendment, Hayakawa said that he had no desire to discourage Americans from learning other languages and in fact he regretted that so few anglophone Americans did so. Nor did he argue against immigration. However, he insisted that a common language was essential to create an integrated society, and he cited the example of other countries, such as Canada, that lacked this asset. The United States, he said "has been strengthened and unified because its newcomers have historically chosen ultimately to forego their native language for the English language." He added that "I am all in favour of bilingual education only insofar as it accelerates the learning of English." Hayakawa's amendment was carried on a roll call by a vote of 78 in favour and 21 against. Perhaps surprisingly, Democrats supported it by a much more overwhelming margin than did Republicans. In fact, only four Democrats, including both senators from Massachusetts, Edward Kennedy and Paul Tsongas, voted against it. California's other senator, Alan Cranston, voted against it, as did Barry Goldwater of Arizona, Gary Hart of Colorado, John Tower of Texas, and Pete Domenici and Harrison Schmitt of New Mexico. Apart from Cranston and Hart, all of these southwestern opponents of the amendment were Republicans.[52]

In the following year, Hayakawa was among the founders of an organization called US English, whose purpose was to make the

United States an officially unilingual nation. Given the extreme difficulty of amending the US Constitution, there was predictably no progress in that direction. However, state constitutions are much easier to amend, so US English concentrated its efforts at that level. California, the stronghold of direct democracy, entrenched English as the official language of the state in its constitution by a referendum in 1986.[53] Arizona, Colorado, and Florida amended their state constitutions to the same effect in 1988, as did Alabama in 1990.[54] The need for such an amendment in Alabama, one of the most unilingual states in the union, was not particularly obvious.

In Texas, the powerful Mexican-American caucus prevented the proposition from receiving the two-thirds majority in both houses of the legislature that was necessary to place it on the ballot. The most influential Texas politician at the time, Vice-President and later President George H.W. Bush, said that the amendment was unnecessary and also endorsed bilingual education. However, voters in the Texas Republican presidential primary of 1988, which Bush won, voted overwhelmingly in a non-binding referendum to make English the official language of both the state and the nation.[55] In New Mexico, with its bilingual tradition and more than two-fifths of its population Hispanic, a constitutional amendment does not seem to have been seriously considered. A number of other states adopted bills endorsing unilingualism but without entrenching the idea in their constitutions.

In response to the emergence of US English, an organization called English Plus was formed to promote the acceptance of other languages, although it acknowledged that English must remain the primary language. "English Plus" laws, although not constitutional amendments, were adopted in New Mexico, Oregon, Rhode Island, and Washington.[56] Hawaii, incidentally, is the only officially bilingual state, having made Hawaiian its second official language in 1978. Puerto Rico has had English and Spanish as its two official languages since it came under American control in 1898.

US English still exists but appears to have lost much of its prominence since the death of Samuel Hayakawa in 1992. In recent years, the controversy over bilingual education seems to have died down, or perhaps it would be more accurate to say that anxiety over the Mexican-American presence in the southwestern states has been deflected from concern about language to concern about immigration.

There is no doubt that the volume of immigration from Mexico in the past few decades has been very large, and much of it has been "illegal" or at least undocumented. In recent years, debates about immigration, its positive and negative consequences, and what should be done about it have tended to focus on Mexico almost exclusively. This is partly because Mexico is the largest single source of immigration, but it also reflects an anxiety that is primarily cultural rather than economic. Indeed, there is little evidence that Mexican immigrants have taken jobs from native-born Americans and much evidence to suggest that their presence has been good for the American economy.

In 1985, the Democratic governor of Colorado, Richard D. Lamm, co-authored a book entitled *The Immigration Time Bomb: The Fragmenting of America*. Seven years later, Peter Brimelow, a journalist and former Canadian, published *Alien Nation*, which predicted dire consequences if the flow of immigration was not reversed.[57] The conservative writer and former presidential advisor Patrick J. Buchanan sought the Republican presidential nomination on an anti-immigration platform in 1992 and ran as a third-party candidate for president in 2000. In a book published soon afterwards, Buchanan referred to the influx of Mexicans into the southwest as the "reconquista" and suggested that when Mexican immigrants and their descendants become a majority of California's population, it could be "America's Quebec," implying that it might attempt to secede from the United States and become part of Mexico.[58] Ironically, as Buchanan is well aware, this scenario would replicate, in reverse, the process by which Texas became part of the United States.

Public authorities have responded to such concerns in various ways. The Immigration Reform and Control Act of 1986 gave an amnesty to about three million illegal immigrants known to be in the country.[59] Two decades later, the number of "illegals" was estimated at twelve million. One motive for replacing the Canada–United States Free Trade Agreement with a North American Free Trade Agreement (NAFTA) including Mexico was to strengthen the Mexican economy, create well-paid jobs south of the border, and thus reduce the incentive to leave Mexico for the United States. In 1996, the Illegal Immigration Reform and Immigrant Responsibility Act made it easier to deport people in the country illegally and harder for such persons to be readmitted.[60] In 2006, Congress voted to construct a security fence along the border to reduce the number of illegal entries, although the surveillance and control of the border had already been greatly strengthened since the turn of the century. Presidents George W. Bush and Barack Obama, both of whom have moderate views on immigration, failed to persuade Congress to adopt measures of immigration reform. Several state governments have denied social benefits to undocumented immigrants or their children, and Arizona in 2010 adopted a controversial and possibly unconstitutional statute seeking to restrict and control the entry of illegal immigrants into the state.

Recent data suggest that immigration from Mexico to the United States has declined sharply in recent years and may currently be no greater than migration in the opposite direction. The Pew Research Center attributes this to various factors, including the poor performance of the United States economy, heightened enforcement of border controls, a rise in deportations, the dangers associated with illegal border crossings, and a decline in Mexico's birthrate.[61] Apparently, the Center does not regard NAFTA as a significant contributing factor. The decline in immigration, unless it is reversed, will increase the probability that Mexican-born persons already living in the United States will become fully integrated into American society. If the trend continues, the hostile response to Mexican immigration is likely to decline and eventually disappear, as hostility to Irish, Chinese, German, Japanese, Jewish, and other waves of immigration did in the past. Furthermore, increasing evidence that English is becoming the universal language of the world should drastically reduce the credibility of the notion that it is under threat in the United States.

In fairness to the American people, it must be said that the anxiety some of them felt and still feel about the future of the English language in their country was based on considerably more credible evidence than could be mustered by anglophone Canadians with similar concerns. The number and percentage of Spanish-speaking people and people of Mexican ancestry in the United States really did increase very dramatically over the past several decades, while the number and percentage of French-speaking people in Canada was actually declining during the same period. Mexico is a large, poor country with a rapidly increasing population that shares a long land border with the United States and has recently been the main source of immigration into that country. France is thousands of miles away from Canada and imports far more migrants than it exports, and its people, quite understandably, have little interest in emigrating to anywhere. "Hispanic" fertility rates in the United States are significantly higher than those of European Americans or African Americans, while the fertility rate of francophones in Quebec declined dramatically during the Quiet Revolution and is similar to those in other parts of Canada.

On the other hand, English-speaking Americans may have less reason to worry about the future of their language than do the French-speaking people of Quebec. It is the French language, not the English language, that must struggle to maintain a place for itself in North America, in the world, and perhaps even in Montreal, which proclaims itself to be the second-largest French-speaking city in the world.

Yet the responses of Americans and both English- and French-speaking Canadians to perceived threats to their respective languages have not been dissimilar. For most people, language is both a part of their identity and a necessary tool of communication, so real or perceived threats to it are likely to be taken seriously. Controversies over language, an old story in Canada and a relatively new one in the United States, have influenced and been influenced by experiences with immigration and by responses to the cultural diversity resulting from immigration. As the next chapter will show, official multiculturalism in Canada was to some extent a by-product of the efforts to manage the relationship between the two official languages. In both the United States and Quebec, on the other hand, the cool or even hostile response to the word "multiculturalism" was also related to linguistic controversies and concerns.

9

Multiculturalism: The Biography of an Idea

"Multiculturalism" is a term constantly used by Canadians, and the phrase "multicultural heritage of Canadians" has been entrenched in Canada's Constitution since 1982, but there is no consensus among either its supporters or its opponents about what "multiculturalism" actually means. It is not even clear whether the word is actually of Canadian origin, and it is certainly used nowadays in other countries, particularly in Australia, the United Kingdom, and the United States. However, it should not be assumed that its meaning in those countries is identical with its meaning, or meanings, in Canada.

Multiculturalism can be understood in at least three ways: as a sociological fact, as a policy or set of policies to which a government or governments are committed, and as a symbol. Of the many policies proclaimed and implemented by governments, only a few become symbols, but policies may become powerful symbols, particularly in countries where the more obvious sources of national cohesion and identity are weak or contested. Three policies that seem to have acquired symbolic status in Canada during the second half of the twentieth century are the single-payer system of health insurance, the practice of committing Canadian soldiers to peacekeeping operations under the auspices of intergovernmental organizations, and the subject of this chapter: multiculturalism.

As described in chapter 7, Canada after World War II experienced a major wave of immigration from Europe, rivalling that of the decade before World War I. At a time when American immigration law still maintained the national-origins quota system for countries outside the Western Hemisphere, it was easier for most Europeans to immigrate to Canada than to the United States. This time, Ontario, rather than the western provinces, received the largest share of the immigrants. While Great Britain remained the largest single source of "New Canadians," large numbers came from the Netherlands, western Germany, and Italy. There were also large numbers of refugees, expellees, and displaced persons from the lands that had been conquered or reconquered by Stalin's armies in the latter part of the war: ethnic Germans, Jews, Ukrainians, Estonians, Latvians, Czechs, Poles, and others. They were joined by many Hungarians after the suppression of the anti-communist rebellion in 1956. Aided by both immigration and the baby boom, Canada's population increased by 30 per cent during the 1950s despite a significant outflow to the United States. By the time of the 1961 census, fewer than 44 per cent of Canadians claimed to be of British or Irish ancestry, 30 per cent were French Canadians, and the rest were persons of various non-British and non-French origins. In the Prairie provinces, apart from the city of Calgary, the non-French ethnic minorities outnumbered persons of British or Irish ancestry. Particularly in those provinces, many of these people were now of the second or third generation and were becoming politically active and articulate. Some of the ethnic minorities and their organizations dating from earlier waves of immigration, such as the Germans, Jews, and Ukrainians, received significant reinforcements from immigrants who arrived in Canada after 1945.

The postwar years also saw cautious steps by the Liberal government to loosen Canada's close ties with the United Kingdom, although this was done more to placate the French Canadians, who formed the core of the Liberal Party's electoral base, than to impress the members of other ethnic groups. The Canadian Citizenship Act was adopted in 1946, judicial appeals to the Imperial Privy Council in London were abolished in 1949, a Canadian was appointed as governor general for the first time in 1952, and public ceremonies were as likely to include the singing of "O Canada" as that of "God Save the King." There were also serious efforts to end the British Parliament's role in amending Canada's Constitution, although this was not actually accomplished until 1982 because of the lack of consensus among the provincial governments. In one bizarre incident, the government apparently even vetoed a request by the Canadian Pacific to call a new Montreal-to-Vancouver passenger train The Royal Canadian. When the train began operating in 1955, it was simply called The Canadian, despite protests by the Progressive Conservative opposition in Parliament.[1] A more useful but even more controversial assertion of Canadian independence occurred the following year when the Liberal government refused to support the British attack on Egypt, which had been intended to regain control of the Suez Canal but ended with a humiliating retreat owing to the opposition of the United States. Prime Minister Louis St Laurent, the son of a French-Canadian father and an Irish-Catholic mother, asserted accurately that the era when "the supermen of Europe" could dominate the rest of the world was drawing to a close.[2]

It was in this period of social and political change, and amid somewhat less obvious developments in Quebec that foreshadowed the coming of the Quiet Revolution a few years later, that a new Progressive Conservative government headed by John Diefenbaker took office in 1957. The party (which added "Progressive" to its name in 1942 in an effort to appeal to prairie farmers) had been out of office since 1935, and Diefenbaker, an opposition member of Parliament since 1940, had never held office at all. Significantly for this narrative, he was the first prime minister to have grown up in western Canada and the first whose ethnic origin and family name were neither British, Irish, nor French. His role in the advent of Canada's official multiculturalism has rarely if ever been acknowledged, but I would argue that it was in fact decisive, albeit not entirely intentional.

Saskatchewan, where Diefenbaker grew up and spent most of his life, became a province when it absorbed the neighbouring territory of Assiniboia in 1905, two years after his family settled there and when Diefenbaker himself was nearly ten years of age. Two decades before that date, it had been home to only a few thousand people, mainly First Nations and French-speaking Métis. As a child, Diefenbaker met Gabriel Dumont, who had been the Métis guerilla commander in the doomed rebellion of 1885.[3] By the time Diefenbaker was in his late teens, Saskatchewan was the third largest province in population and the first in production of wheat, then Canada's principal export commodity. Its population was a mixture of British, French, German, Ukrainian, Russian, Scandinavian, and various other ethnic origins, with a significant number of its settlers having come from, or at least by way of, the United States. The percentage of the population that was neither British, Irish, nor French was the highest of any province and remained so at the time when Diefenbaker was prime minister.

Although his mother was of Scottish ancestry and his father's ancestors had left Germany in the eighteenth century, Diefenbaker

was sensitive about his German origins and especially resented anyone who pronounced the third syllable of his name in the German
manner with a short "a." (President Kennedy committed this faux pas
when he visited Ottawa in 1961, with lamentable consequences for
Canadian–American relations.)⁴ World War I, in which Diefenbaker
served as a Canadian soldier, produced a wave of Germanophobia on
the prairies, especially among the many British-born settlers, who
stood at the top of the social and economic hierarchy. Diefenbaker, a
lifelong monarchist, occasionally pointed out that the British royal
family was itself of German origin.

From his background Diefenbaker drew two conclusions that he
carried with him to the end of his life. First, there must be no invidious distinctions among Canadians based on ethnicity and no special
privileges for any group based on language, culture, or historical
origins. All Canadians should enjoy the same rights in "One Canada,"
a phrase of which Diefenbaker was so fond that he used it as the title
of his memoirs. Second, Canadians whose ethnic origins and cultures were neither British, Irish, nor French, particularly if they came
from western Canada, deserved more respect and social status, and
more political influence, than they had previously received.

There was a certain ambiguity to these ideas, which has persisted
in the Canadian discourse of multiculturalism. "One Canada" and
the aspiration to make everyone equal in rights and status were ideas
not far removed from the republican "melting pot" ideology that
had flourished in the United States during Diefenbaker's youth.
Diefenbaker himself was a fully assimilated ethnic; he spoke no
German and had no German tastes or values to set him apart from
his fellow Canadians. One of his most controversial ideas was to
allow people to designate their ethnic origin as "Canadian" in the
1961 census rather than specifying the ancestry of their immigrant
forebears. This proposal caused such consternation in Quebec,
where it was denounced by the Legislative Assembly, the cardinal
archbishop of Montreal, and many Conservative members of
Parliament, that Diefenbaker had to beat a hasty retreat at the last
moment, even though the census questionnaires had already been
printed.⁵ (In 1996, long after Diefenbaker's death, the census finally
allowed "Canadian" as an ethnic origin, and it proved to be a very
popular choice, especially in Quebec.)

On the other hand, Diefenbaker was nothing if not a monarchist, he
represented an ethnically diverse riding in Canada's most multicultural

province, and in his speeches he often urged ethnic groups to maintain their traditions and cultures, even though his father's family had failed to do so. More concretely, his own courting of ethnic groups and their leaders encouraged and stimulated the ethnic consciousness, especially among Canadians of eastern European ancestry, that paved the way for the emergence of official multiculturalism soon after he left office. Diefenbaker's comments in an interview broadcast on the international service of the CBC while he was prime minister express both of the multicultural themes, diversity and equal opportunity, that would later be adopted by the Liberals. Referring to postwar immigrants he asserted:

> Their coming has enriched the mosaic of Canada and I firmly believe that our strength is based partly on the great diversity of culture. Definitely we have a new blend of Canadianism ...
>
> In Canada we encourage the new citizens to be proud of their heritage and to as quickly as possible absorb themselves in the ways of this country ...
>
> In Canada's parliament we now have representatives of thirteen different ethnic groups, in addition to the British, Irish and French. This would not have been possible twenty-five years ago.[6]

The Progressive Conservative Party in Canada before Diefenbaker became its leader had been predominantly a party of British Protestants, with its strongest support in the Loyalist areas of Ontario and the Maritimes and on ultra-British Vancouver Island. Its Quebec wing, strong in the nineteenth century, had withered away after the Liberals began the practice of alternating between francophone and anglophone leaders and had virtually disappeared after a Conservative prime minister imposed conscription in 1917. The party had few ties to the immigrant communities, most of whose members had arrived in Canada when the Liberals were in office, since the brief intervals of Conservative government in the twentieth century had coincided with periods of war or depression. Its efforts to compensate for this fact by appealing to "New Canadians" had actually begun in 1953, three years before Diefenbaker became leader of the party, when Norman Dunn, a Toronto lawyer, was appointed without salary as a liaison between the party and ethnic minorities, a position he held until his resignation five years later. Dunn calculated that 101 of the 265 parliamentary constituencies were "ethnically sensitive."[7] The extent of his influence is unclear, and he is not even mentioned in John Meisel's academic study of the election that brought Diefenbaker to power.[8] However, it was a start.

Diefenbaker won a minority government in 1957 mainly by making gains in Ontario and the Maritimes, reducing the Liberals to a predominantly francophone party in the House of Commons. In the following year, he won an overwhelming majority of seats, including every constituency in the three Prairie provinces except one. The Conservatives elected to Parliament for the first time in 1957 or 1958 included persons with a variety of ethnic origins, in contrast to those elected in earlier years. Michael Starr, one of several Ukrainian Canadians in the caucus, became the first Ukrainian-Canadian cabinet minister in 1957 and served as minister of labour until Diefenbaker lost office in 1963. Douglas Jung, elected from Vancouver in 1957, was the first person of Asian ancestry ever elected to the Canadian House of Commons. Ed Nasserden, a Lebanese Canadian from Saskatchewan elected the following year, was the second. (At the end of the Diefenbaker era, Lincoln Alexander, also a Progressive Conservative and an ally of Diefenbaker in the party's internal conflicts, would become the first Canadian MP of African ancestry.

The expectations created by Diefenbaker's rise to power are suggested by a letter that a young Ukrainian-Canadian Conservative member of the Ontario legislature, John Yaremko, wrote to the prime minister in the summer of 1957: "Our party has had little contact with various ethnic groups until you, sir, have changed this and made our party a truly national party representing all Canadians equally. We must reach out our hands in welcome. Could there be a reception while the Queen is here so she could meet representative leaders of the ethnic groups? I write to you because I feel strongly about these matters. As perhaps the first 'ethnic' elected to a provincial legislature I represent the most cosmopolitan provincial riding in Canada."[9]

Yaremko, who later became a minister in the Ontario government, was not the first "ethnic" elected to a provincial legislature (his belief that he was indicates how little most Ontarians, then as now, knew about the western provinces), but his riding was certainly cosmopolitan. It had even been represented at Queen's Park by a communist for eight years until Yaremko won it from the incumbent during the Korean War.

One way in which a Canadian prime minister can demonstrate his interest in ethnic minorities is through appointments to the Senate.

Only one of St Laurent's forty-nine senatorial appointees was a person whose ethnic origin was neither British, Irish, nor French; David Croll, a Russian-born Jew from Ontario, was appointed to the upper house in 1955. Diefenbaker soon faced pressure to appoint Ukrainian, Polish, and Italian senators. A spokesman for the Italian Chamber of Commerce complained less than a year after Diefenbaker took office that the Progressive Conservatives were ignoring the contribution of Italian Canadians to Canada and asserted that since Italian Canadians were 3 per cent of the population, they deserved 3 per cent of the seats in both houses of Parliament. Four years later, the prime minister received a number of letters urging appointment of an Italian senator, including one from an Italian-Canadian Progressive Conservative M P, Quinto Martini, who modestly recommended himself for the appointment.[10] Early in 1962, Diefenbaker met with two representatives of the Canadian Polish Congress who urged him to appoint a Polish senator, but when the prime minister mentioned a possible appointee of Polish ancestry, they expressed disapproval on the grounds that the person was a Protestant.[11] Neither of the two alternatives they proposed was appointed.

In the end, Diefenbaker appointed only four senators (out of thirty-two appointments) from ethnic minority groups, all of them from the Prairie provinces. Gunnar Thorvaldson, an Icelandic Canadian from Manitoba, was appointed in 1958, as was James Gladstone, a member of the Blackfoot First Nation from Alberta. John Hnatyshyn, a Ukrainian Canadian from Saskatchewan and the father of future governor general Ramon Hnatyshyn, was appointed in 1959, followed by Paul Yuzyk, a Ukrainian Canadian from Manitoba, in 1963.[12]

Courting the foreign-language press, a significant factor in an era when electronic communication was still relatively new, was another way to make inroads into the ethnic communities. In December 1961, the government hosted a conference of ethnic editors in Ottawa that was attended by Diefenbaker himself, Governor General Georges Vanier, the minister of immigration, and the postmaster general, as well as sixty-nine of the editors. The purpose was said to be to encourage New Canadians to become citizens and to learn one of Canada's official languages. The ethnic newspapers themselves, apart from a few with a pro-communist orientation, provided enthusiastic and favourable coverage of this event. Comments in the mainstream English-language media, however, were somewhat hostile and sarcastic, and the pro-Liberal *Ottawa Citizen* accused the Progressive

Conservatives of trying to buy ethnic votes at the taxpayers' expense.[13] Diefenbaker sent a memo to his minister of citizenship and immigration, Ellen Fairclough, warning that there would be "trouble" (in Parliament, presumably) over this and asking her to find out exactly what the event had cost. She replied that it had cost the government $9,126.15, an amount that seems quaint given the levels of federal expenditures that became routine about a decade later, and that three similar but less conspicuous events had been subsidized, even more modestly, in the 1950s, two of them by the previous Liberal government.[14]

Another symbolic initiative by Diefenbaker's government that appealed to ethnic minorities was his cherished Canadian Bill of Rights, a brief statute adopted by Parliament in 1960. Although it was not entrenched in the Constitution and therefore had very limited effect, it "recognized and declared that in Canada there have existed" certain enumerated rights "without discrimination by reason of race, colour, religion or sex." Diefenbaker often referred to the Bill of Rights in his communications with ethnic groups and devoted considerable space to it in his memoirs, although he personally regretted that provincial misgivings had made it impossible to entrench it in the British North America Act.

Diefenbaker's greatest success in attracting ethnic voters to his party was with those whose origins were in eastern Europe, who responded well to both his enthusiasm for the Canadian mosaic and his anti-communism. Even here there were occasional pitfalls, as when the spokesman for a Serbian-Canadian group complained to the prime minister that a Conservative member of parliament had sent greetings to Croatian Canadians on the anniversary of the independence that Croatia had briefly enjoyed under German protection during the Second World War.[15] There were also small pro-communist factions in most of the east European ethnic communities, and they were naturally not receptive to Diefenbaker's message.

By far the most important of the eastern European groups were the Ukrainians, who at that time were Canada's sixth largest ethnic group after the English, French, Scottish, Irish, and Germans. Some of their early history in Canada was described in chapter 6 of this book. The largest and most influential portion of the Ukrainian-Canadian community was located in Diefenbaker's region of the country, the parkland area of the Prairie provinces that stretches from Winnipeg through Saskatoon to Edmonton, north of the main line of the

Canadian National Railways. In September 1957, the Progressive Conservative premier of Manitoba, Duff Roblin, urged Diefenbaker to make contact with Monsignor Basil Kushnir of the Ukrainian Catholic Church, a Progressive Conservative partisan who had just been elected president of the Canadian Ukrainian Committee.[16] The Conservatives swept the prairies in the following year, transforming a region where they had been in fourth place as recently as 1953 into their strongest bastion. Kushnir met the prime minister after the 1958 election and urged him to stress the identity of ethnic groups in the Canadian mosaic rather than the doctrine of the "melting pot."[17] Another Ukrainian cleric, Bishop Roborecki of Saskatchewan, wrote to Diefenbaker in 1961 offering to help the party in the next election.[18] Under Diefenbaker's leadership, the Conservatives held their prairie fortress in the elections of 1962, 1963, and 1965, which were disastrous for them in the rest of the country.

In July 1962, Monsignor Kushnir, who had been recently elected to another term as president of the Canadian Ukrainian Committee, presented Diefenbaker with the Shevchenko medal, named for Ukraine's greatest poet, at a Ukrainian Canadian Congress in Winnipeg. Diefenbaker replied with a speech in which he praised the Ukrainian "race" (sic) for its contributions to Canada, recalled his own contacts with Ukrainians while growing up in Saskatchewan, and called for "a Canada in which all of the races of man are welcome – to be a Canadian regardless of racial origin."[19]

Diefenbaker's rapport with Ukrainian Canadians, and with Canadians of eastern European origin more generally, was reinforced by his oft-expressed hostility to communism. There is no reason to doubt his sincerity in this regard, but it certainly assisted his goal of broadening the Progressive Conservative Party's electoral base, and it must be noted that he was always more hostile to the Soviet Union and other European communist regimes than he was to the regimes in China and Cuba. His concern with the ethnic vote also influenced Canadian foreign policy, as when he tried to cancel a visit to Ottawa by Yugoslavia's foreign minister and then offended the foreign minister by meeting him for only a few minutes.[20]

On 26 September 1960, Diefenbaker delivered a speech at the United Nations in which he denounced the Soviet domination of eastern Europe and challenged Moscow to allow free elections in Ukraine and other areas within its sphere of influence. For the remainder of his time in office, the prime minister referred repeatedly to this speech, sometimes even claiming, erroneously, that the celebrated incident in which Nikita Khrushchev pounded the United Nations podium with his shoe had been a response to Diefenbaker's remarks. (Khrushchev was not actually present for Diefenbaker's speech, and the shoe incident was more than two weeks later.[21]) Basil Robinson, who served as Diefenbaker's liaison with the Department of External Affairs, wrote in his memoirs that Diefenbaker's insistence on keeping the "captive nations" issue alive was the main source of friction between the prime minister and the department.[22] With hindsight, of course, it must be admitted that Diefenbaker was right about the moral bankruptcy of the eastern European regimes and that the bureaucrats were wrong.

The return of the Liberals to office in April 1963, and their emphasis on bilingualism and official languages as described in the preceding chapter, caused some anxiety among ethnic communities, particularly in the three Prairie provinces where only three Liberals had been elected to the House of Commons. In contrast to Liberal emphasis on the British and French as Canada's two founding peoples, a different concept of Canada, that of the multicultural mosaic, had gained popularity during the Diefenbaker years, especially among Canadians of eastern European ancestry and among those who lived in the western provinces.

As early as 1958, W.S. Kochan, executive director of the Ukrainian Canadian Committee, and Monsignor Basil Kushnir, its president, discussed a list of the committee's demands with Michael Starr, the Ukrainian-Canadian minister of labour. Along with recommendations about foreign policy, immigration, the ethnic question in the census, and the international service of the CBC, the committee maintained that the Canadian Constitution should be amended not only to include a bill of rights but "to guarantee the right of the ethnic cultural identity."[23] In March 1962, the Canadian Ethnic Press Federation, meeting for its biennial convention in Winnipeg, discussed the question "Canada is bilingual, but does that necessarily mean that Canada is bi-cultural? Is Canada multi-cultural?"[24] On 24 January 1963, the same organization sent a letter to the leaders of all four federal political parties urging recognition of the "ethnic fact" and opposing the notion of a bicultural Canada.[25]

The word "multiculturalism," without the hyphen, and the idea that Canadians should cherish it as an important and meaningful distinction between Canada and the United States apparently appeared for the first time in a speech delivered to the Canadian Council of Christians and Jews in Winnipeg in 1963. Ironically, the speaker was an American sociologist from the University of California, Dr Charles Hobart, who subsequently taught at the University of Alberta. Hobart's remarks in Winnipeg were quoted approvingly by Senator Paul Yuzyk, the last of Diefenbaker's "ethnic" appointments to the upper house, in his maiden speech on 3 March 1964. Largely although not entirely because of this speech, Yuzyk is sometimes called "the father of multiculturalism." In his speech he discussed the "third element" and noted that it comprised 26 per cent of Canada's population, an estimate he raised to "almost one-third" in a later part of the same speech. He discussed the Ukrainian contribution to Canada at some length and rejected the notion of a bicultural Canada: "In reality Canada never was bicultural; the Indians and Eskimos have been with us throughout our history; the British group itself is multicultural – English, Scots, Irish, Welsh; and with the settling of the other ethnic groups, which now make up almost one-third of the population, Canada has become multicultural in fact. Furthermore, the projecting of the idea that Canada is bicultural not only excludes the non-British and non-French groups, but denies the multicultural character of the British group, which can only lead to disunity."[26]

Yuzyk called for more appointments of "third element" Canadians to prominent positions, denounced a Liberal minister from Quebec for saying that the speakership of the House of Commons should alternate between British and French Canadians, and described the CBC (a perennial target for abuse by Canadian conservatives) as "the worst offender" in denying Canada's multicultural reality. He also criticized the Royal Commission on Bilingualism and Biculturalism, although he conceded that it had recognized the existence of ethnic groups other than British or French to a limited extent. Interestingly, Yuzyk declared near the end of his speech that "Fundamentally, we are a Christian and democratic nation," a statement that would be considered politically incorrect by proponents of multiculturalism two decades later.

At the time of Yuzyk's speech, the royal commission, as discussed in the previous chapter, was beginning its operations, which would continue over the next five years. The order-in-council setting out its terms of reference referred to "an equal partnership between the two founding races [sic], taking into account the contribution made by the other ethnic groups to the cultural enrichment of Canada and the measures that should be taken to safeguard that contribution."[27] The emphasis, however, was clearly on bilingualism. The Liberal government had apparently recognized Canadians of eastern European ancestry as a potential source of criticism and unhappiness by appointing two of them, one Ukrainian and one Polish, as commissioners. The Italian and Jewish ethnic groups, which were much more inclined to vote for the Liberals, were not represented. In December 1963, the royal commission released a working paper for the use of those preparing briefs. It again referred to "the partnership of the two founding races" as the "mainspring" (a rather odd translation of *idée-force*) of its mandate but noted that "this mainspring is working in a situation where there is the fact of multiculturalism," possibly the first use of this word in a government document.[28] It rejected what it called two extreme positions: that cultures other than English or French should be forgotten or suppressed and that they should receive official recognition.

Between March and June 1964, the royal commission held public hearings in twenty-three cities from coast to coast. In the preliminary report it issued in the following year, the royal commission observed that "people of Ukrainian origin" were overrepresented among those who appeared at the hearings while German Canadians, for example, were under-represented.[29] It also noted the complaints it heard from members of "other ethnic groups," especially in western Canada, that bilingualism and biculturalism would reduce them to the status of "second-class citizens." The expression "New Canadians," which was still widely used in 1964, was apparently not popular with those to whom it ostensibly referred. Furthermore, there was opposition to the bicultural image of Canada: "What image of Canada would do justice to the presence of these varied ethnic groups? This question preoccupied western participants especially, and the answer they often gave was 'multiculturalism,' or, more elaborately, 'the Canadian mosaic.' They asked: If two cultures are accepted, why not many? Why should Canada not be a country in which a multitude of cultural groups live side by side yet distinct from one another, all contributing to a richly varied society? Certainly, it was stated, the mosaic idea was infinitely preferable to the 'melting pot.'"[30]

Beyond these generalities, however, the royal commission found little consensus about what "multiculturalism" and the "mosaic" really meant or how they could or should be put into practice. Moreover, it appeared that the "other ethnic groups," by their own admission, had nothing in common with one another apart from the fact that they were neither British nor French and therefore the idea of a "third force" was unrealistic. Furthermore, many Canadians outside of Quebec disliked the whole idea and favoured "One Canada" with a high degree of assimilation for everyone, French Canadians included. Especially in the western provinces, however, criticism continued, such as this comment in 1965 by William Skoreyko, a Progressive Conservative MP of Ukrainian ancestry from Alberta:

> up to this time that Commission has confined its studies to how English and French speaking Canadians fit into the Canadian way of life.
>
> No one seems to be particularly concerned about the other one third of the population of this country comprising the other ethnic groups. I am not going to dwell on the B and B Commission at any length, but I say to you, Mr Speaker, that any massive concession by any government to any minority group in Canada would just be the beginning of many problems ... I do not think that you can build a united Canada by recognizing one or two races as the only races in this country. They must all be recognized as they have been in the past.[31]

At some point, probably following the unexpected death of co-chairman André Laurendeau on 1 June 1968, the royal commission decided that a fourth and final volume of its report, dedicated to *The Cultural Contribution of the Other Ethnic Groups*, had become politically essential. Released on 23 October 1969, this final volume lacked the scholarly depth of the earlier volumes and showed every sign of being an afterthought. Significantly, only one out of the nineteen research monographs published by the royal commission, and fourteen of the 137 that were not deemed to deserve publication, were devoted to the "other ethnic groups" in Canada. The one that was published dealt with the Italians of Montreal. A study of the Italians of Edmonton by Charles Hobart, whose speech to the Canadian Council of Christians and Jews had introduced the word "multiculturalism" to Canada's public discourse, was among those that were not published.[32] The fourth volume itself skated lightly over an admittedly vast topic, suggesting that an ethnic group was best understood as consisting of those who consciously felt that they belonged to it, and cautioned, as well it might, that the ethnic data in the Canadian census were of little value in determining the size of ethnic groups thus defined. It asserted that the largest ethnic groups in Canada were the British (not precisely defined) and the French. Its recommendations dealt mainly with culture in the narrow sense of the term and with federal cultural agencies such as the C B C and the National Film Board.[33]

By 1971, the royal commission had ended its work, and many of its recommendations to promote the use of French were on the way to being implemented. The fourth and final volume, however, lingered on as an embarrassing reminder, like Banquo's ghost. Prime Minister Trudeau apparently hoped that at least a symbolic recognition of the multicultural mosaic would soften opposition to bilingualism in the western provinces, where the Liberals were highly unpopular. So in September 1971, the prime minister's close friend and colleague Gérard Pelletier, the minister responsible for the federal government's cultural agencies and policies, and Martin O'Connell, the minister without portfolio responsible for citizenship, brought to cabinet a proposal for "a policy of multiculturalism in response to the spirit and recommendations of Book IV of the B & B Commission." The proposal was considered on 20 September by the Cabinet Committee on Science, Culture and Information, which approved it but recommended that it should be considered by the whole cabinet, given its implications for "the government's overall approach to the fundamental questions of national sovereignty and national unity."[34] Three days later, the full cabinet also gave its approval after a discussion in which several ministers "stressed that any policy of multiculturalism should be set firmly within a Canadian context." Trudeau and a number of other ministers said that more emphasis should be placed on self-help by ethnic groups. The prime minister also stressed that the government was not committed to achieving economic equality for all ethnic groups but rather that it hoped to achieve some degree of cultural equality.[35]

In its decision, the cabinet agreed that its policy on multiculturalism should be based on the following four principles:

(i)   the government of Canada will support all of Canada's cultures, and will seek to assist, resources permitting, the development of those cultural groups which have demonstrated a desire and effort to continue to develop, a capacity to grow and contribute to Canada, as well as a clear need for assistance

(ii) the government will assist members of all cultural groups to overcome cultural barriers to full participation in Canadian society
(iii) the government will promote creative encounters and interchange among all Canadian cultural groups in the interest of national unity
(iv) the government will continue to assist immigrants to acquire at least one of Canada's official languages in order to become full participants in Canadian society.[36]

Read carefully, the first principle placed four limitations on the government's commitment to assist ethnic groups in maintaining their cultures. The other three principles contained nothing that any reasonable person could object to. The remainder of the memo recording the cabinet's decision included details of how various government agencies might help to implement the policy. It also recommended that the criteria in the first principle should be made more specific if government expenditure was involved and that any applications to establish radio or television stations broadcasting exclusively in non-official languages should be treated with "extreme caution."

It remained for the prime minister to announce the policy in Parliament, which he did on Friday, 8 October 1971.[37] The date was not accidental, because Trudeau was scheduled to address a Ukrainian Canadian Congress in Winnipeg the following day. Significantly, most of his address to Parliament was delivered in English; the few token paragraphs in French dealt with the details of implementation and the necessity of respecting provincial jurisdiction. The key phrase in Trudeau's parliamentary speech was "multiculturalism within a bilingual framework." This expression was designed to reassure francophones that bilingualism was not in danger while offering enough symbolic recognition to satisfy other ethnic minorities, but it did not really succeed in either objective. Trudeau also anticipated criticism of "multiculturalism" that would be heard increasingly in the years to come when he insisted that adherence to an ethnic group should be considered voluntary and subjective, that the purpose of the policy was to increase freedom of choice, and that "The individual's freedom would be hampered if he were locked for life within a particular cultural compartment by the accident of birth or language." While reassuring to anglophone supporters of "One Canada," this explanation involved dangers in Quebec, as Trudeau presumably knew. The expression "freedom of choice" was anathema to Quebec nationalists, because it was used as a slogan by those who wanted unrestricted access to English-language education in the province.

Reaction to the new policy, if such it was, was initially rather subdued. The leaders of all three opposition parties followed Trudeau's speech with brief statements endorsing it in principle. The coverage of the speech in the *Globe and Mail* the following morning consisted of one sentence on page 7, buried in a column of excerpts from the previous day's House of Commons proceedings. Soon after the 1972 election, Stanley Haidasz of Toronto, one of the few Liberal MPs of eastern European ancestry, was appointed as the first minister of state for multiculturalism. An Advisory Council on Multiculturalism was established in 1973.

Professor Manoly Lupul of the University of Alberta, a prominent Ukrainian-Canadian activist who served on this body from that point until 1980, later wrote that Trudeau had never been seriously committed to multiculturalism.[38] Some credibility is given to this assertion by the fact that in 1969, Trudeau's government had proposed in a White Paper to terminate the special status of Aboriginal (First Nations) peoples so as to facilitate their assimilation into Canadian society.[39] The proposal was withdrawn after it met with almost universal hostility from Aboriginal Canadians.

Whatever the prime minister's views may have been, multiculturalism became a symbol cherished by many Canadians. In 1982, the concept was entrenched in section 27 of the Canadian Charter of Rights and Freedoms, although this was a last-minute response to the requests of ethnic groups that appeared before a parliamentary committee, not a part of the Trudeau government's original plan for constitutional reform. Trudeau's memoirs, published in 1993, did not mention multiculturalism at all, although they devoted ten pages to the Official Languages Act.

Following the federal government's example, most of the anglophone provinces adopted multiculturalism policies of their own. Saskatchewan was the first to adopt a multiculturalism act, in 1974. Ontario, whose premier John Robarts had stated in 1968 that he accepted bilingualism but rejected biculturalism,[40] proclaimed its own policy of multiculturalism in 1977, followed by a statute in 1982. Similar initiatives came from Manitoba and Alberta in 1984,

New Brunswick (the only officially bilingual province) in 1986, Prince Edward Island in 1988, Nova Scotia in 1989, and British Columbia in 1993.

A federal multiculturalism statute had been anticipated but had not yet been adopted by Parliament when the Liberals lost office in 1984. However, Brian Mulroney's Progressive Conservative government was no less committed than the Liberals to making gestures to ethnic groups. To impress Jewish voters, it conferred "honorary citizenship" on the late Raoul Wallenberg, a Swedish diplomat who had saved several thousand Jews from the Nazis and later died in a Soviet prison. As noted in chapter 6 of this book, Mulroney also apologized to the Italian-Canadian community for the internment of fascist sympathizers, mainly in Montreal, during World War II. An act for the preservation and enhancement of multiculturalism in Canada was duly adopted by Parliament in 1988.[41] However, its terms reflected a subtle shift since 1971 in the meaning of the expression. Immigration from Europe had long since tapered off, and most immigrants were now coming from Asia or the Caribbean. The absurd expression "visible minority," which would later be condemned as racist by the United Nations Committee on the Elimination of Racial Discrimination, entered the official Canadian lexicon during the Mulroney era. The focus of multiculturalism shifted, appropriately, from preserving languages and cultures to protecting the new arrivals from racism and ensuring their access to employment.

It was around this time, paradoxically, that opposition to official multiculturalism as it had been defined in the Trudeau era began to be openly expressed, although it remained weak by American standards and never attained real political significance. Some of it came from the very people to whom the policy was supposed to appeal. Two months after the multiculturalism statute received royal assent, Laura Sabia, a Progressive Conservative activist whose parents had been Italian immigrants, accused the government of patronizing ethnic Canadians and "fostering second-class citizenship." She wrote that she did not want to be a hyphenated Canadian and called multiculturalism "a load of garbage."[42] John Nunziata and Maurizio Bevilacqua, two Italian-Canadian Liberal members of Parliament, also attacked the concept of multiculturalism, which Nunziata said was "insulting."[43] Well-known journalists like Jeffrey Simpson, Andrew Coyne, Richard Gwyn, and Robert Fulford joined the chorus over the next few years, as did the former commissioner of official languages, Keith Spicer. The Reform Party, which arose in Alberta in the late 1980s and became the main alternative to the federal Liberals after the implosion of the Progressive Conservatives in 1993, demanded the abolition of official multiculturalism in its program.

In 1994, Neil Bissoondath, a distinguished Canadian novelist who had emigrated from Trinidad (and a nephew of the world-renowned novelist V.S. Naipaul) published a full-length book in which he approvingly quoted Laura Sabia's views on multiculturalism and argued that "personal culture and ethnicity" should be considered a private matter and not a subject of public policy. He also warned that Canada had discarded its past and that "multiculturalism," a concept that implied that Canada had no culture of its own, failed to fill the resulting void.[44] However, a poll conducted for the federal government in 1991 indicated that 61 per cent of Canadians supported multiculturalism and only 24 per cent were opposed.[45]

Stephen Harper, who became prime minister after defeating the Liberals in the general election of 2006, had begun his political career in the Reform Party, which opposed official multiculturalism. However, Harper abandoned most of that party's distinctive policies in the course of merging it with the Progressive Conservatives to form a new and inclusive Conservative Party. The Harper government, and particularly its energetic minister of citizenship, immigration, and multiculturalism, Jason Kenney, has been at least as enthusiastic about multiculturalism as the Liberals, if not more so. Although occasional grumbling is still heard in the media, there is no longer any politically significant opposition to the word in anglophone Canada.

The response to official multiculturalism in Quebec has been entirely different, understandably so since the word first became prominent as an expression of opposition to biculturalism and to the cherished concept of Canada as a partnership of "two founding races." The day before his parliamentary speech introducing the multiculturalism policy, Prime Minister Trudeau sent a letter announcing the policy to Premier Robert Bourassa. The premier's reply, sent more than a month later, indicated "serious reservations" about the new policy, which he said "clearly contradicted" the mandate of the royal commission. Bourassa also noted that the federal policy statement seemed to disassociate language and culture, which he considered questionable. He went on to suggest that if the federal government assumed responsibility for all of the cultures in Canada, Quebec must assume the primary responsibility on its territory for the permanence of the French language and culture. Nonetheless, he pointed out that Quebec was already subsidizing various ethnic groups through programs analogous to those envisaged in Trudeau's policy statement.[46]

Bourassa's comment about Quebec's primary responsibility for the French language perhaps foreshadowed the Official Language Act introduced and adopted by his government in 1974, as well as the more comprehensive Charter of the French Language adopted by René Lévesque's government in 1977. At the same time, both Quebec governments, as Bourassa had pointed out in his letter to Trudeau, pursued policies toward the province's various ethnic and immigrant minorities that were not very different in substance from the federal policy of multiculturalism. Quebec was at this time making the gradual transition from French-Canadian ethnic nationalism, based on *la survivance* of a beleaguered ethnic minority lacking a strong state of its own, to a more inclusive civic nationalism similar to the nationalism of Canada or the United States. Ethnic minorities, including Canadians of British ancestry, had always formed a large part of the Quebec Liberal Party's clientele and did so to an even greater extent after the emergence of the sovereignty movement, but the Parti Québécois, after taking office in 1976, made serious efforts to gain their support also.

Quebec also began actively to seek immigrants, since the sharp decline in its birthrate during the 1960s made this the only alternative to accepting a rapid decline in its share of Canada's total population. Beginning in 1971, a series of agreements with the federal government, based on the fact that immigration was a concurrent jurisdiction under Canada's Constitution, enabled the province to select its own immigrants and to take responsibility for welcoming and integrating them into Quebec society. This was in sharp contrast with the situation in previous years when Quebec governments had deplored immigration, or at least ignored it, and when the hostile attitude of old-fashioned French-Canadian nationalists toward immigrants had virtually driven the latter into the arms of Quebec's anglophone minority, whatever their original language or ethnicity might be.

While the Bourassa government's policy toward minorities had been ad hoc and largely based on the Quebec Liberal Party's traditional contacts with established ethnic groups like the Jews, Greeks, and Italians, the Lévesque government adopted a more systematic approach. In a White Paper entitled *Autant de façons d'être québécois*, the government outlined in 1981 a policy which it called "interculturalism," the essence of which was that immigrants and minorities were welcome in Quebec and were free to retain their own cultures and languages, provided they accepted the fact that French was the public (and, since 1974, the official) language of Quebec.[47] It also renamed Quebec's ministry of immigration, which became the ministry of "immigration and cultural communities." Quebec's anglophones, still regarded as enjoying disproportionate power and influence because of their links with the anglophone majority in Canada, were not considered a "cultural community" *comme les autres*, although ironically the White Paper had been written by a British immigrant named David Payne, who was subsequently elected to the National Assembly in a mainly francophone riding.

Quebec insisted, then and ever since, that its "interculturalism" was entirely different from the federal government's "multiculturalism." The main argument used against the latter was that it allegedly treated the French culture as merely one among many rather than acknowledging its traditional status as the culture of one of the two founding peoples of Canada. As Bourassa had suggested in his letter to Trudeau, this seemed to make it more imperative for Quebec to give priority to the French language and culture, which its policy of "interculturalism" explicitly did. A more recent concern, which will be discussed in chapter 10 of this book, is that section 27 of the Canadian Charter of Right and Freedoms may prevent Quebec from implementing the French republican model of *laïcité*, a model that has gained popularity in Quebec since the report of the Bouchard–Taylor Commission.[48]

Given Trudeau's well-known hostility toward Quebec's neo-nationalism, both before and after he became a federal politician, it was easy for Quebec nationalists to suspect him of harbouring nefarious designs, of which the multiculturalism policy was presumably a part. This was particularly so after he patriated and amended the Canadian Constitution without the Quebec government's consent, an event that followed a few months after the release of *Autant de façons d'être québécois*. The fact that section 27 was part of the much-resented patriation package helped to tar it with the same brush and ensured that multiculturalism would never enjoy legitimacy in Quebec, at least in nationalist circles.

Quebec also argues, as do many anglophone Canadian opponents of multiculturalism, that multiculturalism divides and isolates people while interculturalism promotes their integration into the host society. Yet in spite of this alleged contrast, the similarities between Quebec's "interculturalism" and Canada's "multiculturalism" seem in practice to outweigh the differences. Both Quebec and Canada welcome immigrants with no distinctions based on race, colour, or creed. Both try to integrate the new arrivals into the host society as smoothly as possible, but both permit immigrants to retain their original cultures to the degree that this is feasible – indeed, it is hard to see how they could do otherwise. Both patronize and subsidize ethnic associations. In both Quebec and anglophone Canada, the children of immigrants are educated in the language of the majority: French in Quebec and English elsewhere. In both societies, it can be predicted that most cultural distinctions will disappear after two or three generations, although by that time a fresh supply of immigrants, possibly from different sources, will have replaced those who came earlier. And, as will be argued below, neither Quebec nor anglophone Canada is really very different from the United States in this regard.

Quebec rejects the word "multiculturalism" for historical reasons, but its practices are not much different in substance from those elsewhere in Canada. What makes Quebec appear different from anglophone Canada or the United States is that the requirement to adopt French as one's new "public" language and to educate one's children in that language is made explicit in Quebec, while elsewhere the adoption of English can simply be taken for granted. This difference, which continues to offend some anglophones both within Quebec and elsewhere in Canada, is really a consequence of the numerical weakness of francophones in North America. It is not unreasonable that Quebec should expect immigrants to adopt Quebec's majority language in the same way that immigrants to anglophone Canada or the United States adopt English, but Quebec's circumstances oblige it to use a measure of compulsion to achieve a result that in other places occurs naturally. Quebec's policy of making the rules explicit is more honest than the attempt in anglophone Canada to pretend that there are no rules at all, for Canada's attachment to the word "multiculturalism" conceals more than it reveals. If anyone truly expects to survive in Toronto or Vancouver without learning English or adapting to the North American lifestyle, he or she is certain to be disillusioned.

The United States, like Quebec, has been leery of the word multiculturalism because of the circumstances in which it was brought to the public's attention but has not, in recent years at least, differed greatly from anglophone Canada in practice. As has been noted in previous chapters of this book, the American "melting pot" was an idea developed only at the beginning of the twentieth century and one that has declined in popularity in recent decades. In the nineteenth century, twenty-two American states, or about half of those then in existence, allowed aliens who had not yet been naturalized to vote. German remained a living language in the midwestern states until World War I. In the Union army during the Civil War, many units recruited soldiers exclusively from specific ethnic groups, particularly Irish or German. The same practice reappeared in World War II with the formation of the 442nd Regimental Combat Team of Japanese Americans, as noted in chapter 6. The ideas of Horace Kallen and Randolph Bourne, discussed in chapter 7, were clearly precursors of the Canadian idea of multiculturalism and even preceded the invention of the Canadian "mosaic." While few Americans living today have ever heard of Kallen or Bourne, their ideas would be much less controversial nowadays than they were at the time they were written. More often than not, the United States has tacitly accepted a level of ethnic diversity that few other modern nations have approached.

Admittedly, American acceptance of diversity has its limits, particularly when diversity seems to threaten core principles of the American ideology. Perhaps the most striking contrast between Canada and the United States in their approaches to diversity has been Canada's much greater acceptance of Catholicism.[49] This is not to say that anti-Catholic movements or sentiments have been absent from Canada, but the wise decision of the British authorities to reach an accommodation with what was then the dominant religious organization in their new colony, a decision that led to the Quebec Act of 1774, has had a lasting influence. For example, tax-supported systems of Catholic "separate" schools, which would be unthinkable in the United States, have existed in every province except Nova Scotia and British Columbia and still exist today in Ontario, Saskatchewan, and Alberta. In Ontario at least, they are explicitly guaranteed by the Constitution.

Nine of Canada's twenty-two prime ministers, beginning with John Thompson in 1892, have been Catholics, only four of whom were francophones. Seven of the eleven governors general since 1952, when Canadians began to be appointed to this office, have also been Catholics. The United States has had only one Catholic president, John F. Kennedy, and besides Kennedy, only two Catholics, Al Smith and John Kerry, have ever been chosen as the presidential

candidate of a major party. Smith's religion doomed him to overwhelming defeat in the election of 1928. Kennedy was elected by a
very narrow margin in 1960 and only after he confronted "the religious issue" by delivering a thoughtful address on the separation of
church and state to an audience of Protestant clergy.[50]

This contrast between Canada and the United States reflects the
ideological, rather than ethnic, nature of American nationalism and
the roots of American political thought in the religious controversies
of seventeenth-century England. The Dutch ancestry of Van Buren
and the two Roosevelts and the German ancestry of Hoover and
Eisenhower were not issues when they were elected president, nor
was the Jewish ancestry of Joe Lieberman, the Democratic candidate
for vice-president in 2000 and an aspirant for the presidential nomination in 2004. Barack Obama's successful candidacy in 2008 was
controversial not so much because of the colour of his skin as because
of false allegations that he had not been born in the United States
and was therefore not a "natural-born citizen" as the Constitution
requires every president to be. The lack of controversy about Ronald
Reagan, who was descended from Irish-Catholic immigrants but not
a Catholic himself, confirms that the concern about Kennedy's background that still existed in 1960 was ideological rather than ethnic
in character.

To understand why Americans have reacted unfavourably to the
word "multiculturalism," one must examine the circumstances in
which the word was first brought to their attention. The decade of
the 1960s was an exceptionally turbulent time in the United States,
with an unpopular and unsuccessful war in Vietnam, a sudden surge
of nihilism and radicalism among students at the nation's colleges
and universities, and a probably unprecedented level of social and
cultural change within a very short period of time. Most significantly, it was the time of the civil rights revolution, when African
Americans at last mobilized successfully to claim the rights that were
supposedly guaranteed by the Constitution but had in practice been
denied them since the withdrawal of federal troops from the conquered southern states in 1877. Although almost entirely peaceful in
its methods, the civil rights movement provoked a violent reaction
from many southern whites, often aided and abetted by law enforcement agencies and by state and local governments.

The civil rights movement of southern African Americans had of
course begun as early as 1954 with the Montgomery bus boycott in

Alabama, and it retained its original character for more than a decade under the leadership of Martin Luther King Junior. King and his followers emphasized that African Americans wanted to be integrated fully into the mainstream of American society from which white racism had excluded them. Separating themselves from the mainstream, seeking special privileges as a collectivity (as opposed to individual rights), and protecting a distinct cultural heritage, if any existed, were not part of their agenda. Far more than their white opponents in the southern states, they conformed to the principles of the American creed, both in theory and in practice. They were fully in tune with the civic nationalism that most Americans professed.

Yet even before King's assassination in 1968 and gaining strength afterwards, an alternative movement emerged among African Americans, particularly the urban proletariat in the northern states and in California. Reacting against economic deprivation, the frequently appalling conditions of life in decayed inner cities, and the disproportionate share of casualties in Vietnam that were suffered by African Americans, this movement emphasized a racial and cultural identity separate from that of white Americans. It viewed African Americans as a distinct collectivity, or even a nation, that should enjoy collective rights rather than just the individual civil rights enumerated in the Constitution. Rather than seeking integration into the American mainstream, it emphasized cultural separateness by cultivating a distinct dialect, names, hairstyles, and costumes and inventing an entirely fictitious "African" holiday known as "Kwanzaa" as an alternative to Christmas. It also demanded schools that would teach an African-influenced curriculum rather than the (still not fully achieved) integration into the existing public school system, which had been a major goal of the civil rights movement. At times it embellished its rhetoric with absurd allegations, such as that black Africans had built the Egyptian pyramids, that the HIV virus was the result of a genocidal plot to reduce the African-American population, or even that Karl Marx was of African ancestry.[51]

The word "multiculturalism," as it gradually entered the American consciousness, came to be attached to this radical movement for "Black Power," although not to the original movement for civil rights. Indeed, one American scholar has suggested that "multiculturalism had its roots in the 'black power' movement of the late 1960s."[52] American critics of multiculturalism (in the American sense of the term) devoted much of their critique to African-American separatism and nationalism, even if they had supported the civil rights move-ment.[53] General de Gaulle's visit to Montreal in 1967 and the October Crisis of 1970 had brought Quebec nationalism to the attention of many Americans. Some of them drew a parallel between the separat-ism of "Black Power" and the separatism of Quebec. Learning that "multiculturalism" was a Canadian word and that it had been pro-claimed as official doctrine by a francophone prime minister from Quebec, some Americans jumped to the completely erroneous con-clusion that multiculturalism and Quebec nationalism were closely related. They were in an indirect way but certainly not in the way that these Americans imagined.

Ironically, a movement that really was similar to Canadian multicul-turalism arose in the United States in the 1970s, a few years after its Canadian counterpart, but it arose largely in opposition to "multicultur-alism" American-style. This was the movement of the "white ethnics" or, as it was sometimes called, the ethnic revival. Its bible was *The Rise of the Unmeltable Ethnics*, a book by Michael Novak, an American of Slovakian ancestry, published in the same year that Trudeau pro-claimed the policy of official multiculturalism in Canada.[54] Novak argued that Americans of southern and eastern European ancestry, the descendants of the vast wave of immigration between 1880 and 1914, comprised most of the working class in the industrial states of the northeast and the midwest. Many felt economically deprived by the beginnings of the shift to a knowledge-based service economy, as well as stigmatized by their Catholic religion. They resented radical stu-dents, mainly Protestant or Jewish, who derided patriotism and American values and who refused to fight in Vietnam. They also resented the increasing attention given to the problems of African Americans by an upper- and upper-middle-class "liberal" elite that still consisted mainly of Anglo-Saxon Protestants. (It was at this time that "liberal" suddenly became a term of abuse in American political dis-course.) The working-class white ethnic Americans also suspected with good reason that measures to give African Americans access to better schools, jobs, and housing would probably come at their expense, not at that of the Anglo-Saxon elites who called for such measures.

The "ethnic revival" was dismissed or derided by some academics, such as Richard Alba and Herbert J. Gans, who claimed that the "ethnics" were already fully assimilated and could at most aspire to "symbolic ethnicity."[55] However, it forced some politicians to pay attention. Presidents Nixon, Ford, and Carter all had staff persons in the White House who were responsible for liaison with white ethnic groups. In 1972, Congress adopted, and President Nixon signed, the Ethnic Heritage Studies Act.[56] The purpose of this measure was to develop curricular material related to the history and culture of ethnic groups and their contribution to the American heritage, to provide training for persons to teach these subjects, and to assist ethnic organizations in developing programs or other activities related to their history, culture, and traditions. In fact, the statute had little practical effect, since minimal funding was provided, and it was eventually repealed during the Reagan administration.

In another significant recognition of the ethnic revival, the United States census of 1980 included for the first time an ethnic-origin question similar to that which the Canadian census had included since the Victorian era. Previously, the US census had only enumerated people by race and by place of birth. The 1980 census question, which was repeated in 1990 and 2000, allowed people to specify more than one ethnic origin and also to list their ethnic origin as "American," a choice that proved popular mainly among whites in the southern and border states. By way of comparison, Canada allowed multiple origins beginning in 1986 and recognized "Canadian" as an option beginning in 1996. Despite semantic differences, the North American neighbours seem to be converging in their responses to ethnic diversity.

The different place of the word "multiculturalism" in Canadian and American discourse is not incompatible with this tendency and is completely understandable. Beginning in the 1960s, both countries faced radical demands for change from previously disadvantaged groups: francophone Quebeckers and African Americans, respectively. In both cases, the demand for change initially took a form that did not threaten Canadian or American unity and identity, the Quiet Revolution and the civil rights movement, respectively. In both cases, the initial movement for change was challenged and then partly replaced by more radical and threatening movements: the sovereignty movement in Quebec and the various forms of Afro-American nationalism. In both cases, the mobilization of the largest disadvantaged group produced a response by "ethnics" who felt that their own demands for recognition were being overshadowed and threatened. In neither country was this "ethnic" response considered threatening to national unity or identity, although some dismissed its importance. In Canada, this ethnic response acquired the label of "multiculturalism" while in the United States the same word was applied to the more radical and threatening demands of the large disadvantaged group that had begun the whole sequence of events.

The analogy with Canada and Quebec has also been pressed into service by those who worry about bilingualism and the spread of the Spanish language in the United States, as discussed in the preceding chapter.[57] Indeed, some of the most articulate American critics of "multiculturalism," including S.I. Hayakawa, Peter Brimelow, and Alvin J. Schmidt, had actually lived in Canada and could almost be considered refugees from Canada's political culture. Schmidt, who wrote *The Menace of Multiculturalism*, is a former RCMP officer whose parents were German immigrants in Manitoba.[58] However, that experience has not prevented them from conflating bilingualism and multiculturalism into what they perceive as a single threat, with Canada being presented as an example of what they fear will happen to their adopted country.

American opponents of multiculturalism, as they understand the term, are concerned that their country, which has proudly cherished the motto *E pluribus unum*, is degenerating into a collection of warring tribes whose members identify as African Americans, Hispanics, Native Americans, and so forth rather than simply as Americans. They blame this phenomenon not so much on the minorities themselves but on an ideology of multiculturalism that encourages them to think in this way. But those who share these fears are not entirely united in their views on what should be done about it. Samuel P. Huntington, a distinguished political scientist, insisted in his last book on "the continuing centrality of Anglo-Protestant culture to American national identity."[59] He argued that national unity was preserved, at least until recently, because most immigrants and minorities were close enough to that culture to adapt to it. Michael Lind, on the other hand, favours a more universalistic interpretation of the American creed and denies that the ethnicity or religion of the original settlers is still relevant.[60]

The concern about multiculturalism expressed by these people is not entirely absent in Canada and appears in the writings of people like Neil Bissoondath and Rudyard Griffiths. The similarity of Griffiths's book title to that of Huntington's book is interesting.[61] However, since Canada's original settlers were French and since the country lacks both a revolutionary myth and a clear ideological identity, it is harder in anglophone Canada to specify a plausible alternative to multiculturalism. Perhaps even more significantly, most Canadians appear to have concluded that the "multiculturalism" proclaimed by their federal and provincial governments is harmless and means very little in practice. Indeed, "multiculturalism," may, in the long term, prove to be anglophone Canada's term for the melting pot.[62]

To conclude, "multiculturalism" has come to mean very different things to Canadians and Americans, with the allegedly Canadian origin of the word often causing Americans to confuse it with what, in Canadian terms, is really its opposite. Just as many Canadians like the word because they consider it a symbol of what distinguishes Canada from the United States, some Americans reject it because they consider it a symbol of what they dislike and fear about Canada. The final irony is that while Americans believe "multiculturalism" represents a threat to their national identity, Quebec nationalists believe that the same word threatens the national identity of Quebec. Quebec uses "interculturalism" to distinguish itself from anglophone Canada, just as anglophone Canada uses "multiculturalism" to distinguish itself from the United States. Yet despite the semantic confusion, the similarities between Quebec, anglophone Canada, and the United States in their approaches to ethnic diversity and immigration continue to outweigh their differences.

Recent events, however, have reminded all three societies that there are not always easy answers to relations between a host society and its newly arrived minorities. Religion, which is more fundamental to human identities than physical appearance and more resistant to assimilation than language, has emerged as the elephant in the room in the debate over diversity. This fact should not have been a new or particularly surprising discovery, but it has become increasingly apparent to North Americans and Europeans in the twenty-first century, as the next chapter will describe.

10

Islamophobia

People can be suspicious of one another for a variety of reasons. Physical characteristics, especially the colour of the skin, have been a particular obsession among northern Europeans and their North American descendants and have served as a pretext for colonialism, slavery, mass murder, segregation, and restrictive immigration policies. Language, as described in chapter 8 of this book, has been, and still is, a source of conflict among various groups of North Americans, many of whom have held the view that only one language (their own) should be allowed to flourish in the province, state, or country where they live. Political ideologies and the people who support them have at times inspired fear and hostility since the modern era of ideological politics began in 1776, most notably in the aftermath of the Russian Revolution and again during the early years of the cold war.

Yet of all the causes of discord and hostility among groups of humans, none has had a greater impact in that regard over the whole course of human history than religion. This is not to say that religion, or any particular religion, is a bad thing, as some authors have recently argued. The discord between adherents of different religions is clearly only one aspect of a very complex phenomenon that has many positive aspects as well. Religion is, for millions of people, an important part, and often the most important part, of their identity. As such, it inspires strong feelings, which may include animosity toward people who have a different faith or toward people who have no faith at all.

Since the beginning of settlement by Europeans, the dominant religion in North America has been Christianity in its various forms. Despite recent efforts to airbrush our Christian heritage out of history (such as the detestable practice of calling the years since the birth of Jesus Christ the "Common Era"), its profound influence on our culture and way of life is indisputable. The thirteen British colonies that became the United States were founded or, in the cases of Delaware and New York, acquired at a time when religion played a very large part in English society. With the exception of Maryland, they were founded by Protestants and thus inherited the hostility to Catholicism that had dominated English life since the reign of the first Elizabeth. Thomas Hobbes and John Locke both believed that Catholics could not be tolerated because they owed allegiance to a foreign potentate, the pope. As noted earlier in this book, this idea was still influential in the United States as late as the presidential election campaign of 1960.

French Canada, conversely, was a Catholic colony from which Protestants were deliberately and very effectively excluded until after the British conquest. For pragmatic reasons, the British accepted the Catholic faith of their new acquisition as part of their strategy of indirect rule, even though they were still hostile to Catholicism in principle. However, they also encouraged Protestants to settle there. In what became Lower Canada, and later the province of Quebec, Protestants and Catholics have coexisted reasonably well during most of the time after the conquest. In other parts of British North America, Protestantism was as dominant, or very nearly so, as it was in the United States.

Neither British North America nor the United States had an established church comparable to the Church of England in England, although the North American offshoots of that church (Anglican in Canada and Episcopalian in the United States) enjoyed until quite recent times a social status in North America that was not accorded to other denominations. Some individual states of the United States, however, had established churches well into the nineteenth century, since the Constitution prohibited only the federal government from establishing one. Generally in North America, various forms of Protestantism coexisted quite peacefully with one another, although sects with unusual beliefs, like the Mormons, were at times discriminated against and persecuted.

As described in earlier chapters of this book, the prejudice against Irish-Catholic immigrants, and later against Jewish immigrants, was largely although not entirely directed against their religious beliefs. The Irish Catholics encountered a much less hostile reception in

Catholic Quebec than elsewhere on the continent, and many of them intermarried with French-Canadian Catholics. Particularly outside of Montreal, such marriages often led to French replacing English (or in some cases Irish) as the language of the people concerned and their descendants. Elsewhere in North America, anti-Catholic sentiments lingered for a long time. In Canada, especially Ontario, the Orange Order, an anti-Catholic organization that originated in the northern part of Ireland, was politically influential well into the twentieth century. In both countries, anti-Catholic sentiments are not entirely extinct today, although the most fanatically anti-Catholic North Americans nowadays are usually atheists or agnostics, including former Catholics, rather than devout Protestants.

Jews, who denied the divinity of Jesus Christ and were falsely blamed by some Christians for killing him, took even longer than Catholics to gain acceptance, even though the Old Testament, a collection of Jewish writings, plays a large part in Christian worship. Although the legitimacy of Judaism was accepted somewhat sooner by Protestants than by Catholics and somewhat sooner in the United States than in Canada, it was not fully acknowledged in either country until after World War II, when the expression "Judeo-Christian" began to be used. This belated acceptance was largely a reaction against the mass murder of Jews committed by the German government and by some of its European allies during the war.

The third of the great Abrahamic faiths, Islam, had a very limited presence in North America until recently. (Probably its first, and for a long time only, direct impact on North American history came in the first decade of the nineteenth century when President Thomas Jefferson sent part of the small American navy to fight against Muslim pirates in what is now Algeria.) As a result, most North Americans have been almost totally ignorant of Islam and profoundly suspicious of it. In particular, very few have been aware of the more than coincidental similarity between the beliefs of Muslims and those of Christians and Jews. Not many more have understood the great contribution of Muslims (albeit mainly of Muslims who lived a long time ago) to what is loosely described as "Western" civilization.

Apparently, the first American mosque was founded in Detroit in 1922, but it was the only mosque in the United States until 1934 when one was established in Cedar Rapids, Iowa.[1] The first mosque in Canada was established in Edmonton, Alberta, in 1938. (Larry Shaben, whose Lebanese immigrant parents settled in Edmonton because of the existence of that mosque, became in 1979 the first Muslim to hold a portfolio in a Canadian provincial government.) There were only about twenty mosques in the United States as late as 1972. By 1980, there were 266 mosques in the United States, but more than half of them belonged to an African-American sect known as the Nation of Islam, which was founded in Detroit in 1930 and is not regarded as authentically Muslim by most Muslims outside of the United States.[2] In 1985, there were said to be mosques in 27 Canadian cities.[3]

In the words of one Canadian scholar, "western images of Arabs and Muslims largely overlap."[4] Since there is still a tendency among many North Americans to equate "Muslim" with "Arab," it is important to stress that although the prophet Mohammed was an Arab, the majority of Muslims in the world today are not Arabs. Furthermore, not all Arabs are Muslims. Until very recently, most North Americans of Arab descent were Christians, the descendants of Christian Arabs from what is now Lebanon who emigrated from the Ottoman Empire before World War I. Like most other immigrants, their main motive was to improve their economic situation. At the time, they were usually referred to in North America as "Syrians."[5] After the collapse of the Ottoman Empire and the partitioning of the Middle East between Britain and France, these communities of Christian Arabs were reinforced by new arrivals from Lebanon, some of whom were Muslims. Henry Ford hired 555 Lebanese to work for his company in 1916 and more over the next several years. Dearborn, Michigan, Henry Ford's birthplace and the company's headquarters, still has a larger concentration of Arab Americans than any other city and has attracted more recent Arab immigrants. In the south end of Dearborn, Arabic is still as widely spoken as English.[6]

Under the absurd and invidious practice invented in the 1980s by the Canadian federal government, the Lebanese would be classified today as "visible minorities," but no such category existed when they first arrived on this continent. At first they were denied eligibility for American citizenship on the assumption that they were not "white," but this policy was overturned in 1915.[7] In fact, they could easily be mistaken, and sometimes were, for European Jews, Greeks, or southern Italians. In Canada, some were interned as Ottoman subjects and thus enemy aliens during World War I, but this did not happen in the United States, which was never at war with the Ottoman Empire.

Lebanese Christians often intermarried with people of other ethnic origins. In the words of one writer, they "might have Americanized themselves out of existence" if other Arabs, both Christian and Muslim, had not arrived after World War II. A number of prominent North Americans today are descended in whole or in part from this early Lebanese Christian immigration. They include the consumer advocate Ralph Nader, who won almost three million votes as a presidential candidate in 2000, former United States senators George Mitchell and John Sununu, former secretary of health, education and welfare Donna Shalala, the Ottawa-born popular singer Paul Anka, and professional football players Doug and Darren Flutie. The North American stereotype of "Arabs" rarely includes these people, who have blended quite inconspicuously into the host society, a fact indicating that the stereotype is really based on religion rather than ethnicity.

Islam is of course the newest of the Abrahamic religions, as Judaism is the oldest. Muslims, at least in principle, regard Christians and Jews as "people of the book" whose beliefs should be tolerated and respected, a courtesy that to say the least has not often been reciprocated by Christians. The history of conflict between Muslims and Christians has been long and bitter, creating an underlying current of what could be called Islamophobia in the Western world long before recent events gave rise to the expression. For geopolitical reasons, the two faiths found themselves locked in conflict around the Mediterranean as the boundary between their spheres of influence shifted back and forth. Much of Spain was conquered by Muslims in the eighth century of the Christian era but then reconquered by Christians in the fifteenth. In medieval times, European Christians repeatedly invaded the Middle East, ostensibly to gain control of the sites in Jerusalem associated with the origins of their faith. Large numbers of Muslims (and Jews) were killed by Christians during these "Crusades" before the Christian invaders were finally driven out of the region. In the fifteenth century, the Turks, a central Asian people who had converted to Islam, captured Constantinople (now Istanbul) and from that base expanded up the Danube as far as Hungary before they were driven back into the Balkans and eventually to the outskirts of Constantinople itself.

All of North Africa, which had been Muslim for more than a thousand years, fell under the domination of European Christian powers during the century prior to World War I. By 1914, most of the world's Muslims lived in the British Empire, while the French and Dutch colonial empires included millions more. After World War I, in which the Turks fought on the losing side, England and France divided up the remaining non-Turkish parts of the former Ottoman Empire into "mandates" that were ostensibly supervised by the League of Nations but were in fact treated as colonies. Russia would have gained a large share of the empire as well, including Constantinople, had it not experienced the so-called October Revolution. The Turks expelled the Greek Christians from the lands east of the Aegean Sea, which became the heartland of the new Turkish republic. In 1932, the British used their army and air force to suppress a rebellion in the artificial kingdom of Iraq, which they had established under a puppet king in part of their mandate. During World War II, the British and Soviet governments attacked and occupied Iran, formerly known as Persia, which was then used as a source of oil for the British and a corridor for sending munitions to the Soviets.

Meanwhile, the rise of Zionism, and the promises made to its adherents during World War I by the British government, eventually led in 1948 to the establishment of the Jewish state of Israel, founded by settlers from Europe and heavily dependent on the United States, despite the opposition of all its Muslim neighbours. Several hundred thousand Palestinians, mainly Muslim but including some Christians, were expelled from the territory that became part of the new state. The continuing conflict between Israel and its neighbours after 1948 has had a lasting effect on American views of Muslims, particularly Arab Muslims. For example, the killing of several Israeli athletes by agents of the Palestine Liberation Organization at the 1972 Olympics led the Nixon administration to launch "Operation Boulder" in which hundreds of Arab Americans were interrogated, photographed, and fingerprinted and at least seventy-eight were deported.[8] Nonetheless, President Gerald Ford, in 1976, was the first US president to mention Islam when referring to the religious faiths held by Americans.[9] Perhaps being from Michigan, where many Muslims live, made him more sensitive to their feelings than his predecessors.

As if this long and unhappy history of conflict were not enough, subsequent events made the situation even worse and more complicated. During the early years of the cold war, the United States resented the neutralism espoused by Muslim leaders like Nasser of Egypt and Sukarno of Indonesia but supported and patronized more conservative Muslim regimes in Turkey, Pakistan, Iran, and Saudi Arabia. Jordan and Iraq, ruled by different branches of the Hashemite royal family, remained under British influence, as did Egypt until its monarchy was overthrown in 1952. In 1956, Britain, France, and

Israel jointly invaded Egypt, without consulting the United States, after Nasser nationalized the Suez Canal. This impulsive action was supported by many Canadians of British or Jewish ancestry, but the Liberal government of Canada and the Eisenhower administration in the United States refused to endorse it. When the monarchy in Iraq was overthrown by a revolution in 1958, the United States marines were sent to neighbouring Lebanon.

In 1965, a violent military coup, followed by the murder of more than 300,000 alleged communists, moved Indonesia into the American camp. After Nasser's death in 1970, Egypt also became increasingly pro-American, although no more democratic, under presidents Anwar Sadat and Hosni Mubarak. However, in 1979 a revolution overthrew the pro-American shah of Iran, who had been installed on his throne after the Anglo-Soviet invasion in 1941, and substituted a theocratic regime that was rabidly hostile to the United States. A group of Americans in Iran were held hostage by the new regime and finally spirited out of the country with the assistance of the Canadian embassy after an attempt to rescue them by military means turned into a fiasco. The United States then encouraged the Iraqi dictator, Saddam Hussein, to attack Iran, a country much larger than Iraq, in the hope that he would help to overthrow that country's regime. When he failed to do so, Saddam Hussein turned to the more realistic objective of occupying Kuwait, a small neighbouring state with significant resources of oil that had been under British control until 1961. As a result, the Americans turned against their former ally and fought two wars against him, in 1991 and 2003, leading to his eventual overthrow and execution.

Some Muslims resented American and British support for right-wing regimes, but others were quite content with this. Almost the only subject on which all Muslims agreed was their common resentment of American support for Israel, a support that became more and more enthusiastic and unconditional as Israel fought and won a series of wars against its neighbours. Although few Muslims had much affection for the United States, most were equally hostile, or more so, to communism and the Soviet Union, which made some of them useful to the United States during the cold war.

In 1979, the Soviet Union invaded Afghanistan, a Muslim country that had been within the informal Soviet sphere of influence for many years, and installed a communist regime. The Afghan resistance to this regime, which included the fundamentalist Muslim faction known as the Taliban, were supplied with weapons by the United States, beginning under the Carter administration. After a ten-year war, the Soviet forces withdrew from Afghanistan in defeat, and the Soviet Union itself disintegrated soon afterwards, an event that ended the somewhat incongruous alliance between the fundamentalist Muslim resistance and the United States. In the 1990s, fundamentalist Muslims, including the group known as Al Qaeda, committed a series of violent attacks against American forces and property. This practice culminated in the spectacular destruction of New York's World Trade Center with great loss of life on 11 September 2001, an event permanently engraved on the memory of most North Americans who were living at the time.

This brief summary of international events, however complicated and confusing, is relevant, because the events influenced North American perceptions of Muslims, reinforcing a current of anti-Muslim prejudice that, like the anti-Jewish prejudice described in chapter 5, has very deep roots in European history. The few Muslims who lived in North America before the middle of the twentieth century, and the many who arrived later as immigrants, suffered from this prejudice and hostility. It became worse after the end of the cold war, when Muslims seemed to replace communists as an alleged threat to the North American way of life. In an article published in 1993 and expanded into a book three years later, the noted political scientist Samuel P. Huntington argued that the cold war had been replaced by a "clash of civilizations" in which the Western and Islamic civilizations were two of the principal contestants, although he listed half a dozen others.[10]

However, the freedom, prosperity, and stability of North America made the continent a magnet for Muslims, as it has been for so many others. Some emigrated because of particular events such as the establishment of Israel in 1948, the revolution that overthrew the Egyptian monarchy in 1952, the expulsion of South Asians from Uganda in 1972, the Iranian revolution in 1979, and the sectarian conflict that made Lebanon increasingly dangerous and unstable from 1975 onwards. Others were simply seeking a more prosperous life and were encouraged by the liberalization of Canadian and American immigration policies in the 1960s.

Most Muslim immigrants arrived in North America at a time when one or more Muslim countries were regarded by most North Americans as hostile and potentially threatening to world peace and security. The United States has been a close ally of Israel throughout the existence of that state, it has had extremely hostile relations with Iran for the more than three decades since Iran's revolution, it has been at war in Afghanistan for more than a decade as part of a much-publicized "war on terror," and it has fought two recent wars against Iraq. This contrasts with the experience of, for example, German and Italian immigrants, most of whom arrived in North America long before their native countries began to be perceived as dangerous and hostile.

Because the United States census is prohibited from asking about religion, the number of Muslims in the country can only be estimated. In 1960, the Federation of Islamic Associations in America estimated the number at 1.2 million, while some more recent estimates have suggested that there could be as many as six or seven million.[11] A study by a demographer for the Pew Research Center put the number at 2.35 million in 2007, which would suggest that the estimate of 1.2 million almost half a century earlier was much too high.[12] A significant proportion of American Muslims are native-born Americans of African ancestry who converted to Islam or whose parents or grandparents did so. As noted above, the sect known as the Black Muslims, or more formally as the Nation of Islam, was founded in Detroit in 1930 and is not regarded as orthodox by all Muslims outside of the United States. Its belief that Africans are the chosen race is contrary to orthodox Muslim doctrine, which considers racial differences irrelevant. The more conventional, non-racist interpretation of Islam has, however, been adopted by many African-American Muslims, such as Malcolm X after his pilgrimage to Mecca.

Since the Canadian census collects religious data every ten years, it is much easier to determine the number of Muslims living in Canada than the number living in the United States. In 1931, there were only 645 Muslims in all of Canada, or fewer than there had been twenty years earlier, and in the next three censuses no effort was even made to count them. The number of Muslims reported in the census was 33,370 in 1971, rising rapidly to 98,160 in 1981, 253,260 in 1991, and 579,640 in 2001. By the latter date, there were almost twice as many Muslims as Jews in Canada, while the proportions are probably reversed in the United States. Canadian Jews still outnumbered Canadian Muslims by a fairly slight margin in 1991. A recent estimate puts the number of Muslims in Canada at 700,000, or more than 2 per cent of the population.[13] Almost certainly the percentage of the population of the United States who are Muslim is lower, probably much lower.

In both countries, Muslims are a diverse group. The 2007 Pew Research Center survey suggested that more than one-third of Muslims living in the United States were native-born; between 20 and 42 per cent of these were probably African Americans, according to various estimates. More than half of the foreign-born had arrived in the United States since 1990. Of the foreign-born Muslims, 37 per cent were from Arabic-speaking countries in the Middle East or North Africa, 24 per cent were from South Asia (India, Pakistan, and Bangladesh), and 12 per cent were from Iran.[14] A Canadian study a few years earlier suggested that 45 per cent of all Muslims in Canada, including those born in Canada, were of "Arab or West Asian" origin, including Iran, while about 38 per cent were of South Asian origin, including South Asians from African countries such as Uganda.[15] Other North American Muslims have come from sub-Saharan African countries, from Europe, or from Southeast Asia. Although Indonesia has the largest Muslim population of any country, it has contributed relatively few immigrants to North America.

Data on the religious and political views of North American Muslims suggest that they are much less alienated from their host societies in the United States and Canada than Muslims in Europe, who generally display high levels of alienation. For example, the survey of American Muslims by the Pew Research Center in 2007 found that only 8 per cent felt that suicide bombings of civilian targets in defence of Islam were sometimes or often justified, while the percentage of Muslims in France, Spain, and the United Kingdom who thought so was about twice as high.[16] According to the same survey, the great majority of American Muslims were happy with their lives and with the communities in which they lived.[17]

A survey of Canadian Muslims, also in 2007, indicated that only 17 per cent thought that most or many Canadians were hostile to Muslims. Among Muslims in Britain, Germany, France, and Spain, the percentages with similar impressions of anti-Muslim attitudes in those countries were, respectively, 51, 39, 33, and 31 per cent.[18] However, a study of Arab junior college (CEGEP) students in Quebec conducted in April 2001 found that 72.4 per cent of the Muslims in the sample thought that Canadians were biased against the Muslim religion and 85.1 per cent thought that Islam was misrepresented in the Canadian media.[19] The age of these respondents, the fact that all were ethnically Arab as well as Muslim, and the fact that they all lived in Quebec may explain the difference between these findings and those of the later study, which interviewed a much broader and more representative sample of Canadian Muslims.

The Pew Research Center study of American Muslims in 2007 found that 43 per cent of respondents thought that Muslims coming to the United States should "adopt American customs" while only 26 per cent thought they should "try to remain distinct." Among those who were themselves immigrants, 47 per cent favoured adopting American customs, and only 21 per cent were in favour of remaining distinct.[20] It is possible that many of these Muslim immigrants viewed adopting American customs as a defensive strategy to avoid discrimination, prejudice, and stereotyping rather than supporting that course of action out of conviction. A survey of Canadian Muslims by the Environics polling organization in association with the CBC at about the same time arrived at rather ambiguous conclusions on this issue. Only 15 per cent said that they were in favour of immigrants "blending in" while 65 per cent thought they should try to maintain their religious and cultural practices.[21] However, 55 per cent believed that most Muslims wanted to fit in to Canadian society, and only 23 per cent believed that Muslims generally wanted to remain distinct.[22] These results might suggest that most Muslims wanted to remain distinct themselves but believed their fellow Muslims were less committed to this goal.

Most Muslims in North America, like Muslims elsewhere, take serious issue with some aspects of American, and to a lesser extent Canadian, foreign policy and with the "war on terror" that has preoccupied the governments of both countries at least since 2001. The fact that both the Canadian and American governments are strongly committed to supporting Israel, regardless of which party is in office, is obviously disturbing to Muslims. As noted above, a series of events over the past several decades has kept Muslim countries almost continuously in the news, and the news, at least as viewed and interpreted in North America, has generally not been favourable.

The destruction of New York's World Trade Center on 11 September 2001 in which nearly 3,000 people were killed was of course the most shocking and dramatic event of this kind, although it was by no means the first or the last. Few of the millions of North Americans who saw it are likely to forget the televised image of commercial airliners colliding with the twin towers, which was shown repeatedly throughout the day. For some three million North American Muslims, it was a day of anxiety, as 7 December 1941 must have been for North Americans of Japanese ancestry. Many refused to believe, then or later, that Muslims had been responsible for the disaster, and a variety of conspiracy theories circulated, as is often the case after a tragic and apparently senseless event. Few were as brave as Rasha Abu Ramadan, a Palestinian student at the University of Ottawa, who deplored the loss of life but suggested that the United States was partly responsible for frequent fatal bombings in the occupied territories and that "now the people of America, of Canada, all over the world, know what we're going through."[23]

In the nine weeks following 11 September, there were 520 violent attacks in the United States on people believed to be Arabs or Muslims.[24] A few of the victims were actually Hindus or Sikhs, followers of religions that some North Americans apparently confuse with Islam. In Hamilton, Ontario, a Hindu temple, one of Canada's largest, was destroyed by a firebomb on 15 September, which also damaged a nearby mosque.[25] The person responsible was never apprehended.

President George W. Bush proclaimed a "war on terror," or rather he stepped up the pace of one that had begun with less fanfare under the previous administration. In the index of the New York Times there is only one reference to "terrorism" in the four years from 1968 through 1971, but after the murder of Israeli athletes at the Munich Olympics in 1972, the subject appeared frequently, with references in the last four months of that year covering more than a page of the index. By 1993, the first year of the Clinton administration, references to terrorism covered nearly four pages of the index. In the following year, which saw the first-ever reference in the New York Times to Osama bin Laden, the references to terrorism covered nearly two pages. By 1999 they covered more than four pages. The overwhelming majority of these stories dealing with terrorism featured Muslims or a predominantly Muslim country, and a great many referred to the conflict between Israel and the Palestinians.

According to one compilation of major terrorist attacks on the United States and its interests, twelve of the fourteen such attacks in the years from 1983 to 2000 were conducted by Muslim groups or by the governments of predominantly Muslim countries. The Muslim-linked attacks claimed 993 human lives. (The other two attacks claimed 170 human lives, of which the bombing of a federal building in Oklahoma by right-wing extremists accounted for 168.[26]) The last three items on the list, simultaneous attacks on two American embassies in Africa in 1998 and an attack on a US warship in 2000, were apparently conducted by Al Qaeda, the organization that was responsible for the destruction of the World Trade Center. An earlier incident on the list, in 1993, took place at the World Trade Center itself, although a different Islamist organization was responsible. Thus, terrorism, a technique of warfare that has been used by many groups and many governments (including the United States) throughout history, was increasingly associated with Muslims in the minds of most Americans and of most Canadians also.

Both Canada and the United States adopted legislative measures to facilitate the struggle against terrorism following the destruction of the World Trade Center. The United States Congress adopted three measures, the USA PATRIOT Act, the Homeland Security Act, and the Intelligence Reform and Terrorism Prevention Act. President Bush signed these measures on 26 October 2001, 25 November 2002, and 17 December 2004, respectively.[27]

"USA PATRIOT" is an acronym meaning "Uniting and Strengthening America by Providing Appropriate Tools Required to Intercept and Obstruct Terrorism." It increased the power of the FBI to undertake wiretapping, computer hacking, and other forms of surveillance and to delay indefinitely notifying the targets of the execution of search warrants. It authorized so-called "roving wiretap" orders, which need not specify the location or electronic device to be monitored. Other provisions were directed against money-laundering by possible terrorists and provided for greatly increased security measures along the borders of the United States and at airports. Law enforcement agencies were given increased authority to detain and deport suspected terrorists at their discretion. Several provisions of the act were later found to be unconstitutional. Some of the more controversial provisions were intended to expire eventually but were extended for an additional four years by President Obama in 2011.

In Canada, Jean Chrétien's Liberal government introduced Bill C-36, the Anti-Terrorism Act, which achieved royal assent on 18 December 2001.[28] Its provisions were somewhat similar to those of the USA PATRIOT Act although less elaborate. Some of these provisions were to expire on 1 March 2007 unless renewed. Stephen Harper's Conservative government wished to renew them, particularly since a serious plot by members of Al Qaeda had been discovered in Toronto the year before. However, they lacked a majority in the House of Commons, and the Liberals, although a Liberal government had introduced the act in the first place, refused to vote for an extension. Much of the original act, however, remains in effect.

President Bush, to his credit, stated publicly several times after 11 September 2001 that the United States was not fighting against Islam, that most Muslims were not terrorists, that Islam was a religion of peace and brotherhood, and that Muslims worship the same god as Christians, albeit in a different way.[29] Speaking at the United Nations on 10 November, he asserted that "The war on terror must not serve as an excuse to persecute ethnic and religious minorities in any country."[30] Polls conducted over the next few years suggested that most Americans understood and agreed with him but by no means all. Some prominent evangelical Christians, including Billy Graham's son Franklin Graham, made strongly anti-Muslim remarks. A survey of 700 fundamentalist and evangelical Protestant clergy in 2002 found that 77 per cent of them had an unfavourable view of Islam and only 13 per cent had a favourable view.[31]

On the other hand, a survey of a more representative group of Americans for the Pew Research Center in November 2001, only two months after the bombing of the World Trade Center, found that 59 per cent of respondents had a favourable view of Muslims at that time as compared to only 45 per cent in May of the same year. In a somewhat surprising result, those who described themselves as conservative Republicans were slightly more likely to have a favourable view of Muslims than other persons in the sample.[32] A possible explanation for this is that most Jewish Americans are Democrats and most Americans who are opposed to religion in general describe themselves as liberals.

The destruction of the World Trade Center was followed within less than two years by two American wars, both against Muslim opponents. The first commenced less than four weeks after the attack and was motivated by the understandable desire to destroy the Taliban regime in Afghanistan, which had sheltered the headquarters and principal members of Al Qaeda. The Taliban were quickly removed from power and a new government installed in the Afghan capital of Kabul, but it failed to establish firm control over the entire country. At the time of writing, eleven years after the destruction of the World Trade Center, the United States, Canada, and several other Western nations still had military units operating in Afghanistan against the insurgency there and in support of the Afghan government. Al Qaeda meanwhile shifted its operations across the border into Pakistan, a nominal ally of the United States where its Islamist ideology enjoyed considerable sympathy. It was there that Osama bin Laden, the head of the Al Qaeda organization, was killed in a US military operation on 1 May 2011.

The second war, for which the destruction of the World Trade Center served as a pretext rather than a serious motive, was conducted against Iraq. The United States and several of its allies, including Canada, had fought a brief and successful war against that country under the leadership of the first President Bush in 1991, resulting in the expulsion of Iraqi forces from Kuwait and the restoration of Kuwait's independence. The dictator Saddam Hussein, a brutal tyrant but not a radical Islamist, had remained in office after the successful conclusion of Operation Desert Storm, as the first American war against him was officially known.

In his annual State of the Union address on 29 January 2002, a few months after the destruction of the World Trade Center, the second President Bush referred to Saddam's Iraq, the Islamist theocracy in Iran, and the communist regime in North Korea as constituting an "axis of evil," although he did not specifically state that there was an alliance among them comparable to the original "axis" between Germany, Italy, and Japan in World War II. Bush charged, however, that all three regimes were sponsoring terrorism and were also developing "weapons of mass destruction," a phrase that he used repeatedly during his address.[33] Iraq and Iran were bitter opponents who had recently fought one another in a major war, Saddam Hussein was a Sunni Muslim and the Iranians were Shiites, and neither of them, let alone North Korea, had anything to do with Al Qaeda, which was a fundamentalist Sunni organization. However, few Americans seemed in the mood to make distinctions between different Muslim regimes and factions or to question their president's analysis. It is even possible that the similarity between the names Iraq and Iran confused many Americans into thinking that Saddam Hussein's regime was the same one that had humiliated the United States in the hostage episode of 1979.

On 20 March 2003, the United States launched an attack on the weakest of the three alleged "axis" countries, Saddam Hussein's Iraq. This time Canada, under a Liberal government, refused to take part. Within a few months, the war was effectively over and a new government was established in Baghdad, which eventually executed

Saddam Hussein and several of his associates. No "weapons of mass destruction," whatever that might mean, were ever found. Natalie Maines, the Texas-born lead singer of a country music band called the Dixie Chicks, received death threats and was boycotted by many radio stations after she stated on the eve of the war that she was ashamed that the president of the United States was from Texas. A popular song written soon afterwards in support of the war against Iraq even referred specifically to the destruction of the World Trade Center as a *casus belli*.

Prisoners captured during both of these wars and suspected of being terrorists were taken to a prison that was established at the Guantanamo Bay Naval Base, a leased American enclave on Cuban territory where they were effectively beyond the reach of the United States Constitution and enjoyed no civil rights. Some were tortured, and most were held for years without benefit of habeas corpus. Barack Obama promised to shut down the prison at Guantanamo Bay during his successful election campaign in 2008 but had still failed to deliver on that promise when he was elected to a second term four years later.

One of the captives held at Guantanamo Bay for a decade was a guerrilla soldier named Omar Khadr, who was captured in Afghanistan in 2001 when he was only fifteen years old. The United States charged, and in 2010 convicted, Khadr, who had been born in Toronto to Egyptian immigrant parents and thus was a Canadian citizen, with the "murder" of an American soldier killed in combat. Canadians interested in civil liberties urged the Canadian government to intervene on Khadr's behalf, but the government was at first reluctant even to let him serve out his sentence in a Canadian penitentiary, which the United States administration would have preferred. However, it finally relented, and Khadr returned to Canada in September 2012.

Another Canadian citizen who became a victim of the American anti-terrorist campaign was Maher Arar, a professional engineer who had emigrated from Syria to Canada as a teenager in 1987. In September 2002, he was arrested at New York's international airport where he had stopped over on his way back to Canada from an overseas vacation. A Canadian commission of inquiry later concluded that false information provided by the Canadian government had contributed to this arrest. The American authorities, claiming that Arar had links to Al Qaeda, deported him to Syria, even though he was travelling on a Canadian passport. He was detained in Syria, and apparently tortured, for more than a year before being allowed to return to Canada. The case attracted widespread interest and concern on both sides of the border. The Canadian government formally protested to the US government on Arar's behalf in 2006. The following year, it apologized to Arar himself and paid him more than $10,000,000 in compensation.

During Canada's October crisis of 1970, when a British diplomat and Quebec's minister of labour were kidnapped, and the minister was later killed, by members of a radical Quebec separatist organization, the cartoonist for the Montreal *Gazette* drew a celebrated cartoon. It showed Jean Marchand, then the most influential minister from Quebec in Pierre Trudeau's cabinet, holding a copy of the Montreal telephone directory and proclaiming "We now have a list of suspects." Although few of the Muslims living in Canada and the United States were radical anti-Western Islamists and even fewer would ever have committed a violent act, all were to some extent "suspects" after 11 September 2001 because of their religious beliefs and particularly so if they had been born in an Arabic-speaking country. Ethnic or racial "profiling" by law enforcement and security personnel appeared to be widespread, although the Bush administration issued a directive condemning the practice in 2003.[34]

The Pew Research Centre's survey of Muslim Americans in 2007 found that 53 per cent of those surveyed believed it was more difficult to be a Muslim in the United States since 11 September 2001. Those who were younger, more affluent, or more religious were particularly likely to believe that it had become more difficult to be a Muslim. 54 per cent of Muslim Americans surveyed said that anti-terrorism policies singled out Muslims, while only 31 per cent disagreed. Muslims who had born in the United States were significantly more likely to hold this position than Muslim immigrants: 73 per cent as opposed to 47 per cent. Only 23 per cent of the native-born, but 36 per cent of the immigrants, disagreed with the proposition that anti-terrorism policies singled out Muslims.[35] Possibly the American-born Muslims had higher expectations regarding their government's respect for civil liberties than the immigrants, or possibly some of the immigrants felt that they were being singled out because of their immigrant status or place of birth rather than because of their religion.

When asked to specify the most important problems facing Muslims in the United States, only 19 per cent said there were no problems. The problems most often cited were discrimination, racism, or prejudice (19 per cent), being viewed as terrorists (15 per cent), American ignorance about Islam (14 per cent), stereotyping (12 per cent), and negative portrayals of Muslims in the media (7 per cent).[36] The war against Iraq was opposed by 75 per cent of the sample and supported by only 12 per cent. Opinion on the war in Afghanistan was more evenly divided, with 48 per cent opposed and 35 per cent in favour.[37]

Although Muslims tend to be conservative on social issues and are not particularly far to the left on economic issues, the Republican Party in the United States and the Conservative Party in Canada receive little support from Muslim voters. The Pew survey in 2007 found that only 11 per cent of American Muslims identified as Republicans and 63 per cent identified as Democrats. A survey of Canadian Muslims in the same year indicated that only 7 per cent planned to vote for the Conservatives in the next election compared to 13 per cent for the NDP and 54 per cent for the Liberals.[38] The prominence of evangelical Christians in both the Republican and Conservative parties, as well as the extreme partiality of both parties toward Israel in recent years, probably contribute to their lack of popularity among Muslim voters. In the case of the Republicans, there is the additional fact that recent Republican administrations went to war twice against Iraq and once in Afghanistan. Both wars against Iraq were opposed by the Democrats.

Prime Minister Stephen Harper appointed Muslim member of Parliament Wajid Ali Khan, who had emigrated to Canada from Pakistan many years previously, as his advisor on Muslim affairs in 2007. The experiment seems to have won the government little credit among Muslims, and it ended abruptly when Khan lost his seat to a Liberal in the general election of 2008. Far more attention was attracted by the lengthy feud between the Harper government and the Canadian Arab Federation (CAF), which apparently began when the federation criticized Harper in 2006 for calling Israel's invasion of Lebanon "a measured response." The following year, Jason Kenney, the newly appointed secretary of state for multiculturalism and Canadian identity, allegedly referred to the Canadian Arab Federation as a racist organization while he was attending an international conference on combating discrimination at Bucharest, Romania, adding more fuel to the flames.[39]

In January 2008, Canada announced that it would not attend the United Nations conference on racism in Geneva, which was scheduled to take place in April of the following year. The conference was a follow-up to one in Durban, South Africa, which had taken place a few days before the attack on the World Trade Center in 2001 and had been boycotted by Israel and the United States. The Canadian Arab Federation opposed the Canadian government's decision to boycott the follow-up conference in a statement that referred to Israel's government as racist. Soon afterwards, Jason Kenney, speaking in the House of Commons, said that the government would also not contribute to the travel expenses of non-governmental organizations that attended the conference. Kenney also challenged Omar Alghabra, a Liberal member of Parliament who had emigrated from Saudi Arabia, to state whether or not the Liberal Party agreed that Israel was racist.[40] When a group of Canadian non-governmental organizations, including the Canadian Arab Federation, asked to meet with Kenney to discuss Canada's boycott of the conference, Kenney agreed to meet with all of them except the CAF. A member of Kenney's staff defended the exclusion by claiming that the CAF was anti-Semitic.

The war of words continued to escalate, and in 2009, after Kenney had been promoted from secretary of state to minister of citizenship, immigration and multiculturalism, he announced plans to terminate all government funding to both the Canadian Arab Federation and the Canadian Islamic Congress, organizations that he claimed promoted "hateful sentiments" and anti-Semitism. In response, the president of the Canadian Islamic Congress, Wahida Valiante, pointed out that her organization did not receive any funding from the government to begin with and did not believe in promoting hatred or anti-Semitism. The executive director of the CAF, Mohamed Boudjenane, said that the government funds his organization received were used to help new immigrants become integrated into Canadian life through language training and assistance in seeking employment.[41]

The Israel–Palestine conflict and the campaign against Al Qaeda have not been the only sources of tension between North American Muslims and their neighbours in recent years. To many North Americans, the increasing presence of Islam on a continent where it previously had little influence or visibility seems to threaten their view of North American civilization and culture as essentially Christian. To other North Americans, who do not necessarily view North American civilization and culture as essentially Christian, Islam seems to threaten their perception of the appropriate relationship between religion and the state. The first view resembles that of

North American Christians who, in earlier times, were disturbed by the increasing presence and visibility of Jews. The second view resembles that of Protestants who traditionally feared Catholicism as an alleged threat to the separation of church and state, an issue that preoccupied many Americans when John F. Kennedy was the Democratic Party's presidential candidate in 1960. It also appeals to secularists who are indifferent or even hostile to all religions and who believe that religion should be kept out of the public domain as much as possible.

These two, or really three, points of view of course begin from different premises and conflict with one another on some fundamental issues, but all could focus on Islam as a target of fear and resentment, particularly after the destruction of the World Trade Center and other events had placed Islam under a spotlight. Unlike Judaism, Islam has hundreds of millions of adherents throughout the world; the total number of Muslims in the world is about three times the total population of North America, while the number of Jews on the entire planet is less than the population of Texas. Unlike the Catholic Church, whose influence and power seem to have declined considerably in the half century since Kennedy's religion was a political issue, Islam appears to be gaining rapidly in influence throughout the world in the twentieth century. Birth and fertility rates among Muslims throughout the world are also significantly higher than the global average. Although Islam has no priestly hierarchy and no equivalent to the pope and although the world's Muslims are an exceptionally heterogeneous group in terms of culture, language, politics, and even some specific aspects of their faith, the notion of a "clash of civilizations" between an expanding monolithic Islam and a declining and divided Western and Christian civilization appears credible to many people.

Anxiety of this kind has been much more apparent in Europe in recent years than in North America, partly because Europe is less distant from the Muslim world and has a larger percentage of Muslims than has North America. However, similar anxiety has also appeared in North America and perhaps particularly in the part of North America that most resembles Europe, the province of Quebec. A complete exploration of the resemblances between Europe and Quebec would require a lengthy digression from the primary purpose of this book, but a few interesting parallels may be noted. Quebec resembles most European countries, but differs from Canada and the United States, in that the great majority of its population share a common ancestry and cultural heritage and are descended from people who lived there as long as perhaps four centuries ago. Quebec resembles many European countries, but not Canada or the United States, in that most of its people are nominally Catholic, whatever their actual beliefs. Like some other Catholic countries, Quebec has made the transition (in Quebec's case quite recently and abruptly) from a situation in which the Catholic Church enjoyed tremendous power to a situation in which an aggressive secularism (*laïcité*) has relegated Catholicism to the sidelines. Finally, Quebec resembles Europe in that it is preoccupied with the issue of demographic decline, an issue that has largely (although perhaps unwisely) escaped the attention of most other North Americans.

From the 1840s until the 1960s, Quebec was a society in which the Catholic Church played a dominant role and Catholicism dominated Quebec's sense of its own identity. Almost everyone, apart from the relatively small Protestant and Jewish minorities, attended mass regularly. Clerical and political elites mingled at ceremonial events like the opening of a new bridge or highway. Education and social services were organized along sectarian lines, and the systems of education and social services that served the vast majority of the population were run by the church, to which the province had in effect delegated its responsibility under Canada's federal Constitution. There was no minister of education, because education was run by the church, no birth certificates, because a baptismal certificate sufficed for most purposes, and no civil marriage, because marriage was considered a sacrament. Those with the temerity to seek a divorce had to obtain it through a special act of the federal Parliament in Ottawa. Birth control was forbidden. There were Catholic labour unions and Catholic organizations for youth, women, and farmers. Films unacceptable to the church could not be shown, and public libraries could not lend books that appeared on the papal index.

All of this disappeared over the course of a generation during and after the Quiet Revolution. Attendance at mass declined precipitously, and many churches were closed, demolished, or converted to other uses. The Catholic unions became secular and non-sectarian in 1960. A ministry of education was established in 1964. The state took over social services in 1971. A constitutional amendment in 1993 ended the division of the school system along sectarian lines. Quebec was transformed from the most socially conservative part of North

America to the most socially liberal, with a corresponding decline in the birthrate. Many politicians and intellectuals, especially on the left, became aggressively secular, dedicated to the rigid *laïcité* of republican France. Yet vestiges of Quebec's Catholic heritage survived. There is still a large crucifix behind the president's throne in the National Assembly, and in the Canadian census of 2001 fewer than 6 per cent of Quebec residents declared that they had no religion, compared to almost 20 per cent of the population in the rest of Canada.

Quebec was thus polarized between the secularists, who were mostly politically to the left, supporters of independence, and likely to live in Montreal, and the practising Catholics, who cherished the province's Catholic heritage, were mainly federalists, and were more numerous in the small towns and rural areas. The first group disliked the tendency of religious minorities, particularly Muslims, to advertise their faith in a public way. The second group viewed immigration and minorities as a threat to Quebec's identity and to their own religious beliefs. In the absence of religious minorities, these two groups would have bitterly opposed one another, but the presence of the minorities, of whom they both disapproved although for different reasons, forced them into an uneasy alliance.

In the first decade of the twenty-first century, a number of incidents and disputes involving religious minorities ruffled the normally placid surface of Quebec. Most were trivial, and not all involved Muslims. In one celebrated incident, a school for boys run by ultra-Orthodox Jews objected to a nearby gymnasium through whose plate-glass windows scantily clad young women could be seen using the exercise equipment. Another dispute, which was finally settled by the Supreme Court of Canada, concerned a Sikh student in Montreal who was prohibited by the school board from wearing his kirpan, the ceremonial dagger that male Sikhs are supposed to wear, while attending school.[42] Many Quebeckers viewed the Supreme Court's decision in favour of the Sikh student as evidence that Canada's official multiculturalism, to which Quebec objects on other grounds, as explained in chapter 9, was being carried to excess.

However, the event that finally led the provincial government to take action did involve Islam, or rather it was an anti-Muslim gesture that was symptomatic of the Islamophobia that swept over North America in the first decade of the twenty-first century. On 25 January 2007, the municipal council of Hérouxville, a village of some 1,200 people in the St Maurice valley northeast of Montreal, formally adopted a resolution outlining its *"normes de vie,"* or a code of conduct for potential immigrants who might wish to live there, an apparently superfluous gesture since the village had attracted practically no immigrants at all. Many of the *normes* seemed to be directed against Muslims, and the document was soon denounced by the Canadian Islamic Congress. A few of the more egregious items, such as a prohibition against stoning women in public or covering one's face except at Halloween, were removed a few days later, but the amended version still noted that in Hérouxville women were allowed to drive a car or to walk alone, that parents did not arrange their children's marriages, and that public schools had no space set aside for prayers. (There were also references to the Sikh kirpan and to the gymnasium incident mentioned in the preceding paragraph.)

Two weeks after the publication of this document, Premier Jean Charest announced the formation of a Consultation Commission (they are no longer called royal commissions in anti-monarchist Quebec) on Accommodation Practices Related to Cultural Differences, which was directed to explore the issue, consult with the public, and make recommendations by the end of March 2008. As this was an unwieldy title, it quickly came to be known as the commission on "reasonable accommodation," a phrase borrowed from American jurisprudence. As co-chairmen of the commission, the government appointed two distinguished academics, Gérard Bouchard and Charles Taylor.

Bouchard was a historical sociologist who had published a book on the founding of new societies in which he compared Quebec with Australia,[43] a supporter of independence for Quebec, and the brother of a former Parti Québécois premier, Lucien Bouchard. Taylor was an internationally renowned philosopher who in the same year he was appointed published a brilliant defence of religion and analysis of secularism,[44] a federalist anglophone with some francophone roots, and the brother of a former chancellor of McGill University, Gretta Chambers. Together they released in August 2007 a preliminary consultation document covering forty-four pages in each of Canada's official languages, organized four public forums in Montreal, toured the small towns and rural areas of the province for thirty-one days of public hearings, accepted 900 briefs, heard the oral testimony of 241 persons, and even set up an interactive website. Their final report appeared in May 2008, two months behind schedule.[45]

The report, however, did not fully satisfy either the Catholic traditionalists, the secularists, or the religious minorities, although it tried in its thirty-seven recommendations to offer some comfort to all three groups.[46] The commission concluded that the importance of the events that had led to its formation had been overemphasized by the media. It recommended that in cases of friction between religious minorities and other Quebeckers, a "reasonable accommodation" should be sought without reference to the courts. The government was advised to devote more effort to integrating immigrants into Quebec society but also (more subtly) to ensure that not too many were admitted and that they be encouraged to settle somewhere outside of Montreal. The commission also urged the government to "launch a vigorous campaign to promote interculturalism in Quebec society and to broaden awareness of it" and to fight against Islamophobia, anti-Semitism, and racial discrimination with "exceptional measures."

The most controversial recommendations fell under the heading of secularism. The Bouchard–Taylor report suggested that the government prepare a White Paper on this complicated subject, that judges, Crown prosecutors, police officers, prison guards, and the president and vice-president of the National Assembly be prohibited from wearing religious symbols while on duty, that the crucifix in the National Assembly chamber be relocated to some other part of the building, and that municipal councils abandon the practice of saying a prayer at the beginning of their sessions. In fact, no White Paper on secularism was ever prepared, probably because the Liberal government considered the subject too divisive and controversial. The federal government had allowed Sikh officers in the Royal Canadian Mounted Police to wear their turbans on duty since 1990, citing Canadian human rights legislation as the grounds for this decision.[47] The recommendation regarding the crucifix was rejected by a unanimous vote of the National Assembly itself in which Action Démocratique du Québec, a conservative party dedicated to traditional French-Canadian values, had recently become the official opposition. André Boisclair, the former leader of the Parti Québécois who had been the first to suggest removing the crucifix, had resigned both his leadership and his seat in the assembly while the Bouchard–Taylor inquiry was in progress. After a dismal showing in 2007 under the leadership of the decidedly untraditional Boisclair, the Parti Québécois clearly wished to mend its fences in traditional and rural Quebec. Apparently it succeeded, since it returned to power in 2012.

Rightly or wrongly, many North Americans associate Islam with the subordination of women, and this perception is a major source of distrust toward Islam and toward Muslims as a group. One of the

main arguments used by both the Canadian and American governments to justify the war in Afghanistan was the oppression of women
by the Taliban. Both Quebec and, after some hesitation, Ontario
decided not to allow the use of sharia law to regulate domestic disputes in Muslim families. The Hérouxville *normes* made repeated
references to practices that discriminated against or oppressed
women as examples of customs that were not acceptable.

The fact that many Muslim women cover their hair and a few
cover their entire face when appearing in public seems to bother a
large number of North Americans. In the Pew Research Center's survey of Muslim American attitudes, a slight majority said they were
worried that women whose hair was covered with a hijab would be
treated poorly by their fellow Americans.[48] The number of well-
publicized incidents in Quebec related to this issue may explain in
large part why 75 per cent of respondents in a poll conducted in 2010
thought the Charest government had gone too far in the direction of
"reasonable accommodation." This was only slightly less than the
83 per cent who had held this view prior to the establishment of the
Bouchard–Taylor commission.[49] A Canada-wide survey in 2006
found that although 75 per cent felt Muslim immigrants made a positive contribution to the country and 49 per cent felt immigrants
should be free to maintain their religious and cultural practices, an
overwhelming 81 per cent felt that immigrants should adapt to mainstream Canadian beliefs about the rights and role of women.

Although the relationship of Muslims with the society in which
they live seems decidedly better in North America than in Europe, it
is perhaps too early to say that Muslims are fully integrated or fully
comfortable in North American society, whether in Quebec, anglophone Canada, or the United States. In some ways, their situation
resembles that of Jews in the early decades of the twentieth century
and of Catholics, particularly Irish Catholics, in the nineteenth century. In this connection, it is useful to consider a comment by Will
Kymlicka, a Canadian philosopher who has done much to explore,
and to promote, the meaning of multiculturalism: "Much of the fear
that native-born Canadians express today regarding the integration
of Muslims, for example, is virtually identical to the fear expressed
a century ago regarding the integration of Catholics. Catholics were
perceived to be undemocratic and unpatriotic because their allegiance was to the Pope, and as separatist because they demanded
their own schools. The fear that Catholics would not integrate took

many years to disappear; yet today they are seen as a vital component of the mainstream society into which Muslims are allegedly not integrating."[50]

In the North American response to Muslims today, religious and cultural anxieties are reinforced by political events in Afghanistan, Iran, Iraq, and Palestine in which Muslims appear to clash with the foreign policy objectives of Canada and the United States. In much the same way, the anti-Catholic prejudice of many anglophone Canadians was once reinforced by what they read or heard about the sometimes violent struggles of Irish patriots against Protestant landlords and against the British Empire. Subsequently, anti-Semitism, in North America and elsewhere, was reinforced by reports of the prominent role played by Jews in the Bolshevik revolution. These prejudices and suspicions have faded away with the passage of time, and no one now doubts that Protestantism, Catholicism, and Judaism have much in common or that Catholics and Jews can be patriotic Canadians or Americans. As Kymlicka goes on to predict, the day will come eventually when Muslims of all ethnic origins are equally accepted and equally integrated into North American society. Perhaps a more inclusive expression will replace "Judeo-Christian" to recognize the kinship between the three Abrahamic religions. While this happy outcome may be some distance away and may be delayed by wars and other events in the outside world, the prospects appear more promising in North America than in most European countries.

11

Conclusion

What have we learned from this comparative account of the North American experience with immigration and cultural diversity? Are Canada and the United States fundamentally different in their approaches to these phenomena, as many Canadians believe, or are the Canadian and American approaches essentially the same? Have the two North American federations, or either of them, been success-ful in integrating various minorities into their respective populations, or do they face social disintegration and disaster, as Patrick Buchanan and Samuel Huntington have suggested? Have the immigrants and minorities fared reasonably well on either side, or on both sides, of the border, or do they continue to face discrimination, humiliation, and hardship, as some radical critics of North American society allege? Have the two countries simply reproduced and perpetuated the patterns of behaviour and attitude with which they started on their respective journeys, or have they learned from experience? What can a survey of more than two centuries of history tell us about the future of North America? What will Canada and the United States look like a century from now?

The stereotypes of mosaic and melting pot have some basis in the early history of the two countries, even though neither expression was invented until the twentieth century. As W.L. Morton pointed out more than half a century ago, monarchies are based on vertical ties of allegiance rather than horizontal ties of community.[1] Different groups of people pledging allegiance to the same monarch can thus be governed separately or according to different principles. The per-sonal unions between England and Scotland from 1603 to 1707 and between England and Hanover from 1714 to 1837 can be cited as examples. Even today the "United Kingdom" is really not a united kingdom but a collection of different entities (England, Scotland, Wales, Northern Ireland, Isle of Man, and Channel Islands) that are governed in different ways under the Crown. The American republic, with its eighteenth-century penchant for symmetry and order, could not live with such constitutional untidiness, although it must be conceded that the peculiar status of Puerto Rico may be the exception that proves the rule.

In North America, the most historically significant contrast in governing arrangements is the indirect rule and religious and cultural guarantees enjoyed by the French Canadians after 1774 under the terms of the Quebec Act. Its legacy today is the province of Quebec with its own civil code, French as its only official language, and guaranteed representation on the Supreme Court of Canada. The Quebec Act was one of the grievances mentioned by the Americans in their Declaration of Independence, and needless to say nothing of the sort was provided for Louisiana, New Mexico, or Hawaii when they were acquired by the United States.

The Americans also resented the Royal Proclamation of 1763, which attempted to protect the Aboriginal peoples from English-speaking American settlers on the frontier. George Washington dismissed it at the time as "a temporary expedient to quiet the minds of the Indians." Washington's biographer, Ron Chernow, considers that the "infamous decree" was "shortsighted" and designed only to protect the fur trade.[2] The Aboriginal peoples of Canada, however, still regard this document as their Magna Carta.

In the War of 1812, as was noted in chapter 2 of this book, some Aboriginal tribes fought as allies of the British Crown, not as dependent subjects, although their interests and expectations were betrayed by their British allies in the final terms of the peace treaty. On the western plains, Aboriginal people also preferred the British Crown to the American republic, and because of this the westward expansion of Canada involved much less violence than that of the United States. Even today the politically correct terms for Aboriginal people used on either side of the border indicate a significant ideological contrast. In the United States they are called "Native Americans" and in Canada "First Nations." The American term suggests membership in a single political community, while the Canadian term suggests separateness and implies a promise of self-government, even if the promise has by no means been fully realized.

However, the contrast between the United States and Canada is much less apparent in their treatment of immigrants and of cultural minorities resulting from immigration subsequent to the founding of the two societies. While originally founded on different ideological premises, the United States and Canada have converged ideologically with the passage of time. Canada has evolved, in Frederick Vaughan's words, "from defiant monarchy to reluctant republic."[3] The process began long before Trudeau and his Canadian Charter of Rights and Freedoms made it explicit. Despite the rhetoric of Lord Tweedsmuir and the writings of John Murray Gibbon, many Canadians in Ontario and the western provinces wanted all minorities (including French Canadians) to be submerged in a melting pot that would be uniformly English-speaking and culturally homogeneous. To a large extent, with the help of their provincial governments, the supporters of homogeneity achieved the kind of Canada they wanted, except in Quebec. Certain religious minorities, such as the Mennonites and Hutterites, resisted the trend with some degree of success, but they did so also in the United States. Conversely, there were Americans like Horace Kallen and Randolph Bourne who favoured a cultural mosaic, although the influence of their ideas was very limited during their lifetimes. However, in recent years the melting pot idea has been discarded in a United States that is increasingly diverse and increasingly accepting of its diversity.

In examining the parallel experiences of some large ethnic and immigrant minorities on either side of the border, as was done in the early chapters of this book, one finds some differences but a great many similarities. For example, Irish Catholics may have faced somewhat greater hostility to their religion in the United States than in Canada, where the existence of Quebec made Catholicism seem less dangerous and more familiar, but the influence of the Orange Order in Canada cannot be discounted. The tax-supported Catholic school system disappeared in Manitoba and New Brunswick in the nineteenth century, in Newfoundland in the twentieth, and is increasingly under attack in Ontario. Also, the somewhat lower level of religious hostility to Irish Catholics in Canada was made up for by a much higher level of political hostility to the anti-British and republican ideas associated with Irish nationalism, ideas that Americans generally accepted. Perhaps partly for that reason, a large proportion of the Irish Catholics who entered Canada through the ports of Quebec, Montreal, Saint John, and Halifax moved on, sooner or later, to the United States.

Canadian Jews have remained somewhat more distinct from the larger society than American Jews, with higher levels of religious observance and lower levels of intermarriage with non-Jews. However, this is largely because a much greater proportion of Canadian Jews are only the first or second generation of their families to be born and raised in North America. Significant Jewish immigration to Canada began about half a century later than significant Jewish immigration to the United States, because the transatlantic migration of German Jews in the middle decades of the nineteenth century bypassed Canada almost completely. The German Jews, who fitted easily into the mainstream of American life, paved the way for the Jews from eastern Europe, who arrived in both countries around the turn of the century, to be accepted more rapidly by Americans than by Canadians. This was probably also a factor in the more liberal response of the United States to Jewish refugees from Nazism in the 1930s. On the other hand, Canada has received a proportionately greater number of Jews in recent years, including Jews from North Africa (many of whom speak French) and the Middle East. Apart from the timing of migration, the degree of assimilation may be related to cultural and religious factors. Reform Jews, much more numerous in the United States, are more likely to assimilate (and to marry outside their faith) than Orthodox Jews. North Africans face greater cultural barriers to assimilation than Russians, and Russians face greater cultural barriers than Germans.

It is difficult to see much difference between the two countries in their treatment of Chinese, Japanese, and other "Orientals" over the years since East Asians began to arrive on this continent in significant numbers. From the arrival of gold-seekers in California in 1849 and in British Columbia a decade later, to the building of the transcontinental railways with the help of Chinese labourers, to the federal laws excluding Chinese immigrants from both countries, to the racist state and provincial laws of west-coast jurisdictions, to the compulsory relocation of Japanese, naturalized and otherwise, during World War II, to the gradual decline of racism after the war, the parallels have been so striking as to seem more like a single shared history than the histories of two distinct nations. The fact that persons of Chinese ancestry are proportionately much more numerous in Canada today than in the United States is largely a function of the fact that Hong Kong was ruled as a British colony until 1998. (For similar reasons, Canada has proportionately far more people from the English-speaking Caribbean, and from India and Pakistan, than does the United States, but proportionately fewer from the Dominican Republic, the six republics of Central America, the Philippines, Korea, and Vietnam.)

From the 1920s until the 1960s, the United States largely closed the door to immigration from Europe through its quota system, which gave large quotas to prosperous England and Germany and to Ireland with its small population of around four million but very small quotas to the countries where there was a significant demand for opportunities to emigrate. Canada did not do so and as a result received proportionately more immigrants from Europe in the 1920s and proportionately far more after 1945. As noted in chapter 7 of this book, it was during the years of post–World War II immigration that Canada began for the first time to appear more culturally diverse than the United States and that the familiar stereotypes of mosaic versus melting pot became more plausible and more popular than ever before.

The reason for this contrast in immigration policies, however, probably had little to do with Canada's monarchical traditions. The main reason for it was that Canada still perceived itself, correctly, as an underpopulated country that needed additional settlers, a need that was reinforced by the constant outflow of Canadians (who were exempted from the American quota system) to the United States. While the United States had officially closed its frontier in 1890, Canada was still distributing free land on the prairies to immigrants in the 1920s. As late as the 1950s, Canada still had only four people per square mile (and less than seven per square mile excluding the northern territories) while the outflow of Canadians to the United States continued. However, Canada's perception that it needed more people did not go as far as welcoming the arrival of Asians, who were largely barred from entering both countries, or of African Americans. Regarding the latter group, incidentally, Canada had been more liberal before Confederation, when it welcomed many refugees from American slavery via the so-called Underground Railroad. Most of these people, or their descendants, returned to the United States after slavery was abolished.

One interesting question about American immigration policy prior to 1965 is why Western-Hemisphere nations were exempted from the quota system. The demand for low-priced Mexican labour in the southwest may have been a factor, but probably more important was the fact that the largest source of Western-Hemisphere immigration at that time was Canada. Given the usual American perception that Canadians are indistinguishable from themselves (apart from our peculiar habit of swearing allegiance to a monarch), Canadians were probably viewed as harmless and useful immigrants who already spoke English, had suitably pale complexions, were unlikely to be communists, and would not upset the ethnic balance of forces in American society. Some New Englanders had a less benign view of French-Canadian immigration, but that was a local concern in a region with declining political influence and had little impact on the United States as a whole.

In the 1960s, both countries finally removed overt racial and ethnic discrimination from their immigration policies, although they continued to be selective in their choice of individual immigrants. By this time, the increasing prosperity and stability of western Europe and the slow growth of its population had reduced the supply of potential immigrants from that region, while the communist regimes in eastern Europe made it extremely difficult for their citizens to leave. Thus, people from outside of Europe, particularly Asians, were the principal beneficiaries of the new and more liberal policies in Canada and the United States. On the whole, Asian immigrants to both countries have been quite well received by Americans and Canadians in recent years, in contrast to the reception their predecessors encountered in earlier times. The significant volume of Asian immigration since the 1960s has proved very beneficial to both countries, and it is encouraging that most Americans and Canadians, particularly younger ones, seem to realize this. Higher levels of education, a greater familiarity with the outside world through air travel and the Internet, and the discrediting of racist theories after the defeat of their most enthusiastic supporters in World War II have all contributed to this happy outcome, although pockets of prejudice and discrimination certainly remain.

Latin-American immigration to the United States has also increased sharply since the 1960s but would presumably have done so even without the reforms in immigration policy, since Latin-American countries had been exempted from the quota system when that system existed. Canada has also received immigrants from Spanish-speaking America but in much smaller numbers, given its more limited historical, cultural, and economic ties with that part of the world. The rapid increase in immigration from Mexico in particular and the growing number of Spanish-speaking people in the United States has produced a backlash, particularly in the southwestern states, as described in chapter 8 of this book. While some Canadians may view this phenomenon as evidence of their own moral superiority to Americans, something in which they are always eager to believe, it is very doubtful that they would have acted any differently from their American neighbours if Canada shared a long land border with a large developing country speaking a different language. The anglophone Canadian response to the rather modest efforts by the federal and some provincial governments to preserve the francophone minorities outside of Quebec certainly provides no grounds for complacency or self-righteousness in this regard.

While immigration policy was changing in the 1960s, with eventual consequences that were not fully foreseen at the time, other social and cultural changes were taking place in both the United States and Canada. The civil rights movement in the United States and Quebec's Quiet Revolution in Canada both drew attention to the most fundamental ethnic cleavages in the two societies, the legacy of slavery in one case and of conquest in the other. African Americans and French Canadians both mobilized to demand the equality that had long been denied them in practice and in the African-American case also in law. The parallel is obviously not exact, but in both cases governments were persuaded to take action, and inequalities were eventually reduced, although not eliminated, while the more extreme manifestations of discontent and frustration gradually subsided.

"Multiculturalism" in Canada and the "ethnic revival" in the United States, which emerged almost simultaneously, were both byproducts of these dramatic developments as other minorities vented their own frustrations and sought attention from governments that, in their view, were excessively preoccupied with responding to the Quiet Revolution and the civil rights movement. In both cases, it was the European ethnic minorities resulting from earlier waves of immigration who expressed such sentiments, fearing that their own heritages would be forgotten, and their voices unheard, by governments preoccupied with more pressing problems. Governments responded to some degree, particularly in Canada, but it is doubtful that much changed as a result. Of far greater consequence than anything that governments did or failed to do for the European ethnic minorities was the transformation wrought by the new wave of immigration that has made North America multi-racial and multi-religious as well as multicultural.

Language, race (a term that should probably be used within quotation marks), and religion have all tended to divide the human species into competing groups, and all have at various times provoked violence between or among the competing groups in North America and elsewhere. For historical reasons, "race" (European versus African) has been a central preoccupation in the United States, and language (English versus French) has been a central preoccupation in Canada. These historically determined national obsessions, if one may call them that, have influenced the North American response to other aspects of human diversity that became apparent later in their respective histories as waves of immigration transformed the cultural landscape of the continent. The addition of more "races" and more languages to the mixture made both societies more complex, although the traditional bipolarity, in both cases, remained paramount.

In future, however, it may be religion that will create the most difficult problems of social adjustment as governments strive to maintain a delicate equilibrium between followers of various religions, between religious fundamentalists and religious liberals, and between people sympathetic to religion and those who reject it entirely. The religion of immigrants is much more likely to survive unto the third or fourth generation than is their mother tongue. The fact that different faiths have different views regarding the appropriate relations between state, society, and religion, and the fact that even those who share a Christian and European heritage have achieved no consensus among themselves on these matters, make the situation still more complex. In addition to the traditional categories of believers, agnostics, and atheists there is a growing number of people, especially younger people, who describe themselves as "spiritual" but seem to have no specific religious beliefs. How they will fit into the equation remains to be seen.

While there are many differences between Canada and the United States, the conclusion to be drawn from this comparative study is that their experiences with, and approaches to, the management of cultural diversity are really quite similar, at least when viewed in comparison with the rest of the world. Over a period of a few centuries – a short time in relation to the whole history of human civilizations – both have attracted and absorbed large numbers of immigrants from a variety of sources, integrated them into the mainstream society through essentially non-coercive means, and transformed them, or their descendants, into useful citizens, most of whom are proud to be Americans or Canadians as the case may be and who have no desire to live anywhere else.

We tend to take this achievement for granted, like the air that we breathe, but it has few parallels elsewhere, with the exception of Australia and perhaps one or two other countries. Whatever the secret of our success has been, even other stable and prosperous democracies like the United Kingdom, France, Germany, and Japan have not really discovered it. Canadians are inclined to call the secret "multiculturalism" and to believe that it distinguishes their country from the United States. Most, but by no means all, Americans reject that label, and some of them still prefer to invoke the old metaphor of the melting pot, but the process and the outcomes are not fundamentally different in the two countries. A label is only a label, and Canadians and Americans use different words for many everyday objects as well as for more abstract phenomena like the one under discussion. If they derive satisfaction from these differences in semantics, as many Canadians appear to do, so be it.

Any attempt at an explanation of why both the United States and Canada have done so well in integrating their immigrants must be highly tentative, but a few suggestions may be offered. A high material standard of living and an abundance of land and natural resources are obviously part of the explanation, although perhaps not as much so as many North Americans believe. The English language is certainly an asset, since it is familiar in much of the world and fairly easy to learn; no one who has struggled to remember the genders of French nouns or the genders and case endings of German nouns will disagree with the latter statement. Our traditions of individualism and self-reliance, rooted in the philosophy of John Locke and the theology of Protestantism or perhaps even further back in the common law of medieval England, encourage new arrivals to strive for economic success and social integration while allowing them to retain those aspects of their original heritages that still appeal to them.

Yet perhaps the most important asset of all is experience. Through no particular virtue of their own but simply as a result of their respective foundings in a large, rich, and thinly populated continent, both Canada and the United States developed in a peculiar way. Beginning with small groups of original settlers, each developed incrementally by adding new groups of settlers, often differing in culture from the originals, in a process that proved to be continuous, although it moved much faster at some times than at others. Each layer of immigration and settlement was placed on top of the layers that had preceded it. The experience of absorbing each new cohort of immigrants facilitated absorbing the next cohort when it arrived. The new arrivals, particularly if they ranked fairly low in socio-economic status, contributed to the upward mobility of those ethnic groups who had arrived earlier and thus helped to make immigration acceptable to the population as a whole. Perhaps the best metaphor to describe what happened is neither a mosaic nor a melting pot but an onion. From the outside, the onion appears as a single object, but when cut to reveal the inside it is seen to be a series of layers that have been added one at a time, making the object larger with the passage of time but not really altering its essential shape and structure. At the same time, the layered structure gives the onion strength and cohesion.

David Hackett Fischer has demonstrated how different regions of the United States retain a remarkable number of cultural attributes inherited from the part of England that provided each region with its original cohort of European settlers several hundred years ago, even though the great majority of their people no longer have any English ancestry at all.[4] The synthesis that results from successive layers of settlement creates a society that combines continuity with growth and cohesion with diversity. The phrase "a nation of immigrants," which is often used in both countries, expresses the fact that immigration seems a natural, normal, and healthy process rather than the anomaly it is perceived to be in most European nations. Unlike European nation-states or Japan, neither the United States nor Canada can plausibly claim biological descent from a single source, but the absence of such a belief, sometimes viewed as a weakness, enables them to continue the process of adding new layers to the original entity, a process that has never really ended.

Much of what has been asserted in the last few paragraphs applies only partially to one important part of North America: the province of Quebec. Immigration policy is a concurrent jurisdiction under Canada's federal Constitution, and Quebec since the Quiet Revolution has taken much more advantage of this fact than the other provinces. Through agreements with the federal government, it has its own process of selecting immigrants and has assumed most of the responsibility for integrating them after they arrive. All Quebec governments in recent years have encouraged immigration and accepted cultural diversity, at least in theory. Quebec's policy of "interculturalism" does not differ much in substance from federal "multiculturalism" except for the fact that Quebec gives priority to the French language while the federal government is formally neutral between English and French. However, in practice the people of Quebec have not moved as far or as fast along the road that leads away from European-style ethnic nationalism as have other North Americans. The majority of Quebec's people are still descended from pre-conquest French settlers while in the rest of Canada probably less than half the population has family roots extending even as far back as 1867. Few Quebeckers would agree that Quebec is "a nation of immigrants." Political discourse is also pervaded by anxiety for the future of the French language on a continent where English and Spanish are much more widely spoken. So in practice Quebec's response to immigration remains more like that of a western European democracy than like that of anglophone Canada or the United States.

Even in anglophone Canada and the United States, the "nation of immigrants" mentality does not mean that all has been sweetness and light on either side of the border, for some problems remain. The process of building new nations out of immigration and diversity has excluded and marginalized the descendants of those original North Americans who were here when the first settlers from England and France arrived, creating a social and economic problem to which there are no easy answers in either the United States or Canada. The descendants of people who were brought from Africa as slaves, either to North America itself or to the islands of the Caribbean, also continue to suffer from discrimination, racial prejudice, and a lower average standard of material well-being than the rest of the population in both the United States and Canada.

Even those who came to North America as voluntary immigrants faced, more often than not, a mixture of hostility, fear, and contempt, doubts that they could really "fit in," fear that they would take the jobs of those already here or impose an alien culture and style of life on their neighbours, contempt for their beliefs, their physical attributes, or their behaviour, and sometimes suspicion that their loyalty to a foreign nation, church, or ideology would pose a permanent danger to society. While racism and xenophobia have declined, neither has been totally eradicated. The myths and stereotypes applied to each new group of arrivals often resembled those that had been applied to their predecessors. Muslims and Sikhs today often endure the same prejudice and discrimination that were directed against Irish Catholics and Jews in earlier times. Arabs and Iranians today, like Germans and Japanese in earlier times, may be viewed by some as potential enemies and threats to national security. The good news is that such attitudes tend to decline as a new and less familiar group of immigrants arrives and the earlier immigrants or their descendants come to be viewed as normal, familiar, and harmless.

The process has never ended, although the volume of immigration rises and falls in response to both domestic and global circumstances, and it will continue. Northwestern Europe was once the main source of immigrants until it was replaced by eastern and southern Europe. Eastern and southern Europe in turn were replaced by Asia and Latin America. As Asia and Latin America become more prosperous and as their fertility rates decline, they in turn will probably be replaced by Africa, the poorest of the continents and the one with the most rapidly growing population. Given the historical legacy of anti-African racism that dates from the era of the trans-Atlantic slave trade, the next wave of immigrants will probably not be universally welcomed, but then none of their predecessors were universally welcomed either at the time they arrived.

Nation-building through immigration, or the ability to attract immigrants and then to integrate them into the host society, will nonetheless be North America's greatest asset in the twenty-first century. Germany, Italy, Japan, and Russia face a future of demographic decline with no end in sight. The United Kingdom and France are in a somewhat better situation because of immigration that comes mainly from their former overseas colonies, but neither the British monarchy (which practises a sort of multiculturalism) nor the French republic (which emphasizes uniformity) seems able to fully integrate its immigrants into the host society or to use their talents and skills to best advantage. That fact is both a cause and a consequence of the hostility to immigration that is evident in both of those countries.

Both the United States and Canada have learned, by trial and error, how to integrate their immigrants and turn them into Americans and Canadians, and thus it seems likely that both the United States and Canada will continue to grow and flourish. Even if the people who live in North America a century or two from now may differ from most present-day North Americans in some of their physical characteristics, they will still be recognizably Canadians and Americans, just as the descendants of Irish, Jewish, Italian, and Ukrainian immigrants are today. So perhaps in conclusion the last word should go to Finley Peter Dunne and his alter ego, Mr Dooley:

> "I think th' counthry is goin' to th' divvle," said Mr. Hennessy, sadly.
>
> "Hinnissy," said Mr. Dooley, "if that's so I congratylate th' wurruld."
>
> "How's that?" asked Mr. Hennessy.
>
> "Well," said Mr. Dooley, "f'r nearly forty years I've seen this counthry goin' to th' divvle, an' I got aboord late. An' if it's been goin' that long an' at that rate, an' has got no nearer thin it is this pleasant Chris'mas, thin th' divvle is a divvle iv a ways further off thin I feared."[5]

Notes

CHAPTER ONE

1 Zangwill.
2 Foster; John Murray Gibbon.
3 For example, Kernerman; Kymlicka.
4 Mackey.
5 McRoberts.
6 Bibby, *Mosaic Madness*; Gwyn.
7 Kennedy.
8 Glazer.
9 Reitz and Breton, 30.
10 Porter; Kaufmann.
11 J.W. Pickersgill, *The Mackenzie King Record 1939–1944*, 515 (Toronto: University of Toronto Press 1960).
12 For example, Handlin; Olson.
13 For example, Kelley and Trebilcock; Knowles.
14 For example, Coogan.
15 Hansen.
16 Hawkins.
17 The classic presentation of this theory by a political scientist is Pierson, *Politics in Time: History, Institutions and Social Analysis*. See also Mahoney, 507–48.
18 Stevenson, *Parallel Paths*.

CHAPTER TWO

1 On the seigneurial system, see Eccles, 34, 57, 70, 79–80.

2 Steven Pincus, *1688: The First Modern Revolution* (New Haven: Yale University Press 2009).

3 Colley.

4 Daniels, *Coming to America*, 41–3.

5 Ibid., 89–90.

6 Colley, 11–54.

7 Lawson, 57.

8 Colley, 127, 131.

9 Lawson, 109.

10 Ibid., 76.

11 Ibid. See also Lanctot, 25–6.

12 Guindon, "The Crown, the Catholic Church and the French Canadian People."

13 Edward Gibbon, vol. I, 25–6.

14 Morton, 85.

15 Fuchs, 13.

16 Dinnerstein, Nichols, and Reimers, 20.

17 Quoted in Daniels, *Coming to America*, 109–10.

18 Quoted in Philip Gleason, "American Identity and Americanization," 33.

19 Hamilton, Madison, and Jay, 38.

20 Forrest McDonald and Ellen Shapiro McDonald, "The Ethnic Origins of the American People, 1790," *William and Mary Quarterly* 37 (1980).

21 Fuchs, 7–12.

22 Elazar, 229–57.

23 Fischer.

24 Kohn, 149.

25 Alan Taylor, 101–23.

26 Ibid., 45–72.

27 Ibid., 235–67.

28 Ibid., 441–58.

29 Clark, 195.

30 Grant, 37.

31 Fuchs, 110.

CHAPTER THREE

1 Kerby A. Miller, 137.

2 Ibid., 147.

3 Fischer, 605–782.

4   Coogan, 258–60. The others listed are Polk, Buchanan, Andrew Johnson, Grant, Arthur, Cleveland, Benjamin Harrison, McKinley, and Wilson.

5   Stevenson, *Ex Uno Plures*, 270–2.

6   Akenson, table at 57.

7   Ignatiev, 37.

8   Kivisto and Ng, 76.

9   Dinnerstein, Nichols, and Reimers, 114.

10 Fay, 137–43.

11 Daniels, *Coming to America*, 79–80.

12 Greeley, "The Success and Assimilation of Irish Protestants and Irish Catholics in the United States."

13 Maguire, 309, 312. A similar view of the expression was expressed in Davin, 64.

14 The best overview of the Famine is in Donnelly.

15 Donnelly, 171.

16 Kerby A. Miller, 292.

17 Dinnerstein, Nichols, and Reimers, 81, 89.

18 Takaki, *A Different Mirror*, 159.

19 Wilson, *Thomas D'Arcy McGee: The Extreme Moderate 1857–1868*, 61.

20 Jacobson, 41.

21 Ibid., 46–7.

22 Dunne, 19.

23 Gleason, "American Identity and Americanization," 35.

24 Letter to Joshua Speed, 24 August 1855, in Lincoln, 105–6.

25 Wiley, 329–30.

26 Akenson, 194.

27 McGowan, 19.

28 O'Day and Stevenson, 76–7.

29 Peter M. Toner, "New Brunswick Schools and the Rise of Provincial Rights," in Hodgins et al.

30 Wilson, *Thomas D'Arcy McGee: The Extreme Moderate 1857–1868*, 283.

31 Clinton, 401.

32 Mark McGowan, "Between King, Kaiser, and Canada," in David A. Wilson, ed., *Irish Nationalism in Canada*, 97–120.

33 Shanahan.

34 Stevenson, *Parallel Paths*, 157.

35 Banks, 44–52.

36 Shanahan, 301.

37 For the definition of "charter groups," see Porter, 60–3.

38 Coogan, 261.

39 Kenny, 113.

40 Reedy.

41 Erie, 5.

42 Ibid., 89.

43 Ibid., table 2, 20–1.

44 Reedy, 47–50.

45 Dinnerstein, Nichols, and Reimers, 174.

46 Ignatiev, 163–4.

47 Reedy, 28–9.

48 Sharon Doyle Dreidger, 183.

49 Ibid., 188–9.

50 Burns, 33–4, 51–2, 62, 67–8, 122.

51 McGowan, 36.

52 See the interview with Hanley in Burns, 85–9, and also Sharon Doyle
   Dreidger, 354–61.

53 Thomas Sowell, an African-American scholar, has suggested some intrigu-
   ing parallels between Irish Americans and African Americans. Sowell,
   Ethnic America, 289–90.

54 Kerby A. Miller, 498.

55 Greeley, "The Success and Assimilation of Irish Protestants and Irish
   Catholics in the United States."

56 Schlesinger, *Robert Kennedy and His Times*, 5–7.

57 The message was sent by the Hon. Jason Kenney to a conference attended
   by Gerry Adams, which took place in Toronto on 7 November 2009.

CHAPTER FOUR

1 Ward, x.

2 Stuart Creighton Miller, 16–37.

3 Takaki, *Strangers from a Different Shore*, 92–3.

4 Ibid., 79.

5 Dinnerstein, Nichols, and Reimers, 19.

6 Takaki, *Strangers from a Different Shore*, 82.

7 Sowell, *Ethnic America*, 137.

8 Olson, 188.

9 Takaki, *Strangers from a Different Shore*, 101–2.

10 Ibid., 116.

11 Ibid., 112.

12 Bain, 205–7.

13 Takaki, *A Different Mirror*, 181.

14 Takaki, *Strangers from a Different Shore*, 84–5.

15 Ward, 170, table 1.

16 De Kiewiet and Underhill, 264.

17 Stevenson, *Ex Uno Plures*, 161–6, 174–6.

18 Lavallée, 218–20.

19 Takaki, *Strangers from a Different Shore*, 79.

20 Stuart Creighton Miller, 173–5; Takaki, *Strangers from a Different Shore*, 94–5.

21 Stuart Creighton Miller, 175–82; Takaki, *Strangers from a Different Shore*, 95–9.

22 Saxton, 158.

23 Ibid., 80–91.

24 Ibid., 104–5.

25 Ibid., 133.

26 Ibid., 177–8.

27 Vigdor, 105, table 5.1.

28 Takaki, *Strangers from a Different Shore*, 112.

29 Department of Commerce and Labor, "Enforcement of the Chinese Exclusion Laws: General Instructions," 24 June 1905. Microfilm in Immigration History Research Center, University of Minnesota, reel P-5033, 674–5.

30 Ibid., "To Immigration Officers and Others Concerned," 11 January 1911. Microfilm in Immigration History Research Center, University of Minnesota, reel P-5033, 673.

31 Takaki, *A Different Mirror*, 201–3.

32 Department of Commerce and Labor, various documents. Microfilm in Immigration History Research Center, University of Minnesota, reel P-5028, 432–52.

33 Stevenson, *Ex Uno Plures*, 175.

34 Ibid., 273.

35 Ward, 42.

36 Stevenson, *Ex Uno Plures*, 175.

37 Ward, 59, 61.

38 Ibid., 170–1, tables 1 and 2.

39 McClain and McClain.

40 Fritz, 50.

41 Ibid., 50–6.

42 Salyer.

43 (1899) A.C. 580.

44 (1903) A.C. 151.

45 LaForest, 83–101 (Appendix A).

46 Ward, 58–9.

47 Ibid., 75.

48 Ibid., 91.

49 Woodsworth, *Strangers within Our Gates*, 170–89.

50 Goutor, 33–84.

51 Ibid., 77.

52 *Quong Wing v. R.* (1914) 49 S.C.R. 44.

53 Goutor, 78.

54 *House of Commons Debates*, 30 April 1923, 2,312–13.

55 Ibid., 30 April 1923, 2,316.

56 Ibid., 30 April 1923, 2,326–7.

57 Ibid., 4 May 1923, 2,485–7.

58 Daniels, *Coming to America*, 304–5.

59 Roy, 161–2.

60 *House of Commons Debates*, 11 February 1947, 307–8.

61 Roy, 264–5.

62 *House of Commons Debates*, 11 February 1947, 319–21.

63 Ibid., 11 February 1947, 322.

64 Ibid., 11 February 1947, 335.

65 Roy, 173–4.

66 Kivisto and Ng, 306–10.

67 Dinnerstein, Nichols, and Reimers, 275.

68 Bloemraad, 36, table 2.

69 *Statistical Abstract of the United States 1994*, 11, table 8; *Statistical Abstract of the United States 2004–05*, 10, table 8.

70 Kivisto and Ng, 308–9.

71 UCLA AASC, "2011 Statistical Portrait of Asian Americans, Native Hawaiians, and Other Pacific Islanders," www.aasc.ucla.edu/archives/stats2011.asp.

72 Bloemraad, 34–6, tables 1 and 2.

73 UCLA AASC, "2011 Statistical Portrait of Asian Americans, Native Hawaiians, and Other Pacific Islanders," 1–2, www.aasc.ucla.edu/archives/stats2011.asp.

74 Statistics Canada, "Profiles of Ethnic Communities in Canada," vol. 2006, no. 1, "The Chinese Community in Canada," 4–7, www.statcan.gc.ca/pub/89-621-x/89-621-x2006001-eng.htm.

75 "Ottawa Stuns, Angers Ethnic Groups by Refusing to Grant Financial Redress," *Globe and Mail*, 16 December 1994.

76 "MPs Hand out Compensation for Chinese Head Tax," *CTV News*, 20 October 2006.

77 Foner, 59.

78 Angus Reid Group, 49–52.

79 Statistics Canada, "Profiles of Ethnic Communities in Canada," vol. 2006, no. 1, "The Chinese Community in Canada," 7, www.statcan.gc.ca/pub/ 89–621–x/89–621–x2006001–eng.htm.

CHAPTER FIVE

1 An account of her life and background is in Karp, 146–52.

2 Waxman, 3.

3 Fuchs, 8.

4 Troper, 9–14.

5 Karp, 374 (Appendix 1).

6 Ibid.

7 Ibid., 375 (Appendix 2).

8 Rosenberg, 47.

9 Zolberg, 229.

10 Karp, 345–6.

11 Ruth Z. Murphy and Sonia Grodka Blumenthal, "The American Immigrant in the Community," *Annals of the American Academy* 367 (September 1966).

12 Waxman, 15–7.

13 Karp, 342.

14 Ibid., 219.

15 Ibid., 376–7 (Appendix 3).

16 Kallen, *Culture and Democracy in the United States*, 111–4.

17 Kelley and Trebilcock, 74–5.

18 Sowell, *Ethnic America*, 80–2.

19 Ibid., 89.

20 Karp, 378 (Appendix 4).

21 Waxman, 10.

22 Jacobson, 163–4.

23 Ibid., 75–7.

24 Ibid., 169–70.

25 Karp, 304.

26 Zolberg, 230.

27 Sowell, *Ethnic America*, 95.

28 Higham, 277–80.

29 Immigration History Research Center, University of Minnesota, US Immigration and Naturalization Service, files 71–42, reel 1, Hoover to Caminetti, 16 April 1920.

30 Higham, 282–5; Karp, 269–70.

31 Steinberg, 222–7.

32 Frost, 128.

33 Bumsted, 182.

34 Knowles, 113.

35 Tulchinsky, 136–9, 283–301.

36 Foster, 29, 46.

37 Rosen, 4.

38 Karp, 376–7 (Appendix 3).

39 Mayer.

40 Rosen, 28–9.

41 Ibid., 79.

42 Franklin D. Roosevelt papers, Presidential Office Files, file 76–C (Jewish), Ralph Senesi to FDR, 8 June 1939.

43 Rosen, 60–7, 75–8, 133.

44 Ibid., 91–104.

45 Evans, 599.

46 Zolberg, 290.

47 Abella and Troper, xxii.

48 Ibid., 126–47.

49 Bumsted, 207.

50 Zolberg, 305.

51 Karp, 251–3.

52 Royal Commission on Bilingualism and Biculturalism, *Report: Book III, The Work World*, part 1, 23 (Ottawa: Queen's Printer 1969).

53 Gotlieb, 584, 604.

54 Weinfeld, 159–69.

55 Zenner, 124.

56 Weinfeld, 359–61.

57 Stuart Schonfeld, "The Jewish Religion in North America: Canadian and American Comparisons," *Canadian Journal of Sociology* 3, no. 2 (1978): 228.

58 Takaki, *A Different Mirror*, 9.

59 Karp, 320.

60 Troper.

61 Waxman, 121–3.

CHAPTER SIX

1 Churchill, *The Grand Alliance*, 476–82.
2 Daniels, *Coming to America*, 146, table 6.6.
3 Tolzmann, 205–8.
4 Ibid., 209–10.
5 Ibid., 223.
6 Dinnerstein, Nichols, and Reimers, 168–9.
7 Sowell, *Ethnic America*, 58.
8 Tolzmann, 257–66.
9 The estimates are from Dinnerstein, Nichols, and Reimers, 161, and Tolzmann, 262.
10 Lehmann, 127–30.
11 Jonathan Wagner.
12 Melnycky, 3.
13 Higham, 210.
14 Wittke, 163.
15 Thompson, 75–6.
16 Higham, 202.
17 Ibid., 218.
18 Thompson, 79–80.
19 Helling, 52.
20 Ibid., 50.
21 Grenke.
22 Manuel Meune, "Berlin, Canada," *Queen's Quarterly* 112, no. 2 (summer 2005): 283–91.
23 Wittke, 182–3.
24 Higham, 248.
25 Harrington, 685.
26 Hawgood.
27 Higham, 204 ff.; Fuchs, 59.
28 Tolzmann, 298–301.
29 Quoted in Hamilton, 105.
30 Martynowyck, 4.
31 Census of Canada 1911, vol. 2, table 11; Census of Canada 1921, vol. 1, table 24.
32 Martynowyck, 161–2.
33 Avery, 34–5.
34 Martynowyck, 317–18.

35 Kordan, 25–9.
36 Martynowyck, 324–5.
37 Kordan, 6.
38 Luciuk.
39 Kordan, 72–3.
40 Ibid., 41.
41 Ibid., 116–17.
42 Young, 243.
43 Halich, 24.
44 Kuropas, 20–1.
45 Ibid., 72.
46 Ibid., 24–5.
47 Helling, 80–1.
48 Lorenzkowski.
49 Churchill, *Their Finest Hour*, 620.
50 Liberati.
51 Principe, 36.
52 *House of Commons Debates*, 13 June 1940, 748–51.
53 Helling, 82–3.
54 Bayor, 61–3.
55 Ibid., 71.
56 Ibid., 147.
57 Tolzmann, 334.
58 Scherini, 290–1.
59 Kashima, 18–19.
60 Daniels, *Concentration Camps*, 2.
61 Harold Innis, editor's preface in Young, Reid, and Carrothers, vii–xix.
62 Young, Reid, and Carrothers, xxiii.
63 Ward, 115–16.
64 Young, Reid and Carrothers, xxiv.
65 Daniels, *Concentration Camps*, 16.
66 Ibid., 11.
67 *Cunningham v. Tomey Homma* [1903] A.C. 151.
68 *A.G. Canada v. A.G. British Columbia* [1930] A.C. 111.
69 Lucy.
70 Kashima, 15.
71 Ibid., 35.
72 Ibid., 36–7.
73 Daniels, *Concentration Camps*, 33.
74 Ibid., 75–7.

75 Kashima, 129.
76 Ibid., 134, 136.
77 Daniels, *Concentration Camps*, 130–43.
78 Ibid., 166.
79 Granatstein and Johnson, 113–14.
80 Ibid., 110.
81 Roy, 17.
82 Daniels, *Concentration Camps*, 182.
83 *House of Commons Debates*, 10 March 1943, 1,127.
84 Adachi, 252.
85 Ibid., 256.
86 Ibid., 321.
87 Ibid., 281.
88 *House of Commons Debates*, 4 August 1944, 5,915–17.
89 Daniels, *Concentration Camps*, 191.
90 Census of Canada 1951, vol. 1, table 32.
91 "PM Apologizes to Italian-Canadians for War Treatment," *Globe and Mail*, 5 November 1990.

CHAPTER SEVEN

1 Horace M. Kallen, "Democracy versus the Melting Pot," 98.
2 Ibid., 116.
3 Bourne, "Trans-national America," 265.
4 Ibid., 276.
5 Ibid., 268–9.
6 Daniels, *Coming to America*, 276–7.
7 Ibid., 280.
8 Ibid., 280–1.
9 Ibid., 282–3.
10 Berger, *The Writing of Canadian History*, 128–31.
11 Avery, 90–1.
12 Ibid., 101.
13 Ibid., 100, 120.
14 Ibid., 101.
15 Lyndon B. Johnson Presidential Library, LBJ papers, legislative background, Immigration Law 1965, folder 1, "Four Presidents Urge Reform."
16 *Congressional Record*, 26 June 1952, 8,225–6, 8,267.
17 George, 196–7.

18 John F. Kennedy Presidential Library, JFK papers, Senate files, Legislation Introduced or Co-sponsored, box 630, press release, 29 August 1957.

19 John F. Kennedy, *A Nation of Immigrants*, New York: B'nai Brith 1958.

20 John F. Kennedy Presidential Library, JFK papers, Senate files, Legislation Introduced or Co-Sponsored, box 630, "Kennedy Introduces Three Point Immigration Program," press release, 18 May 1959.

21 *New York Times*, 9 May 1961.

22 Stephen T. Wagner, 376.

23 Lyndon B. Johnson Presidential Library, LBJ papers, national security file, files of Gordon Chase, immigration: Schwartz to Feldman, 14 June 1963.

24 Schwartz, 119.

25 Full text of Kennedy's message to Congress proposing the bill is in the *New York Times*, 24 July 1963.

26 John F. Kennedy Presidential Library, Abba Schwartz papers, box 7, Immigration Legislation, 1963.

27 John F. Kennedy Presidential Library, AFL-CIO papers (microfilm), reel 9, Statement on Immigration Reform, 15 August 1963.

28 Schwartz, 118.

29 Full text of Johnson's message to Congress proposing the bill is in the *New York Times*, 14 January 1965.

30 Lyndon B. Johnson Presidential Library, LBJ papers, office files of White House aides, Bill Moyers, box 1, immigration, memo for the president from acting attorney general re Congressman Feighan's immigration proposals, 4 February 1965.

31 Documents pertaining to the committee are in Lyndon B. Johnson Presidential Library, LBJ papers, White House central files, box 63, confidential file, folder LE/HI to LE/LE3 (1 of 2).

32 "U.S. Public Is Strongly Opposed to Easing of Immigration Laws," *Washington Post*, 31 May 1965.

33 Lyndon B. Johnson Presidential Library, LBJ papers, office files of White House aides, Mike Manatos, box 8, Rodman to Manatos, 21 July 1965.

34 Lyndon B. Johnson Presidential Library, LBJ papers, legislative background, Immigration Law 1965, folder 6, "The Road to Final Passage, Part 4," Valenti to LBJ, 22 July 1965.

35 Lyndon B. Johnson Presidential Library, LBJ papers, White House central files, legislation, box 74, LE/IM, O'Brien to LBJ, 30 July 1965.

36 *Congressional Record*, 25 August 1965, 21820–1.

37 Lyndon B. Johnson Presidential Library, LBJ papers, legislative background, Immigration Law 1965, folder 6, LBJ to McCormack, 25 August 1965.

38 Lyndon B. Johnson Presidential Library, LBJ papers, legislative background, Immigration Law 1965, folder 6, Valenti to LBJ, 25 August 1965.
39 *Congressional Record*, 22 September 1965, 24,783.
40 The full text is in *Laws of the 89th Congress, 1st session*, 3 October 1965, 883–97.
41 Lyndon B. Johnson Presidential Library, LBJ papers, White House central files, LE/IM, Rosenthal to Moyers, 31 August 1965.
42 Lyndon B. Johnson Presidential Library, LBJ papers, White House central files, LE/IM, Udall to LBJ, 23 September 1965.
43 *New York Times*, 26 May 1966.
44 Lyndon B. Johnson Presidential Library, LBJ papers, oral histories, AC 75–15, Richard M. Scammon, interviewed 3 March 1969.
45 Ueda, 45.
46 Daniels, *Coming to America*, 410.
47 Library and Archives Canada, RG 26, vol. 100, file 3–18–1, part 1.
48 *House of Commons Debates*, 1 May 1947, 2644–7.
49 Library and Archives Canada, RG 26, vol. 100, file 3–18–1, part 2, memo from Mitchell, 12 June 1948.
50 Library and Archives Canada, Louis St Laurent papers, MG26 L, vol. 55, file I-20–2, Immigration, French-secret, 1948.
51 P.C. 2856, 9 June 1950.
52 Canadian data compiled from Knowles, 273–5, table A.1. American data from Daniels, *Coming to America*, 410, table 17.1.
53 Daniels, *Coming to America*, 410.
54 Cabinet committee on immigration policy, minutes of meeting 27 May 1947, in Library and Archives Canada, RG 26, vol. 100, file 3–18–1, part 1.
55 Library and Archives Canada, RG 26, vol. 100, file 3–18–1, part 2, unsigned memo to cabinet, 1 September 1948.
56 Library and Archives Canada, RG 26, vol. 100, file 3–18–1, part 2, memo to cabinet from A.L. Joliffe, 12 April 1948.
57 P.C. 1956–785, 24 May 1956.
58 *House of Commons Debates*, 11 February 1947, 319–21; 29 April 1955, 3319–20.
59 Library and Archives Canada, Cabinet Conclusions, 25 July 1957.
60 P.C. 1958–7, 2 January 1958.
61 Library and Archives Canada, Cabinet Conclusions, 24 October 1958. See also Library and Archives Canada, RG 2, vol. 2,741, cabinet document 237/58, 11 August 1958.
62 Library and Archives Canada, Cabinet Conclusions, 12 August 1958.

63 Library and Archives Canada, RG 2, vol. 2,742, cabinet document 127–59, 23 April 1959.

64 P.C. 1959–310, 19 March 1959.

65 P.C. 1959–507, 23 April 1959. For the background, see Library and Archives Canada, Cabinet Conclusions, 14, 20, and 23 April 1959.

66 Library and Archives Canada, RG 2, vol. 2,743, cabinet document 386–59, 26 November 1959. This memo from Fairclough to the cabinet attaches a copy of the draft.

67 Library and Archives Canada, RG 26, vol. 99, file 3–15–1, part 6. Contains the department's views, with a cover letter signed by Norman Robertson on 31 December 1959.

68 Library and Archives Canada, RG 26, vol. 99, file 3–15–1, part 7, Baskerville to Davidson, 20 January 1961. The quotation is from an attached document, apparently written by Baskerville's executive assistant, D. Sloan.

69 Library and Archives Canada, RG 26, vol. 100, file 3–15–1, part 8, Fairclough to cabinet, 16 October 1961.

70 Library and Archives Canada, RG 26, vol. 100, file 3–15–1, part 8, Citizenship Branch to deputy minister, 27 October 1961.

71 Library and Archives Canada, RG 26, vol. 100, file 3–15–1, part 8, Baskerville to Davidson, 10 November 1961.

72 Library and Archives Canada, RG 26, vol. 100, file 3–15–1, part 9, Davidson to Fairclough, 3 January 1962.

73 Library and Archives Canada, Cabinet Conclusions, 18 January 1962.

74 Library and Archives Canada, RG 26, vol. 100, file 3–15–1, part 8, Fairclough to Diefenbaker, 23 November 1961.

75 *House of Commons Debates*, 19 January 1962, 9–11.

76 Library and Archives Canada, Cabinet Conclusions, 5 March 1964.

77 Library and Archives Canada, RG 2, vol. 6,261, cabinet document 359–64, memo to cabinet from René Tremblay, 10 August 1964.

78 Library and Archives Canada, Cabinet Conclusions, 13 August 1964.

79 Marchand.

80 The origins of the point system are described in Kent, 409–13.

81 Library and Archives Canada, RG 2, vol. 6,320, cabinet document 687–66, Marchand to cabinet, 25 November 1966.

82 Library and Archives Canada, Cabinet Conclusions, 10 August 1967.

83 Knowles, 199–210.

84 Canada, Manpower and Immigration, *Immigration Statistics 1968* (Ottawa: Queen's Printer 1969).

85 Statistics Canada, *Tracking Immigration Trends*, www.statscan.ca/english/ Estat/guide/track.htm.
86 See note 52.
87 Calculated from Daniels, *Coming to America*, 410, table 17.1.

CHAPTER EIGHT

1   Kloss, 112–13.
2   Ibid., 28–31.
3   *Meyer v. Nebraska*, 262 U.S. 390 [1923].
4   Tatalovich, 65–9.
5   N.E.S. Griffiths, 5–6.
6   Canada, *Statutes*, 1870, ch. 3.
7   Manitoba, *Statutes*, 1890, chs 14, 37, 38.
8   Thompson's memorandum of 21 March 1891 on the subject is in Library and Archives Canada, RG 2, series 1, vol. 475.
9   Canada, *Statutes*, 1875, ch. 49, and 1877, ch. 7.
10 Ibid., 1891, ch. 22.
11 Bélanger, 296.
12 Silver.
13 Bélanger, 301–4.
14 Ibid., 304–6.
15 Joy, 28.
16 Mark McGowan, "Gauthier, Charles Hugh," in *Dictionary of Canadian Biography*, vol. 15.
17 Joy. The book was first published privately in 1967.
18 A translation of the editorial is in Cook and Behiels, 250–2.
19 The origins of the royal commission are described in Fraser, 25–41. The author is Canada's commissioner of official languages.
20 Canada, *Statutes*, 1968–69, ch. 54.
21 Bourgeois.
22 *A.G. of Manitoba v. Forest*, [1979] 2 S.C.R. 1032.
23 *Mahé v. Alberta*, [1990] 1 S.C.R. 342.
24 Andrew, 1–2.
25 Quebec, *Statutes*, 1974, ch. 6.
26 Ibid., 1977, ch. 5.
27 *Ford v. Quebec (Attorney General)*, 1988 2 S.C.R. 12.
28 Daniels, *Coming to America*, 308.
29 The full text of the treaty is at http://www.mexica.net/guadhida.php.

30 Kloss, 49.
31 Ibid., 130–1.
32 Jennifer E. Glick and Jennifer Van Hook, "The Mexican-Origin Population of the United States in the Twentieth Century," 575, table 3, www.utexas.edu/lbj/uscir/binpapers/v2a-3glick.pdf.
33 Ibid., 576, table 4.
34 Ibid., 575–6.
35 Ibid., 576, table 4.
36 Gonzalez, 117.
37 Ibid., 138–40.
38 Jennifer E. Glick and Jennifer Van Hook, "The Mexican-Origin Population of the United States in the Twentieth Century," 572, table 1, www.utexas.edu/lbj/uscir/binpapers/v2a-3glick.pdf.
39 "The 1930 Census in Perspective," http://www.1930census.com/us_census_history.php.
40 D'Vera Cohn, "Hispanic? Latino? Or ... ?" Pew Research Center 2012, http://www.pewsocialtrends.org/2012/04/04/hispanic-latino-or.
41 United States Census Bureau. "The Foreign-Born Population in the United States: 2010," (issued May 2012): 2.
42 Jennifer E. Glick and Jennifer Van Hook, "The Mexican-Origin Population of the United States in the Twentieth Century," 575, table 3, www.utexas.edu/lbj/uscir/binpapers/v2a-3glick.pdf.
43 Thernstrom, Orlov, and Handlin, 632, table 1.
44 www.census.gov/hhes/socdemo/language/data/acs/Table2.xls.
45 Data from United States Census Bureau, "2004 American Community Survey," http://en.wikipedia.org/wiki/Spanish_language_in_the_United_States.
46 United States Census Bureau, Public Information Office, release CB 11-CN.146, 26 May 2011.
47 Gonzalez, 172.
48 Ibid., 211.
49 Thernstrom, 619–22.
50 Lau v. Nichols, 414 U.S. 563 [1974].
51 Thernstrom, 624–5.
52 All the information in this paragraph is from http://usenglish.org/view/26.
53 Tatalovich, 13.
54 Ibid., 22.
55 Ibid., 160–8.
56 Ibid., 16–20.
57 Gonzalez, 194–5.
58 Buchanan, 123–46.

59 Public Law 99–603, 100 Stat. 3359.
60 Public Law 104–208, 100 Stat. 3009–546.
61 Jeffrey Passel, D'Vera Cohn, and Ana Gonzalez-Barrera, "Net Migration from Mexico Falls to Zero – and Perhaps Less," Pew Research Center (2012) http://www.pewhispanic.org/2012/04/23.

CHAPTER NINE

1 *House of Commons Debates*, 22 February 1955, 1,377–8; 28 February 1955, 1,551–3; 1 March 1955, 1,595.
2 Quoted in Newman, 44.
3 Diefenbaker, 26.
4 Robinson, 198.
5 Library and Archives Canada, Diefenbaker papers, MGO1/XII/C/88, Léger to Diefenbaker, 5 January 1961; MGO1/VI, vol. 413, file 580, Lemieux to Diefenbaker, 18 January 1961.
6 Library and Archives Canada, Diefenbaker papers, MGO1/XII/F/408, includes a transcript of the interview.
7 Library and Archives Canada, Diefenbaker papers, MGO1/VI, vol. 35, file 045 (Dunn).
8 Meisel.
9 Library and Archives Canada, Diefenbaker papers, MGO1/VI, vol. 35, file 045 (language and ethnic groups-ethnic groups), Yaremko to Diefenbaker, 20 August 1957.
10 Library and Archives Canada, Diefenbaker papers, MGO1/VI, vol. 35, file 045 (language and ethnic groups-ethnic groups-Italian) contains all the relevant documents.
11 Library and Archives Canada, Diefenbaker papers, MGO1/XII/C/167, prime minister's memo, 12 February 1962.
12 Library and Archives Canada, Diefenbaker papers MGO1/VI, vol. 278, file 324 (Yuzyk) contains several letters from Ukrainian Canadians expressing approval of Yuzyk's appointment.
13 Library and Archives Canada, Diefenbaker papers, MGO1/XII/C/168 contains a copy of the editorial and other press clippings about the conference.
14 Library and Archives Canada, Diefenbaker papers, MGO1/XII/C/167, Diefenbaker to Fairclough, 9 January 1962; Fairclough to Diefenbaker, 10 January 1962.
15 Library and Archives Canada, Diefenbaker papers, MGO1/VI, vol. 37, file 045 (language and ethnic groups-ethnic groups-Serbia), P. Susovich to Diefenbaker, 8 May 1958.

16 Library and Archives Canada, Diefenbaker papers, MG01/XII/A/441, Roblin to Diefenbaker, 11 September 1957.

17 Library and Archives Canada, Diefenbaker papers, MG01/VI, vol. 348, file 391.517, private memo for the prime minister, 16 May 1958.

18 Library and Archives Canada, Diefenbaker papers, MG01/XII/C/167, Roborecki to Diefenbaker, 27 December 1961.

19 Transcript of speech is in Library and Archives Canada, Diefenbaker papers, MG01/XII/C/141.

20 Robinson, 190–1.

21 Newman, 259–60.

22 Robinson, 226.

23 Library and Archives Canada, Diefenbaker papers, MG01/VI, vol. 37, file 045 (Ukr), Kochan to Starr, 27 December 1958.

24 Copy of convention program is in Library and Archives Canada, Diefenbaker papers, MG01/XII/C/168.

25 Library and Archives Canada, Diefenbaker papers, MG01/VI, vol. 576, file 912.6.

26 *Senate Debates*, 3 March 1964, 50–8, at 55.

27 Royal Commission on Bilingualism and Biculturalism, *Preliminary Report*, appendix I, 151–2.

28 Ibid., appendix IV, 183–7.

29 Ibid., 29.

30 Ibid., 51.

31 *House of Commons Debates*, 9 April 1965, 195.

32 A complete list of the research studies, both published and unpublished, may be found in Christopher R. Adamson, Peter C. Findlay, Michael K. Oliver, and Janet Solberg, "The Unpublished Research of the Royal Commission on Bilingualism and Biculturalism," *Canadian Journal of Political Science* 7 (1974): 709–20.

33 Royal Commission on Bilingualism and Biculturalism, *Report, Book IV*, 228–30.

34 Library and Archives Canada, cabinet document 981/71, 21 September 1971.

35 Library and Archives Canada, Cabinet Conclusions, 23 September 1971.

36 Canada, Privy Council Office, Record of Cabinet Decision, meeting of 23 September 1971.

37 *House of Commons Debates*, 8 October 1971, 8,545–6.

38 Lupul, "The Political Implementation of Multiculturalism."

39 *Statement of the Government of Canada on Indian Policy* (Ottawa: Department of Indian Affairs and Northern Development 1969).

40 *Legislature of Ontario, Debates*, 27 February 1968, 271.

41 Canada, *Statutes*, 35–36–37 Elizabeth II, ch. 31.

42 Laura Sabia, "Stop Pandering to Ethnics," *The Standard* (St Catharines), 27 September 1988.

43 Quoted in Jeffrey Simpson, "Balking at Multiculturalism," *Globe and Mail*, 29 September 1989.

44 Bissoondath, 219, 223–4.

45 Angus Reid Group Inc.

46 Library and Archives Canada, Trudeau papers, MG26, O7, vol. 37, file 040.2, Bourassa to Trudeau, 11 November 1971.

47 For a fuller discussion of interculturalism, see Gagnon and Iacovino.

48 Lampron.

49 Westhues.

50 For the text of his speech, see White, 391–3.

51 The last of these allegations appears in Herbert W. Vilakazi, "Was Karl Marx a Black Man?" *Monthly Review* 32 (2): 42–58.

52 Tatalovich, 248.

53 e.g., Schlesinger, *The Disuniting of America*.

54 Novak.

55 Gans; Alba.

56 Public Law 92–318. See "Implementation of Schweiker Ethnic Studies Bill," *Congressional Record*, 30 September 1972, E8253–4.

57 e.g., Huntington, *Who Are We?*

58 Schmidt.

59 Huntington, *Who Are We?* 30.

60 Lind.

61 Rudyard Griffiths.

62 Daniel Stoffman, "Surface Multiculturalism: An Ideology, Not a Fact," *Globe and Mail*, 22 August 2009.

CHAPTER TEN

1 The Cedar Rapids mosque is identified as the first in Philipp, 732–3. However, the foundation of the Detroit mosque in 1922 is mentioned in other sources.

2 Lovell.

3 Yvonne Y. Haddad, "Islam," in *The Canadian Encyclopedia*, 905–7 (Edmonton: Hurtig 1985).

4 Eid, 25.

5 Marvasti and McKinney, 4.

6 Abraham.

7 Marvasti and McKinney, 10–11.

8 Ibid., 56–7.

9 Lovell, 107.

10 Huntington, "The Clash of Civilizations?" and *The Clash of Civilizations and the Remaking of World Order*.

11 Pew Research Center, 11.

12 Ibid., 10.

13 "Glad to Be Canadian, Muslims Say", CBC News, 13 February 2007.

14 Pew Research Center, 15.

15 The federal government's Ethnic Diversity Survey (2002), cited in Breton, *Different Gods*, 29.

16 Pew Research Center, 53.

17 Ibid., 29–30.

18 "Canada's Muslims, an International Comparison," CBC News in Depth, 13 February 2007.

19 Eid, 154, 161.

20 Pew Research Center, 33.

21 "Glad to Be Canadian, Muslims Say", CBC News, 13 February 2007.

22 "Canada's Muslims, an International Comparison", CBC News in Depth, 13 February 2007.

23 "Woman Understands Palestinian Reaction," *The Standard* (St Catharines), 12 September 2001.

24 Marvasti and McKinney, xii.

25 "Cause of Hamilton Temple Fire Unknown," *The Standard* (St Catharines), 17 September 2001.

26 Piszkiewicz, 141–3 (appendix 1).

27 Public Law 107–56, 115 stat. 272; Public Law 107–296, 116 stat. 2135; Public Law 108–458, 118 stat. 3638.

28 Canada, *Statutes*, 2001, ch. 40.

29 See, for example, his remarks at the Islamic Center of Washington, 17 September 2001, remarks prior to discussions with Muslim community leaders, 26 September 2001, and remarks prior to discussions with King Abdullah II of Jordan, 28 September 2001, all in *Public Papers of the Presidents of the United States: George W. Bush* (2001: Book II).

30 Remarks to the United Nations General Assembly in New York City, 10 November 2001, in *Public Papers of the Presidents of the United States: George W. Bush* (2001: Book II).

31 Data supplied by Ontario Consultants on Religious Tolerance and accessed at www.religioustolerance.org.

32 See previous note.
33 The text of the address is in *Public Papers of the Presidents of the United States: George W. Bush* (2002: Book I).
34 Marvasti and McKinney, 152–4.
35 Pew Research Center, 35–6.
36 Ibid., 36.
37 Ibid., 49.
38 "Glad to Be Canadian, Muslims Say," CBC News, 13 February 2007.
39 Canadian Arab Federation, "Minister Jason Kenney's History with CAF," 9 March 2009. The text of Kenney's speech that was released to the press does not contain these words, but they may have been spoken in response to a question or in an impromptu addition to the text.
40 *House of Commons Debates*, 29 January 2008, 2,310–11.
41 "Kenney Says Some Canadian Arab Groups Express Hatred toward Jews," CBC News, 17 February 2009.
42 *Multani v. Commission scolaire Marguerite-Bourgeoys*, 2006 1 S.C.R. 256.
43 Bouchard.
44 Taylor.
45 Bouchard and Taylor.
46 Government of Quebec, "The 37 Recommendations in the Final Report of the Bouchard–Taylor Commission," press release, 22 May 2008. For a collection of critical comments on the report, see Gagnon. For a more positive appraisal, see Jeffrey Simpson, "Bouchard–Taylor Commission Tells Quebec to Grow Up," *Globe and Mail*, 24 May 2008.
47 *House of Commons Debates*, 15 March 1990, 9,307–9.
48 Pew Research Center, 37.
49 "Sondage Léger Marketing–Le Devoir – Le gouvernement Charest trop 'accommodant,'" *Le Devoir*, 18 February 2010.
50 Kymlicka, 55.

CHAPTER ELEVEN

1 Morton, 85.
2 Chernow, 137.
3 Vaughan.
4 Fischer.
5 Dunne, 244.

Bibliography

Abella, Irving, and Harold Troper. *None Is Too Many: Canada and the Jews of Europe.* 3rd edn. Toronto: Key Porter Books 2000

Abraham, Sameer Y. "Detroit's Arab-American Community: A Survey of Diversity and Commonality." In *Arabs in the New World: Studies on Arab-American Communities*, edited by Sameer Y. Abraham and Nabeel Abraham, 84–108. Detroit: Wayne State University Center for Urban Studies 1983

– and Nabeel Abraham, eds. *Arabs in the New World: Studies on Arab-American Communities.* Detroit: Wayne State University Center for Urban Studies 1983

Abu-Laban, Baha. *An Olive Branch on the Family Tree: The Arabs in Canada.* Toronto: McClelland and Stewart 1980

Adachi, Ken. *The Enemy That Never Was.* Toronto: McClelland and Stewart 1991

Akenson, Donald Harmon. *Being Had: Historians, Evidence and the Irish in North America.* Mississauga, ON: P.D. Meany 1985

Alba, Richard. *Ethnic Identity: The Transformation of White America.* New Haven, CT: Yale University Press 1990

– "The Twilight of Ethnicity among Americans of European Ancestry: The Case of Italians." *Ethnic and Racial Studies* 8 (1985): 134–58

Altschuler, Glenn C. *Race, Ethnicity, and Class in American Social Thought 1865–1919.* Arlington Heights, IL: Harlan Davidson 1982

Anderson, J.T.M. *The Education of the New-Canadian.* Toronto: J.M. Dent 1918

Andrew, J.V. *Bilingual Today, French Tomorrow: Trudeau's Master Plan and How It Can Be Stopped.* Richmond Hill, ON: BMG Press 1977

Angus Reid Group. *Multiculturalism and Canadians: Attitude Study 1991*. Ottawa: Multiculturalism and Citizenship Canada 1991

Avery, Donald. *"Dangerous Foreigners": European Immigrant Workers and Labour Radicalism in Canada 1896–1932*. Toronto: McClelland and Stewart 1979

Bain, David Haward. *Empire Express: Building the First Transcontinental Railroad*. New York: Viking 1999

Bangarth, Stephanie. *Voices Raised in Protest: Defending the North American Citizens of Japanese Ancestry, 1942–1949*. Vancouver: University of British Columbia Press 2008

Banks, Margaret. *Edward Blake, Irish Nationalist: A Canadian Statesman in Irish Politics*. Toronto: University of Toronto Press 1957

Banting, Keith, et al. *Belonging? Diversity, Recognition and Shared Citizenship in Canada*. Montreal: Institute for Research in Public Policy 2007

Barone, Michael. *Our Country: The Shaping of America from Roosevelt to Reagan*. New York: Free Press 1990

Bauer, Julien. *Les minorités au Québec*. Montreal: Boréal Express 1994

Bayor, Ronald H. *Neighbors in Conflict: The Irish, Germans, Jews and Italians of New York City, 1929–1941*. Baltimore: Johns Hopkins University Press 1978

Bélanger, Réal. *Wilfrid Laurier : quand la politique devient passion*. Quebec City: Les Presses de l'Université Laval 1986

Bell, David V.J. *The Roots of Disunity: A Study of Canadian Political Culture*. rev. edn. Toronto: Oxford University Press 1992

Berger, Carl. *The Sense of Power*. Toronto: University of Toronto Press 1970

– *The Writing of Canadian History*. 2nd edn. Toronto: University of Toronto Press 1986

Berry, John, et al. *Multiculturalism and Ethnic Attitudes in Canada*. Ottawa: Minister of Supply and Services 1977

Bibby, Reginald W. *Fragmented Gods: The Poverty and Potential of Religion in Canada*. Toronto: Irwin 1987

– *Mosaic Madness*. Toronto: Stoddart 1990

– *Unknown Gods: The Ongoing Story of Religion in Canada*. Toronto: Stoddart 1993

Biles, John, Meyer Burstein, and James Frideres. *Immigration and Integration in Canada in the 21st Century*. Kingston: School of Policy Studies, Queen's University 2008

Bissoondath, Neil. *Selling Illusions: The Cult of Multiculturalism in Canada*. Toronto: Penguin Books 1994

Bloemraad, Irene. *Becoming a Citizen: Incorporating Immigrants and Refugees in the United States and Canada*. Berkeley and Los Angeles: University of California Press 2006

Boissevain, Jeremy. *The Italians of Montreal: Social Adjustment in a Plural Society*. Ottawa: Queen's Printer 1970

Bouchard, Gérard. *Genèse des nations et cultures du Nouveau Monde*. Montreal: Boréal 2001

– and Charles Taylor. *Building the Future: A Time for Reconciliation*. Quebec City: Government of Quebec 2008

Bourgeois, Daniel. *The Canadian Bilingual Districts: From Cornerstone to Tombstone*. Montreal and Kingston: McGill-Queen's University Press 2006

Bourne, Randolph. *The History of a Literary Radical and Other Papers*. New York: S.A. Russell 1956

– "Trans-national America." In Randolph Bourne, *The History of a Literary Radical and Other Papers*, 260–84. New York: S.A. Russell 1956

Breton, Raymond. *Different Gods: Integrating Non-Christian Minorities into a Primarily Christian Society*. Montreal and Kingston: McGill-Queen's University Press 2012

– *Ethnic Relations in Canada: Institutional Dynamics*. Montreal and Kingston: McGill-Queen's University Press 2005

– Jeffrey Reitz, and Victor Valentine. *Cultural Boundaries and the Cohesion of Canada*. Montreal and Kingston: Institute for Research on Public Policy 1980

Buchanan, Patrick J. *The Death of the West*. New York: St Martin's Press 2002

Bumsted, J.M. *Canada's Diverse Peoples: A Reference Sourcebook*. Santa Barbara: ABC Clio 2003

Burns, Patricia. *The Shamrock and the Shield: An Oral History of the Irish of Montreal*. Montreal: Véhicule Press 1998

Cameron, Elspeth, ed. *Multiculturalism & Immigration in Canada*. Toronto: Canadian Scholars Press 2004

Carment, David, and David Bercuson, eds. *The World in Canada: Diaspora, Demography, and Domestic Politics*. Montreal and Kingston: McGill-Queen's University Press 2008

Castles, Stephen, and Mark J. Miller. *The Age of Migration: International Population Movements in the Modern World*. 4th edn. New York: Guilford Press 2009

Champion, C.P. *The Strange Demise of British Canada*. Montreal and Kingston: McGill-Queen's University Press 2010

Chan, Sucheng, ed. *Entry Denied: Exclusion and the Chinese Community in America 1882–1943*. Philadelphia: Temple University Press 1991

Chennells, David. *The Politics of Nationalism in Canada*. Toronto: University of Toronto Press 2001

Chernow, Ron. *Washington: A Life*. New York: Penguin Press 2010

Churchill, Winston S. *The Grand Alliance*. Boston: Houghton Mifflin 1950

– *Their Finest Hour*. Boston: Houghton Mifflin 1949

Clark, S.D. *The Developing Canadian Community*. 2nd edn. Toronto: University of Toronto Press 1968

Clinton, Bill. *My Life*. New York: Alfred A. Knopf 2004

Colley, Linda. *Britons: Forging the Nation 1707–1837*. New Haven: Yale University Press 1992

Coogan, Tim Pat. *Wherever Green Is Worn: The Story of the Irish Diaspora*. New York: Palgrave 2001

Cook, Ramsay, and Michael Behiels, eds. *The Essential Laurendeau*. Toronto: Copp Clark 1976

Dahlie, J., and T. Fernando, eds. *Ethnicity, Power and Politics in Canada*. Toronto: Methuen 1981

Daniels, Roger. *Coming to America: A History of Immigration and Ethnicity in American Life*. 2nd edn. New York: Harper Collins 2002

– *Concentration Camps: North America*. 2nd edn. Malabar, FL: Kreiger 1991

Davin, Nicholas F. *The Irishman in Canada*. London: Sampson, Low, Marston 1877

Day, Richard. *Multiculturalism and the History of Canadian Diversity*. Toronto: University of Toronto Press 2000

De Kiewiet, C.W., and F.H. Underhill, eds. *The Dufferin–Carnarvon Correspondence 1874–1878*. Toronto: The Champlain Society 1955

Diefenbaker, John. *One Canada: The Crusading Years 1895–1956*. Toronto: Macmillan 1975

Dinnerstein, Leonard, Roger L. Nichols, and David M. Reimers. *Natives and Strangers: A Multicultural History of Americans*. New York: Oxford University Press 1996

Donnelly, James S., Jr. *The Great Irish Potato Famine*. Gloucester: Sutton 2001

Driedger, Leo. *Multi-ethnic Canada: Identities and Inequalities*. Toronto: Oxford University Press 1996

Driedger, Sharon Doyle. *An Irish Heart: How a Small Immigrant Community Shaped Canada*. Toronto: Harper Collins 2010

Dunne, Finley Peter. *Mr. Dooley on Ivrything and Ivrybody*. New York: Dover Publications 1963

Eccles, W.J. *France in America*. New York: Harper and Row 1972

Eid, Paul. *Being Arab: Ethnic and Religious Identity Building among Second Generation Youth in Montreal*. Montreal and Kingston: McGill-Queen's University Press 2007

Elazar, Daniel. *The American Mosaic*. Boulder, CO: Westview Press 1994

Erie, Steven P. *Rainbow's End: Irish-Americans and the Dilemmas of Urban Machine Politics, 1840–1985*. Berkeley and Los Angeles: University of California Press 1988

Evans, Richard J. *The Third Reich in Power*. New York: Penguin Books 2006

Ewing, Katherine Pratt, ed. *Being and Belonging: Muslims in the United States since 9/11*. New York: Russell Sage Foundation 2008

Fay, Terence J. *A History of Canadian Catholics*. Montreal and Kingston: McGill-Queen's University Press 2002

Fernando, Shanti. *Race and the City: Chinese Canadian and Chinese American Political Mobilization*. Vancouver: University of British Columbia Press 2006

Fischer, David Hackett. *Albion's Seed: Four British Folkways in America*. New York: Oxford University Press 1989

Foner, Nancy. *From Ellis Island to JFK: New York's Two Great Waves of Immigration*. New Haven: Yale University Press 2000

Foster, Kate A. *Our Canadian Mosaic*. Toronto: YMCA 1926

Fraser, Graham. *Sorry, I Don't Speak French: Confronting the Canadian Crisis That Won't Ever Go Away*. Toronto: McClelland and Stewart 2006

Fritz, Christian G. "Due Process, Treaty Rights and Chinese Exclusion, 1882–1891." In *Entry Denied: Exclusion and the Chinese Community in America 1992–1943*, edited by Sucheng Chan, 25–56. Philadelphia: Temple University Press 1991

Frost, Stanley Brice. *McGill University for the Advancement of Learning, 1895–1971*. Kingston and Montreal: McGill-Queen's University Press 1984

Fuchs, Lawrence H. *The American Kaleidoscope: Race, Ethnicity and the Civic Culture*. Hanover, NH: University Press of New England 1990

Gagnon, Alain-G., and Raffaele Iacovino. "Framing Citizenship Status in an Age of Polyethnicity: Quebec's Model of Interculturalism." In *Canada: The State of the Federation 2001*, edited by Hamish Telford and Harvey Lazar, 313–42. Kingston: Institute of Intergovernmental Relations 2002

Gagnon, Bernard, ed. *La diversité québécoise en débat*. Montreal: Québec Amérique 2010

Gans, Herbert G. "Symbolic Ethnicity: The Future of Ethnic Groups and Cultures in America." *Ethnic and Racial Studies* 2 (1979): 1–20

Gardner, Michael. *Harry Truman and Civil Rights*. Carbondale and Edwardsville: Southern Illinois University Press 2002

George, Neil James. "The Interplay of Domestic and Foreign Considerations in United States Immigration Policy." PHD dissertation, Case Western University, 1975

Gibbon, Edward. *The Decline and Fall of the Roman Empire*, vol. I. New York: Modern Library n.d.

Gibbon, John Murray. *Canadian Mosaic: The Making of a Northern Nation*. Toronto: McClelland and Stewart 1938

Gimpel, James, and James Edwards. *The Congressional Politics of Immigration Reform*. Needham Heights, MA: Allyn and Bacon 1999

Glazer, Nathan. *We Are All Multiculturalists Now*. Cambridge, MA: Harvard University Press 1997

– and Daniel P. Moynihan. *Beyond the Melting Pot: The Negroes, Puerto Ricans, Jews, Italians and Irish of New York City*. 2nd edn. Cambridge, MA: Massachusetts Institute of Technology Press 1970

Gleason, Philip. "American Identity and Americanization." In *Harvard Encyclopedia of American Ethnic Groups*, edited by Stephen Thernstrom, A. Orlov, and O. Handlin. Cambridge, MA: Harvard University Press 1980

– *Speaking of Diversity: Language and Ethnicity in Twentieth Century America*. Baltimore: Johns Hopkins University Press 1992

Gonzalez, Juan. *Harvest of Empire: A History of Latinos in America*. New York: Penguin 2001

Good, Kristin R. *Municipalities and Multiculturalism: The Politics of Immigration in Toronto and Vancouver*. Toronto: University of Toronto Press 2009

Gordon, Milton M. *Assimilation in American Life*. New York: Oxford University Press 1964

Gotlieb, Allan. *The Washington Diaries 1981–1989*. Toronto: McClelland and Stewart 2006

Goutor, David. *Guarding the Gates: The Canadian Labour Movement and Immigration, 1872–1934*. Vancouver: University of British Columbia Press 2007

Granatstein, J.L., and Gregory A. Johnson. "The Evacuation of the Japanese Canadians, 1942: A Realist Critique." In *On Guard for Thee: War, Ethnicity and the Canadian State, 1939–1945*, edited by Norman Hillmer, Bohdan Kordan, and Lubomyr Luciuk, 101–29. Ottawa: Minister of Supply and Services 1988

Grant, Ulysses S. *Personal Memoirs of U.S. Grant, Two Volumes in One*. New York: Charles L. Webster 1894

Greeley, Andrew M. "The Success and Assimilation of Irish Protestants and Irish Catholics in the United States." *Social Science Review* 72, no. 4 (July 1988): 229–35

– *Why Can't They Be Like Us? Facts and Fallacies about Ethnic Differences and Group Conflicts in America*. New York: Institute of Human Relations Press 1969

– and William C. McCready. *Ethnicity in the United States: A Preliminary Reconnaissance*. New York: Wiley 1974

Greenfeld, Liah. "The Reality of American Multiculturalism: American Nationalism at Work." In *Contemporary Majority Nationalism*, edited by Alain-G. Gagnon, André Lecours, and Geneviève Nootens, 181–96. Montreal and Kingston: McGill-Queen's University Press 2011

Grenke, Art. "The German Community of Winnipeg and the English-Canadian Response to World War I." *Canadian Ethnic Studies* 20, no. 1 (1988): 21–44

Griffiths, N.E.S. "Acadia." In *The Canadian Encyclopedia*, 5–6. Edmonton: Hurtig 1985

Griffiths, Rudyard. *Who We Are: A Citizen's Manifesto*. Vancouver: Douglas and McIntyre 2009

Guindon, Hubert. *Quebec Society: Tradition, Modernity, and Nationhood*. Toronto: University of Toronto Press 1988

– "The Crown, the Catholic Church and the French Canadian People: The Historical Roots of Quebec Nationalism." In his *Quebec Society: Tradition, Modernity and Nationhood*, 94–111. Toronto: University of Toronto Press 1988

Gwyn, Richard. *Nationalism without Walls: The Unbearable Lightness of Being Canadian*. Toronto: McClelland and Stewart 1995

Halich, Wasyl. *Ukrainians in the United States*. Chicago: University of Chicago Press 1980

Halter, Marilyn. *Shopping for Identity: The Marketing of Ethnicity*. New York: Schocken Books 2000

Hamilton, Alexander, James Madison, and John Jay. *The Federalist Papers*. New York: Mentor Books 1961

Hamilton, Robert M. *Canadian Quotations and Phrases*. Toronto: McClelland and Stewart 1952

Handlin, Oscar. *The Uprooted: The Epic Story of the Great Migrations That Made the American People*. 2nd edn. Boston: Little Brown 1973

Hansen, Marcus Lee. *The Mingling of the Canadian and American Peoples*. New Haven, CT: Yale University Press 1940

Harrington, Mona. "Loyalties, Dual and Divided." In *Harvard Encyclopedia of American Ethnic Groups*, edited by Stephen Thernstrom, A. Orlov, and O. Handlin, 676–86. Cambridge, MA: Harvard University Press 1980

Hawgood, John A. *The Tragedy of German-America*. New York: G.P. Putnam 1940

Hawkes, Arthur. *The Birthright: A Search for the Canadian and the Larger Loyalty*. Toronto: J.M. Dent 1919

Hawkins, Freda. *Critical Years in Immigration: Canada and Australia Compared*. Montreal and Kingston: McGill-Queen's University Press 1989

Hayward, Victoria. *Romantic Canada*. Toronto: Macmillan 1922

Helling, Rudolf A. *A Socio-economic History of German-Canadians*. Wiesbaden: Franz Steiner Verlag 1984

Herberg, Will. *Protestant-Catholic-Jew: An Essay in American Religious Sociology*. rev. edn. New York: Anchor Books 1960

Higham, John. *Strangers in the Land: Patterns of American Nativism 1860–1925*. 2nd edn. New York: Atheneum 1963

Hillmer, Norman, and Adam Chapnick, eds. *Canadians of the Mind*. Montreal and Kingston: McGill-Queen's University Press 2007

– Bohdan Kordan, and Lubomyr Luciuk, eds. *On Guard for Thee: War, Ethnicity and the Canadian State, 1939–1945*. Ottawa: Minister of Supply and Services 1988

Hodgins, Bruce, et al., eds. *Federalism in Canada and Australia: The Early Years*. Waterloo, ON: Wilfrid Laurier University Press 1978

Hollinger, David A. *Postethnic America*. New York: Basic Books 1995

Hryniuk, Stella, and Lubomyr Luciuk, eds. *Multiculturalism and Ukrainian Canadians*. Toronto: University of Toronto Press 1993

Huntington, Samuel P. "The Clash of Civilizations?" *Foreign Affairs* 72, no. 3 (summer 1993): 22–49

– *The Clash of Civilizations and the Remaking of World Order*. New York: Simon and Schuster 1996

– *Who Are We? The Challenge to America's National Identity*. New York: Simon and Schuster 2004

Iacovetta, Franca. *Gatekeepers: Reshaping Immigrant Lives in Cold War Canada*. Toronto: Between the Lines 2006

– Roberto Perin, and Angelo Principe, eds. *Enemies Within: Italian and Other Internees in Canada and Abroad*. Toronto: University of Toronto Press 2000

Igartua, José. *The Other Quiet Revolution*. Vancouver: University of British Columbia Press 2006

Ignatiev, Noel. *How the Irish Became White*. New York: Routledge 1995

Jacobson, Matthew Frye. *Whiteness of a Different Color*. Cambridge, MA: Harvard University Press 1998

Joshee, Reeve, and Lauri Johnson, eds. *Multicultural Education Policies in Canada and the United States*. Vancouver: University of British Columbia Press 2007

Joy, Richard J. *Languages in Conflict*. Toronto: McClelland and Stewart 1972

Kallen, Horace. *Culture and Democracy in the United States*. New York: Boni and Liveright 1924

– "Democracy versus the Melting Pot." In his *Culture and Democracy in the United States*, 67–125. New York: Boni and Liveright 1924

Kaplan, William, ed. *Belonging: The Meaning and Future of Canadian Citizenship*. Montreal and Kingston: McGill-Queen's University Press 1993

Karp, Abraham J. *Haven and Home: A History of the Jews in America*. New York: Schocken Books 1985

Kashima, Tetsuden. *Judgment without Trial: Japanese-American Imprisonment during World War II*. Seattle: University of Washington Press 2003

Kaufmann, Eric P. *The Rise and Fall of Anglo-America*. Cambridge, MA: Harvard University Press 2004

Kelley, Ninette, and Michael Trebilcock. *The Making of the Mosaic: A History of Canadian Immigration Policy*. Toronto: University of Toronto Press 1998

Kelley, Robert. *The Cultural Pattern in American Politics: The First Century*. New York: Knopf 1979

Kennedy, John F. *A Nation of Immigrants*. New York: Harper and Row 1964

Kenny, Kevin. *The American Irish: A History*. London: Longmans 2000

Kent, Tom. *A Public Purpose*. Montreal and Kingston: McGill-Queen's University Press 1988

Kernerman, Gerald. *Multicultural Nationalism*. Vancouver: University of British Columbia Press 1995

Kirkconnell, Watson. *Canadians All: A Primer of Canadian National Unity*. Ottawa: Director of Public Information 1941

Kivisto, Peter, and Wendy Ng. *Americans All: Race and Ethnic Relations in Historical, Structural and Comparative Perspective*. 2nd edn. Los Angeles: Roxbury 2005

Kloss, Heinz. *The American Bilingual Tradition*. Rowley, MA: Newbury House 1977

Knowles, Valerie. *Strangers at Our Gates: Canadian Immigration and Immigration Policy, 1540–2007*. rev. edn. Toronto: Dundurn Press 2007

Kohn, Hans. *American Nationalism: An Interpretative Essay*. New York: Collier Books 1961

Kordan, Bohdan S. *Enemy Aliens, Prisoners of War: Internment in Canada during the Great War*. Montreal and Kingston: McGill-Queen's University Press 2002

Kuropas, Myron B. *The Ukrainian-Americans: Roots and Aspirations 1884–1954*. Toronto: University of Toronto Press 1991

Kymlicka, Will. *Finding Our Way: Rethinking Ethnocultural Relations in Canada*. Toronto: Oxford University Press 1998

LaForest, Gerald V. *Disallowance and Reservation of Provincial Legislation*. Ottawa: Queen's Printer 1965

Lampron, Louis-Philippe. "La gestion du pluralisme religieux au Québec – comment déroger à la Charte canadienne sans déroger à la liberté de religion." *Le Devoir*, 8 March 2010

Lanctot, Gustave. *Canada and the American Revolution 1774–1783*. Toronto: Clarke Irwin 1967

La Selva, Samuel. *The Moral Foundations of Canadian Federalism*. Montreal and Kingston: McGill-Queen's University Press 1996

Lavallée, Omer. *Van Horne's Road*. Toronto: Fitzhenry and Whiteside 1974

Lawson, Philip. *The Imperial Challenge: Quebec and Britain in the Age of the American Revolution*. Montreal and Kingston: McGill-Queen's University Press 1989

Lehmann, Heinz. *The German Canadians 1750–1937: Immigration, Settlement and Culture*. St John's: Jesperson Press 1986

Lemieux, Lucien. *Histoire du Catholicisme québécois, les XVIIIe et XIXe siècles*. Montreal: Boréal 1985

Liberati, Luigi Bruti. "The Internment of Italian Canadians." In *Enemies Within: Italian and Other Internees in Canada and Abroad*, edited by Franca Iacovetta, Roberto Perin, and Angelo Principe, 76–98. Toronto: University of Toronto Press 2000

Lincoln, Abraham. *Selected Speeches and Writings*. New York: Vintage Books 1992

Lind, Michael. *The Next American Nation*. New York: Free Press 1996

Loney, Martin. *The Pursuit of Division: Race, Gender, and Preferential Hiring in Canada*. Montreal and Kingston: McGill-Queen's University Press 1998

Lorenzkowski, Barbara. "Spies, Saboteurs and Subversives: German-
    Canadian Internees and the Wartime Discourse on the Canadian Home
    Front." In *A Chorus of Different Voices: German-Canadian Identities*,
    edited by Angelika E. Sauer and Matthias Zimmer, 167–85. New York:
    Peter Lange 1998
Lovell, Emily Kalled. "Islam in the United States: Past and Present." In *The
    Muslim Community in North America*, edited by Earle H. Waugh, Baha
    Abu-Laban, and Regula B. Qureshi, 93–110. Edmonton: University of
    Alberta Press 1983
Lower, Arthur R.M. *Canadians in the Making*. Toronto: Longmans, Green
    1958
Luciuk, Lubomyr. *Roll Call: Lest We Forget*. Canmore, AB: Ukrainian
    Canadian Civil Liberties Association 1999
Lucy, Roger V. *The Armoured Train in Canadian Service*. Ottawa: Service
    Publications 2005
Lupul, Manoly R. "The Political Implementation of Multiculturalism."
    Journal of Canadian Studies 17, no. 1 (spring 1982): 93–102
– *The Politics of Multiculturalism: A Ukrainian-Canadian Memoir*.
    Edmonton and Toronto: Canadian Institute of Ukrainian Studies Press
    2005
McClain, Charles J., and Laurene Wu McClain. "The Chinese
    Contribution to the Development of American Law." In *Entry Denied:
    Exclusion and the Chinese Community in America 1992–1943*, edited
    by Sucheng Chan, 3–24. Philadelphia: Temple University Press 1991
McGowan, Mark. *The Waning of the Green: Catholics, the Irish and
    Identity in Toronto, 1887–1922*. Montreal and Kingston: McGill-
    Queen's University Press 1999
Mackey, Eva. *The House of Difference: Cultural Politics and National
    Identity in Canada*. Toronto: University of Toronto Press 2000
McLemore, S. Dale, Harriet D. Romo, and Susan Gonzalez Baker. *Racial
    and Ethnic Relations in America*. 6th edn. Boston: Allyn and Bacon
    2001
McRoberts, Kenneth. *Misconceiving Canada: The Struggle for National
    Unity*. Toronto: Oxford University Press 1997
Maguire, John Francis. *The Irish in America*. London: Longmans, Green
    1868
Mahoney, James. "Path Dependence in Historical Sociology." *Theory and
    Society* 29 (2000): 507–48
Malcolmson, Scott L. *One Drop of Blood: The American Misadventure
    of Race*. New York: Farrar Straus Giroux 2000

Marchand, Hon. Jean. *White Paper on Immigration*. Ottawa: Queen's Printer 1966

Martynowych, Orest T. *Ukrainians in Canada: The Formative Period, 1891–1924*. Edmonton: Canadian Institute of Ukrainian Studies Press 1991

Marvasti, Amir, and Karyn D. McKinney. *Middle Eastern Lives in America*. Lanham, MD: Rowman and Littlefield 2004

Mayer, Arno J. *Why Did the Heavens Not Darken: The "Final Solution" in History*. New York: Pantheon Books 1988

Meisel, John. *The Canadian General Election of 1957*. Toronto: University of Toronto Press 1962

Melnycky, Peter. "The Internment of Ukrainians in Canada." In *Loyalties in Conflict: Ukrainians in Canada during the Great War*, edited by Frances Swyripa and John H. Thompson, 1–24. Edmonton: Canadian Institute of Ukrainian Studies 1983

Miller, Kerby A. *Emigrants and Exiles: Ireland and the Irish Exodus to North America*. New York: Oxford University Press 1985

Miller, Stuart Creighton. *The Unwelcome Immigrant: The American Image of the Chinese 1785–1882*. Berkeley and Los Angeles: University of California Press 1969

Morton, W.L. *The Canadian Identity*. Toronto: University of Toronto Press 1961

Newman, Peter C. *Renegade in Power: The Diefenbaker Years*. Toronto: McClelland and Stewart 1963

Novak, Michael. *The Rise of the Unmeltable Ethnics*. New York: Macmillan 1972

Nurse, Andrew, and Raymond B. Blake, eds. *Beyond National Dreams: Essays on Canadian Citizenship and Nationalism*. Markham, ON: Fitzhenry and Whiteside 2009

O'Day, Alan, and John Stevenson, eds. *Irish Historical Documents since 1800*. Dublin: Gill and Macmillan 1992

Olson, James Stuart. *The Ethnic Dimension in American History*. New York: St Martin's Press 1979

Painter, Nell Irvin. *The History of White People*. New York: W.W. Norton 2010

Pal, Leslie A. *Interests of State: The Politics of Language, Multiculturalism and Feminism in Canada*. Montreal and Kingston: McGill-Queen's University Press 1993

Palmer, Howard, ed. *Immigration and the Rise of Multiculturalism*. Toronto: Copp Clark 1975

Paquet, Gilles. *Deep Cultural Diversity: A Governance Challenge*. Ottawa: University of Ottawa Press 2008

Perlmutter, Philip. *The Dynamics of American Ethnic, Religious and Racial Group Life: An Interdisciplinary Overview*. Westport, CT: Praeger 1996

Pew Research Center. *Muslim Americans: Middle Class and Mostly Mainstream*. Washington: Pew Research Center 2007

Philipp, Thomas. "Muslims." In *Harvard Encyclopedia of American Ethnic Groups*, edited by Stephen Thernstrom, A. Orlov, and O. Handlin, 732–3. Cambridge, MA: Harvard University Press 1980

Pickus, Noah. *True Faith and Allegiance: Immigration and American Civic Nationalism*. Princeton: Princeton University Press 2005

Pierson, Paul. *Politics in Time: History, Institutions and Social Analysis*. Princeton: Princeton University Press 2004

Piszkiewicz, Dennis. *Terrorism's War with America*. Westport, CT: Praeger 2003

Porter, John. *The Vertical Mosaic: A Study of Social Class and Power in Canada*. Toronto: University of Toronto Press 1965

Principe, Angelo. "A Tangled Knot: Prelude to 10 June 1940." In *Enemies Within: Italian and Other Internees in Canada and Abroad*, edited by Franca Iacovetta, Roberto Perin, and Angelo Principe, 27–51. Toronto: University of Toronto Press 2000

Purewal, Shinder. "The Politics of Multiculturalism, 1963–1971." MA thesis, Simon Fraser University, 1992

Reedy, George. *From the Ward to the White House: The Irish in American Politics*. New York: Scribner's 1991

Reimers, David M. *Still the Golden Door: The Third World Comes to America*. New York: Columbia University Press 1992

Reitz, Jeffrey G. *The Survival of Ethnic Groups*. Toronto: McGraw-Hill Ryerson 1980

– and Raymond Breton. *The Illusion of Difference: Realities of Ethnicity in Canada and the United States*. Toronto: C.D. Howe Institute 1994

Ringer, Benjamin B., and Elinor R. Lawless. *Race, Ethnicity and Society*. New York: Routledge 1989

Robinson, Basil Robinson. *Diefenbaker's World: A Populist in Foreign Affairs*. Toronto: University of Toronto Press 1989

Rosen, Robert N. *Saving the Jews: Franklin D. Roosevelt and the Holocaust*. New York: Thunder's Mouth Press 2006

Rosenberg, Stuart E. *America Is Different: The Search for Jewish Identity*. London and New York: Thomas Nelson and Sons 1964

Roy, Patricia E. *The Triumph of Citizenship: The Japanese and Chinese in Canada, 1941–67.* Vancouver: University of British Columbia Press 2007

Royal Commission on Bilingualism and Biculturalism. *Preliminary Report.* Ottawa: Queen's Printer 1965

– *Report: Book IV, The Cultural Contribution of the Other Ethnic Groups.* Ottawa: Queen's Printer 1969

Rudin, Ronald. *The Forgotten Quebecers: A History of English-Speaking Quebec.* Quebec: Institut québécois de recherche sur la culture 1985

Ryan, Phil. *Multicultiphobia.* Toronto: University of Toronto Press 2010

Salaita, Steven. *Anti-Arab Racism in the USA.* London: Pluto Press 2006

Salins, Peter D. *Assimilation, American Style.* New York: Basic Books 1997

Salyer, E. "'Laws Harsh as Tigers': Enforcement of the Chinese Exclusion Laws, 1891–1924." In *Entry Denied: Exclusion and the Chinese Community in America 1882–1943*, edited by Sucheng Chan, 57–93. Philadelphia: Temple University Press 1991

Sauer, Angelika E., and Matthias Zimmer. *A Chorus of Different Voices: German-Canadian Identities.* New York: Peter Lang 1998

Saxton, Alexander. *The Indispensable Enemy: Labor and the Anti-Chinese Movement in California.* Berkeley: University of California Press 1995

Scherini, Rose D. "When Italian Americans Were 'Enemy Aliens.'" In *Enemies Within: Italian and Other Internees in Canada and Abroad*, edited by Franca Iacovetta, Roberto Perin, and Angelo Principe, 280–305. Toronto: University of Toronto Press 2000

Schlesinger, Arthur, Jr. *The Disuniting of America.* New York: W.W. Norton 1992

– *Robert Kennedy and His Times.* Boston: Houghton Mifflin 1978

Schmidt, Alvin J. *The Menace of Multiculturalism: Trojan Horse in America.* Westport, CT: Praeger 1997

Schwartz, Abba. *An Open Society.* New York: William Morrow 1968

Shanahan, David. "The Irish Question in Canada." PhD dissertation, Carleton University, 1989

Silver, A.I. *The French-Canadian Idea of Confederation 1864–1900.* Toronto: University of Toronto Press 1982

Smith, Rogers M. *Civic Ideals: Conflicting Visions of Citizenship in United States History.* New Haven, CT: Yale University Press 1997

Sowell, Thomas. *Ethnic America: A History.* New York: Basic Books 1981

– *Migrations and Cultures: A World View.* New York: Basic Books 1996

Stein, Janice Gross, et al. *Uneasy Partners: Multiculturalism and Rights in Canada.* Waterloo, ON: Wilfrid Laurier University Press 2007

Steinberg, Stephen. *The Ethnic Myth: Race, Ethnicity and Class in America*. New York: Atheneum 1981

Stevenson, Garth. *Ex Uno Plures: Federal-Provincial Relations in Canada 1867–1896*. Montreal and Kingston: McGill-Queen's University Press 1993

– *Parallel Paths: The Development of Nationalism in Ireland and Quebec*. Montreal and Kingston: McGill-Queen's University Press 2006

Swyripa, Frances, and John Herd Thompson, eds. *Loyalties in Conflict: Ukrainians in Canada during the Great War*. Edmonton: Institute of Ukrainian Studies 1983

Takaki, Ronald. *A Different Mirror: A History of Multicultural America*. rev. edn. New York: Back Bay Books 2008

– *Strangers from a Different Shore: A History of Asian Americans*. New York: Penguin 1989

Tatalovich, Raymond. *Nativism Reborn? The Official Language Movement and the American States*. Lexington: University of Kentucky Press 1995

Taylor, Alan. *The Civil War of 1812*. New York: Knopf 2010

Taylor, Charles. *A Secular Age*. Cambridge, MA: Harvard University Press 2007

Telford, Hamish, and Harvey Lazar, eds. *Canada: The State of the Federation 2001*. Kingston: Institute of Intergovernmental Relations 2002

Thernstrom, Abigail M. "Language: Issues and Legislation." In *Harvard Encyclopedia of American Ethnic Groups*, edited by Stephen Thernstrom, A. Orlov, and O. Handlin. Cambridge, MA: Harvard University Press 1980

Thernstrom, Stephen, A. Orlov, and O. Handlin, eds. *The Harvard Encyclopedia of American Ethnic Groups*. Cambridge, MA: Harvard University Press 1980

Thompson, John H. *The Harvests of War: The Prairie West 1914–1918*. Toronto: McClelland and Stewart 1978

Thorne, Christopher. *Allies of a Kind: The United States, Britain, and the War against Japan, 1941–1945*. New York: Oxford University Press 1978

Tierney, Stephen, ed. *Multiculturalism and the Canadian Constitution*. Vancouver: University of British Columbia Press 2007

Tolzmann, Don Heinrich. *The German-American Experience*. Amherst, NY: Humanity Books 2000

Tracey, Lindalee. *A Scattering of Seeds: The Creation of Canada*. Toronto: McArthur and Company 1999

Troper, Harold. *The Defining Decade: Identity, Politics and the Canadian Jewish Community in the 1960s*. Toronto: University of Toronto Press 2010

Tulchinsky, Gerald. *Canada's Jews: A People's Journey*. Toronto: University of Toronto Press 2008

Ueda, Reed. *Postwar Immigrant America: A Social History*. Boston and New York: Bedford and St Martin's Press 1994

Vaughan, Frederick. *The Canadian Federalist Experiment: From Defiant Monarchy to Reluctant Republic*. Montreal and Kingston: McGill-Queen's University Press 2003

Vigdor, Jacob L. *From Immigrants to Americans: The Rise and Fall of Fitting In*. Lanham, MD: Rowman and Littlefield 2009

Wagner, Jonathan. *A History of Migration from Germany to Canada 1850–1939*. Vancouver: University of British Columbia Press 2006

Wagner, Stephen T. "The Lingering Death of the National Origins Quota System: A Political History of United States Immigration Policy 1952–1965." PhD dissertation, Harvard University, 1986

Wallis, Maria, and Augie Fleras, eds. *The Politics of Race in Canada*. Toronto: Oxford University Press 2009

Ward, W. Peter. *White Canada Forever: Popular Attitudes and Public Policy towards Orientals in British Columbia*. 3rd edn. Montreal and Kingston: McGill-Queen's University Press 2002

Waters, Mary C. *Ethnic Options: Choosing Identities in America*. Berkeley and Los Angeles: University of California Press 1990

Waugh, Earle, Baha Abu-Laban, and Regula Qureshi, eds. *The Muslim Community in North America*. Edmonton: University of Alberta Press 1983

Waxman, Chaim I. *America's Jews in Transition*. Philadelphia: Temple University Press 1983

Weinfeld, Morton. *Like Everyone Else ... But Different: The Paradoxical Success of Canadian Jews*. Toronto: McClelland and Stewart 2001

Westhues, Kenneth. "Stars and Stripes, the Maple Leaf, and the Papal Coat of Arms." *Canadian Journal of Sociology* 3, no. 2 (1978): 245–61

Whitaker, Reg. *Double Standard: The Secret History of Canadian Immigration*. Toronto: Lester and Orpen Dennys 1987

White, Theodore H. *The Making of the President 1960*. New York: Athaneum 1961

Wiley, Bell Irvin. *The Life of Johnny Reb*. Baton Rouge: Louisiana State University Press 1978

Wilson, David A., ed. *Irish Nationalism in Canada*. Montreal and
    Kingston: McGill-Queen's University Press 2009
– *Thomas D'Arcy McGee: Passion, Reason and Politics 1825–1857*.
    Montreal and Kingston: McGill-Queen's University Press 2008
– *Thomas D'Arcy McGee: The Extreme Moderate 1857–1868*. Montreal
    and Kingston: McGill-Queen's University Press 2011
Wittke, Carl. *German-Americans and the World War*. Columbus: Ohio
    State Archaeological and Historical Society 1936
Wood, Peter. *Diversity: The Invention of a Concept*. San Francisco:
    Encounter Books 2003
Woods, Eric. "Multiculturalism and Identity in Canada: A Case Study of
    Ukrainian-Canadians." MA thesis, University of Saskatchewan, 2006
Woodsworth, J.S. *My Neighbor*. Toronto: Missionary Society of the
    Methodist Church 1911
– *Strangers within Our Gates*. 3rd edn. Toronto: Missionary Society of
    the Methodist Church 1911
Young, Charles H. *The Ukrainian Canadians: A Study in Assimilation*.
    Toronto: Nelson 1931
– Helen Reid, and W.A. Carrothers. *The Japanese Canadians*. Toronto:
    University of Toronto Press 1938
Zachariah, Mathew, Allan Sheppard, and Leona Barratt, eds. *Canadian
    Multiculturalism: Dreams, Realities, Expectations*. Edmonton:
    Canadian Multicultural Education Foundation 2004
Zangwill, Israel. *Works of Israel Zangwill: The Melting Pot*. New York:
    The American Jewish Book Company 1921
Zenner, Walter P. "Jewishness in America: Ascription and Choice." *Ethnic
    and Racial Studies* 8 (1985): 117–33
Zolberg, Aristide R. *A Nation by Design: Immigration Policy in the
    Fashioning of America*. Cambridge, MA: Harvard University Press 2006

Index